REGNUM STUDIES IN GLOBAL CHRISTIANITY

God Has Not Left Himself Without Witness

REGNUM STUDIES IN GLOBAL CHRISTIANITY

(Previously GLOBAL THEOLOGICAL VOICES series)

Series Preface

In the latter part of the twentieth century the world witnessed significant changes in global Christian dynamics. Take for example the significant growth of Christianity in some of the poorest countries of the world. Not only have numbers increased, but the emphasis of their engagement has expanded to include ministry to a wider socio-cultural context than had previously been the case. The *Regnum Studies in Global Christianity* series explores the issues with which the global church struggles, focusing in particular on ministry rooted in Africa, Asia, Latin America and Eastern Europe.

Not only does the series make available studies that will help the global church learn from past and present, it provides a platform for provocative and prophetic voices to speak to the future of Christianity. The editors and the publisher pray particularly that the series will grow as a public space, where the voices of church leaders from the majority world will contribute out of wisdom drawn from experience and reflection, thus shaping a healthy future for the global church. To this end, the editors invite theological seminaries and universities from around the world to submit relevant scholarly dissertations for possible publication in the series. Through this, it is hoped that the series will provide a forum for South-to-South as well as South-to-North dialogues.

Series Editors

REGNUM STUDIES IN GLOBAL CHRISTIANITY

God Has Not Left Himself Without Witness

Ivan M. Satyavrata

First published 2011 by Regnum Books International

Regnum is an imprint of the Oxford Centre for Mission Studies
St. Philip and St. James Church
Woodstock Road
Oxford, OX2 6HR, UK
www.ocms.ac.uk/regnum

09 08 07 06 05 04 03 8 7 6 5 4 3 2 1

British Library Cataloguing in Publication Data
A catalogue record for this book is available from the British Library

ISBN - 978-1-506475-84-4

Typeset by Words by Design
Cover design by Words by Design

The publication of this title was made possible by the the financial assistance of the Boys and Girls Missionary Crusade (BGMC) Fund of the (US) Assembly of God World World Mission through the Eurasia Office (Director Omar Beiler)

Distributed by 1517 Media in the US and Canada

Contents

Contents v

Acknowledgements viii

Abbreviations ix

Foreword vii

Introduction 1

The Background and Statement of the Problem 1
The Definition and Scope of the Project 3
A Brief Introduction to Fulfilment Theology 9
Models of Fulfilment 11
Prophetic or Promise-fulfilment 11
Logos-historical fulfilment 12
Evolutionary fulfilment 14
A Definition of Fulfilment 15
Pedagogical value of other religions 15
Christ's universality set within essential continuity 15
Decisiveness of Christ 15
Background and Development of the Protestant Fulfilment Tradition in the Nineteenth Century 16
The Conservative Protestant Missionary Attitude to Other Religions 16
The Emergence of the Protestant Missionary Fulfilment Approach 21
Fulfilment Approaches in the Pre-independence Indian Context 25
Fulfilment in Renascent Hindu Approaches to Christ: Keshub Chunder Sen (1838-84) 26
Fulfilment in Indian Christian Apologists: Nehemiah Goreh (1825-95) 31
Fulfilment in the Advaitic Christian Tradition: Brahmabandhab Upadhyay (1861-1907) 34
Fulfilment in the Bhakti Christian Tradition: N.V. Tilak (1862-1919) 39
Summary Evaluation 42
Conclusion 46

Fulfilment in John Nicol Farquhar's 'The Crown of Hinduism' 47

The Man and His Background (1861-1929) 48
Fulfilment in Farquhar's Earlier Literary Contribution 50
Fulfilment in 'The Crown of Hinduism' 59

A Critical Analysis of Farquhar's Fulfilment Approach 68
Farquhar's Conception of Fulfilment 68
The Pedagogical Value of Hinduism 72
Objection 1: Christ offers the solution to a need which Hinduism does not feel. 72
Objection 2: The evidence is forced to fit the theory. 76
Evolutionary Continuity and Progressive Revelation 78
Objection 3: Opposition to the use of evolutionary theory. 78
Objection 4: The Jewish-Christian fulfilment model cannot be applied to the Hindu-Christian relationship. 81
Christ, the Crown of Hinduism 83
Objection 5: The fulfilment approach reflects an attitude of condescension. 85
Summary Evaluation 85

Fulfilment in Krishna Mohan Banerjea's Vedic Theology 91

The Man and His Background (1813-1885) 92
His Theological Development 96
The Emergence of Fulfilment in Banerjea's Early Thought 98
Christianity as the Fulfilment of Hinduism in Banerjea's Thought 103
A Critical Analysis of Banerjea's Fulfilment Approach 112
Use of the Vedas 122
Primeval Revelation 126
Christ and Prajapati 131
Summary Evaluation 134

Fulfilment in Sundar Singh's Bhakti Spirituality 139

The Man and His Background (1889-1929) 139
Bhakti Mysticism and Sundar Singh's Fulfilment Framework 145
The Background and Sources of Sundar Singh's Bhakti Mystical Orientation 146
Bhakti Mysticism as a Framework of Continuity in Sundar Singh's Fulfilment View 154
God 155
Divine Revelation 158
Salvation 162
Fulfilment of the Bhakti Religious Quest 167
Christ and Non-Christian Religious Experience 168
Christ as Fulfilment 175
Fulfilment and the Sadhu Ideal 180
A Critical Analysis of Sundar Singh's Understanding of Fulfilment 184
The Pedagogical Value of Hindu Religious Experience 185
Revelation and the Intuitive Knowledge of God 188
The Logos-Christ of Mystical Experience 191
Summary Evaluation 193

A Critical Evaluation of the Contributions of Farquhar, Banerjea, and Sundar Singh to Fulfilment Thought 197

The Socio-political Impulse for the Emergence of Fulfilment Approach in Pre-independence India 197
A Comparative Theological Assessment of the Fulfilment Conceptions of Farquhar, Banerjea and Sundar Singh 199
Fulfilment and the Pedagogical Value of Hinduism 199
Fulfilment and Continuity-Discontinuity 207
Fulfilment and the Decisiveness of Christ 214
A Cumulative Description of the Fulfilment Proposal 219
The 'Cosmic' Trajectory 223
The 'Word' Trajectory 224
The 'Spirit' Trajectory 225
Convergence 226

Christ and the Other Religions in Fulfilment Theology 228

An Evaluation of the Fulfilment Proposal 228
Fulfilment and the Religions 229
Fulfilment and Christ 232
Criticisms of the Fulfilment Proposal 236
Criticism 1: Fulfilment Theology is a Form of Imperialism 237
Criticism 2: Fulfilment theology is a theology of and for the high castes 240
Conclusion: Towards a Recovery of Protestant Fulfilment Theology 241

Bibliography 248

Acknowledgements

This book has its origin in a Doctor of Philosophy research project at the Oxford Centre for Mission Studies (OCMS). I owe much to several people for their support and encouragement in this project. I am deeply indebted to my Director of Studies, Dr. Gavin D'Costa, Professor of Christian Theology, Department of Theology and Religious Studies, University of Bristol, for his expert and patient guidance. I am thankful to Dr. Vinay Kumar Samuel, of OCMS for his help in the original conception of this thesis, and his and Mrs. Colleen Samuel's encouragement at several stages of my research. My Supervisors, Dr. Christopher Sugden, OCMS, and Dr. David Samuel, TAFTEE, Bangalore, offered helpful suggestions and comments on my work.

I am greatly indebted personally to the Rev. Dr. John Stott and to the Langham Research Scholarships Trust (now Langham Partnership International), as well as the Assemblies of God World Missions, USA, for providing the financial assistance for my studies. My thanks are also due to AGWM personnel, Dr. David Grant and Dr. John Higgins, and the Board of Directors of Southern Asia Bible College (SABC), for their willingness to grant me periodical leaves of absence and for supporting our family in various other ways. I also benefited from the consistent encouragement of several friends too numerous to list by name, including staff and scholars at OCMS, my colleagues at SABC, and various members of our extended family.

This work would never have been published but for the efforts of special friends. Dr. Wonsuk Ma, Executive Director, OCMS, both initiated the proposal and helped facilitate a publication grant. I was able to devote some time to preparing this manuscript for publication through the facility of the Dr. J. Philip Hogan Chair at the Assemblies of God Theological Seminary (AGTS), Springfield, Missouri, USA. My family and I owe a huge debt of gratitude to Dr. Byron Klaus, President of AGTS, Lois Klaus, and the faculty and staff community at AGTS for their support and gracious hospitality. I am especially grateful to Susan Starkey, Administrative Assistant to President Klaus, for her careful editing of the final manuscript.

I could not have concluded this journey successfully without the support and prayers of my dear wife, Sheila, and sons, Rahul and Rohan. Above all I thank the Triune God who graciously enabled me to complete this project – it is to the praise of his glory that I humbly dedicate this volume!

Abbreviations

CIIS	Centre for Indian and Inter-religious Studies
CISRS	The Christian Institute for the Study of Religion and Society
CLS	The Christian Literature Service
ISPCK	The Indian Society for Propagating Christian Knowledge
IVP	Inter Varsity Press
OUP	The Oxford University Press
RV	Rg Veda
SCM	The Student Christian Movement
SPCK	The Society for Propagating Christian Knowledge
UTC	The United Theological College
VPC SSS	Various Private Collections about Sadhu Sundar Singh
WCC	The World Council of Churches

Dedication

Lovingly dedicated to John & Faith Higgins, true Friends in Mission

Foreword

From Abraham's conversation with Melchizedek to Paul's speech in Athens, the Bible portrays many encounters between people who knew the living God in the context of covenant revelation and others who stood on different ground and yet are presented as having some knowledge of God and some impulse to seek after God and worship him. What are we to make of such encounters, and how are we to envisage the spiritual reality that lies behind them in terms of God's relationship with those who were not (or not yet) standing within that salvific covenant tradition? And how are we to articulate the relationship between their pre-existing religious understandings and the faith declared to them in the name of the biblical God, founded on his words and deeds climaxing in Jesus Christ?

Substitute for the small governing council of Athens, heirs to the few centuries of Greek religion and philosophy that formed the worldview from which they listened to Paul, the millions of Indians over countless generations whose worldview has been shaped for two millennia by the philosophy and religion of the Vedas and other scriptures of what was eventually categorized as "Hinduism", and you begin to see the scale of the task confronting Christian mission in that land through all its centuries – not to mention the scale of the task that Ivan Satyavrata attempts in this book.

The Bible affirms two great truths, as integral and essential to each other as the dynamic relation of breathing in and breathing out. There is the universality of the Bible's teaching about humanity; and there is the particularity of the Bible's teaching about God's revealing and saving action in and through Jesus of Nazareth.

So, on the one hand, all human beings are made in God's image, live in God's created world that reveals his existence, power and kindness, are known individually to God in all their thoughts, motives and actions, are loved by God and accountable to God. All human beings, however, participate in the universality of sin and rebellion against God and stand under judgment. Given this double truth about human beings, there is a corresponding double truth about all human religion: simply because it is human, it shares something of the image of God, contains elements of the truth and the revelation of God and expresses human longing for the God who made us. But likewise, simply because it is human, it shares the reality of human sin and rebellion, provides a powerful way of obscuring the radical demands of God, and entangles us in idolatries and darkness. There is, then, a paradoxical ambiguity about all religion that mirrors our ambiguous human condition. And this double-edged truth, according to the Bible, is universal. We will find in any and all religions that which reflects the goodness of God in whose image we are made, and that which reflects the depravity of our fallen rebellion.

And, on the other hand, the Bible affirms that salvation rests not in our human capacity or accomplishment – religious or otherwise – but only in what the living God has chosen to do within human history for the salvation of humanity and the ultimate redemption of all creation. That unique and particular story of salvation is told in the Bible itself, and of course comes to its climax and final accomplishment in the cross and resurrection of Jesus of Nazareth. Therefore, alongside the universality of what the Bible says about humanity as a whole, we have to place the uniqueness, finality, and decisiveness of Jesus Christ as the heart and soul of Christian witness and mission.

How then does the one hand relate to the other hand? When people come out of a religious tradition that contains elements of truth and revelation alongside the marks of human ignorance and sin, and meet the living God in and through encounter with Jesus Christ and put their faith in him – how are they (or we) to express the relationship between their Christ-centred faith and their prior religious understanding and practice? That has been a divisive issue of Christian mission from the very beginning (it can be seen in the conflict between Christian believers from Jewish and Gentile backgrounds in the New Testament itself).

In this book, Dr Satyavrata explores a significant strand of Christian theologizing on this issue associated with the word "fulfilment". From having been a major and influential way of articulating the relationship in the early 20th century, it has suffered neglect more recently, particularly in evangelical missiology and missionary practice. His thorough analysis of three major figures in Indian Christian history and their antecedents is richly illuminating. Again and again we will find theological insights and approaches in their writings that anticipate by decades the debates that still generate heat and argument today. How quickly we forget!

Dr Satyavrata is concerned to do more than merely summarize or analyse, however. He is keenly aware of "both hands" of the issue, as expressed above, and seeks not only to critique his three exemplars by the criteria of sound Christian confession of the central decisiveness of Jesus Christ and his saving work, but also to articulate a theologically defensible synthesis of what we can most learn from them in our generation.

It is a particular joy for me to commend this book, having known Ivan Satyavrata since the days we studied together – as teacher and student in many Old Testament classes at Union Biblical Seminary, Pune, India - through his years of doctoral work as a distinguished Langham Scholar, and in the subsequent years of his seminary and church leadership in India. May this fruit of his own research bear more fruit among those who read and heed his work.

Christopher J.H. Wright
International Director,
Langham Partnership International

Introduction

The Background and Statement of the Problem

The Christian Church has had to address the question of the common ground between the Christian faith and other religions since its earliest inception. While the issue is thus by no means new, in recent years the relationship of Christian faith to other religious traditions has begun to occupy a position of prominence in the contemporary world of theological reflection. In the two-third's world context of a desperate struggle for social harmony amidst growing religious fundamentalism and militancy, the issue is not merely of academic interest but one with critical existential and socio-political consequences.

The current debate has generated a considerable amount of literature on the subject,[1] giving rise to a wide range of responses to the fundamental question: Is there a way of relating Christian faith and experience to other religions which ascribes genuine value to the religious experience of people of other faiths while affirming the essential truth claims of the Christian faith? An assumption implicit in much of the contemporary discussion on this question is that the modern experience of religious plurality has forced this issue upon the Church.[2] It is, however, the original constituting fact of the Christian faith – the Christ-event, and claims of decisiveness[3] and universality integral to it – that has given rise to the intrinsic missionary nature of the Christian faith since its inception. This fact has compelled the Church to address the issue of the

---

[1] Early available treatments of the broad gamut of issues include: A. Race, *Christians and Religious Pluralism* (New York: Orbis, 1982); P.F. Knitter, *No Other Name? A Critical Survey of Christian Attitudes to World Religions* (New York, Orbis, 1985); and G. D'Costa, *Theology and Religious Pluralism* (Oxford: Basil Blackwell, 1986). Two multi-author contributions of almost watershed significance are J. Hick and P. Knitter, eds. *The Myth of Christian Uniqueness: Towards a Pluralistic Theology of Religions* (New York: Orbis, 1987), and a critical response, G. D'Costa, *Christian Uniqueness Reconsidered: The Myth of a Pluralistic Theology of Religions* (New York: Orbis, 1990).

[2] As implied, for instance, in Knitter, *No Other Name,* 2-6; Race, *Christians and Religious Pluralism,* x; and M. Barnes, *Christian Identity and Religious Pluralism: Religions in Conversation* (Nashville, Abingdon, 1989), 8-11.

[3] In this study the term decisiveness and its cognates will normally be preferred to other related terms such as absoluteness, uniqueness, and finality to denote how the Church has historically viewed the definitive significance of God's action in the Christ-event. A case for the greater precision and appropriateness of this term over the others has been cogently argued by O.V. Jathanna, *The Decisiveness of the Christ-event and the Universality of Christianity in a World of Religious Plurality: With Special Reference to Henrik Kraemer and Alfred George Hogg as well as to William Ernest Hocking and Pandipeddi Chenchiah* (Berne: Peter Lang, 1981), 22-35.

relation of Christian faith to other religions since the earliest stages of its contact with the non-Christian world.

Evangelical Christians professing a firm commitment to active missionary engagement tend to take the original missiological context of the issue seriously and, consequently, focus on one end of the dialectic – the decisiveness of Christ. Their treatments, however, frequently display a marked lack of sensitivity to the genuine religious aspirations of peoples of other faiths.[4] Pluralists, on the other hand, often lose sight of the original missiological context which gave birth to this issue, and out of a genuine concern to defend the legitimate religious aspirations of peoples of other faiths, respond in ways that seem to compromise the integrity of the Christian tradition.[5]

Christianity came not into a religious vacuum, but into a world of living religions. Wherever the Christian faith went, there was already an existing religious tradition of some kind, a "tradition of response",[6] expressing the awareness of the transcendent within the particular context. The original membership of the Church thus consisted of converts from different religions.

---

[4] As typical illustrations, R. Gundry, 'Salvation According to Scripture: No Middle Ground', *Christianity Today* 22 (1977), 14-16; J. Cottrell and S.E. Burris, 'The Fate of the Unreached: Are They Lost Without Special Revelation?', *International Journal of Frontier Missions* 10:2 (1993), 67-72; Sproul, *Reason to Believe* (Grand Rapids: Zondervan, 1982), 52-56; for a fuller list, see Sanders, *An Investigation into the Destiny of the Unevangelized* (Grand Rapids: Eerdmans, 1992), 78-79. There are, however, indications of a more sensitive and sympathetic response in evangelical treatments in recent years, see W.G. Phillips, 'Evangelicals and Pluralism: Current Options', *The Evangelical Quarterly* 64 (1992), 229-244; C. Pinnock, *A Wideness in God's Mercy* (Grand Rapids: Zondervan,1992); Sanders, *An Investigation Into the Destiny of the Unevangelized*, 131-286; and especially J.G.R. McDermott, *God's Rivals: Why has God Allowed Different Religions? Insights from the Bible and the Early Church* (Downers Grove, IL: InterVarsity Press, 2007).

[5] See, for example, the critiques of pluralism in G. D'Costa, 'Other Faiths and Christianity' in A.E. McGrath, ed., *The Blackwell Encyclopedia of Modern Christian Thought* (Oxford, Blackwell, 1993), 413; L. Newbigin, 'Religious Pluralism and the Uniqueness of Jesus Christ', *International Bulletin of Missionary Research* 13.2 (1989), 50-54; K. Flanagan, 'Theological Pluralism: A Sociological Critique' in I. Hammett, ed., *Religious Pluralism and Unbelief: Studies Critical and Comparative* (London: Routledge), 1990), 90-91; K. Surin, 'Towards a "Materialist" Critique of Religious Pluralism' in I. Hammett, ed., *Religious Pluralism and Unbelief: Studies Critical and Comparative* (London: Routledge, 1990), 123-26; A. Hastings, 'Pluralism: The Relationship of Theology to Religious Studies in I. Hammett, ed., *Religious Pluralism and Unbelief: Studies Critical and Comparative* (London: Routledge, 1990), 235-39.

[6] John Taylor's expression in *The Go-Between God – The Holy Spirit and the Christian Mission* (London: SCM Press, 1972), 182f, which K. Bediako employs in *Theology and Identity: The Impact of Culture Upon Christian Thought in the Second Century and in Modern Africa* (Oxford: Regnum Books, 1992), 436, in applying the early fathers' inclusive approach to pre-Christian tradition in the African context.

As the Christian gospel spread to new lands down through the centuries, and as vast numbers of peoples of diverse cultures and religions responded to it from within their traditions, the Church has accumulated for itself a wide variety of traditions of encounter. These may be found in every culture where the Christian gospel has made an impact, providing valuable resources for reflection on the issue in focus.

These "traditions of encounter", which represent the accumulated resources of two millennia of the Church's experience of relating to people of other faiths, receive inadequate attention in many recent approaches to this problem. Most scholars concede in theory the importance of the Church's history of encounter with other religions, but only a few seem to treat the past experience of the Church as having any real value in shaping the Christian response today.[7] Although some features we observe may be discarded as archaic or irrelevant, any attempt to arrive at an informed solution to the problem cannot afford to ignore the rich resources of religious experience and inter-faith engagement represented by these "traditions of encounter".

The task is thus multi-faceted and complex, but essential for a responsible Christian response to the phenomenon of other religions. The present study attempts to make a small contribution towards this broader project by drawing from one such "tradition of encounter" within the Indian context: the appropriation of Christ by converts in pre-independence India (1820 to 1947).[8]

The Definition and Scope of the Project

The followers of Christ in India have had to grapple with the question of the relationship between Christian faith and other religions for centuries. Although the theological tradition of India has not been wholly ignored in this regard, significant strands of creative thinking – especially from the earlier formative years – seem to have been left largely untouched and undeveloped. The Christian tradition in India is strewn with illustrations of converts to Christian faith in whom the tension between allegiance to Christ and love for their ancestral tradition was deeply personalised. Several of these found a

---

[7] For instance: E.J. Sharpe, *Faith Meets Faith: Some Christian Attitudes to Hinduism in the Nineteenth and Twentieth Centuries* (London: SCM Press, 1970; P. Hacker, *Theological Foundations of Evangelization* (St. Augustin: Steyler Verlag), 1980; F.A. Sullivan, *Salvation Outside the Church? Tracing the History of the Catholic Response* (London: Chapman, 1992); and Jacques Dupuis, *Toward a Christian Theology of Religious Pluralism* (New York: Orbis, 1997). For a rare illustration of a focussed treatment that takes serious account of the Indian Christian experience, see J. Lipner, 'A Modern Indian Christian Response', in *Modern Indian Responses to Religious Pluralism*, ed. H.G. Coward (Albany: State University of New York, 1987), 291-314.

[8] This focus on the pre-independence period is determined by the formative significance of the theological discussion during these crucial years; see n. 10 below.

satisfactory resolution to their struggle by regarding faith in Christ as in some way fulfilling the highest aspirations of their pre-Christian religious experience.

Our study focuses on this fulfilment stream as articulated in the experience of Indian Christian converts during the pre-independence period (1820 to 1947).[9] The reasons for locating this study in this period are: (1) the encounter between Protestant missionary Christianity and Hinduism during this period represents an important theological ferment in which critical questions regarding the relationship of Christianity to Hinduism were first raised and discussed in the modern period;[10] (2) the origins of an authentic Indian Christian identity and theological tradition may be traced to the pioneering indigenization efforts of the converts of this period;[11] (3) these converts, moreover, offer creative and original insights into fundamental issues in the Christian-Hindu encounter. Hence, the principal subjects of our study are located in this period.

The importance of this fulfilment stream may be observed in the fact that the vast majority of indigenous approaches to other faiths during this period reflect some form of the fulfilment concept, whether or not the term is explicitly used.[12] In analysing the attitude to other religions within this Indian fulfilment stream, we seek to relate it to the fulfilment tradition that emerged as the predominant Protestant missionary apologetic approach of the nineteenth century, and then evaluate it theologically in relation to a broader historical Christian theory of other religions – fulfilment theology.

The essential question guiding this study is: What value do the fulfilment approaches of representative Indian Christian converts from the pre-independence period have in helping relate the Christian faith to other religions in a way which affirms the particular truth claims of the Christian tradition and yet ascribes genuine worth to the religious experience of people of other faiths?

Chapter one considers preliminary questions of definition, background and context. The wide range of views and variety of nuances covered by the term fulfilment necessitates that we address the problem of definition early. Our procedure requires us to distinguish several levels at which the fulfilment

---

[9] Ram Mohan Roy is widely regarded as the first Indian to have engaged in serious scholarly interaction with the Christian faith; the period under consideration is thus dated from the publication of his *Precepts of Jesus* in 1820, to 1947, the year of India's independence; R. Boyd, *An Introduction to Indian Christian Theology* (Delhi: ISPCK, 1991), 19.

[10] According to Sharpe, *Faith Meets Faith*, 1, xiii-xiv, the second half of the nineteenth century was marked by "the most extensive confrontation" of the Christian faith with non-Christian religions since the first century.

[11] Lipner, 'A Modern Indian Christian Response', 291-292.

[12] Thus several of the figures treated in Boyd's standard textbook on Indian Christian thought either explicitly use the term fulfilment, or reflect the fulfilment impulse without actually using the term as such; Boyd, *An Introduction to Indian Christian Theology*, 37, 54, 67, 106, 280-310.

impulse is expressed, and to introduce a frame of reference for the purpose of conceptual and terminological clarity.

The term fulfilment is used in the following three senses: (1) fulfilment *approach* (or view)[13] is the term used to denote expressions of the fulfilment concept (theme/impulse) in the thought of specific individuals like Farquhar or Banerjea; (2) fulfilment *tradition* (or proposal) is used to connote a group of approaches with certain family resemblances which give them the status of a school of thought, such as the nineteenth century evolutionary fulfilment tradition or the fulfilment tradition of the early fathers; (3) fulfilment *theology* is used to represent a broad theory of religion,[14] a theological perspective of other religions expressed in various forms and periods in church history, which has the basic fulfilment concept (or theme/impulse) at its core. In this context we will also introduce a typology of three fulfilment models for identifying and distinguishing between various forms of fulfilment theology.

The distinction between these three levels of usage of the term fulfilment is integral to the differentiation of the three stages of the task. In the first inductive and analytical stage, we examine the fulfilment *approaches* of a leading representative of the nineteenth century Protestant fulfilment tradition and two representative Indian converts. The second synthetic stage involves a comparative evaluation of the three fulfilment approaches we have considered, first, to see whether the approaches of Indian converts can be held together in a theologically coherent fulfilment proposal; and, second, to explore the extent to which they may be able to complement the nineteenth century Protestant fulfilment *tradition.* The final evaluative stage of the project will assess how investigation of this Indian Christian tradition of encounter contributes to the plausibility of the broader fulfilment *theology* scheme.

It is thus essential to our procedure that we first clarify our understanding of the fulfilment concept and then seek to describe individual fulfilment approaches, various fulfilment traditions, and fulfilment theology in relation to this broad definition of the fulfilment concept. We define the fulfilment concept in relation to three principal models which emerged at critical moments of defining significance in the Christian encounter with other traditions: (1) in the emergence of the gospel from its theological cradle, the Jewish faith; (2) in the early Church's encounter with Greek culture in the second and third centuries; and, (3) in the nineteenth century Protestant missionary encounter with the religions of India. Our definition of the fulfilment concept will thus be based on common features drawn from our outlines of these three models.

---

[13] The alternative expressions are offered in each case as stylistic variations in view of the frequent usage of each term.

[14] Whaling, 'Religion Theories of', in *The Blackwell Encyclopedia of Modern Christian Thought*, ed. A.E. McGrath (Oxford: Blackwell, 1993), 548-549.

In setting the context, we first outline the background and development of the nineteenth century Protestant fulfilment tradition. For many years, Eric Sharpe's competent historical survey remained the standard introduction to this tradition.[15] A series of recent works have investigated different aspects of this tradition from a variety of perspectives.[16] Of special significance is a historical study of the nineteenth century British fulfilment tradition that includes a theological analysis and assessment.[17] In our sketch of this tradition, we trace its emergence against the background of the confrontational Protestant missionary posture which dominated the first half of the nineteenth century, identify the principal factors which contributed to the growth in influence of the Protestant fulfilment tradition, and outline the course of its development prior to the Edinburgh World Missionary Conference in 1910. This provides the necessary background for our consideration of the fulfilment approach of John Nicol Farquhar, and the context for our subsequent comparison and synthesis.

The immediate ferment within which fulfilment approaches emerged within the Indian context was the wide range of indigenous[18] responses to Christ during the same period.[19] Our survey of the responses of Indian converts will evaluate the influence of the fulfilment concept in shaping the Christian

---

[15] Sharpe, *Not to Destroy but to Fulfil: The Contribution of J.N. Farquhar to Protestant Missionary Thought in India before 1914* (Uppsala: Swedish Institute of Missionary Research, 1965).

[16] Martin Maw focuses on B.F. Westcott's fulfilment view and the contribution of the Cambridge Mission to Delhi; M. Maw, *Visions of India: Fulfilment Theology, the Aryan Race Theory, and the Work of British Protestant Missionaries in Victorian India* (Frankfurt: Peter Lang, 1990). Although Kenneth Cracknell does not specifically focus on fulfilment theology, he deals with the theologies of religion of thirteen leading theologians and missionary thinkers of the period; K. Cracknell, *Justice, Courtesy and Love: Theologians and Missionaries Encountering World Religions (1846-1914)* (London: Epworth, 1995). Wesley Ariarajah's evaluation of the twentieth century Protestant attitude to other faiths, focuses on the Edinburgh, Jerusalem, and Tambaram missionary conferences; S.W. Ariarajah, *Hindus and Christians: A Century of Protestant Ecumenical Thought* (Grand Rapids: Eerdmans, 1991).

[17] P.M. Hedges, *Preparation and Fulfilment: A History and Study of Fulfilment Theology in Modern British Thought in the Indian Context* (Bern: Peter Lang, 2001).

[18] The term indigenous has a variety of theological and missiological connotations, but unless otherwise indicated, in this study it will be used in its normal sense of native or belonging naturally to.

[19] Although our focus in this study is upon converts, the Hindu response to Christ was complex and nuanced. At one end were converts who still struggled to maintain their Hindu cultural identity after joining the Church; some Hindus attempted to initiate new syncretistic Hindu-Christian movements; others expressed strong attraction and devotion to Christ while remaining within the orthodox Hindu fold; at the other end of the spectrum were Hindus who unequivocally rejected the Christian message; for some illustrations, see M.M. Thomas, *The Acknowledged Christian of the Indian Renaissance* (Madras: CLS, 1976).

attitude to other religions in India, and provide the necessary context for our more detailed examination of the fulfilment approaches of the second and third principal subjects of our study, Krishna Mohan Banerjea and Sadhu Sundar Singh.

Chapter two examines the fulfilment view of John Nicol Farquhar (1861-1929),[20] a leading representative of the nineteenth century Protestant fulfilment tradition. Farquhar only gave structured expression and clarity to a line of thinking which preceded him in Europe as well as in India, but his precise scholarship and systematic articulation of the fulfilment approach has caused him to be widely regarded as a leading proponent of fulfilment theology in the modern period.[21] The importance of Farquhar has been called into question in recent years.[22] Although Farquhar's best-known work, *The Crown of Hinduism*, describes most of the salient features of his fulfilment approach, a survey of the earlier stages in the development of his thought illuminates some essential aspects of his later view. The most significant criticisms of his view will be evaluated, and comments offered regarding his influence on Protestant fulfilment thought. Our discussion of Farquhar's fulfilment approach is methodologically critical since it provides a framework for analysing the fulfilment approaches of the two Indian subjects of our study.

Chapters three and four present substantial assessments, respectively, of the fulfilment approaches of two representative Indian converts: Krishna Mohan Banerjea (1813-1885) and Sadhu Sundar Singh (1889-1929).[23] They have been selected for detailed treatment for the following reasons: (1) both were converts – Banerjea from Hinduism and Sundar Singh from Sikhism – who remained deeply immersed in their pre-Christian culture even after their conversion, and yet evidence firm commitment to the witness of the Christian tradition; (2) they represent two successive generations of thought, and each articulates a distinctive fulfilment approach from within two different strands of Hindu religious tradition. Banerjea was a Brahmin convert and sought to relate Christian faith to the pure theism of the Vedas; although Sundar Singh was a Sikh by birth, his approach to Christ and his understanding of fulfilment were clearly conditioned by his marked bhakti devotional orientation; (3) both have

---

[20] M.M. Thomas and P.T. Thomas, *Towards an Indian Christian Theology: Life and Thought of some Pioneers* (Tiruvalla: New Day Publications of India, 1992), 80.

[21] His name is thus consistently associated with the emergence of fulfilment theology in the modern period; see, for instance, E.C. Dewick, *The Christian Attitude to Other Religions* (Cambridge: Cambridge University Press, 1953), 49; F. Whaling, *Christian Theology and World Religions: A Global Approach,* 1986), 85; B. Stanley, *The Bible and the Flag: Protestant Missions and British Imperialism in the Nineteenth and Twentieth Centuries* (Leicester: Apollos, 1990), 164; J. Brockington, *Hinduism and Christianity* (Basingstoke: MacMillan, 1992), 177.

[22] Cracknell, *Justice Courtesy and Love*, 172-173; Hedges, 'A History and Study of Fulfilment Theology', 7; Hedges, *Preparation and Fulfilment* 2001: 5.

[23] Thomas and Thomas, *Toward an Indian Christian Theology*, 22, 162.

received insufficient scholarly attention from the theology of religions perspective,[24] even as they continue to exercise considerable influence upon grass-roots level Christian witness in the Indian context.[25]

Chapter five focuses on the synthetic dimension of our project. Farquhar's fulfilment approach was representative of a type of attitude to other faiths that received widespread acceptance among leading members of the Protestant missionary community at the historic World Missionary Conference at Edinburgh in 1910, becoming, in Sharpe's words, "an item of Christian orthodoxy for a whole generation of Indian missionaries" in the period immediately following the conference.[26] In the years leading up to the Tambaram Conference of the International Missionary Council in 1938, serious objections began to be raised against the fulfilment approach contributing to the decline in its influence.

It is at this point that the fulfilment approaches of Indian converts offer resources for complementing and strengthening the modern Protestant fulfilment tradition. Based on their study of Hindu texts and their own first-hand experience, they represent, cumulatively, an empirically credible response to some of the criticisms of the nineteenth century Protestant fulfilment tradition. Their insights thus can help clarify and confirm, as well as correct and complement some aspects of Farquhar's view. Our comparative evaluation of the fulfilment approaches of Farquhar, Banerjea, and Sundar Singh will thus

---

[24] Their contributions to theology of religions are thus generally mentioned only in passing within broader descriptions of their thought. This omission is unfortunate given that: (1) they represent a phase which is of critical significance for the theology of Christian-Hindu encounter; and, (2)] their religious experience which overlapped two traditions offers a valuable resource for understanding the relation between these two traditions. Lipner's treatment of Banerjea is one of few exceptions Lipner, 'A Modern Christian Response', 303-306; Hedges strangely subsumes his brief treatment of Banerjea and other select Indian thinkers under the chapter title, 'Missionary Usage', and includes a paragraph sketch of Sundar Singh in his conclusion; Hedges, *Preparation and Fulfilment*, 137-154; 389-390.

[25] Banerjea's influence is more indirect, through the perpetuation of his ideas by D.P. Titus, *Fulfilment of the Vedic Quest in the Lord Jesus Christ* (Nainital: Sat Tal Ashram, 1982); R.C. Das, *Convictions of an Indian Disciple* (Bangalore: CISRS, 1966) and several less known writers at a popular level. The life and teachings of Sundar Singh continue to shape the collective consciousness of much of Indian Christianity, especially, though not exclusively, of the evangelical and Pentecostal type; see E.J. Sharpe, 'The Legacy of Sadhu Sundar Singh', *International Bulletin of Missionary Research* 14 (1991), 165-166. The ongoing relevance of the contributions of both figures is underlined by the publication of significant compilations of their writings in recent years: T.D. Francis, *The Christian Witness of Sadhu Sundar Singh: A Collection of His Writings* (Madras, CLS, 1989), and K.P. Aleaz, *From Exclusivism to Inclusivism: The Theological Writings of Krishna Mohun Banerjea (1813-1885)* (Delhi: ISPCK, 1998).

[26] E.J. Sharpe, 'The Legacy of J.N. Farquhar', *Occasional Bulletin of Missionary Research* 3, 2 (1979), 62.

enable us to outline a framework for a cumulative and theologically coherent Protestant fulfilment proposal.

This research project attempts to strengthen the case for the legitimacy and value of fulfilment theology. Our concluding proposal in chapter six addresses two important contemporary criticisms of fulfilment theology, and offers justification for the coherence of its response over alternative proposals to the problem posed in our thesis question: how can we affirm the particular truth claims of the Christian tradition while ascribing genuine value to non-Christian religious experience? Finally, we consider the implications of our study for the recovery of Protestant fulfilment theology in the light of its apparent decline in the twentieth century.

A Brief Introduction to Fulfilment Theology

Fulfilment theology is broadly based on a theory of the relation between Christianity and other religions which holds that "...all religious traditions have partial access to truth, to spirituality and to transcendence, but Christianity has access to them in their fullness."[27] Although the scope of this study does not permit us to trace in detail the biblical and historical roots of fulfilment theology, it is important to recognise that the belief that Christianity fulfils other religions can be traced almost continuously throughout the history of the Church.

We begin with Jesus' attitude to Judaism reflected in the words of Matthew 5:17: "Do not think that I have come to abolish the Law or the Prophets; I have not come to abolish them but to fulfil them" (TNIV). Although the theme in its original New Testament context applied primarily to the fulfilment of Jewish messianic expectations in the Incarnation of Christ,[28] resources for a secondary application to other non-Christian cultures may be found in certain New Testament evangelistic texts: the concept of *Logos* in the prologue of John's gospel,[29] the addresses of Paul to Gentile audiences in Acts 14 and 17,[30] and

---

[27] Whaling, 'Religion Theories', 548; Whaling, *Christian Theology and World Religions*, 83, delineates three forms of fulfilment: fulfilment of the common essence of religion, fulfilment of other religious traditions, and fulfilment of process. Dhavamony's classification corresponds closely to that of Whaling, but distinguishes only the first two categories; M. Dhavamony, 'The Cosmic Christ and World Religions', *Studia Missionalia*, 42 (1993), 179-181.

[28] Dewick, *The Christian Attitude*, 77-82; R.N. Longenecker, *The Christology of Early Jewish Christianity* (Grand Rapids: Baker Book House, 1970), 65-66, 79-81; V. Poythress, *The Shadow of Christ in the Law of Moses* (Brentwood: Wolgemuth & Hyatt, 1991), 264-67, 363-77.

[29] A.C. Bouquet, 'Revelation and the Divine *Logos*', in *The Theology of the Christian Mission*, ed. G. H. Anderson (London: SCM), 1961), 183-98; G.R. Beasley-Murray, *Word Biblical Commentary, John*, vol. 36 (Waco: Word Books, 1987), 1, 8-10; L. Morris, *The Gospel According to John* (Grand Rapids: Eerdmans, 1995), 102-108.

Paul's creation theology in Romans 1 & 2.[31] The early fathers' approach to non-Christian philosophy and religion was also based on a fulfilment reading of the New Testament.[32]

Although the Christianization of Europe caused the problem of the relationship of Christianity to non-Christian religions to be relegated to the background, all through the middle ages, significant schools of thought within Christendom accepted in theory the principle that all goodness and truth – regardless of where they may be found – find their highest fulfilment in Christ.[33] This fulfilment impulse, however, seems to have existed alongside a more confrontational posture which viewed the Christian encounter with other religions essentially as a meeting of truth with falsehood.[34]

It is difficult to define a term employed over two millennia of Christian tradition with a wide range of theological nuances. Hedges gives fulfilment a context-specific definition in relation to its expression in modern British Protestant thought.[35] Based on an analysis of its various nineteenth century definitions and expressions, he defines a classical form of fulfilment theology based on a quintessential foundation or essence summed up in four key phrases: progressive revelation; man as a religious animal; divine providence; and Logos theology.[36] The strength of Hedges' definition is its inductive approach. Its weakness is that, although he recognises the existence of a broader historical stream of fulfilment theology, it is difficult to apply consistently his discussion of the nineteenth century British Protestant fulfilment tradition to a theological critique of fulfilment approaches in other contexts.

In keeping with the objectives of our study, our procedure will offer a working definition of the broad fulfilment concept, which will then clarify

---

[30] The literature on Paul's speech in Acts 17 is vast; for a detailed bibliography, see F.F. Bruce, *The Acts of the Apostles* (Grand Rapids: Eerdmans, 1990), 379-380, 354-56, 381-85; also L. Legrand, 'The Missionary Significance of the Areopagus Speech' in *God's Word Among Men*, ed. G. Gispert-Sauch, (Delhi: Vidyajyoti, 1973), 60-69; L. Legrand, 'The Unknown God of Athens: Acts 17 and the Religion of the Gentiles', *The Indian Journal of Theology* 30 (1981), 158-166.

[31] J.D.G. Dunn, *Word Biblical Commentary: Romans 1-8*, vol. 8 (Dallas: Words Books, 1988), 57-58, 71, 105; D. Moo, *The Wycliffe Exegetical Commentary: Romans 1-8* (Chicago: Moody Press, 1991), 99-101, 122, 145-48.

[32] C. Saldanha, *Divine Pedagogy: A Patristic View of Non-Christian Religions* (Rome: Las, 1984), 158-86; Hacker, *Theological Foundations*, 35-50; Dupuis, *Toward Christian Theology*, 53-83.

[33] For a brief sketch of fulfilment thought in the Eastern Orthodox, Roman Catholic, and Reformed Churches during the pre-nineteenth century period, see Dewick, *The Christian Attitude*, 121-26; for medieval developments see also Sullivan, *Salvation Outside the Church?*, 30-123; and Dupuis, *Toward a Christian Theology*, 84-122.

[34] Sharpe, *Faith Meets Faith*, 2-10.

[35] Hedges, *Preparation and Fulfilment*, 26-43.

[36] Hedges, *ibid.*, 28-45.

variously in the specific contexts in which the term is employed. We begin by outlining the principal models of fulfilment that have emerged historically at critical moments of defining significance in the Christian encounter with other faiths.

Models of Fulfilment

The following classification focuses on the salient features of each model, highlighting the important distinctions between them, enabling us to discern elements of commonality and diversity in our definition of fulfilment.[37]

PROPHETIC OR PROMISE-FULFILMENT[38]

This fulfilment model was forged within the ferment of the original defining moment of the Gospel's emergence from its theological cradle, the Jewish faith. Derived from the original application of Jesus' words in Matthew 5:17, this model describes the approach of the first-century Christians to Old Testament Judaism. Based on the biblical conception of divine salvation history, this is the most basic expression of the fulfilment theme: the Messiah was promised, predicted, and prefigured in the Old Testament – the incarnation, crucifixion and resurrection of Christ took place in fulfilment of Old Testament predictions.

Although Judaism as a religious movement understandably rejected the claim that the coming of Christ in some way marks the fulfilment of the Old Testament promise and the completion of its story, historically Christianity has defined itself as the fulfilment of Judaism.[39] The attitude of the earliest Christians to their Jewish heritage and the New Testament account of Jesus' own attitude to his ancestral faith and culture, thus constitute the primary biblical resources for the construction of a coherent fulfilment approach.

Although this model originally applied to Jewish-Christian fulfilment, early and tentative attempts to relate Christianity to non-Christian religions often follow a similar pattern, in which non-Christian religious texts are appealed to for evidence of prophetic predictions or promises fulfilled in the Christian gospel. This approach, while attractive in its simplicity, becomes contentious at two points.

---

[37] Although this classification is not patterned after any existing fulfilment typology, we will indicate points of correspondence with other schemes where appropriate.

[38] This model corresponds approximately, if not precisely, to what Whaling describes as 'fulfilment of other religious traditions'; Whaling, 'Religion, theories of', 458.

[39] D'Costa offers a coherent justification of this position in response to the charge of supposed inherent anti-Semitism in this view; G. D'Costa, 'One Covenant or Many Covenants? Toward a Theology of Christian-Jewish Relations', *Journal of Ecumenical Studies* 27 (1990), 441-47.

According to one school of thought, the promise-fulfilment model both lacks theological validity and undermines the integrity of the Jewish faith.[40] Furthermore, some of those who affirm the legitimacy of this model in describing the relationship of Christian faith to Judaism would object to its application to Christianity and non-Jewish faiths.[41] For others, however, this model does express meaningful continuity between Christian and pre-Christian religious experience, if other non-Christian religions are not thereby accorded the *sui generis* status of Old Testament Jewish faith.[42] This original fulfilment model is of critical importance since approaches in subsequent gospel-culture encounters have often been patterned after it, although its prescriptive value may be a moot point in scholarly research.[43]

LOGOS-HISTORICAL FULFILMENT

The clear articulation of this model first emerged in the second defining moment of the Church's encounter with Greek culture in the second and third centuries. As the Church began to spread outside of Palestine it was confronted by a new cultural challenge – the world of Greek philosophy and religion. The Christian movement was no longer just a Jewish sect, but a faith which claimed universality and a missionary mandate. The questions were now significantly more complex: What part do non-Jewish religions have in the economy of God? Are there any legitimate religious aspirations or valid points of contact in them? How were the claims of Christian faith to be related to different forms of pre-Christian religion?

The earliest theologians of the church formulated their attitude to non-Christian religions in the context of these questions. The response generally took the form of uncompromising hostility to what was commonly regarded as paganism, but we also find some of the most generous recognitions of the work of God outside the Church prior to the modern period. Although the early Fathers are our main source of reflection for this period, the Fathers based their teaching on the theological resources of the New Testament.[44]

The various Fathers viewed non-Christian religions in different ways, but it is possible to identify a broad common framework that undergirds their approach. The Fathers sometimes treated Greek philosophy and literature as a

---

[40] For a summary description and rebuttal of its main arguments, see D'Costa, 'One Covenant or Many Covenants?', 442-452.

[41] The view of some conservative objectors to fulfilment, Dewick, *The Christian Attitude*, 82.

[42] L.H. De Wolf, 'The Interpenetration of Christianity and the Non-Christian Religions', in *The Theology of the Christian Mission*, ed. G.H. Anderson (London: SCM, 1961), 208-209.

[43] *Ibid.*, 252-254.

[44] Their views are of considerable importance not only because of their chronological proximity to the New Testament period, but also because their writings represent the earliest in-depth engagement with non-Jewish religion and philosophy.

kind of Old Testament, but their theological engagement of the Greek culture both built upon the promise-fulfilment approach and explicated it further. Saldanha uses the concept of pedagogy to summarise the dialectic in the Fathers' attitude to other religions, designating the elements of continuity and discontinuity within it by the terms preparation and transcendence respectively.[45] The essential challenge they seem to have faced was to hold the two elements together. They succeeded in their attempt to do so as a result of their view of salvation-history, and their vision of the universal scope of the divine economy.

Although critical of certain aspects of cultic religion they regarded as demonic and contrary to the Christian gospel, they seem to have discerned beneath these elements an underlying continuity in the history of God's dealings with humankind.[46] They grounded their approach in a universal salvation-history framework, comprising both Old and New Testaments, creation and redemption, the whole of history from beginning to end, within which there was a progressive development in the revelation by the Logos, culminating in the incarnation of this Logos in Jesus Christ. Within this vision of the universal economy of God with the Logos at the centre, non-Christian philosophies find their place as providential pedagogical systems orientated towards Christ, their ultimate consummation and fulfilment. Thus, the same incarnate Logos who sets the Christian faith apart in its uniqueness and transcendence, also brings together non-Christian philosophies and Christianity in "a preparation-fulfilment" relationship.[47]

The Fathers saw no other way in which humanity could come to know the transcendent God except through revelation by the *Logos*, who has been active through various stages of history from the time of creation itself. They accordingly saw some measure of revelation, faith and grace among the Greeks even before the coming of Christ, but distinguished different kinds of participation in the *Logos* by the pagan, Jew and the Christian. They were thus, for the most part, careful to distinguish the revelation accorded to the Jews through the Law from the light of nature present in Gentile philosophies, and the divine inspiration of the Old Testament prophets from the illuminating action of the *Logos*. Pre-Christian participation in the *Logos* was likewise viewed in qualitatively different terms in what they saw as a temporary stage in an ongoing progression towards perfection and fulfilment in the incarnate *Logos*, the Christ of history.[48]

---

[45] Saldanha, *Divine Pedagogy*, 152-153.
[46] Saldanha, *ibid.*, 161, 151.
[47] Saldanha, *ibid.*, 161.
[48] Saldanha, *ibid.*, 176-180, 185-186.

EVOLUTIONARY FULFILMENT

The specific location of our study is the evangelical Protestant missionary encounter with the religions of India, which began in the early nineteenth century. There were two opposing tendencies affecting the Christian attitude to other faiths during this period. On one hand, the dominant missionary attitude to non-Christian religions in the early half of the century was hostile and imperialistic. On the other hand, the eighteenth-century Orientalists' serious scholarly engagement with the textual resources of these religions gave impetus to a more irenic attitude. This attitude eventually found expression in a distinctive and historically unique model of fulfilment towards the late nineteenth and early twentieth century, which received widespread acceptance following the ecumenical Protestant missionary conference at Edinburgh in 1910.

As the name suggests, this model was developed in the nineteenth century under the influence of Darwin's evolutionary theory on the scientific study of religion. The model eventually reached and became popular in the mission field as well. It recognizes the presence of fragments of truth in all religions, and sees all the religions of the world as being at various stages in an evolutionary scheme of development within which the lower religions are fulfilled by the higher religions.

Most exponents of the evolutionary model would agree that Christianity is at the end of this continuum and represents the fulfilment of the religious instincts and desires of all religions, but divergence of interpretation exists as to what this signifies. One approach sees fulfilment in Christ or Christianity in more absolute terms, as the final stage of this evolutionary process.[49] Others, however, view this fulfilment in more dynamic terms, and see fulfilment as an ongoing process, involving further explication of the significance of Christ as a consequence of engagement with other religious traditions.[50]

We will see that this model does bear some degree of continuity with the thought of the early Fathers in its attempt to ground itself in a *Logos* Christology, the empirical recognition of elements of truth in other religions, and the acceptance of a salvation-history continuum in which the *Logos* himself is active in the economy of salvation. Its main distinctive, the

---

[49] M. Monier-Williams, *Indian Wisdom* (London: William H. Allen, 1875); M. Monier-Williams, *Modern India and the Indians* (London: Trubner, 1878); M. Monier-Williams, *The Holy Bible and the Sacred Books of the East, 4 Addresses* (London, SPCK, 1900); T.E. Slater, *The Higher Hinduism in Relation to Christianity* (London, 1903), 27-28, 29-30.

[50] Max Muller and Westcott, see pp.22, 23. Although there is nothing corresponding to evolutionary fulfilment in Whaling's classification, at this point it overlaps with what he refers to as fulfilment of process. Whaling's third category, 'fulfilment of the essence of religion', includes various forms of fulfilment which hold that there is a philosophical or mystical essence common to all religions, which Christianity contains more fully than others; Whaling, *Christian Theology*, 83, 85-86.

evolutionary framework, however, is also the most significant point of divergence from the theological orientation of the early Fathers.

A Definition of Fulfilment

This sketch of three influential models of fulfilment shows that the fulfilment concept finds expression in a wide range of views concerning the relationship of Christianity to other religions. It is, however, possible to identify some points of generic commonality in these views, which distinguish them from alternative viewpoints, and help define the essential nature of the fulfilment concept.

PEDAGOGICAL VALUE OF OTHER RELIGIONS

Fulfilment approaches neither absolutize nor demonise religions. They view religions as, objectively, containing some elements of the true knowledge of God, and, subjectively, reflecting legitimate expressions of the need for self-transcendence. While the different models give varying degrees of value to these rays of truth or intimations of reality in other religions, all agree that these are not in themselves adequate pictures of truth and require something more to be complete. These religions, however, have genuine value in preparing people to receive the truth in its fullness.

CHRIST'S UNIVERSALITY SET WITHIN ESSENTIAL CONTINUITY

The sharp distinction between Christian and non-Christian salvation history is minimized in fulfilment approaches. This is done in various ways: by emphasizing the universality of God's cosmic covenant, by universalization of salvation-history, or by extending the scope of divine grace. Christianity is thus viewed as a cosmic religion in which the truths and values of all religions as well as all human religious aspirations can be incorporated. In the nineteenth century this continuity was provided by the evolutionary scheme. Christ is thus not just the Saviour of Christians, but of all people, and non-Christian religions are viewed as part of a theology of history, as providential systems orientated towards Christ, the universal Saviour.

DECISIVENESS OF CHRIST

All models of fulfilment accept the provisional nature of other religions with varying degrees of emphasis. While the degree of value ascribed to non-Christian religions by each model varies, all agree that these religions express human anticipations of something fuller – the fullness offered only in Christ. Other religious traditions thus possess only provisional legitimacy: when the more perfect revelation of truth and grace in Christ becomes known, it transforms, subsumes, or replaces pre-Christian religion.

Some forms of fulfilment interpret the decisiveness of Christ dynamically, as not unidirectional, but a two-way fulfilment: not only do the aspirations of other religions find fulfilment in Christ, but, conversely, Christocentric criteria may be applied in identifying elements of truth in these religions. These elements may then be incorporated into Christian faith as part of the indigenization process, entailing criticism, purification, and growth of the existing tradition and practice of Christianity.

With this clarified understanding of the fulfilment concept we now turn our attention to examining its expression in the nineteenth-century Protestant missionary encounter with the cultural and religious tradition of India.

Background and Development of the Protestant Fulfilment Tradition in the Nineteenth Century

The nineteenth century missionary movement opened up several new frontiers for the engagement of the Christian faith and non-Christian cultures.[51] Protestant Christianity in particular, which had thus far been largely restricted within the shores of Europe, now found itself for the first time in contact with various indigenous religions of the world. The Christian engagement with the Hindu world at this time in India presented a unique challenge to missions, and became the immediate context within which fulfilment approaches emerged in India.[52] Protestant missionary attitudes took on two forms of expression during this period. The dominant posture in the early half of the century was theologically conservative and confrontational towards other religions. There was also a minority irenic attitude, which in the closing decades of the century expressed itself in an increasingly influential fulfilment approach.

The Conservative Protestant Missionary Attitude to Other Religions

Nineteenth century Protestant missions were essentially the outcome of the late eighteenth and early nineteenth century 'Evangelical Awakening' in Britain.[53] The theology of British missionaries in the nineteenth century was thus significantly shaped by the beliefs of this awakening.[54] One of its deepest convictions, the ultimate lost-ness of the heathen apart from Christ, provided a sense of absolute priority and urgency to Christian mission. It was also, in some measure, responsible for the missionary task being perceived as a

---

[51] Although the Lutheran mission to Tranquebar, South India, began in 1706, and the Roman Catholic missionary presence originated with Vasco de Gama's arrival on the West coast of India in 1498, the nineteenth century missionary movement marks the earliest genuine attempt of Protestantism to engage indigenous cultures and religions theologically; C.B. Firth, *An Introduction to Indican Church History* (Madras: CLS, 1989), 49f, 131.

[52] Hedges, *Preparation and Fulfilment*, 131.

[53] Stanley, *The Bible and the Flag*, 55-61.

[54] Cracknell, *Justice, Courtesy and Love*, 3-34.

straightforward conflict between the revealed truth of God and false and idolatrous religious systems.[55] The predominant attitude of British missionaries towards Indian religion and culture was thus severely critical and denunciatory, especially in the earlier decades of the nineteenth century.[56]

Antony Copley describes the confrontational and narrow exclusivist theology of this period as a "fiercely embattled, bigoted ideology" of Mission.[57] Evangelical statesmen and clergy set the tone back home in Britain.[58] According to Wilberforce, "The Hindu divinities were absolute monsters of lust, injustice, wickedness and cruelty. In short, their religious system is one grand abomination",[59] and Charles Grant: "Indian civilization was barbaric because its religion was degrading. It was both dangerous and a violation of the Christian spirit even to tolerate such a culture."[60] A missionary educator, William Hastie, denounced Indian religion as a mass of "senseless mummeries, loathsome impurities...every conceivable form of licentiousness, falsehood, injustice, cruelty, robbery, murder..."[61] Hinduism was characterised in such terms as 'under Satanic influence", "the grandest embodiment of Gentile error", and "naked idolatry of the most gross and vulgar description".[62]

Sharpe cautions against too harsh a judgment of the missionaries, convinced that although most were motivated by sincere intentions, their approach was simply circumscribed by the limitations of their theological framework and their fragmentary knowledge of Hinduism.[63] Sharpe's attempt to justify the missionary attitude finds support in Maw's observation regarding the lack of education and ignorance in most missionary quarters of basic issues in inter-religious engagement.[64]

---

[55] Stanley, *The Bible and the Flag*, 61-67.

[56] Although our focus is on British attitudes, this reflects the trend in Western missions as a whole. The attitude on the continent during this period was, if anything, even more conservative and resistant to change, Sharpe, *Not to Destroy but to Fulfil*, 24, especially n. 1.

[57] A. Copley, *Religions in Conflict: Ideology, Cultural Contact and Conversion in Late-Colonial India* (Oxford: Oxford University Press, 1997), xiii, 13; cf. T.V. Philip, *Krishna Mohan Banerjea: Christian Apologist* (Madras: CLS, 1982), 68-72, 75.

[58] D. Kopf, *British Orientalism and the Bengal Renaissance: The Dynamics of Indian Modernization: 1773-1835* (Berkeley: University of California, 1969), 136-143.

[59] Great Britain, *Hansard's Parliamentary Debates* (June 22, 1813), 164, quoted in Kopf, *British Orientalism*, 142.

[60] Quoted in Kopf, *British Orientalism*, 134.

[61] *Hindu Idolatry and English Enlightenment* (Edinburgh, 1882), 30, 33; quoted in Maw, *Visions of India*, 8.

[62] All cited in Sharpe, *Not to Destroy but to Fulfil*, 26-28.

[63] Sharpe, *Not to Destroy but to Fulfil*, 25, 28-34; Sharpe, *Faith Meets Faith*, 9; cf. S. Jayakumar, *Dalit Consciousness and Christian Conversion: Historical Resources for a Contemporary Debate* (Delhi: ISPCK, 1999), 169-171.

[64] Maw, *Visions of India*, 8-10.

The missionary attitude of this period is, however, hard to defend in the light of the contrast with the evangelistic approach of the Lutheran missionaries of the Tranquebar Mission in the previous century.[65] The Lutheran pioneer missionary, Bartholomaeus Ziegenbalg, conducted a vigorous religious dialogue with learned members of the Hindu community.[66] He researched the sources of Hinduism in considerable depth and was sympathetic towards the Hindu tradition. Whilst cautioning against the "horrible errors" and "darkness of Satan" present in Hinduism, he recognizes the existence of common ground and expresses positive appreciation for certain elements of truth – the light of nature – within the Hindu tradition.[67] For instance, in a letter written in 1710 he observes:

> I do not reject everything they teach, rather rejoice that for the heathen long ago a small light of the Gospel began to shine...Of course, one will find many 'unreasonable stories' but one will find here and there such teachings and passages in their writings which are not only according to human reason but also according to God's Word.[68]

Ziegenbalg thus discovered grounds for recognizing elements of partial truth and the knowledge of God in the Hindu tradition over a century earlier. The nineteenth century evangelical missionaries were of the same pietistic stock as their eighteenth century counterparts of the Tranquebar Mission.[69] Furthermore, the state of knowledge concerning non-Christian religions had advanced significantly as a result of the work of the Orientalists. Sharpe's justification of the condemnatory Protestant posture towards Hinduism in the nineteenth century is thus difficult to sustain.

There were, on the other hand, several non-theological factors which also contributed to the perpetuation of this confrontational missionary attitude in the nineteenth century:[70] (1) the cultural imperialism implicit in the colonial educational policy and underlying the educational philosophy of some

---

[65] F. Fenger, *A History of the Tranquebar Mission* (Tranquebar: Evangelical Lutheran Mission Press, 1863); E.A. Lehmann, *It Began at Tranquebar: The Story of the Tranquebar Mission and the Beginnings of Protestant Christianity in India Published to Celebrate the 250th Anniversary of the Landing of the First Protestant Missionaries at Tranquebar in 1706* (Madras: CLS, 1956).

[66] The evidence includes accounts of 54 conversations with and 99 letters from non-Christian partners in dialogue and enquirers; H. Grafe, 'Hindu Apologetics at the Beginning of the Protestant Mission Era in India', *Indian Church History Review* 6, 1 (1972), 44-50.

[67] Lehmann, *It Began at Tranquebar*, 31-32; cf. Grafe, 'Hindu Apologetics', 64-67.

[68] Lehmann, *ibid.*, 31-32.

[69] Sharpe, *Not to Destroy but to Fulfil*, 25f.

[70] Sharpe, *ibid.*, 29-34.

missionaries;[71] (2) the mission compound mentality which alienated the missionary from the surrounding culture and totally dissociated the convert from his cultural roots; (3) the growing success of the Christian mission among the lower castes and outcastes, remote from the Hindu social structure, marginalized issues of Christian-Hindu encounter by reinforcing the rejectionist attitude towards Hinduism;[72] and, (4) the ongoing conservative influence within Western churches and mission agencies.

We should be careful not to generalize overly the situation at this point. The East India Company had for long maintained, out of political expediency, a policy of cautious tolerance towards both Hinduism and Islam, and even patronized and supported these religions.[73] Not all Protestant missionaries of this period possessed unmitigated contempt towards Hinduism. An irenic missionary perspective received scholarly undergirding in the work of the Orientalists – officers and civil servants of the East India Company who, beginning in the last quarter of the eighteenth century, engaged in careful research into Indian culture, language and religion. Thus careful and judicious research into the literature of the vedic period by British Oriental scholars such as W. Jones, H.T. Colebrooke, W. Robertson, C. Wilkins and H.H. Wilson, helped forge a sympathetic and enlightened view of Indian culture and civilization, which influenced the Protestant missionary attitude of this period.[74]

The Orientalists' scholarly enterprise was undergirded by the belief in the essential cultural unity of all mankind based on common origins, of special significance for the emergence of the nineteenth century fulfilment approach.[75] Max Muller later built upon this hypothesis in what eventually became known

---

[71] The colonial imperialistic project, to which some educational missionaries tacitly subscribed, was fuelled by the conviction that the British Empire had been divinely entrusted with the task of reviving an Indian civilization in decay and decline. The influence of the Enlightenment on the educational missionary enterprise is thus significant in this regard, especially in the priority given to the cultural 'civilising' objective over the evangelistic 'christianising' mandate in the educational missions debate; T.A. Metcalf, *Ideologies of the Raj* (Cambridge: Cambridge University Press, 1996), 1-27; J.C. Ingleby, 'Education as a Missionary Tool: A Study in Christian Missionary Education by English Protestant Missionaries in India with Special Reference to Cultural Change' (Ph.D. thesis, Oxford Centre for Mission Studies, 1998), 51-98.

[72] As an illustration of the success of the confrontational conservative approach among outcastes, see Jayakumar, *Dalit Consciousness*, 168-172.

[73] Sharpe, *Not to Destroy but to Fulfil*, 27-28.

[74] Kopf, *British Orientalism*, 19f, 31-41; Jones, for instance, urged Protestant missionaries to stop depreciating Indian theology and ethics, and to respect the religious institutions of India, G.D. Bearce, *British Attitudes towards India 1784-1858* (London: Oxford University Press, 1961), 21-24.

[75] Kopf, *British Orientalism*, 31f, 207; see the influence of this view on Farquhar, 45.

as the 'Aryan race' theory,[76] his distinctive ethnological hypothesis of the common origins of the European and Indian Aryan peoples in an original Central Asian Aryan race. Muller envisioned an emerging renaissance of Aryan civilization, with the coming together of the European and Indian Aryan races in the modern era. While Muller's Aryan race theory must be distinguished clearly from fulfilment theology, Maw illustrates its influence on the emergence of the fulfilment approach in nineteenth century India.[77]

In addition to the contribution of the British Orientalists, other factors provided a fresh impetus to the irenic Protestant attitude in the nineteenth century. The latter half of the nineteenth century witnessed a religious revival, a Counter-Reformation within Hinduism, which followed intense mid-century controversies and conflicts between the Christian missionary and Hindu communities.[78] The perception that Christianity was a denationalizing force, fuelled by a newfound pride in India's past, intensified the Hindu resistance to the Christian missionary assault and strengthened the forces of religious and political nationalism. The missionaries faced their strongest opposition from educated Hindus as the nationalist movement approached its peak in the closing years of the nineteenth century. Thus growing frustration with the failure of the confrontational approach to evangelise the Hindu compelled them to seriously re-evaluate their traditional attitude.[79]

Meanwhile, in Europe, the influence of the evolutionary hypothesis and the rise of historical criticism were beginning to have a positive influence on the development of a more sympathetic attitude to Hinduism. Furthermore, as a result of the increase in factual knowledge of the non-Christian religions, the 1890s saw the development and introduction of the discipline called the science of religion or comparative religions in many theological seminaries in the West.[80]

---

[76] According to this theory, the Aryan race was regarded as responsible for all the progress made by human civilization, and hence morally superior to non-Aryan races, a notion repudiated by anthropologists in the second quarter of the twentieth century; Maw, *Visions of India*, 24-34.

[77] Maw, *Visions of India*, 39-74 traces its influence especially on the fulfilment approaches of Slater and Banerjea.

[78] The Arya Samaj and the Theosophical Society became rallying points for strident anti-Christian propaganda during this period. Swami Vivekananda and the Ramakrishna Mission played an important role in restoring Hindu confidence in their ancestral religion and undermining Christian missionary polemic; Sharpe, *Not to Destroy but to Fulfil*, 144-146, 153-156.

[79] Philip, *Krishna Mohan Banerjea*, 74-81; S.M. Pathak, *American Missionaries and Hinduism* (Delhi: Munshiram Manoharlal, 1967), 230-233; J.N. Farquhar, *The Crown of Hinduism* (1913; repr., New Delhi: Oriental Books: London: OUP, 1971), 17-18, explicitly refers to the Hindu nationalist opposition as one of the factors that prompted his formulation of the fulfilment approach.

[80] Sharpe, *Not to Destroy but to Fulfil*, 38-43.

These factors, in varying degrees, influenced the trend towards a sympathetic interpretation of Hinduism.[81] Although this irenic attitude, which expressed itself in various forms of the fulfilment approach, gained credence in the last few decades of the nineteenth century, it is difficult to date precisely this change in the Protestant missionary posture.[82] Sharpe suggests that despite the growing popularity of the irenic missionary posture in the last quarter of the nineteenth century, it remained a minority view; the period was a preparatory stage, which anticipated the broader acceptance of the fulfilment approach in the early years of the twentieth century.[83]

The Emergence of the Protestant Missionary Fulfilment Approach

The earliest original ideas which contributed to the emergence of the Protestant fulfilment approach in the nineteenth century were expressed in the writings of four notable theologians: Richard Trench (1807-1886), Frederick D. Maurice (1805-1872), Rowland Williams (1817-1870), and John B. Morris (1812-1880).[84] Trench, Maurice, and Williams were influenced by the same Cambridge school of liberal theology, and hence, reflect a similar openness to truth in other religions while affirming that all the nobler longings of the "heathen world" are satisfied in Christianity.[85]

The precursor of the nineteenth century missionary fulfilment approach in India was the British evangelical scholar, John Muir (1810-1882).[86] Muir provided a vital bridge between the Orientalists' scholarship and Protestant missions. He encouraged missionaries to adopt a respectful and conciliatory attitude towards Indian culture based on an intimate knowledge of Hinduism, and the recognition of traces of truth and excellence in the Hindu scriptures.[87] However, three figures who exercised the most significant influence upon the

---

[81] Pathak, *American Missionaries and Hinduism*, 220-233.

[82] Philip, *Krishna Mohan Banerjea*, 80 and Stanley, *The Bible and the Flag*, 164 observe the change as beginning in the 1870s; Copley, *Religions in Conflict*, 251 sees it as taking place in the 1880s; Hedges, *Preparation and Fulfilment*, 226 is convinced that the fulfilment approach "was most widely accepted" by the 1890s; Pathak, *American Missionaries and Hinduism*, 233-234 views the 1910 Edinburgh Conference as the decisive moment in this regard.

[83] Hedges' evidence for the earlier widespread acceptance of the fulfilment approach in Anglican circles is convincing, but its broader ecumenical acceptance is difficult to gauge conclusively prior to the Edinburgh Missionary conference in 1910; Hedges, *Preparation and Fulfilment*, 269-275; cf. Sharpe, *Not to Destroy but to Fulfil*, 107-108; Sharpe, *Faith Meets Faith*, 17-19.

[84] See Hedges' competent treatment of these figures; Hedges, *Preparation and Fulfilment*, 51-98].

[85] Maw, *Visions of India*, 155-157.

[86] Sharpe, *Not to Destroy but to Fulfil*, 36-37.

[87] J. Muir, *An Essay on Conciliation* (Calcutta, 1849), 54-58.

development of the missionary fulfilment tradition in nineteenth century India were Max Muller, Monier-Williams, and B.F. Westcott.[88]

Muller was convinced that the essential truths about God were accessible to the unaided human reason, and since the Divine Spirit was at work in revelation in people of all religions, all religions must contain some truth.[89] Placing all the religions of the world at various stages within an evolutionary scheme, he maintained that non-Christian religions were part of the divine education of the human race, preliminary stages in the history of the world's progress towards Christianity.[90] He believed that the truths of other religions would have something to contribute towards a future world religion, continuous and yet different from Christianity, a religion that would be "the fulfilment of all the religions of the past", the ultimate answer to the deep aspirations that God's Spirit has placed in all religions.[91]

In contrast to Muller, Monier-Williams insisted on the absolute supremacy of historical Christianity, "the only divine system capable of regenerating the entire human race", "the only message of salvation", and "the only power of God unto salvation to Jew, Greek, Hindu and Mohammedan".[92] All other religious systems were thus for him ultimately false. However, his belief that non-Christian religions were corruptions of some original revelation to humanity convinced him that fragments of truth which reflect elements of that primordial revelation, signs of the work of God's Spirit, could be found in them.[93]

Max Muller and Monier-Williams shared a similar evolutionary understanding of fulfilment, and were both convinced that all religions were

---

[88] Hedges, *Preparation and Fulfilment*, 112-126, 99-112, 193-202, deals with all three figures. Sharpe, *Not to Destroy but to Fulfil*, 15, n. 4 was clearly not convinced of Westcott's fulfilment orientation, a significant error of judgment in the light of Maw's analysis and Hedges' counter-critique of Westcott's fulfilment view; cf. Maw, *Visions of India*, 130-165.

[89] F.M. Muller, *The Life and Letters of the Rt. Hon. Friedrich Max Muller, Edited by his Wife, II* (London: Longmans, Green, 1902), 70, 110, 290-291; F.M. Muller, *Chips from a German Workshop I* (London, 1867-1875), xxvii.

[90] Muller, *Life and Letters of the Rt. Hon. Friedrich Max Muller*, 491, 346, 391. From the middle of the nineteenth century, Darwin's biological theory of evolution began to assume the nature of an all-pervasive ideology as it began to be applied to other disciplines such as science, sociology, religion and ethics. Matthew Arnold sought to establish an evolutionary interpretation of religion, a key factor which influenced the thought of Max Muller, Monier-Williams, Slater and other nineteenth century exponents of fulfilment theory; W.P. Hall and R.G. Albion, *A History of England and the British Empire* (Boston: Ginn & Co., 1937), 784-789; cf. Sharpe, *Not to Destroy but to Fulfil*, 39-43.

[91] Muller, *Life and Letters of the Rt. Hon. Friedrich Max Muller*, 141, 383.

[92] Monier-Williams, *Modern India and the Indians*, 202, 189; Monier-Williams, *Indian Wisdom*, xxxviii, 143.

[93] See the concurrence with Banerjea's view of primeval revelation, 107.

ultimately the expressions of a fundamental and deep-seated religious instinct in man, but differed regarding the amount of truth-content and value that could be ascribed to this instinct. For Monier-Williams, Christianity represented absolute truth, the ultimate consummation of all religious aspirations, a "full-stop" in the evolutionary continuum; Max Muller, in contrast, viewed Christianity as a higher stage in the religious evolution of man, which pointed beyond itself to further levels of religious attainment, incorporating other religious insights as well.

Muller and Monier-Williams clearly influenced the fulfilment views of missionary thinkers, although this influence is more explicit in some – like J. Robson, W. Miller, T.E. Slater, than others – like Farquhar.[94] Muller's influence on one of the earliest Indian fulfilment thinkers, K.C. Sen, is stated quite explicitly in one of his essays.[95]

B.F. Westcott was another crucial figure in the Cambridge tradition of Maurice, Trench, and Williams, who helped shape the new missionary attitude to the religions of India.[96] Westcott's fulfilment approach was similar to that of Max Muller, although his starting point was not the empirical data of non-Christian religions but his belief in the universal revealing activity of the *Logos*. According to his dual consummation view of fulfilment, the predictions and aspirations of other religions find their consummation in Christianity, while Christian faith itself moves closer toward its consummation in the transformation it experiences in its encounter with other religious traditions.[97]

Westcott was convinced that each culture and religion contained its own particular fragment of revelation, and the Church's engagement with the eastern races would lay open fresh depths within the gospel hitherto undiscovered. The final form of Christianity would involve a gathering together of fragments of truth present in cultures scattered all over the earth and weaving them together into one coherent whole in the task of relating all religions to the *Logos*.[98] Westcott's view received support and affirmation in a volume of essays written by seven bishops and edited by Bishop H.H. Montgomery of the Society for the Propagation of the Gospel.[99] This sanction of the fulfilment approach in the highest ecclesiastical circles undoubtedly affected the response on the mission field as well.[100]

---

94 Sharpe, *Not to Destroy but to Fulfil*, 54, 87, 98, 101, 125-126; see p.48, n.8.

95 F.M. Muller, *Biographical Essays* (London: Longmans, Green, 1884), 36, 80f.

96 Hedges, *Preparation and Fulfilment*, 193, 195-196, 201; Cracknell, *Justice, Courtesy and Love*, 60-71.

97 Maw, *Visions of India*, 11-12.

98 Maw, *Visions of India*, 11, 165.

99 H.H. Montgomery, ed. *Mankind and the Church: An Attempt to Estimate the Contribution of Great Races to the Fulness of the Church of God (by seven bishops)* (London: Longmans, Green, 1907), xii-xiii.

100 For Westcott's influence upon the missionary community in India, see Maw, *Visions of India*, 166-253; Hedges, 'A History and Study of Fulfilment Theology', 217-227.

A significant figure Westcott influenced was T.E. Slater, the first active evangelical missionary in India who tried to develop a fulfilment approach.[101] Following Muir's example, Slater felt that the missionary must have an attitude of real sympathy toward as well as a detailed knowledge of Hinduism.[102] While Slater's position is clearly evolutionist, his evolutionary theory is in the line of Monier-Williams rather than Max Muller.[103] All religions have presentiments or fragments of the truth, but are imperfect in relation to Christianity, which is the absolute religion, on a higher evolutionary level than all the others.[104]

Maw makes a fair case for the influence of Westcott and the Cambridge University Mission upon Slater's thought, although he is careful to highlight points of divergence.[105] Slater represents an early stage of the appropriation of the ideas of fulfilment proponents like Max Muller, Monier-Williams and B.F. Westcott from within the evangelical missionary community in India. He was a pioneer who indicated the way for a line of thinking among a whole generation of missionary scholars.[106]

The last few decades of the nineteenth century saw the fulfilment approach receiving progressively wider acceptance until it developed into an influential school of thought by the early years of the twentieth century.[107] At the World Missionary Conference at Edinburgh in 1910, in the context of the findings of Commission IV devoted to the missionary's approach to non-Christian religions, the verdict became overwhelmingly clear. The evidence indicates that for a large majority of missionaries the fulfilment approach represented the most promising strategy for the completion of the missionary task.[108] J.N. Farquhar, whose thought we consider in the following chapter, was one of several leading fulfilment thinkers who submitted contributions to the conference.[109]

---

[101] For details of Slater's life and thought, see Sharpe, *Not to Destroy but to Fulfil*, 94-105; Cracknell, *Justice, Courtesy and Love*, 108-119; Hedges, 'A History and Study of Fulfilment Theology', 161-188.

[102] Slater, *The Higher Hinduism in Relation to Christianity*, 1.

[103] Slater in fact sought Monier-Williams' approval of his views; Sharpe, *Not to Destroy but to Fulfil*, 101.

[104] Slater, *The Higher Hinduism in Relation to Christianity*, 291.

[105] For the influence of Muller and Westcott on Slater, see Maw, *Visions of India*, 51-74, 339-345; also Hedges, 'A History and Study of Fulfilment Theology', 167-168.

[106] For instance, Farquhar's acquaintance with Slater's work is beyond dispute, although the extent of explicit influence difficult to confirm; Sharpe, *Not to Destroy but to Fulfil*, 52, 98, 104, 208.

[107] Sharpe, *Not to Destroy but to Fulfil*, 236-240.

[108] Sharpe's assessment is cautious, hinting that the 'triumph' of fulfilment was not as complete as suggested in the first part of the report; Sharpe, *Not to Destroy but to Fulfil*, 278-297, 309-310, 322-323, but both Maw, *Visions of India*, 325f, 363, 366-378, 390-393 and Cracknell, *Justice, Courtesy and Love*, 197-227, 253-260 concur regarding the Conference's firm affirmation of the fulfilment view.

[109] Maw, *Visions of India*, 331.

In concluding this section of our discussion, we make the following summary observations. First, the positive attitude to religions found growing acceptance as an alternative to the confrontational Protestant missionary posture in the second half of the nineteenth century, and succeeded in reducing some of the cultural and political tensions on the mission field. Second, a prominent feature of the fulfilment approaches of this period, which attracted much criticism, was the influence of evolutionary theory.[110] Third, the main strength of the fulfilment approaches of this period was that they were not *a priori* theological or philosophical constructs, but were based on rigorous study of religious texts and often forged in the context of practical inter-religious engagement.

We turn then to the more immediate context of our study: the evidence of indigenous expressions of the fulfilment impulse within the pre-independence Indian context.

Fulfilment Approaches in the Pre-independence Indian Context

Our intent in this section of our enquiry is to assess the influence of the fulfilment impulse in shaping the Christian attitude to other religions in India in the pre-independence period. The survey includes a description of the approaches to other faiths of select representatives within four important strands of Indian Christian thought. The individual thinkers selected for treatment are either representative of a particular Indian theological tradition, or representatives of original and distinctive lines of thought, but all have three vital features in common.[111]

First, each in his own way sought to penetrate the heart of the Christian faith, but all manifest clear evidence of having been deeply influenced by the person and message of Christ. Second, all share a common non-Christian ancestry and respond to Christ with their religious and cultural roots deeply embedded within various Hindu traditions. Third, all belong to the high caste Hindu community in India, with the centre of gravity of their thinking in the Sanskritic tradition.[112]

---

110 Sharpe, *Not to Destroy but to Fulfil*, 272; we will examine this more closely in our assessment of Farquhar's fulfilment approach in the following chapter.

111 Much of Indian Christian thought, especially during this early period, is in the nature of spontaneous theological reflection rather than structured systems of thought, making categorization into clearly-defined schools difficult. There is, hence, no standard scheme of classification. Two possible exceptions to this would be the Christian bhakti line of approach, which developed around Sadhu Sundar Singh, A.J. Appasamy, N.V. Tilak and others, and the now influential Roman Catholic advaitic tradition, first inaugurated by Brahmabandhab Upadhyay, and revived in recent years through the work of Pierre Johanns, Jules Monchanin, Henri Le Saux, and Raimundo Pannikar, among others.

112 This dominance of high caste figures in the formulation of indigenous Christian theology was largely due to sociological rather than theological factors. The Hindu

First, the following investigation will involve a brief assessment of the background and essential impulses of select Indian fulfilment responses to Christ. Second, we will also look for threads of continuity or evidence of mutual influence between the fulfilment responses in the different Indian theological strands. Third, we will need to offer an explanation for the widespread appropriation of the fulfilment concept as a unifying phenomenon among converts, and evaluate the extent to which their views are authentically Indian theological responses rather than western imperialistic impositions.[113]

The first Indians to address Christian theological issues seriously and extensively in scholarly writings were not orthodox Christians but some of the nineteenth century pioneers of the Hindu renaissance in India. The earliest indigenous interpretations of Christ in India were attempted by Ram Mohan Roy, K.C. Sen and other leaders of the Brahmo Samaj, an influential Hindu reform movement which emerged in early nineteenth century Bengal.[114] We begin our survey with a consideration of the fulfilment approach within this reform movement.

Fulfilment in Renascent Hindu Approaches to Christ: Keshub Chunder Sen (1838-84)

Our consideration of the renascent Hindu approach to Christ will be limited to the teachings of one of the foremost leaders of the Brahmo Samaj, Keshub

---

social structure granted the Brahmin caste privileged access to the Hindu scriptures and exclusive control of the performance of religious rituals. The Brahmin caste, for the most part, thus constituted the educated elite in the nineteenth century. The missionaries focussed a significant portion of their efforts on trying to convert this influential segment of Hindu society. The Sanskritic tradition over which the Brahmins had almost total monopoly was thus frequently regarded by non-Brahmanical castes as an instrument of high-caste oppression and privilege, and Christian missionary efforts among lower castes and outcastes tended to receive a positive response when they displayed a negative attitude towards this tradition, see Lipner, 'A Modern Indian Christian Response', 310-311.

[113] This is a frequent and sometimes implied assumption in much of the criticism of the fulfilment approach. For instance, after acknowledging its reputable theological lineage, Ignatius Puthiadam, 'Diversity of Religions in the Context of Pluralism and Indian Christian Life and Reflection', in M. Amaldoss, John, T.K., and G. Gispert-Sauch (eds.), *Theologizing in India* (Bangalore: Theological Publications in India, 1981), 417, 425f asserts that the fulfilment view is one of the positions "...associated with a dominant and expansionist Western culture"; cf. Pieris, *An Asian Theolgoy of Liberation* (New York, Orbis, 1988), 47, 59f; cf. S.J. Samartha, *One Christ...Many Religions: Toward a Revised Christology* (New York, Orbis, 1990), 99.

[114] K. Baago, *Pioneers of Indigenous Christianity* (Madras: CLS, 1969), 12; for a detailed bibliography on the Brahmo Samaj, see D.C. Scott, ed., *Keshub Chunder Sen* (Madras: CLS, 1979), 347-351.

Chunder Sen, a key figure in the development of Indian Christian theology.[115] According to Scott, [116] the crucial formative influences upon Sen's life and thought were, "Vaisnava *bhakti* with its yogic mysticism and incarnational theology, and a devotion to Jesus Christ, dissociated from the western trappings of organized Christianity".[117]

Sen's response to the person and message of Christ evolved through various stages, with Christ moving progressively closer to the centre of his religious experience. His view of the relationship between Christianity and Hinduism must be understood within the context of his conception of the ultimate religion as a syncretistic but Christ-centred harmony of religions. He saw Christ as having come to fulfil what was best in all of the world's religions, and was convinced that Hindus could discover fulfilment of their national instincts and aspirations in the message of Christ.[118] Three distinct but overlapping strands run through Sen's conception of fulfilment.

First, the fulfilment idea is expressed explicitly in terms of prophetic fulfilment. In one of his later lectures, Sen explicitly applies the words of Jesus in Matthew 5:17 to his own Hindu tradition:

> Will he [Christ] not fulfil the Indian scripture? I am reminded of the passage in the Gospel in which he says, 'I am not come to destroy, but to fulfil.' The Mosaic dispensation only? Perhaps the Hindu dispensation also. In India he will fulfil the Hindu dispensation.[119]

Sen here seems to view the Hindu tradition in much the same way as a Jewish Christian would regard the Old Testament, perceiving no qualitative distinction between the Old Testament Hebrew and Hindu dispensations, both

---

[115] Scott, *Keshub Chunder Sen*, xii. Compelling reasons for beginning our survey with Sen include: (1) His profession of a genuine personal experience of Christ; (2) Most of the standard textbooks on Indian Christian theology begin with an assessment of various Brahmo responses to Christ; (3) Many of the conceptions and categories used by subsequent Indian thinkers were first stated by Sen; (4) Sen was the first Indian to have used the term fulfilment to describe the relationship of Christ to other religions; Boyd, *An Introduction to Indian Christian Theology*, 19ff, 27; Thomas, *The Acknowledged Christ*, 1-99; Scott, *Keshub Chunder Sen*, xiii.

[116] Scott's work includes an edited selection of Sen's more important works, an introductory biographical sketch, and a selected bibliography of his original works and secondary sources. (Henceforth, we note citations from Sen by page numbers from this work unless otherwise indicated).

[117] Scott, *Keshub Chunder Sen*, xii.

[118] Scott 'India Asks: Who is Christ?' in *Keshub Chunder Sen*, 201-202; H. Staffner, *Jesus Christ and the Hindu Community* (Anand: Gujarat Sahitya Prakash, 1988), 9f.

[119] Scott, 'Who is Christ?', in *Keshub Chunder Sen*, 214; cf. Scott, 'Behold the light of Heaven in India', *Keshub Chunder Sen*, 173.

of which are fulfilled – in the same sense – in Christ.[120] He thus appeals to his fellow-countrymen to direct their devotion to Christ in fulfilment of their indigenous prophetic aspirations:

> Behold Christ cometh to us as an Asiatic in race, as a Hindu in faith, as a kinsman and a brother, and he demands your heart's affection. Will you not give him your affection? He comes to fulfil and perfect that religion of communion for which India has been panting, as the hart panteth after the waterbrooks...[121]

Sen was, however, less concerned with the historical person of Christ than with the pre-existent *Logos-Cit.*[122] He prefers what he refers to as the larger "spirit-Christ", with whom is identified all goodness and truth wherever it be found, to the "narrow" or "smaller" Christ of Nazareth.[123] His view of Christ is accordingly not exclusive but all-inclusive, and he appeals to the testimony of the Church Fathers in support of this view of an "all-pervading" and "eternal" *Logos*-Christ.[124]

We thus observe a strand of thought in Sen, which at some points approaches the *Logos*-fulfilment view of the early fathers. He thus concurs with the early fathers in affirming that long before he came into the world, Christ had a spiritual existence as "the Word, the divine *Logos*, the right Reason" and dwelt within Socrates and other poets, philosophers and moral teachers. Thus, there are germs of truth in every Christian or non-Christian philosophical system, which must be fragments of the *Logos* or the Eternal Word. The partial truth that these fragments of the Divine Word reveal prepares the way for the Christian Dispensation and is perfected in it. Christ, who alone manifests this *Logos*-Light in full measure, brings together the partial and incomplete light of the *Logos* in these fragments of truth and makes them one.[125]

A critical point of contrast between the Christocentricity of Sen and the fathers, however, is that for Sen, Christ was fundamentally the universal *Logos*-Christ to be appropriated in the context of all cultures and religions through mystical experience.[126] Thus, whereas the fathers' "larger" *Logos*-Christ was firmly grounded in the "smaller" Christ of history, the bedrock of Sen's

---

[120] Sen's acknowledgment of errors in the Hindu scriptures is thus matched by his ecletic attitude to the Bible, Scott, 'Christ and Christianity', in *Keshub Chunder Sen*, 139.

[121] Scott, 'Who is Christ?', in *Keshub Chunder Sen*, 215f.

[122] *Cit* – Sen's Sanskrit designation for the *Logos*, meaning intelligence or wisdom, derived from the famous definition of *Brahman* as *Sat-Cit-Ananda*; Boyd, *An Introduction to Indian Christian Theology*, 28, 34.

[123] Scott, 'Why take the smaller Christ?', in *Keshub Chunder Sen*, 327.

[124] Scott, 'Our Reply', in *Keshub Chunder Sen*, 316; Scott, 'That Marvellous Mystery – The Trinity', in *Keshub Chunder Sen*, 237.

[125] Scott, 'Christ in Socrates', in *Keshub Chunder Sen*, 300f; Scott, 'Fragments of the 'Word' in India', in *Keshub Chunder Sen*, 331f.

[126] M.C. Parekh, *Brahmarshi Keshub Chunder Sen* (Rajkot, 1931), 25f, 33.

religious faith is not the Christ of history but the *Logos*-Christ of mystical experience present in every human heart.[127] Furthermore, in contrast to the early fathers, Sen does not distinguish the universal illuminating presence of the *Logos* from the divine inspiration of the Old Testament prophets. Christ is already present in every true Brahmin and in every one of us as the holy Word or the eternal Veda, and Sen challenges his hearers to experience the Christ, 'the light that lighteth every man that cometh into the world', who is already in them.[128]

Another major point of difference between the *Logos* fulfilment tradition of the early fathers and that of Sen is the qualitative differentiation the fathers made between Christian and pre-Christian participation in the *Logos*. Whereas for Sen it was enough to appropriate the universal *Logos* through mystical experience, the fathers regarded any participation in the pre-incarnate activity of the *Logos* as provisional, a preparatory stage in an ongoing progression towards actual historical fulfilment in the Christ-event.

A third dimension in Sen's conception of fulfilment is indicated in his *Logos* Christology, which incorporates within it a belief in the ongoing evolution of the *Logos*, giving it a dynamic eschatological thrust towards the future. The basis of this is the concurrence of the Hindu and Christian belief in creation as the continued evolution of the *Logos* with the modern theory of evolution:

> Creation means not a single act, but a continued process.... The Hindu, too, like the Christian, believes in the continued evolution of the *Logos*, and its graduated development through ever-advancing stages of life.... Such precisely is the modern theory of evolution.[129]

While the climax of this "continued evolution of the *Logos*" is Jesus Christ, the creative process does not stop with fulfilment in Christ. The goal of this process is not just the production of one Christ, but to universalise the divine sonship of Christ – to make every man Christ. Christ was only the way, a means, not the end, and the ultimate purpose of creation is only fulfilled through the multiplication of Christ in every human being.[130] Sen thus concurs with Max Muller in his conviction that fulfilment in Christ is not an absolute

---

[127] Scott, 'Light of Heaven', in *Keshub Chunder Sen*, 176. This judgment does not deny the normative value accorded to the historical Jesus and his divine humanity in some of Sen's writings, although, *contra* Pape, the *Logos*-Christ is clearly more central to his scheme than what he sometimes disparagingly refers to as the "flesh-Christ", Scott, 'Christ in all Rational Beings', in *Keshub Chunder Sen*, 329; Scott, 'Trinity', in *Keshub Chunder Sen*, 238; cf. Thomas, *The Acknowledged Christ*, 69, and W.R. Pape, 'Keshub Chunder Sen's Doctrine of Christ and the Trinity: A Rehabilitation', *The Indian Journal of Theology* 25 (1976): 55-71; 64-66, 68.

[128] Scott, 'Trinity', in *Keshub Chunder Sen*, 238; Scott 'Who is Christ?', in *Keshub Chunder Sen*, 217.

[129] Scott, 'Trinity', in *Keshub Chunder Sen*, 225f.

[130] Scott, 'Trinity', in *Keshub Chunder Sen*, 226-227.

end in itself, but points beyond to higher levels of religious attainment in an ongoing process of evolutionary development.[131]

In his *Biographical Essays*, Max Muller explicitly indicates his influence on Sen's view:

> K.C. Sen rejoiced in the discovery that, from the first, all religions were but varying forms of one great truth.... That the principle of historical growth or natural evolution applied to religion also, as I had tried to prove in my books on the Science of Religion, was to him the solution of keenly felt difficulties...[132]

Thus, although there appear to be several facets to Sen's understanding of fulfilment, the influence of Max Muller's nineteenth century evolutionary fulfilment view appears to be the most determinative. Sen's fulfilment approach is thus vulnerable to the same criticism as other nineteenth century fulfilment approaches conditioned by evolutionary philosophy. They bear a common weakness: the absence of adequate biblical or theological criteria for identifying the activity of the *Logos*-Christ in the world.

Sen's view of fulfilment is of critical importance since he was one of the earliest Indians to address the issue of the relation between Christ and non-Christian religious experience in an informed manner. His ideas may be faulted for their lack of systematic formulation and consistency, but despite the somewhat tentative and undeveloped nature of his ideas, they remain brilliant in their originality and depth.[133] The richness of his articulation of the fulfilment concept is seen in the extent of influence his ideas have had on subsequent expressions of fulfilment thought.[134]

Sen has perhaps justly been charged with being favourable towards the West, especially towards British rule in India.[135] It is true that Sen's staunch support of British rule in India, and his conviction that it had a crucial role to play in the advent of the New Dispensation alienated him from some of his Indian contemporaries.[136] These facts must not, however, be allowed to obscure the depth and strength of his Hindu identity. Although highly critical of many aspects of Hinduism and especially of the polytheistic idolatry, he always retained a deep affection for his ancestral faith.

---

[131] Scott, 'Light of Heaven', in *Keshub Chunder Sen*, 173-174; cf. 27.

[132] F.M. Muller, *Biographical Essays* (London: Longmans, Green, 1884), 80.

[133] There is, for instance, a lack of adequate integration between the prophetic, *Logos* and evolutionary fulfilment elements in Sen's approach. He shifts from one to the other in keeping with the context and flow of his rhetoric, see Scott, 'Light of Heaven', in *Keshub Chunder Sen*, 173-176; Scott, 'Who is Christ?', in *Keshub Chunder Sen*, 215, 217; Scott, 'Trinity', in *Keshub Chunder Sen*, 225-227, 246, 237-239; see Thomas, *The Acknowledged Christ*, 68.

[134] We will observe some instances in the fulfilment approaches surveyed in this section.

[135] Scott, 'Jesus Christ: Europe and Asia', in *Keshub Chunder Sen*, 56; Scott, 'Who is Christ?', in *Keshub Chunder Sen*, 199.

[136] Scott, *Keshub Chunder Sen*, 27, 31.

Sen's fervent attraction and devotion to Christ was balanced by an equally passionate rejection of what he perceived as the western trappings of Christian faith and practice.[137] Moreover, in Sen's assessment, the Asian heritage in religion, metaphysics, and culture was not merely a medium of communication but contained truth and value, which finds fulfilment in Jesus Christ and his universal Church.[138] Despite the pronounced influence of western evolutionary thought on his framework, Sen's fulfilment view is still a genuine attempt to respond to the person and message of Christ from within the Hindu religious and cultural framework.[139]

Fulfilment in Indian Christian Apologists: Nehemiah Goreh (1825-95)[140]

The nineteenth century encounter between Christianity and Hinduism in India also witnessed the conversion to Christ of a number of educated Hindus who were destined to play a crucial role in shaping an indigenous Indian Christian identity. Their approach has sometimes unjustly been identified with the largely negative approach of the western missionaries of this period.[141] However, although they often employed the method of textual research and historical and philosophical enquiry in persuasive apologetic appeals to their fellow-countrymen, in contrast to the cultural insensitivity of the missionary approaches, they were deeply committed to preserving both their cultural roots and national identity.[142] The better known among these were Lal Behari Day and Krishna Mohan Banerjea in Bengal, and Nehemiah Goreh and Pandita Ramabai in Maharashtra.[143] Of these, Banerjea and Goreh both specifically addressed the issue of fulfilment.

Banerjea's fulfilment conception will be examined more closely in chapter three. Nehemiah Goreh, originally, Nilakanta Sastri Goreh, was a high caste Brahmin by birth and a Sanskrit scholar of considerable stature. In the public testimony of his conversion, Goreh leaves us in no doubt of his emotional attachment to his ancestral religion and of his deep roots in the Sanskrit philosophical tradition, although he does so with characteristic reserve and

---

137 Scott, 'Jesus Christ', in *Keshub Chunder Sen*, 64-65; Scott, 'Who is Christ?', in *Keshub Chunder Sen*, 200ff.

138 Thomas, *The Acknowledged Christ*, 70.

139 Boyd, *An Introduction to Indian Christian Theology*, 38f.

140 The standard biography of Goreh is that of C.E. Gardner, *Life of Father Goreh* (London: Longman's, 1900). The only other available full-length treatment of Goreh's life and work is by B.A.M. Paradkar, *The Theology of Nehmiah Goreh* (Bangalore: CISRS, 1969).

141 Philip, *Krishna Mohan Banerjea*, 70ff.

142 Lipner, 'A Modern Indian Christian Response,' 292.

143 Thomas, *The Acknowledged Christ*, 38.

humility.[144] His early years of training as a Chitpavan Brahman in Benares thus ensured that despite the influence of western rationalism and orthodoxy, Goreh stayed close to his cultural tradition and refused to become westernised. He strongly emphasised the Asian origin of Christianity and had a deep distaste for the western trappings of the Church.[145]

In *A Rational Refutation of the Hindu Philosophical Systems*,[146] his *magnum opus*, Goreh displays an extremely negative attitude towards Hinduism. In this work, he undertakes a detailed logical examination of the six main Hindu philosophical systems, in an attempt to demonstrate that philosophical Hinduism is rationally and epistemologically untenable. Boyd observes, however, that Goreh "…loved his Hindu fellow-countrymen, felt at home in their society, and was convinced that in some unknown way God had been preparing their hearts and minds to receive the Christian revelation."[147]

This intuition was the basis of a more irenic attitude towards other faiths that emerges in two of Goreh's later works.[148] He thus acknowledges the possibility of these false religions containing some elements of truth:

> But is it not rather the truth that all false religions… contain many glorious truths, taught, or at least commended, by natural reason? And Christianity which is the purest form of natural religion… does not reject what is true in these false religions, but rather purifies, improves and retains it.[149]

Goreh was convinced that the light of God in general revelation had prepared the sincere Hindu to appreciate and accept the truths of Christian faith, and speaking as someone standing within the Hindu tradition, writes:

> Providence has certainly prepared *us,* the Hindus, to receive Christianity, in a way in which, it seems to me, no other nation – excepting the Jews, of course – has been prepared. Most erroneous as is the teaching of such books as the *Bhagavadgita*, the *Bhagvata*, etc., yet they have taught us something of *ananyabhakti* (undivided devotedness to God), of *vairagya* (giving up the world),

---

[144] He is sometimes regarded as one of the most deeply versed in the Hindu tradition of all Indian Christians; Boyd, *An Introduction to Indian Christian Theology*, 40. Hedges' summary treatment mistakenly underestimates the degree of Goreh's influence, Hedges, *Preparation and Fulfilment,* 151.

[144] Boyd, *An Introduction to Indian Christian Theology*, 54-55.

[145] Boyd, *ibid.*, 54-55.

[146] N. Goreh, *A Rational Refutation of the Hindu Philosophical Systems* (Calcutta: Bishop's College Press, 862). (Original Hindi title: *Shaddarshana Darpana*, 1860).

[147] Boyd, *An Introduction to Indian Christian Theology*, 55.

[148] *On Objections against the Catholic Doctrine of Eternal Punishment* (Calcutta: Bishop's College Press, 1868) and *Proofs of the Divinity of Our Lord stated in a Letter to a Friend* (1887), both of which are not accessible; citations from these works are thus from secondary sources.

[149] *Objections*, 80f; quoted in Paradkar, *Theology of Nehemiah Goreh*, 22.

of *namrata* (humility), of *ksama* (forbearance), etc., which enables us to appreciate the precepts of Christianity.[150]

He indicates that this light of general revelation has manifested itself in orthodox Hinduism in certain ideas, which point beyond themselves to fulfilment in Christ. These concepts, including the acceptance of the possibility of miracles and the idea of incarnation, could legitimately be regarded as a *preparatio evangelii* within Hinduism. In illustrating this from his own experience, Goreh explains how Hinduism prepared him for the idea of a divine incarnation:

...I never found fault *in idea* with its [Hinduism's] teaching that God becomes Incarnate. Indeed, many stories of Krishna and Rama, whom the Hindu religion teaches to be incarnations of God, used to be very affecting to us.... And thus our countrymen have been prepared, to some extent, to appreciate and accept the truths of Christianity.[151]

Goreh thus views Christ as the consummation or fulfilment of the anticipations and yearnings of his Hindu ancestors. Christians and Hindus share the belief that the highest goal of man is union with God, but the conviction that God alone can make provision for salvation is distinctively Christian. His exposition of the benefits of Christ's sacrificial death, appropriated through the sacrament of Holy Communion, clarifies how Christ fulfils the deepest longings of Hinduism. Hindu aspirations for union with God are fulfilled when their sins are cleansed by participation in the Eucharist, as they become one with the Father, and thus partake of the divine nature.[152] His explication of the fulfilment concept reaches its climax in his concluding suggestion that the unity with Brahman his forefathers aspired after for centuries, finds its true and proper realization only in the Christian experience of union with God.[153]

The absence of a detailed treatment of the fulfilment theme in any of Goreh's writings makes analysis and categorisation difficult. However, a distinct resonance with the *Logos* fulfilment idea is reflected in the following passage:

May God, in his infinite mercy, grant, my dear countryme-on, that you quench not the divine light which he has lighted in your breasts; that, on the contrary, you may follow its leading; that you meekly and patiently try, by it, the Christian

---

[150] *Proofs*, 75; quoted in Boyd, *An Introduction to Indian Christian Theology*, 55.

[151] *Proofs*, 76-77; cf. *Objections*, 81; both quoted in Boyd, *An Introduction to Indian Christian Theology*, 56.

[152] Boyd, *An Introduction to Indian Christian Theology*, 53f.

[153] *Objections*, 41-42; quoted in Boyd, *An Introduction to Indian Christian Theology*, 54.

> Scriptures; that you take hold on their priceless promises; and that, in the end, you may inherit, as your everlasting portion, the joy of the Heavenly Kingdom.[154]

This reference to the witness of the "divine light", which God has placed within the hearts of his Hindu fellow countrymen echoes the language of K.C. Sen's *Logos* fulfilment conception, but the correspondence between the two fulfilment approaches is only superficial. For Sen, the presence and activity of the pre-incarnate, universal *Logos* has ultimate value in and of itself, whereas for Goreh, truth outside of Christ only has value as *preparatio evangelii*, pointing forward to historical fulfilment in Christ. As in the early fathers, the historic Christ-event is the controlling focus of Goreh's *Logos* fulfilment scheme.

Goreh's understanding of fulfilment, with Banerjea's vedic theology, represents the earliest indigenous Christian approach to Hinduism which emerged in nineteenth century India.[155] Despite the perception that he was essentially a proponent of orthodox western theology, he was nevertheless convinced that God had not left himself without witness in Hinduism, willing to view the light discerned in the best traditions of Hinduism as pointing towards fulfilment in the true light in Christ.[156]

Fulfilment in the Advaitic Christian Tradition: Brahmabandhab Upadhyay (1861-1907)[157]

In the early years of the nineteenth century encounter between Christianity and Hinduism, the advaita Vedanta school of Hindu philosophy was viewed with great suspicion by Christian thinkers, and generally dismissed as a form of pantheism. Brahmabandhab Upadhyay,[158] a brilliant and ardent disciple of K.C. Sen, inaugurated a new school of indigenous thought which sought to employ the advaitic school of Hindu thought in the service of Christian theology in the Indian context. Upadhyay's contribution was crucial in the early stages of the

---

[154] Goreh, *A Rational Refutation*, 280.

[155] Boyd, *An Introduction to Indian Christian Theology*, 44f, 51f.

[156] Lipner, 'A Modern Indian Christian Response', 300; cf. Boyd, *An Introduction to Indian Christian Theology*, 56-57.

[157] The most authoritative account of the life and contribution of Upadhyay is that of J. Lipner, *Brahmabandhab Upadhyay: The Life and Thought of a Revolutionary* (New Delhi: OUP, 1999). The only comprehensive biography of Upadhyay prior to this was by B. Animananda, *The Blade: Life and Word of Brahmabandhav Upadhyay* (Calcutta: Roy and Sons, n.d.), which Lipner dates in 1946, Lipner, *Brahmabandhab Upadhyay*, xxii, n.25. All quotations, unless otherwise indicated, are from Part I of an anthology of Upadhyay's writings by J. Lipner and G. Gispert-Sauch, *The Writings of Brahmabandhab Upadhyay (including a Resume of his Life and Thought)*, vol. 1 (Bangalore: UTC, 1991).

[158] The name he assumed following his baptism; his original name was Bhabani Charan Banerjea.

development of Indian Christian thought. The tradition he inaugurated has exercised an ongoing influence especially upon the shape of Roman Catholic theological reflection in India.[159]

A Bengali Hindu Brahmin by birth, Upadhyay belonged to a category of educated and somewhat westernised Bengalis known as the *bhadralok* or the cultured folk.[160] After some years in the Brahmo Samaj, he was drawn to the Christian faith and was baptized in the Anglican Church, but eventually became a devout member of the Roman Catholic Church.[161] Upadhyay's theological orientation was determined by an absorbing passion for a meaningful synthesis between Christianity and Hinduism, the ultimate object of which was "winning over India to the Holy Catholic Church".[162] He explained his firm allegiance to Hindu culture and tradition as a committed Roman Catholic in the following terms:

> By birth we are Hindu and shall remain Hindu till death.... In customs and manners, in observing caste or social distinctions, in eating and drinking... our thought and thinking is emphatically Hindu.... In short, we are Hindus so far as our physical and mental constitution is concerned, but in regard to our immortal souls we are Catholic. We are *Hindu* Catholic.[163]

Upadhyay considered his mission to be in direct continuity with the work of Sen in establishing a basis for the unity of all religions. Like Sen, Upadhyay believed that all religions find their fulfilment and are reconciled with one another in Christ.[164] In a lecture shortly before his conversion, he tried to show

---

[159] There has been an increasing recognition of the significance of Upadhyay's work in India and abroad in the latter half of the twentieth century, Gispert-Sauch, 'The Sanskrit Hymns of Brahmabandhav Upadhyay', *Religion and Society* 19 (1972), 60; Lipner and Gispert-Sauch, *The Writings of Brahmabandhab Upadhyay*, xiv. For some modern proponents of this advaitic Christian school of thought, see J. Mattam, 'Interpreting Christ to India Today: The Calcutta School', *The Indian Journal of Theology* 23 (1974), 191-205; J. Mattam, 'Modern Catholic Attempts at Presenting Christ to India', *The Indian Journal of Theology* 23 (1974), 206-218.

[160] For more details on the *bhadralok* phenomenon, see Lipner, *Brahmabandhab Upadhyay*, 9-15.

[161] For a detailed account of factors leading to his conversion to Roman Catholicism, see Lipner, *Brahmabandhab Upadhyay*, 77-99.

[162] *The Tablet*, London January 3, 1903), 7; quoted in Mattam, 'Interpreting Christ to India Today', 192.

[163] Upadhyay, 'Are We Hindus?' *Sophia* (weekly) (July 1898), 24f. The term Hindu Christianity has a variety of connotations ranging from the renascent Hindu responses to Christ of K.C. Sen, P.C. Mozoomdar and others, to the consciously Christian approaches of converts such as Banerjea, Upadhyay, and Tilak, who attempted to remain culturally integrated within Hindu society even though they embraced the Christian faith. For Upadhyay it captured the conviction that it was possible to be a Christian in faith while remaining culturally a Hindu.

[164] Upadhyay, 'Ourselves', *The Harmony* (August 1890), 2-3.

that the sinlessness of Jesus made him unique among all the prophets, and that he thus fulfilled Hindu aspirations for the advent of a sinless Guru.[165] Thus, from the early years of his theological development, Upadhyay clearly believed that Christian faith must fulfil, not destroy what was true and good in Hinduism: "Our object is to present to our countrymen the right and full Christianity – a Christianity which fulfils all the accumulated goodness of our ancient country..."[166]

It is possible to distinguish two phases in Upadhyay's subsequent reflection concerning the relationship between Hinduism and Christianity.[167] In the early years following his conversion, Upadhyay attempted to find a natural foundation for the supernatural religion of Christ in the ancient theistic religion of the Vedas. In a series of articles he drew attention to parallels between the Old Testament and the Vedas, such as humanity's descent from one progenitor and original sinlessness, the universal flood, and to the idea of "the One True God" present in India's primitive religion.[168]

Although Upadhyay, at this stage, seems to have consciously sought points of correspondence between the Vedas and the Old Testament, he did not intend to supplant the authority of the Old Testament with that of the Vedas.[169] Rather, using the Old Testament as a normative grid, he attempts to demonstrate that elements of truth in the Vedas may be used to support a doctrine of theism, and most naturally connect with the specific truths of Christian faith in which they are brought to fulfilment.[170] He described his task at this stage in the following terms:

> But though the religion of Christ is beyond the grasp of nature and reason, still its foundation rests upon the truths of nature and reason.... It is on account of the close connection between the natural and the supernatural that we have taken upon ourselves the task of expounding the Hindu Scriptures systematically and of fishing out the Theistic truths from the deluge of Pantheism, Idolatry and Anthropomorphism... to form, as it were, a natural platform upon which the

---

[165] Animananda, *The Blade*, 35; Lipner, *Brahmabandhab Upadhyay*, 79.

[166] 'An Exposition of Catholic Belief as Compared with the Vedanta', Sophia (monthly) (January 1898], 19; cf. 'Our Attitude Towards Hinduism' *Sophia* (monthly) (January 1895), 4.

[167] See Kuttianimattathil's summary assessment of Upadhyay's theological method; J. Kuttianimattathil, *Practice and Theology of Interreligious Dialogue: A Critical Study of the Indian Christian Attempts since Vatican II* (Bangalore: Kristu Jyoti Publications, 1995), 33.

[168] Upadhyay, The Origin of Man', *Sophia* (monthly) (January 1894), 196f; 'Theism in the Vedas', Sophia (monthly) (March 1894) in Baago, *Pioneers of Indigenous Christianity*, 127.

[169] The project of Chenchiah and other radical thinkers in later years, who wanted the Hindu scriptures to supplant the Old Testament in the Indian context.

[170] Upadhyay, 'Hinduism', *Sophia* (monthly) (January 1895), 5.

> Hindus taking their stand may have a view of the glorious supernatural edifice of the Catholic religion of Christ.[171]

Baago compares the "Thomistic *Logos*-theology" of Upadhyay during this period with the *Logos spermatikos* approach of the early Christian apologists.[172] Undergirding this approach was the conviction that a primitive pure theism constituted the common foundation and lay at the heart of all religions.[173] Thus, within Upadhyay's Thomistic nature-grace framework, the revealed or supernatural truths of grace could build upon the religious insights of natural reason already present in non-Christian cultures.[174]

From about 1897, vedantic theism – Upadhyay's distinctive reinterpretation of the Vedanta – began to replace vedic theism as the natural basis for the reception of Christian truth.[175] Convinced that "…the Vedanta must be made to do the same service to the Catholic faith in India as was done by the Greek philosophy in Europe", he adopted Sankara's advaita as the most reliable guide and authority for the interpretation of the Vedanta.[176] Upadhyay's most important contribution in this direction was his attempt to show that the conception of Brahman as *Saccidananda* in the Vedanta prefigured on the level of natural reason the fuller revealed Christian doctrine of the Trinity.[177] His understanding of the nature of the Trinity as *Saccidananda* finds its richest expression in a Sanskrit hymn he composed, which Lipner describes as "…straightforward fulfilment theology at its most brilliant."[178]

---

[171] Upadhyay, *ibid.*, 6.

[172] Baago, *Pioneers of Indigenous Christianity*, 35; Upadhyay, 'Hindu Philosophy and Christianity', *Sophia* (monthly) (July 1897), 17-19.

[173] Updahyay, 'Our Attitude Towards Hindu Reformers', *Sophia* (monthly) (February 1896), 12-13.

[174] Lipner, *Brahmabandhab Upadhyay*, 124-127, 178-183.

[175] According to Lipner, this "relatively abrupt" transition was a consequence of Upadhyay's reassessment of advaitic philosophy's potential as a preparation for the Catholic faith, in the context of the growing popularity of Vivekananda's new interpretation of advaita as a nationalist ideology; Lipner, *Brahmabandhab Upadhyay*, 183-190.

[176] 'The Clothes of Catholic faith', *Sophia* (monthly) (August 1898); quoted in Animananda, *The Blade*, 74-75; cf. K.P. Aleaz, 'The Theological Writings of Brahmabandhav Upadhyay Re-Examined', *The Indian Journal of Theology* 28, 2 (1979), 58-59.

[177] *Saccidananda* Brahman denotes that Brahman is self-existent (*Sat*), has self-knowledge (*Chit*), and experiences perfect internal harmony, self-satisfaction and bliss (*Ananda)*. It was Keshub Chunder Sen who had first indicated an inspired interpretation of the Trinity in the vedantic conception of *Brahman* as *Saccidananda* (*Sat-Chit-Ananda*); Aleaz, 'Theological Writings of Brahmabandhav Upadhyay Re-Examined', 61f, 75; cf. Lipner, *Brahmabandhab Upadhyay*, 191-194.

[178] Lipner, *Brahmabandhab Upadhyay*, 201; for detailed expositions of the hymn, see Lipner, *Brahmabandhab Upadhyay*, 199-204 and Gispert-Sauch, 'The Sanskrit Hymns', 65-74.

However, for Upadhyay, the unique revelation of God in Christ alone affirms and explains the nature of God as *Sat-Chit-Ananda*, and hence he saw this conception as providing a vital key for the crucial task of reconciling Hinduism and Christianity in Christ.[179] Upadhyay sought to reinterpret the advaita tradition in a way that enabled him to draw essential correspondences between vedantic and neo-Thomistic ideas. This vedantic natural theology would then serve as a platform on which the supernatural truths of Catholic faith could legitimately rest.[180]

The earlier vedic-Christian strand in Upadhyay's theology bears a marked resemblance to Banerjea's approach in the *Arian Witness*.[181] Like Banerjea, Upadhyay sought to trace the similarities between the Hindu and Christian scriptures to a common primitive theistic faith based on a primeval revelation given to the whole human race.[182] The natural-supernatural framework of Upadhyay's thought, however, fits more closely with the *Logos* fulfilment model, the relationship between the old and the new being described in terms of: "…root and trunk, base and structure, as outline and filling."[183]

Upadhyay's original theological insights ushered in a whole new attitude to the Christian-Hindu encounter that continues to wield a powerful influence upon contemporary Indian Christian thought.[184] Although his fulfilment view was grounded in a western Thomistic natural-supernatural framework, he remained culturally a Hindu and passionately patriotic until the end of his life. He responds to Christ as one deeply rooted within his Hindu tradition, and found his experience and identity as a Hindu-Christian most adequately expressed in the fulfilment approach.

---

179 Upadhyay, 'Christ's Claim to Attention', *The Twentieth Century* 1, 5 (May 1901), 193-194.

180 Upadhyay, 'Vedantism and Christianity', *Sophia* (weekly) (September 29, 1900), 228. This conclusion is in keeping with Lipner's careful assessment, and *contra* Aleaz' view that Upadhyay's unique contribution to Indian theology was his discovery that the Christian doctrines were already present in the Vedanta alongside its obvious errors; Aleaz, 'The Theological Writings of Brahmabandhave Upadhyay Re-Examined', 56; cf. Lipner, *Brahmabandhab Upadhyay*, 196, n. 22; also Lipner, 'A Modern Indian Christian Response', 308-309.

181 Banerjea's vedic-Christian approach antedates that of Upadhyay and will be examined more closely in Chapter 3.

182 Updahyay, 'The Catholic Religion and Other Religions', *Sophia* (monthly) (July 1898), 23-24. Lipner sees the possible influence of the concept of primeval revelation as employed by Banerjea and other converts prior to Upadhyay's time, although Upadhyay does not make any explicit reference to Banerjea's work; Lipner, *Brahmabandhab Upadhyay*, 180, n. 3.

183 Upadhyay, 'Catholic Faith', *Sophia* (monthly) (August 1898); quoted in Animananda, *The Blade*, 73.

184 Mattam, 'Interpreting Christ to India Today', 192; cf. Lipner and Gispert-Sauch, *The Writing of Brahmabandhab Upadhyay*, xlv.

Fulfilment in the Bhakti Christian Tradition: N.V. Tilak (1862-1919)

The bhakti school in Hinduism has held a great attraction for Indian Christians because of its conception of God as a loving, personal being distinct from his creation, who bestows grace upon his creatures and can be worshipped with feelings of deep love and personal devotion.[185] A significant number of Hindu converts from the bhakti tradition seem to have viewed the bhakti framework as providing the most appropriate preparation for and expression of the Christian faith in the Indian context.[186] Several of the proponents of this school were poet-mystics, and the best known of these Christian bhakti poets was Narayan Vaman Tilak.

Narayan Vaman Tilak, [187] a Chitpavan Brahmin convert and renowned Maharashtrian poet, was a saint, poet and activist, rather than a systematic theologian. Although we do not find structured theological statements on any aspect of his thought, his poetry and hymns express original theological insights of considerable value in the quest for a deeper understanding of the Christian-Hindu religious encounter.[188] Tilak's patriotism was the starting point of an ardent quest for the ideal religion that would provide a suitable spiritual foundation for a great and prosperous India. At the end of his search and his study of the New Testament, he found himself irresistibly attracted to Christ, and became convinced that Christ was the Guru whom India and the world was looking for.[189]

Tilak was passionately devoted to Christ and deeply committed to his Hindu spiritual heritage, and his intense love for both remained with him all his life. He did his best to dispel the misconception that becoming a Christian involved renouncing one's traditional cultural heritage and separating oneself from the Hindu community.[190] According to Winslow, Tilak was convinced that: "…if

---

[185] For the Christian approach to Hindu *bhakti*, see A.J. Appasamy, *Christianity as Bhakti Marga* (Madras: CLS, 1930); S. Neil, *Bhakti: Hindu and Christian* (Madras: CLS, 1974); A.F. Thompson, 'Christian Views of Hindu *Bhakti*', in *Hindu-Christian Dialogue: Perspectives and Encounters*, ed. H.G. Coward (Delhi: Motilal Banarsidass, 1993), 176-190.

[186] The better-known among these were H.A. Krishna Pillai, Kahanji Madhavji, and Narayan Vaman Tilak; Boyd, *An Introduction to Indian Christian Theology*, 112f. We examine this approach more closely in chapter four in the *bhakti*-conditioned framework of Sadhu Sundar Singh.

[187] Two early definitive biographies of Tilak are by Winslow (1930) and his wife, Lakshmibai Tilak, *I Follow After* (trans. E. Josephine Inkster; Madras: Oxford University Press, 1950). Other useful introductions to Tilak's life and thought are: P.S. Jacob, *The Experiential Response of N. V. Tilak* (Bangalore/Madras: CISRS/CLS, 1979; and H. L. Richard, *Christ-Bhakti: Narayan Vaman Tilak and Christian Work among Hindus* (Delhi: ISPCK, 1991).

[188] Richard, *Christ-Bhakti*, 81; Jacob, *The Experiential Response of N. V. Tilak*, x.

[189] P.S. Jacob, 'Interfaith Dialogue: N.V. Tilak's Experiential Model', *Indian Church History Review* 27, 2 (1993): 108.

[190] Staffner, *Jesus Christ and the Hindu Community*, 65.

Christ could be presented to India in His naked beauty, free from the disguises of Western organisation, Western doctrines and Western forms of worship, India would acknowledge Him as the supreme Guru, and lay her richest homage at His feet."[191]

In the early years following his conversion, Tilak's attitude to Hinduism was essentially confrontational, and his criticism of certain aspects of Hinduism often expressed itself in anti-Hindu rhetoric. His overall approach was, nevertheless, sensitive:

> There is truth in Hinduism and we must not accuse and hurt Hindus, but find common points and then present the gospel.... Always study their side. Do not say all is false, idol worship is sin, there is no life in it, and so on.... Look for similarities to build a bridge...[192]

Seven or eight years after his conversion, Tilak underwent a spiritual crisis which radically deepened his personal experience of communion with Christ. Richard observes that the spiritual and emotional resources of *bhakti*, which lay suppressed in the depths of his being, were now released in a deeply Indian lyrical and musical expression of devotion to Christ.[193] This phase in Tilak's experience led him to break out of traditional Christian worship styles into more contextually relevant approaches, and to reinterpret his Hindu devotional heritage in the light of his experience of Christ.[194]

Tilak's earlier critical attitude thus gave way to a more positive approach to Hinduism in later years, when he became convinced that the knowledge of God imparted to India through the bhakti poet-saints had prepared India for the gospel of Christ. He recommended the study of older Hindu literature and devotional poetry, believing that the devotional writings of Namdev, Tukaram, Jnanesvara and other saints of Maharashtra could serve as preparation for the reception of the Christian gospel. He thus cautions Christian missionaries against imposing a foreign version of the Christian faith in India, and advises them to show respect and reverence for the ancient religious traditions and sages of India.[195]

The significance of this attitude is clarified when he says, "We esteem all the world's saints as prophets of God, and the sayings of the Hindu saints form our first old testament."[196] For Tilak, the Hindu scriptures seem to have functioned as a kind of Old Testament, preparing Hindus to receive the truth of

---

[191] J.C. Winslow, *Narayan Vaman Tilak: The Christian Poet of Maharashtra* (Calcutta: Association Press, 1930), 118.

[192] *Dyanodaya* 57, 25 (June 23, 1898), quoted in Richard, *Christ-Bhakti*, 65-66.

[193] Richard, *Christ-Bhakti*, 77.

[194] Richard, *ibid.*, 78-80.

[195] Winslow, *Narayan Vaman Tilak*, 60.

[196] Quoted in Jacob, *The Experiential Response of N.V. Tilak*, 45.

the Gospel message.[197] Tilak illustrates this from his own experience with his famous claim, "I have come to the feet of Christ over the bridge of Tukaram", indicating that his study of Tukaram had prepared him to receive the message of Christ.[198]

In further elaborating this understanding of the relationship between Christian and *bhakti* Hindu experience based on his own spiritual pilgrimage, Tilak explains how the teaching of *bhakti* saints like Tukaram and Jnanesvara positively influenced his movement towards Christ:

> The traditional way of union with the Supreme through *bhakti*, which Hindu mystics have conceived and Hindu devotees experienced, may be summed up in the four words, *samipata* (nearness), *salokata* (association), *Sarupata* (likeness), and *sayujyta* ('yokedness' or union); this has helped me to enter into the meaning of that series of Christ's sayings – 'Come after Me', 'Take My yoke upon you', 'Become like unto Me', 'Abide in Me'.[199]

Tilak's positive attitude to the Hindu tradition is, however, balanced by a clear conviction regarding the decisiveness of God's revelation in Christ. He affirms that in contrast to Tukaram and other bhakti saints, Jesus alone spoke with a clear voice about God and is the only Saviour: "Nothing but the religion of Jesus… can enable our beloved India to understand what God's idea of sin is, nor reclaim the sinner, nor regenerate, nor make him perfect as his Father in heaven is perfect."[200]

He was, however, convinced that Hindus must be invited to accept Christ not as the supplanter of their spiritual heritage, but as its fulfilment:

> Christ came not to destroy, but to fulfil and his learned disciples have ever interpreted the literature of the world in a discerning and constructive way. Our task is not to condemn indiscriminately, but rather to appreciate the best that there is in persons, to hold up to them their own acknowledged best, and then to try lovingly to make that best of theirs still better.[201]

Tilak's thought is couched in poetic language and embedded in lyrical verse, making a conceptual analysis of his fulfilment ideas somewhat difficult. His approach to the Hindu devotional literature as a kind of Old Testament is similar to what we have earlier categorised as the prophetic fulfilment model. His project was in some ways similar to that of Upadhyay in its attempted synthesis of the person and message of Christ with Indian culture and tradition. However, in contrast to the well-grounded *Logos*-fulfilment framework of

---

[197] Richard, *Christ-Bhakti*, 85; cf. Staffner, *Jesus Christ and the Hindu Community*, 67.

[198] Reported by Winslow, *Narayan Vaman Tilak*, 59.

[199] Quoted in Winslow, *Narayan Vaman Tilak*, 56-57.

[200] *Dyanodaya* 59:23 (June 7, 1900), and 76:21 (May 24, 1917); quoted in Richard, *Christ-Bhakti*, 86.

[201] *Dyanodaya*, 71:37 (September 12, 1912); quoted in Richard, *Christ-Bhakti*, 12.

Upadhyay's thought, Tilak's approach, while fresh and creative, lacks theological sophistication.

The main strength of Tilak's fulfilment approach was its contextual authenticity, emerging out of his attempt to assert the continuity of his Christian experience with his pre-Christian religious and cultural heritage. His attempt led him to make a decisive break with the established church towards the closing years of his life, following which he launched an indigenous Christian movement called *Devacha darbar*.[202] This step was the climax of a life-long struggle to free the person and message of Christ from its western image, and his deep identification with the Indian culture and tradition.[203] His principal contribution to fulfilment thought thus lay in his application of the fulfilment concept in practical inter-religious engagement rather than in theoretical structured formulations.

Summary Evaluation

Our survey of the approaches to other faiths in the crucial formative years of Indian theological reflection in the pre-independence period focussed on four select representatives: Keshub Chunder Sen, Nehemiah Goreh, Brahmabandhab Upadhyay, and Narayan Vaman Tilak. Their fulfilment approaches express various levels of commitment to Christ on one hand, and allegiance to nationalist aspirations and ancestral religion on the other. Apart from these two factors, the diversity of fulfilment approaches was shaped by the specific contexts and distinct impulses conditioning each of their responses.

Sen was probably the first within the Indian context to have used the term fulfilment to describe the relationship of Christ to other religions. It is thus appropriate that subsequent views be outlined in relation to his original conception. Sen's understanding of fulfilment seems to be essentially in line with Muller's evolutionary fulfilment approach, but also includes elements of *Logos* and prophetic fulfilment within its scheme.[204] Despite Boyd's conclusion that the Brahmo Samaj view of Christ "…was fundamentally different from the Christian faith as handed down in the Bible and received by the Church",

---

[202] In his mother tongue, *Marathi*, this means "God's Court", which he described as "a brotherhood of the baptized and unbaptized disciples of Christ", Richard, *Christ-Bhakti*, 100.

[203] Richard points out that Tilak himself was "living proof of at least partial validity in the fulfilment school;" Richard, *Christ-Bhakti*, 18-19, 89-90.

[204] Chenchiah presents us with another form of Indian fulfilment thinking conditioned by evolutionary theory, which needs closer investigation. His distinctive version of fulfilment by transcendence views religions as moving towards Christ, who offers something new and different without parallel in any other religion; D.A. Thangasamy, *The Theology of Chenchiah* (Bangalore: CISRS, 1967), 154-162, 196-197, 215; see Jathanna's analysis, Jathanna, *The Decisiveness of the Christ-event*, 359-370, 430-432.

Christ was clearly the centre of Sen's experience and the apex of his theological framework.[205]

Sen's vision of a Christ-centred harmony of religions was pursued further in a syncretistic direction by one of his disciples, Manilal Parekh.[206] In the earlier stages of his spiritual pilgrimage from Jainism through theism to a Christocentric *bhakti*, Parekh's journey was similar to the fulfilment path outlined by his spiritual mentor. Thus, the teaching of the famous nineteenth century Gujarati reformer, Swami Narayana, convinced him "that God incarnates himself for the redemption of mankind", leading him first to faith in Christ and then eventually to seek Christian baptism.[207]

In the later stages of his thought Parekh's quest seems to have been for a harmony of religions with its fulfilment in his conception of a universal personal religion called *Bhagavata dharma*.[208] The touchstone and essence of this harmony of religions is clearly the personal theism of *bhakti*, discernable in various religious traditions, but most distinctly observed in Christianity and Vaisnavism.[209] Parekh's view requires closer analysis, but this sketch illustrates the syncretistic trajectory in Sen's fulfilment approach.

Upadhyay, on the other hand, took Sen's original proposal in a Christocentric direction. Although, like Parekh, the basic impulse for Upadhyay's quest also came from Sen's vision of a Christ-centred harmony of religions, unlike Sen and Parekh, Upadhyay was a committed Roman Catholic, and his theological framework remained fundamentally Thomistic. The Vedanta, in his expression of the *Logos* fulfilment model, thus represented the highest point which unaided reason has attained to in the Indian context, providing the foundation for a natural theology, which finds fulfilment in the supernatural revelation in Christ.

At the opposite end of the spectrum from Sen's Christ-centred, harmony of religions' view of fulfilment is Goreh's apologetic approach. The absolute decisiveness of Christ is clearly the starting point of Goreh's approach, and his concept of fulfilment a tentative attempt to build a bridge from the light of God in general revelation within Hinduism to an acceptance of the full revelation of God in Christ. He was convinced that this bridge must be crossed if the Hindu is to experience fulfilment of the anticipations and longings of the religion of his birth. Goreh and Sen approach the *Logos* fulfilment idea from diametrically opposite directions. While the universal *Logos*-Christ is basic to Sen's view,

---

205 Boyd, *An Introduction to Indian Christian Theology*, 38-39.

206 R. Boyd, *Manilal C. Parekh: Dhanjibhai Fakirbhai* (Madras: CLS, 1974), 24, 32-33.

207 Boyd, *Manilal C. Parekh*, 4, 25, 37f.

208 Parekh broadened the use of this term, originally used to describe the reformed Hinduism of the Prarthna and Brahmo Samaj, to denote the true worship of and friendship with the one God, and loving fellowship among his people; Boyd, *Manilal C. Parekh*, 18-19, 53, 85f.

209 Boyd, *Manilal C. Parekh*, 10.

Goreh grounds his conception of *Logos*, like the early fathers, in the Christ of history.

Although Tilak's theological orientation is similar to that of Goreh, his *bhakti* orientation and deeper Christian appropriation of the Hindu cultural tradition sets him apart. He claimed most explicitly to have come to faith in Christ as the culmination of his spiritual journey along the path indicated by the *bhakti* poet-saints of India. In this respect and in his explicit adoption of the *bhakti* devotional framework, his approach was close to that of Parekh. But while *bhakti* represented the ultimate destination for Parekh, for Tilak, the *bhakti* devotional literature and poetry had a provisional and preparatory function, pointing beyond to prophetic fulfilment in Christ.

Our survey of the expressions of the fulfilment concept within these different strands of the Indian tradition thus indicates the essential originality and individuality of each fulfilment approach. While Sen's vision of fulfilment may have inspired Upadhyay and Parekh, among others, there is little evidence of any significant degree of mutual influence between the various fulfilment views examined.

On the other hand, although the fulfilment approaches of this period are not carefully formulated theological statements, various forms of the basic fulfilment concept emerge frequently and consistently. How is this widespread appropriation of the fulfilment concept explained given the apparent minimal degree of mutual influence between the various views? A possible explanation is suggested by a consideration of the two factors: the common focus of these Indian thinkers on issues of national identity and indigeneity; and, their common acceptance of the normativity of the New Testament Jewish-Christian fulfilment approach.

To begin with, our representative thinkers shared a concern to demonstrate the contextual relevance of the message of Christ to India. Sen passionately rejected what he perceived as the western trappings of Christianity, and abhorred the denationalisation that frequently marked Indian converts to Christianity. Goreh, likewise, refused to become westernised, wanting to affirm allegiance to his traditional culture and religion. Upadhyay remained deeply rooted within his Hindu cultural tradition and passionately patriotic until the end of his life.[210] Tilak's quest for the ideal religion was grounded in his patriotism, and led him to a more Indian expression of Christ-centred discipleship.

With this common concern in focus, these thinkers drew their insights from a variety of sources, of which the only common factor appears to have been their experience of Christ as mediated through the Christian scriptures. A reasonable hypothesis which could explain their common appropriation of the fulfilment concept is that, following their experience of Christ, they allowed the New Testament account of Christ's and the early Christians' reading of the

---

[210] Lipner, *Brahmabandhab Upadhyay*, 362-384.

Jewish scriptures to shape their own approach to their pre-Christian tradition. The widespread and consistent presence of fulfilment as a unifying phenomenon among converts thus seems to have been the consequence of an application of the Jewish-Christian fulfilment approach to their pre-Christian religion and culture in the light of their common contextual concerns.[211]

Despite diverse forms of expression and lack of sophisticated formulation, the consistent and widespread emergence of fulfilment approaches among converts in pre-independence India is convincing evidence that the fulfilment concept has critically influenced the Christian attitude to other faiths in the Indian context.

To what extent are the views we have considered authentically Indian responses rather than western imperialistic impositions? The charge of imperialism directed frequently against the fulfilment approach essentially has two dimensions. First, a theological aspect inherent in the seemingly absolute claim Christians make concerning Christ's decisiveness and universal lordship.[212] Second, and of more immediate relevance to this stage of our discussion, the cultural imperialism allegation frequently associated with the colonial missionary enterprise.[213] In this form it refers originally to the effort of the Anglicist party of British educators to use education as a tool for imposing European culture in place of Indian culture, but is frequently applied to the missionary enterprise as a whole.[214] This is an issue that will come up at different points in our discussion, and will be addressed more substantially towards the conclusion of our study. An important contribution to our overall argument that emerges at this stage is our observation of the fundamentally indigenous quality of the Indian fulfilment approaches we have examined.

It is possible to demonstrate some western influence upon all the thinkers we have looked at, with the exception of Tilak: evolutionary theory on Sen, rationalism on Goreh and Thomistic theology on Upadhyay. To the extent that these influences, along with the biblical sources that helped shape the fulfilment approach, were essentially of foreign origin, these fulfilment approaches cannot claim to be purely indigenous.

On the other hand, we have also observed that the fulfilment approaches of these converts arose out of a fundamental desire to keep their pre-Christian cultural roots intact, and celebrate what they regarded as true and good in the religion and culture of their birth. It is in this sense that the emergence of fulfilment approaches in India may be legitimately regarded as an indigenous theological development rather than an induced imperialistic response.

---

[211] This is a hypothesis which will need to be tested when we consider the fulfilment approaches of Banerjea and Sundar Singh in Chapters 3 and 4.

[212] Race, *Christians and Religious Pluralism*, 68; Stanley, *The Bible and the Flag*, 184.

[213] Copley, *Religions in Conflict*, 36-38.

[214] Ingleby, 'Education as a Missionary Tool', 397-404.

Conclusion

In this chapter we have tried, first, to define the problem this study seeks to address in relation to its background and context, and to outline the rationale, scope and methodology of the project. We introduced the central theme of our study, first sketching three models of fulfilment, on the basis of which we then outlined a working definition of the fulfilment concept.

Second, in setting the context for our study, we described two main Protestant missionary attitudes during the nineteenth century: a dominant conservative and confrontational posture, and a more irenic minority attitude, which eventually found expression in various fulfilment approaches. The work of the British Orientalists, the rise of religious nationalism in India, and the emergence of the science of comparative religions in Europe contributed to the growing influence of this irenic attitude in the closing decades of the century. Evolutionary philosophy became a prominent common feature of the Protestant missionary fulfilment tradition that emerged in the closing years of the nineteenth century, and received the missionary community's sanction at the World Missionary Conference at Edinburgh in 1910.

Our final task was to survey representative fulfilment approaches that emerged as indigenous responses to Christ within India during the same period. We observed that: (1) The frequency and consistency with which converts seem to adopt some form of the fulfilment concept confirms its significance in shaping the Christian attitude to other religions in the Indian context during this period; (2) The widespread adoption of the fulfilment concept despite the absence of signs of mutual influence is the result of a common New Testament-inspired Christian reading of indigenous religious sources; (3) Although the western influence is indisputable, the fundamental desire of converts to root their appropriation of Christ firmly within the Hindu culture and tradition confirms the integrity of their views as authentic Indian responses to Christ.

We turn our attention in the next chapter to the fulfilment approach of a leading representative of the nineteenth century Protestant fulfilment tradition, John Nicol Farquhar.

Fulfilment in John Nicol Farquhar's 'The Crown Of Hinduism'

We have examined the ferment from within which the fulfilment tradition emerged in nineteenth century Protestant missionary theology. The dominant evangelical faith of the late nineteenth century, strongly polemical towards other faiths, continued to provide the impetus for an ongoing encounter with other religions on the mission field. However, an irenic attitude towards other religions began to grow in influence and was adopted by an increasing number of Christian missionaries by the turn of the century. Nowhere was this more evident than in India, or the trend better exemplified than in the work of the Scottish missionary to India, John Nicol Farquhar.[1]

This chapter is devoted to a theological assessment of Farquhar's fulfilment approach. After an overview of his life and ministry, we trace the emergence and development of his fulfilment approach, especially focusing on its statement in *The Crown of Hinduism*.[2] Our critical analysis of Farquhar's approach based on the fulfilment grid outlined in our opening chapter will include an evaluation of some important criticisms of his view and a theological assessment.

---

[1] To date, Eric J. Sharpe's various published studies continue to be the main sources for the life and contribution of Farquhar. Sharpe's first book on Farquhar (1962) was essentially biographical; E.J. Sharpe, *J.N. Farquhar: A Memoir* (Calcutta: YMCA), 1962; in his later landmark work, Sharpe undertakes a fairly rigorous assessment of Farquhar's contribution to the development of Protestant mission theology in India in the second half of the nineteenth and early twentieth centuries; E.J. Sharpe, *Not to Destroy but to Fulfil: The Contribution of J.N. Farquhar to Protestant Missionary Thought in India before 1914* (Uppsala: Swedish Institute of Missionary Research), 1965. Other shorter publications on Farquhar include: E.J. Sharpe, *John Nicol Farquhar and the Missionary Study of Hinduism* Aberdeen: Scottish Institute of Missionary Studies), 1971; E.J. Sharpe, *Faith Meets Faith: Some Christian Attitudes to Hinduism in the Nineteenth and Twentieth Centuries* (London: SCM. Press, Ltd.,1977),19-32; E.J. Sharpe, 'The Legacy of J.N. Farquhar', *Occasional Bulletin of Missionary Research* 3, 2 (1979): 61-64; and K. Cracknell, *Justice, Courtesy and Love: Theologians and Missionaries Encountering World Religions (1846-1914)* (London: Epworth,1995),167-173 and a recent significant evaluation of his thought by Hedges, 'A History and Study of Fulfilment Theology in Modern British Thought' (Ph.D. thesis, University of Wales, 2001), 277-340, 347-392. Brief sketches and references to Farquhar's fulfilment view in other works are too numerous to list, but highlight the importance of his work.

[2] J.N. Farquhar, *The Crown of Hinduism* (1913; repr., New Delhi: Oriental Books, 1971).

The Man and His Background (1861-1929)[3]

Farquhar was born in Aberdeen, Scotland, and brought up as a member of an independent evangelistic society called the Evangelical Union, a type of Scottish Protestant Congregationalism.[4] He grew up imbibing the revivalist and evangelistic fervour, the intellectual rigour, and the positive attitude to interdenominational co-operation fostered by the Evangelical Union.[5] Farquhar was converted to Christ at the age of twenty-four as a result of a close friendship with his childhood acquaintance, Euphemia Watson, who eventually became his wife in 1891.[6] He entered Aberdeen Grammar School in 1882, then Aberdeen University, before going on to study classics at Christ Church in Oxford; he graduated in 1889 with a B.A. degree in Literae Humaniores.[7]

Farquhar's regular studies did not include any theology and, hence, apart from some knowledge of New Testament exegesis, acquired through informal study, his personal theological framework at this stage remained largely undeveloped. Among the various possible influences on Farquhar's life, conclusive evidence exists for the direct influence of only Andrew Martin Fairburn, principal of Mansfield College, Oxford.[8] Four essential features of Fairbairn's thought became distinguishing marks of Farquhar's theological method and framework in later years: (1) his willingness to apply the findings of historical and critical study to his study of the Bible and theology, without compromising his commitment to essentials of Evangelical theology; (2) his emphasis on the person and teachings of Christ as the foundation of Christian theology; (3) his acceptance of evolution as a working hypothesis; and, (4) his interest in the study of comparative religion.[9]

On completing his studies at Oxford, Farquhar was accepted by the London Missionary Society as a candidate for educational missionary work abroad, and was appointed as a teacher of the Society's institution at Bhowanipur in

---

[3] We are largely dependent upon Sharpe's seminal research for biographical details of Farquhar's life and ministry; see Sharpe, *Not to Destroy*, 109.

[4] Sharpe, *A Memoir*, 6.

[5] Sharpe, *Not to Destroy*, 109-116.

[6] Sharpe, *A Memoir*, 7.

[7] For details of Farquhar's early life, see Sharpe, *A Memoir*, 1-16.

[8] The influence of Max Muller and Monier-Williams is possible, but must remain a moot point due to lack of conclusive evidence. Despite the absence of any express acknowledgment of dependence, the factors which make Fairbairn's influence upon Farquhar quite probable include: (1) their almost certain personal acquaintance based on common membership of the Evangelical Union; (2) Fairbairn's ministry in Aberdeen for five years while Farquhar was still an apprentice draper; (3) the personal tone of Fairbairn's letter of recommendation on the occasion of Farquhar's missionary candidacy; and, (4) Farquhar's membership of Fairbairn's circle during his Oxford years placed him within the sphere of his theological influence; Sharpe, *Not to Destroy*, 125-130; Cracknell, *Justice, Courtesy and Love*, 74, 167-168.

[9] Sharpe, *Not to Destroy*, 121, 128-130.

Calcutta.[10] He arrived at the Bhowanipur institution in early February 1891 at a time when it was difficult to carry out any programme of direct evangelism in the prevailing atmosphere of hostility towards Christian mission. The London Missionary Society (LMS) College was patterned after the Church of Scotland institution in Calcutta, started by Alexander Duff in 1830, and was presumably based on his mission philosophy.[11] Farquhar seems to have become frustrated with the lack of evangelistic opportunity, and disillusioned with the ineffectiveness of educational work as a tool for high caste conversions.[12]

In January 1902, Farquhar moved from the L.M.S. to the Young Men's Christian Association (YMCA) in order to devote more time to evangelistic work.[13] He went on to serve first as National Student Secretary and then Literary Secretary of the Indian YMCA. The terms of his last appointment enabled him to devote all his energies to the task of producing apologetic literature.[14] His ministry responsibilities included evangelism, leading Bible classes, conducting private interviews, and producing evangelistic literature. He acquired a formidable reputation among the Calcutta missionary community for effectiveness in personal evangelism.

Farquhar focused on the central truths of the Christian gospel, avoided theological controversy, and displayed sympathy and cultural sensitivity when communicating to non-Christian audiences.[15] A grassroots practitioner rather than an abstract theologian, his views were forged in the heat of practical Christian-Hindu encounter and informed by a careful study of religious texts. His quest for a more irenic evangelistic approach towards Hinduism was in response to the challenge of growing political and religious nationalism and Hindu militancy.[16]

Following his retirement in 1923, he accepted appointment as professor of comparative religion in the University of Manchester, and received honorary doctorates from the universities of Oxford and Aberdeen shortly before his demise in 1929.[17] We turn now to consider Farquhar's early literary activity,

---

[10] Sharpe, *ibid.*, 123-124, 131-133.

[11] Duff viewed western higher education as a means of undermining the hold of Hinduism upon upper caste youth, and preparing them to respond favourably to the Christian faith. For Duff's philosophy of higher education as a tool of mission, see Sharpe, *Not to Destroy*, 63-67; cf. J.C. Ingleby, 'Education as a Missionary Tool: A Study in Christian Missionary Education by English Protestant Missionaries in India with Special Reference to Cultural Change' (Ph.D. thesis, Oxford Centre for Mission Studies, 1998), 347-368.

[12] Sharpe, *Not to Destroy*, 139.

[13] For details, see Sharpe, *Not to Destroy*, 147-153, 156-163.

[14] Sharpe, *ibid.*, 161, 183, 219-221, 270.

[15] Sharpe, *ibid.*, 181-182.

[16] Sharpe, *ibid.*, 20-21.

[17] Sharpe, 'The Legacy of J.N. Farquhar', 61.

and the light it sheds on the development of his apologetic approach in the years leading up to the publication of *The Crown of Hinduism*.

Fulfilment in Farquhar's Earlier Literary Contribution

Farquhar was a prolific writer; Sharpe admits that his extensive research, which includes forty entries comprising twenty-two books or monographs and eighteen articles, was not exhaustive.[18] He was convinced that in the prevailing climate of hostility, the most effective instrument for presenting Christ to the educated Hindu was apologetic literature sympathetic to the cultural heritage of India.[19] Farquhar's contribution also included recruiting and motivating others to enlist in the task of producing this new kind of literature.[20] Our focus in the following assessment is limited to those items of Farquhar's contribution that illuminate the development of his fulfilment approach.

Farquhar's publication of *The Crown of Hinduism* in 1913, the fullest and clearest statement of his fulfilment approach, placed him at the forefront of the movement towards a more sympathetic and positive Christian approach to Hinduism. But the process leading to the development of his approach began at least a decade earlier, and in his writings of these years we observe the interplay of four distinct impulses.

Farquhar's principal impulse was clearly a simple but uncompromising loyalty to Christ and the Gospel. He was first and foremost a missionary who viewed his task as assisting in the work of "spreading the Gospel of Christ among the heathen", and persuading "a people to change its religion".[21] The supremacy and decisiveness of Christ as a non-negotiable theological truth, and the obligation to communicate this fact as an absolute missiological mandate, together constituted an essential starting point of Farquhar's apologetic method.[22]

Second, Farquhar was an educational missionary. Missionary higher education viewed itself as contributing to a process of modernization based on the enlightenment project of discovering neutral and objective truths. Modernity was thus seen as preparing the ground for reception of the Christian

---

[18] Sharpe also examined vast amounts of unpublished material such as letters, reports, and other papers; Sharpe, *Not to Destroy*, 18; cf. 362-364, 368-369.

[19] Sharpe, *Not to Destroy*, 236-243.

[20] Farquhar thus accepted editorial responsibility for a number of works, such as *The Religious Quest of India Series*, *The Heritage of India Series*, and *The Religious Life of India Series*; for details, see M.D. David, *The YMCA and the Making of Modern India: A Centenary History* (New Delhi: National Council of YMCAs of India, 1992), 481-482; cf. Sharpe, 'The Legacy of J.N. Farquhar', 61.

[21] According to his candidature papers; Sharpe, *Not to Destroy*, 131-133.

[22] Sharpe, *Not to Destroy*, 305-309 lists loyalty to Christ along with sympathy towards Hinduism and quality scholarship as the three components of Farquhar's theological method.

gospel by providing the educated Hindu with a "value-free" intellectual framework, which would eventually undermine his traditional religious beliefs and culture. Some of these assumptions of the missionary philosophy of higher education emerge repeatedly in Farquhar's writings.

Third, Farquhar arrived in India when religious and political nationalism was on the rise. The nationalist spirit accompanied by the growth of strong anti-Western sentiments intensified between 1902 and 1905, and the atmosphere became even more antagonistic towards Christian mission after 1905.[23] The need for an irenic approach that would remove cultural hindrances to the favourable reception of the Christian faith in India was thus felt more acutely.

Fourth, in his quest for a credible and neutral framework on which to base his Christian apologetic, Farquhar turned to the science of religions.[24] In an early article he stated his intention thus: "...we want a broader foundation to build on... a criticism that will set Christianity clearly and distinctly in its relations with other faiths."[25] In the same article he specified the two main principles undergirding the scientific study of religion: the essential unity of the whole human race, and the understanding of human life as an organic process of development, both of which were reflected in his subsequent apologetic approach.[26]

Farquhar's earliest writings reflect his acceptance of the liberal critical and scientific method along with an evangelical insistence on personal commitment to Jesus Christ.[27] His discussion of the impact of modern thought on the Christian faith reveals his acceptance of the evolutionary hypothesis in historical investigation.[28] In "Science of Religion" he invites the missionary to explore a new apologetic approach based on the science of religion, grounding his appeal in the attempts of the early Christian apologists to develop a theory of relations between Christianity and other religions, and the logical attraction of such a scientific theory.[29] These early impulses continued to guide Farquhar's theological development in subsequent years.

---

[23] Sharpe, *-254.*, 191-193, 209-227, 243-254.

[24] The comparative study of religions based essentially on an evolutionary framework of religious development, later known as Comparative Religion; see Sharpe, *Not to Destroy*, 45-46.

[25] J.N. Farquhar, 'The Science of Religion as an Aid to Apologetics', *Harvest Field* 12 (1901), 369.

[26] Farquhar, 'The Science of Religion', 370-371.

[27] J.N. Farquhar, *The Crossbearer: Being Extracts from the Gospel According to St. Matthew, Translated, Analysed and Explained in an Brief Commentary* (Calcutta: Methodist Publishing House, 1900); J.N. Farquhar, *Christ and the Gospels: A Letter to the Thinking Men of Calcutta* (Calcutta, 1901); J.N. Farquhar, *Criticism and Christianity: A Letter to the Thinking Men of Calcutta and Bengal* (Calcutta, 1901).

[28] Farquhar, *Criticism and Christianity: A Letter to the Thinking Men of Calcutta and Bengal* 2.

[29] Farquhar, 'Science of Religion', 369-370.

Farquhar's editorship of the YMCA monthly journal, *The Inquirer*, provided him with the needed opportunity for ongoing literary activity.[30] The first few issues reflect a fairly conservative stance towards other religions,[31] but his basic irenic posture is reflected consistently throughout.[32] Many core concepts of his later fulfilment approach began to be formulated during this period, such as his conviction of the organic unity of life,[33] the driving impulse behind his quest for a unifying theory of religion,[34] and his belief in the universal Fatherhood of God.[35] He clearly stated his views in a series of articles published in 1903 entitled, 'Is Christianity the Only True Religion?'[36]

Starting from what is to him a self-evident premise that there can be only one true and universal religion, Farquhar bases his apologetic on the method of contrast. Whereas Christianity satisfies the fundamental instincts of the universal human religious consciousness in its quest for a personal God, an incarnation, the ultimate atoning sacrifice and an enduring ethical system, Hinduism, as a system, will not survive the demands of the modern age due to its justification of polytheism, caste and idolatry, and its inadequate foundation for morality.[37] The universal breadth of the Christian vision enables Christians to recognize principles of true religion and elements of spiritual and ethical truth in the Hindu tradition in the same way as the early Church Fathers did in Greek philosophy and religion.[38]

Within its Christ-centred vision, Christianity acknowledges "...that God has spoken in many religions, and recognizes that Christ is the light that lighteth every man that cometh into the world."[39] The concluding article of this series introduces the term fulfilment for the first time in Farquhar's writings. The assertion that Christianity is the only truly universal religion that satisfies the modern mind, completes the glimpses of truth and fulfils the longings of other religions, represents an early, rudimentary expression of the fulfilment view.[40]

Farquhar applied his fulfilment approach early in a rigorous study of the main text of religious nationalism in India, the *Bhagavad Gita*, resulting in the

---

[30] He took over its editorship with the August 1902 issue.

[31] *Inquirer* 4:1 (September 1902), 6; *Inquirer* 4:6 (February 1903), 8.

[32] He concedes, for instance, that those who follow all the light they have may be saved without explicit knowledge of the gospel, and is willing to acknowledge the "genuine religious insights of the non-Christian world", *Inquirer* 4:5 (January 1903), 2-3; *Inquirer* 4:11 (July 1903), 3. Sharpe's perception of a progression in Farquhar's thought in *Inquirer* from exclusiveness towards a more open inclusivist posture is, thus, not convincing.

[33] *Inquirer* 3:12 (August 1902), 6.

[34] *Inquirer* 4:2 (October 1902), 7-8.

[35] *Inquirer* 3:12 (August 1902), 4.

[36] *Inquirer* 4:10 (June 1903) – 5:1 (September 1903).

[37] *Inquirer* 4:10 (June 1903), 1-3; 4:12 (August 1903), 1.

[38] *Inquirer* 4:11 (July 1903), 1-2.

[39] *Inquirer* 4:12 (August 1903), 2.

[40] *Inquirer* 5:1 (September 1903), 6.

publication of three works on the subject.[41] He concluded that the existence of the mythical figure of Krishna in the *Gita* reflects the need for a saviour, a need unfulfilled within Hinduism, which Christ alone is able to satisfy: "Rightly read, the Gita is a clear-tongued prophecy of Christ, and the hearts that bow down to the idea of Krishna are really seeking the incarnate Son of God."[42]

Missing from Sharpe's careful chronicle of Farquhar's theological development is reference to a paper he read at the North India Conference of Christian Workers. He recommends a positive approach in the Christian witness to the Hindu based on recognition of the divine origin of Hindu religious instincts:

> If we believe that God's creative hand gave man his religious instincts, then we must necessarily believe that these instincts, however much perverted by human sin, will, in their struggles to express themselves, shew their divine origin; and if we believe that the Light which lighteth every man has actually been shining in every human heart, then we shall expect to catch even in the darkest caverns of their religion some gleam of the True Light.[43]

Farquhar remains convinced that, despite some false and even immoral forms of expression, these instincts have prepared Hindus to receive the fuller light of Christian truth, and should be appealed to in gospel presentations.[44] After relating several Hindu ideas to Christianity, he concludes that a "right instinct" is involved in every aspect of Hinduism, and every element can be shown to point properly to Christ.[45] Echoing Banerjea's language, he asserts that "...every important Christian truth is foreshadowed in Hinduism, though buried in heaps of rubbish"; the task of the Christian worker is to discover these and indicate how they are fulfilled in Christ.[46] In a paper read at the Calcutta Missionary Conference the following year, Farquhar insists that the unsympathetic denunciation of Hinduism alienates the Hindu community, and that a sympathetic attitude is an essential prerequisite for a proper understanding of Hinduism.[47]

---

[41] J.N. Farquhar, *Gita and Gospel* (Calcutta, 1903); J.N. Farquhar, *Permanent Lessons of the Gita* (Madras, 1903); and J.N. Farquhar, *The Age and Origin of the Gita* (Madras, 1904).

[42] Farquhar, *Gita and Gospel*, 59; cf. *Inquirer* 4:6 (February 1903), 4.

[43] J.N. Farquhar, 'How to Present the Response in the Christian Faith to Hindu Religious Aspirations', *The Harvest Field* 15:12 (1904), 461.

[44] Farquhar, *ibid.*, 461-462.

[45] Farquhar, *ibid.*, 462-471.

[46] Farquhar, *ibid.*, 472; cf. 154.

[47] J.N. Farquhar, 'Missionary Study of Hinduism', *The Harvest Field*, 16, 5 (1905): 177. A footnote in this paper indicates Farquhar's acquaintance with and essential agreement with the ideas of two earlier fulfilment thinkers, T.E. Slater and F.W. Kellett; see Sharpe, *Not to Destroy*, 94-106; cf. 29, n. 111.

Farquhar's sympathetic sensitivity towards Hinduism was matched by a strong sense of optimism regarding the future of Christianity in India, which bordered on triumphalism. In 'Christianity in India'[48] he argued that despite the slow advance of Christian missions in India, Protestant Christianity was destined to take the place of Hinduism as the religion of India.[49] His analysis of the Hindu resistance to outside influences led him to conclude that the intellectual, moral, social, and religious upheaval generated by the demands of modernity and the onslaught of Christian mission have penetrated "the protective armour of Hinduism".[50] This triumphalistic tone was to become characteristic of Farquhar's fulfilment view in later years.

One of the earliest and clear statements of Farquhar's fulfilment approach is evidenced in a lecture delivered at the World's Student Christian Federation Conference at Oxford in 1909:

> The method I refer to consists in setting forth Christianity as the fulfilment of all that is aimed at in Hinduism, as the satisfaction of the spiritual yearnings of her people, as the crown and climax of the crudest forms of her worship... [this method] sets forth every part of Hinduism as springing from some real religious instinct and having a value of its own, and thus gives the religion the full credit for every fragment of moral and religious help it contains; yet it sets Christ supreme over all, and proclaims Him to be the consummator of religion.[51]

The essential impulse of Farquhar's method is set forth here explicitly: to state the relationship between Christianity and Hinduism in a way that would enable the people of India to see in Christ the fulfilment of their deepest religious aspirations. Christianity is presented here as the "fulfilment", "satisfaction", the "crown and climax" not just of the high points, but of every aspect of Hindu faith and practice. This fulfilment relates to "all that is aimed at in Hinduism", the underlying "spiritual yearnings", and the "religious instinct" at the core of each expression. Ascribing significance and legitimacy to the best as well as the worst in Hinduism became hereafter an important component of his fulfilment view, but also attracted much conservative criticism.

In two articles published in 1910, Farquhar clarified his understanding of fulfilment even further. 'The Greatness of Hinduism' offers a philosophical

---

[48] J.N. Farquhar, 'Christianity in India', *The Contemporary Review* 93 (1908): 597-616.

[49] He had advanced a similar thesis four years earlier in a pamphlet entitled, "The Future of Christianity", arguing that the evolutionary principle of the stronger overcoming the weaker species assured the ultimate victory of Christianity in India; Sharpe, *Not to Destroy*, 205.

[50] Farquhar, 'Christianity in India', 597-609.

[51] 'Lessons from Experience in India' in Report of the Conference of the World's Student Christian Federation held at Oxford, England [1909], 72, quoted in Sharpe, *Not to Destroy*, 255-256.

justification for Hinduism as a religion: Its lofty theory of God and the world; its sophisticated organisation based on the authority of the Brahmins, the divine quality and inspiration of the Vedas and other sacred literature; the grandeur and heroic achievements of the ascetic ideal; the sincerity of the Hindu spiritual quest reflected in various theistic movements; and the pervasive breadth and penetrative power of its appeal, all contribute to making Hinduism one of the greatest religions of the world.[52]

The article goes on to apply the modernity principle undergirding the educational missionary enterprise in showing that the spirit of nationalism is the direct outcome of the influence of Western education on the Indian spirit.[53] The concepts of patriotism and nationalism are thus held up as illustrations of culturally neutral and universally relevant discoveries of modernity.[54] The recovery of the sacred literature of the East by European scholars has influenced the rise of religious nationalism. But India's encounter with the West has given rise to impulses for progress in politics, education, and social reform, ultimately incompatible with ancient Hindu ideals. He concludes that many of the hallowed institutions of Hindu religion and culture are gradually breaking down, "...shattered by the impact of modern thought and religion..."[55]

'The Crown of Hinduism' carries forward the argument of 'Greatness' by explaining how Christianity would become the one religion of India without destroying its national cultural and religious heritage.[56] Although Farquhar anticipates the eventual collapse of Hinduism as a system, he remains convinced that the rich religious literary tradition of India would always continue to nourish and resource the people of India. He makes a bold claim in justifying this conviction:

> God has spoken in India. Men have heard His voice and have repeated His utterances... no religion will ever captivate and satisfy the heart of India that does not enrich itself with these spiritual treasures.... Every part of India's religion is significant. Every element springs from some living religious instinct.[57]

Farquhar's two prerequisites for a religion with the potential for replacing Hinduism in India are relevance to the demands of modernity, and continuity with all aspects of the Hindu religious spirit. He goes on to show how Christianity fulfils both these prerequisites in a way that contemporary Hindu

---

[52] J.N. Farquhar, 'The Greatness of Hinduism', *The Contemporary Review* 97 (1910): 645-55.
[53] Farquhar, *ibid.*, 655-656.
[54] Farquhar, *ibid.*, 657.
[55] Farquhar, *ibid.*, 658-662.
[56] J.N. Farquhar, 'The Crown of Hinduism', *The Contemporary Review* 98, 535 (1910): 56-68.
[57] Farquhar, *ibid.*, 57-58.

renaissance movements could not.[58] He concludes that, despite the wide gulf that separates them, the "natural and strong" lines of connection between Hinduism and Christianity are:

> … lines of development, that Hinduism is a rudimentary faith, Christianity its culmination. The Hindu who becomes a Christian loses nothing. All that his old faith offered him he enjoys again in Christianity, only at a more advanced stage of evolution… [Christianity is thus]… the evolutionary crown of Hinduism.[59]

The Indian Christianity of the future will incorporate within it a re-born Hinduism, emerging from a Christ-centred reinterpretation of the Hindu tradition:

> Christ's authority will be maintained supreme in all things. Everything must pass the scrutiny of His spirit…. Thus the New Testament will remain the focus of all Revelation, the central sun in the light of which everything must be read and estimated. But the greater books of Hinduism will form a sort of second Old Testament, set like stars around the sun…[60]

The reference to a "second" Old Testament and the use of the star analogy indicate that Farquhar regarded the Hindu religious literature as having some revelatory value. He also recommends a Christological interpretation of the Hindu tradition in the Christian approach to Hinduism. This article clarifies two complementary elements critical to Farquhar's fulfilment view in later years: the triumphalism implicit in its aspiration to replace Hinduism, and the concern for preservation of a Hindu tradition reborn in Christ.

In 1910, Farquhar also published 'Christ and the Religions of the World',[61] primarily for an educated British audience. This article, which effectively summarises the salient features of his fulfilment approach prior to the publication of *Crown of Hinduism*, subsequently became the focus of the fulfilment debate in India.[62]

Farquhar begins by justifying the pressing need for a reasonable and coherent approach towards other religions.[63] His approach is governed by a twofold concern. At one end is the recognition that every element of religion "…springs from some genuine instinct, deep seated in the mystery of our common religious nature".[64] The other pole is the conviction that Christianity

---

[58] Farquhar, *ibid.*, 58-60.

[59] Farquhar, *ibid.*, 67; 60-67.

[60] Farquhar, *ibid.*, 67-68.

[61] J.N. Farquhar, 'Christ and the Religions of the World', *Student Movement* 12 (1919): 195-98.

[62] For details of this debate conducted primarily in the Methodist journal, *Indian Witness*, see Sharpe, *Not to Destroy*, 309-23.

[63] Farquhar, 'Christ and the Religions of the World', 195.

[64] Farquhar, *ibid.*, 195-96.

represents the pinnacle of humanity's religious development, the "final religion", in which all other religions find consummation:

> Now, if Christ has given us the final religion… clearly all our religious instincts will find satisfaction in Christianity…. If Christ is able to satisfy all the religious needs of the human heart, then all the elements of pagan religions, since they spring from these needs, will be found reproduced in perfect form, completely fulfilled, consummated in Christ.[65]

These two impulses are held together most adequately in the New Testament theme of fulfilment expressed in Christ's declaration: "I came not to destroy but to fulfil" (Matt. 5:17). Farquhar acknowledges the primary application of these words to the evolution of Judeo-Christian religion, but sees adequate grounds for including non-Christian religions within their scope.[66] His understanding of how Christ fulfils the Old Testament serves as a controlling model for the relationship of Christian faith to other religions.

In claiming that the Old Testament prophecies are fulfilled in himself, Christ did not seem to be concerned with the details, and on occasion appeared to abrogate certain aspects. The Old Testament prophecies instead give expression "…to natural longings of the human religious consciousness", aspirations regarding the coming of the Kingdom of God and the Messiah, all of which Christ fulfils. He thus draws the principle that Christ feels himself "…related to every natural religious instinct and aspiration of the human spirit."[67]

In applying this principle to other religions, Farquhar explicitly clarifies his acceptance of the evolutionary framework. Ideas present in rudimentary and material form in the earlier, "lower" religions, appear in more spiritual form in the purer, "higher" religions. Farquhar observes a greater correlation between corresponding truths in Hinduism and Christianity than Judaism and Christianity. Ideas within Hinduism such as that of a sacred revelation, a holy people, a divine priest who is also himself the sacrifice, incarnation and the self-abandoned pursuit of God, have however been buried under other crippling misconceptions detrimental to Hindu religious life and culture. Thus, although the legitimate spiritual yearnings of Hinduism find their satisfaction in Christ, death is a prerequisite for fulfilment: "Hinduism must die into Christianity, in order that all that her philosophers, saints and ascetics toiled for may live."[68]

This life through death metaphor, crucial to Farquhar's later more detailed argument in *Crown*, is introduced here for the first time. It captures implicitly two essential features of Farquhar's fulfilment view not expounded in detail in this article. First, an implicit triumphalism, stated clearly first in 'Future of Christianity', restated four years later in 'Christianity in India', and then

[65] Farquhar, *ibid.*, 196.
[66] Farquhar, *ibid.*, 196.
[67] Farquhar, *ibid.*, 196-197.
[68] Farquhar, *ibid.*, 197.

expounded more fully in 'Greatness' and 'Crown'. The evolutionary principle of the weaker giving way to the stronger resulted in a positive optimism regarding the ultimate displacement of Hinduism by Christianity as the dominant religion of India.

'Crown' tempers this triumphalism by explaining the life impulse in fulfilment, which seeks the preservation of the rich cultural and religious heritage of India, an emphasis also captured in this article. The presence of fragments of spiritual and ethical truth within the literary tradition of Hinduism is evidence that God has not left himself without witness within it. These elements must be preserved and will continue to nourish Indian society even after the demise of the Hindu system. Indian Christianity must incorporate within itself a Christ-centred reinterpretation of the Hindu tradition. Other religions, likewise, may be similarly related to Christian faith on the basis of an evolutionary fulfilment continuum. Presentiments of Christian truth present in other religions in rudimentary or undeveloped form find completion in Christianity, "...the evolutionary crown of all".[69]

This is the fullest summary statement of Farquhar's view of the relationship of Christianity to other religions up to this point. The advantages of this view are listed: a sympathetic framework for the study of religions and approach to people of other faiths; a reasonable explanation of how Christ's supremacy is related to and fulfils the aspirations of other religions; and, its safeguard against syncretistic compromise: "...everything must pass the scrutiny of the spirit of Christ".[70]

In summary, Farquhar's fulfilment apologetic was driven by a quest for a comprehensive unifying theory of the relation between religions and motivated by a desire to relate Christ to the deepest religious aspirations of India. He sought to give non-Christian religions their rightful place while affirming the incontestable supremacy of the Christian faith. He recognised fundamental instincts of religious consciousness within every human heart and religion, and sought to uncover religious instincts behind every aspect of Hindu belief and practice.

Farquhar adopted the evolutionary theory as a formal scheme of continuity between religions. The theological content for this scheme was derived from his application of Jesus' employment of the fulfilment concept in the New Testament to explain the continuity of his message with Old Testament Judaism. In applying this to Hindu-Christian continuity, Farquhar employs the "life through death" metaphor, capturing both the idea of the replacement of the rudimentary truths of Hinduism by their fullness in Christ, and the preservation of the treasures of Hindu tradition through fulfilment in Christ.

The essential contours of Farquhar's fulfilment view were thus already clearly defined prior to its comprehensive and definitive statement in *Crown*.

---

[69] Farquhar, *ibid.*, 197.
[70] Farquhar, *ibid.*, 198.

This fundamental continuity between the ideas in Farquhar's earlier writings and in *Crown* has led his chief commentator to assert that *Crown* contained nothing original not found in his earlier work.[71] This is also the basis for a recent claim that his earlier writings have little value for assessing his fulfilment approach.[72]

Our investigation of Farquhar's earlier writings prior to the publication of *Crown* is, however, methodologically crucial for the following reasons: (1) it helps identify the original impulses and influences shaping his thought; (2) some of the specific components of his later view are illuminated more clearly in his early writings;[73] and (3) we are able to recognize movement or shifts, if any, between his early and later thought.

In 1913, Farquhar published *The Crown of Hinduism*, an apologetic treatise that set forth his fulfilment view most clearly, systematically and comprehensively.[74]

Fulfilment in "The Crown of Hinduism"

The Crown of Hinduism was Farquhar's response to the need for an effective apologetic approach to the Hindu, which would remove the misconception that the Christian gospel was anti-national and destructive of the Indian religious and cultural heritage. The value of this work is not so much in its conceptual originality as its breadth and scope: it attempts to establish Farquhar's thesis of Hindu-Christian fulfilment in relation to all the main features of Hinduism.

Farquhar's project is skilfully outlined in the introduction to the work in four stages. First, he describes how enhanced modern communication has contributed to heightened interest in other religions, and a desire to share one's religious treasures with people of other faiths. He restates two critical presuppositions of the Science of Religion mentioned earlier: a recognition of the unity of the religious life of humanity, and the possibility of a unifying framework provided by the evolutionary hypothesis.[75]

---

[71] Sharpe, *Not to Destroy*, 329-330; Sharpe's assertion is slightly overstated; we will see that there is at least one significant feature of Farquhar's fulfilment view stated in *The Crown of India* which marks a development on his earlier position, see p.63.

[72] P.M. Hedges, *Preparation and Fulfilment: A History and Study of Fulfilment Theology in Modern British Thought in the Indian Context* (Bern, Peter Lang: 2001), 282-83.

[73] Thus insights from Farquhar's earlier writings illuminate certain crucial points at which our evaluation differs from Hedges' interpretation; see pp.70-71.

[74] One of four full-length and notable works which he published; the other three are of little relevance to our study: J.N. Farquhar, *A Primer of Hinduism* (Oxford, 1914), a text-book on Hinduism; J.N. Farquhar, *Modern Religious Movements in India* (New York: MacMillan Co., 1915, which earned him an Oxford D.Litt.; and his *magnum opus*, J.N. Farquhar, *An Outline of the Religious Literature of India* (London, Oxford University Press, 1920).

[75] Farquhar, *The Crown of Hinduism*, 12.

He clarifies that his fulfilment view has been forged in the context of an urgent need for "a clear statement of the practical relationship of Christianity to the other great religions".[76] The Church feels this need as it seeks to understand its mission to the people of other faiths and to respond to outside objections to its sense of missionary obligation. The growing opposition to Christian mission and conversion thus requires that these be justified in a clear statement of Christian belief regarding the relation of Christian faith to other religions.[77]

In introducing how the informed Christian views other religions, Farquhar asserts the "underlying unity in all religions": from the lowest to the highest there are "gleams of light" and "suggestions of truth", giving every religion "value" to its followers. Consequently, every religion has some legitimacy in enabling humanity to reach God. "We must believe that it is possible for every human being, no matter what his circumstances may be, to find his way to God, if he truly use all the light he has."[78]

The theological basis for this continuity rests primarily on the Christian acknowledgement of the universal Fatherhood of God, and the fact that Christ is the universal light, although various religions possess different degrees of light. Followers of the grossest forms of religion possess some degree of access to God, for he accepts religious people of all nations without prejudice.[79] The condition for reaching God is the same in every religion: "…utter sincerity, the turning of his whole soul toward the light, the frank acceptance of truth into his heart, straightforward obedience to the very highest he knows."[80] However, newer and fuller truth received through the light of additional revelation makes the old way invalid and ineffectual.[81]

The fact that non-Christian religions have led multitudes of men and women to God, and continue to mediate a true and fruitful religious experience, is evidence that each possesses some truth. He, however, distinguishes the observation that all religions "contain" some measure of truth from the absolute claim that all these religions are true.[82] The irreconcilable differences and fundamental contradictions between various religions are evidence of the superiority of some religions over others, with Christianity clearly occupying the highest place.[83]

In setting the stage for an explicit statement of his broader thesis, Farquhar declares: "The needs of the new time… can be met only by Christianity. Not in arrogance, not in partisanship, do we say this, but with wide open eyes and

[76] Farquhar, *ibid.*, 15.
[77] Farquhar, *ibid.*, 25.
[78] Farquhar, *ibid.*, 26.
[79] Farquhar, *ibid.*, 26-27.
[80] Farquhar, *ibid.*, 27.
[81] Farquhar, *ibid.*, 28.
[82] Farquhar, *ibid.*, 28-29.
[83] Farquhar, *ibid.*, 31.

with full consciousness of the stupendous character of the claim we make."[84] The specific objective of his book is thus to demonstrate the validity of his fulfilment approach in relation to Hinduism.

Farquhar's starting point is the common objection to the missionary enterprise as being an imperialist assault on the spirit of nationalism: "Christianity is objected to not as being untrue, but as being destructive and denationalizing."[85] He insists, however, that the real challenge to Hinduism is that posed by modernity itself and the educated modern Hindu, the most vociferous critic of his own tradition. The disintegration of the Hindu system highlights the urgent need for a new system more appropriate to the changing demands of modernity.[86]

The heart of Farquhar's response to the charge that Christianity is destructive and denationalizing is rooted in Jesus' call to discipleship which involves giving up the old way of life including one's old religion:

> The Christian idea, that the individual should renounce his old national religion, is not an excrescence, but belongs to the very heart of Christ's system.... That His call, 'Follow me', should lead to the surrender of the old religion on the part of the individual, and in the end to the death of the old religion, is in full accordance with the leading principles of His teaching.[87]

This principle of "life through death" thus applies not just to individuals but to each of the national religions as well, since it is the national character of each of these religions that limits their fullest and most universal expression.[88] The "precious truths" in Hinduism and the "aspirations and dreams" of Hindus can only come to fruition as the ancient Hindu system falls into the ground and dies: "Hinduism must die in order to live. It must die into Christianity."[89]

This principle of death leading to life leads us to the theological core of Farquhar's argument, encapsulating his understanding of progressive revelation: "God's method of revelation is not the presentation, once for all, of a complete system of truth expressed in a book from all eternity, but a gradual and historical process."[90] Jesus' commitment to progressive revelation thus caused him to both affirm the faith of Israel, and yet seek to transform it into a new religion.

Farquhar illustrates the idea of progressive revelation, first, in the emergence of Christian faith from Judaism. Although Judaism was not a complete revelation of God's will, it was his instrument to prepare Israel for the

---

84 Farquhar, *ibid.*, 33.
85 Farquhar, *ibid.*, 33.
86 Farquhar, *ibid.*, 36-43.
87 Farquhar, *ibid.*, 49.
88 Farquhar, *ibid.*, 50.
89 Farquhar, *ibid.*, 51.
90 Farquhar, *ibid.*, 51.

coming of Christ. Christ viewed the Old Testament as pointing forward to himself, summing up His relationship to it in the words: 'I am come not to destroy, but to fulfil' (Matt.5:17).[91] The Old Testament is thus related to the New Testament as the bud is to the flower: the Christian interprets the Old Testament "through Christ... in consonance with the Spirit of Christ".[92]

This understanding of Judaism as a pedagogy to Christ is, likewise, applied to the Graeco-Roman religions. Glimpses of spiritual truth and genuine light shone through them, finding their most complete realization in Christ. The early Greek apologists believed that Greek philosophy was a preparation for the coming of Christ, and that everything of value in Graeco-Roman civilization, philosophy, literature, and art has been preserved and has flowered in Christianity.[93]

Christ, likewise, does not come to destroy anything of value in the Hindu culture and religion. He is, in fact, already "breathing life" into the Hindu culture, affirming all that is of value in it.[94] Christ is the criterion by which all aspects of Hindu religion and culture must be tested, but he is "...not the Destroyer but the Restorer of the national heritage...." The chief purpose of *Crown* is thus to demonstrate that the "gleams of light" within Hindu faith and worship find their logical "consummation" in Christ, to show that Christianity is "...the Crown of Hinduism."[95]

The principle of life through death enables Christianity to function as a universal religious system while providing freedom for application to specific national and cultural contexts. This is, of course, what we describe today as 'Contextualization'. Farquhar's definition of Christianity is of crucial significance in this regard:

> When we say that Christianity is the Crown of Hinduism, we do not mean Christianity as it is lived in any nation, nor Christianity as it is defined and elaborated in detail in the creed, preaching, ritual, liturgy, and discipline of any single church, but Christianity as it springs living and creative from Christ Himself.[96]

This definition raises the question of whether it is possible to identify a pure form of Christianity that Farquhar envisages apart from a particular cultural expression. Farquhar's main concern, however, is not so much to locate a purified Christianity, as to dispel the impression that Christianity is inextricably bound up with Western forms of expression, and to demonstrate the cultural

---

[91] Farquhar, *ibid.*, 52-53.
[92] Farquhar, *ibid.*, 52.
[93] Farquhar, *ibid.*, 53.
[94] Farquhar, *ibid.*, 54.
[95] Farquhar, *ibid.*, 54-55.
[96] Farquhar, *ibid.*, 58.

translatability of the message of Christ as recorded in the New Testament.[97] He maintains that Christ did not leave behind detailed rules and regulations, but rather laid down spiritual principles for which His followers then had to work out the detailed contextual application.

Christians should distinguish the universal and context-specific aspects of the Gospel: "...in seeking to transfuse the life of Christ into the Hindu people, Christians must be constantly on their guard, laying aside all that is merely Western or temporary, and offering only the Bread of Life Himself."[98] The Christian mission cannot be viewed as an imperialistic enterprise, since the presentation and response to the person and principles of Christ have little to do with the issue of national identity.[99]

Farquhar concludes this opening chapter with a critical and revealing point regarding his fulfilment view. In distinct resonance with the "dual consummation" view of Westcott, Farquhar insists that our understanding of Christ remains incomplete until every constituent of the human community contributes its interpretation:

> He [Christ] is human; and the riches that are in Him can be set forth only by the united efforts of the whole human family. There are many elements in His life and teaching which are acknowledged by the Church, yet have never been fully worked out in thought or in life....[100]

India has a unique contribution to make in Farquhar's eschatological vision of the universal Lordship of Christ. Truth hitherto latent within the Christian gospel will rise to the surface and find fulfilment as it encounters the rich religious tradition of India:

> Then will the wonderful religious genius of India reveal its power anew in its interpretation of Christ. Aspects of His example and of His message which are latent in the West will in India find free and full expression.... Aspects of Christ which the hard practical West has failed to utilize will prove fruitful beyond our dreams in the Christian experience of the richly dowered Hindu race.[101]

This aspect of Farquhar's understanding of fulfilment introduced for the first time in *Crown* is often overlooked. Further analysis will consider its significance more closely.[102] In subsequent chapters, Farquhar reviews various

---

[97] He emphasises the fact that his understanding of Christianity is grounded almost exclusively on the New Testament account of Christ; Farquhar, *The Crown of Hinduism*, 64.
[98] Farquhar, *The Crown of Hinduism*, 61.
[99] Farquhar, *The Crown of Hinduism*, 61-63.
[100] Farquhar, *The Crown of Hinduism*, 63.
[101] Farquhar, *The Crown of Hinduism*, 64.
[102] Maw and Hedges both overlook this element, an omission which significantly affects their interpretation of Farquhar's thought, see p.70-71.

aspects of Hinduism in order to demonstrate the tenability of his thesis. The Indo-Aryan religion, the Hindu family, the doctrine of *karma*, the caste system, Vedanta, asceticism, image-worship, the Hindu sects, the concept of incarnation, and the Hindu religious organism are each examined in turn, and their relation to corresponding ideas in Christianity explored from the perspective of his fulfilment approach. All derive some validity from elements of truth that undergird them, but are variously either partial, weak, or inadequately developed in their present form, pointing to higher and fuller expression in Christ.

Farquhar regards the Indo-Aryan faith very favourably since it represented a movement towards ethical theism and produced a body of highly theistic religious literature.[103] He sees the concept of sacrifice as representing the heart of Rigvedic worship, and in a close parallel to Banerjea's fulfilment theory,[104] points out the striking proximity of the Rigvedic religion to Christian faith:

> ...this early [Rigvedic] faith stands much nearer to Christianity than it does to Hinduism. A transition from the religion of the *Rik* to Christianity would be much simpler and more natural than a transition to Hinduism.... Those who have leaned on animal sacrifice turn with deep religious joy to the perfect moral sacrifice of the death of Christ....[105]

Indicating other points of correspondence between Indo-Aryan and Christian faith, such as worship of a holy law-giver, the concept of life after death, the positive attitude to the world, and the healthy social and family freedom, he concludes in language that echoes that of Banerjea:

> ... if the beliefs we now hold are the true spiritual successors of the simple ideas found in the primitive religion, then we may well claim that to us has descended the heritage of the early faith. In this sense, then, the religion of Christ is the spiritual crown of the religion of the *Rgveda*.[106]

This resonance with Banerjea's ideas raises questions of possible influence. The internal evidence, however, seems to indicate Farquhar's strong independence as a scholar. Thus, as Hedges notes, despite the dominance of the sacrificial motif in fulfilment approaches from Banerjea to Slater, Farquhar acknowledges its significance without exploring it in detail.[107] There are only

---

[103] Farquhar, *The Crown of Hinduism*, 66-72.

[104] Farquhar, *The Crown of Hinduism*, 67, 73, 76; see pp.131-134.

[105] Farquhar, *The Crown of Hinduism*, 75-76.

[106] Farquhar, *The Crown of Hinduism*, 77.

[107] The Preface acknowledges the significant omission of a detailed treatment of sacrifice, but a summary interpretation of its significance is offered in the opening and concluding chapters, Farquhar, *The Crown of Hinduism*, 3, 449-450; cf. Hedges, 'A History and Study of Fulfilment Theology', 301-302, 349-350. Hedges, *Preparation and Fulfilment*, 285, 329-330.

two explicit indications of Farquhar's familiarity with Banerjea's work: a passing reference to Banerjea, Kellett and Sen in a later article,[108] and, mention of "Dr. Banerjea's" name in a copy of 'Missionary Study of Hinduism' annotated by Farquhar himself.[109]

This slight evidence makes Farquhar's acquaintance with Banerjea's work almost certain, and the lack of more explicit interaction with Banerjea's thought difficult to explain. His failure to use the arguments of Slater, Banerjea, and others on the familiar theme of sacrifice perhaps suggests the originality and integrity of his scholarship. The importance of the theme and the extent of research involved may have warranted, in his view, separate, more thorough treatment.

Farquhar's analysis of the Hindu family draws attention to both its oppressive aspects and the positive aspects, hidden below the surface.[110] Traditional Hindu family values have already been eroded as a result of the Christian influence introduced by the Hindu social reform movement.[111] The Christian teaching on family is continuous with the noblest ideals of the Hindu family: "...in it all the noblest ideals of the Hindu family reappear, but in completed form...."[112] The divine truths revealed in Christ thus enable Hinduism "...to raise its best customs to their height, to universalize its highest laws, and to correct its glaring abuses."[113]

Farquhar views the all-pervasive Hindu doctrine of *karma* fundamentally as a theory of morality.[114] The average Indian mind has been conditioned by the western conception of humanity's potential for progress and captivated by a dynamic vision of the future. The educated Indian's commitment to active philanthropy and nation-building is evidence of the practical negation of the doctrine of *karma* and transmigration.[115] The essential weakness of the Indian moral theory is that it has "...no divine personality at its centre, [it] is a mechanical, automatic system; and the supreme God of the religion is non-moral."[116] The implication is obvious: this weakness of the moral impulse within Hinduism is complemented and fulfilled by the Christian view of a personal moral law-giver.

According to Farquhar, the universal basic quest of the human spirit for human equality, complete social freedom, and social justice undermines the

---

[108] J.N. Farquhar, 'The Relation of Christianity to Hinduism', *International Review of Missions* 3 (1914): 431.

[109] The specific title referred to has been removed in the process of binding; Sharpe, *Not to Destroy*, 208, n. 8.

[110] Farquhar, *The Crown of Hinduism*, 78-103.

[111] Farquhar, *ibid.*, 113-118.

[112] Farquhar, *ibid.*, 132.

[113] Farquhar, *ibid.*, 133.

[114] Farquhar, *ibid.*, 145.

[115] Farquhar, *ibid.*, 148-152.

[116] Farquhar, *ibid.*, 152.

hold of the caste system in India.[117] The Christian doctrine of the Fatherhood of God provides the only adequate religious basis for "the social law" of the equality of all people, the idea of total social freedom, and the concept of social justice for all.[118] Christian society is the evolutionary goal of all living forms of society.[119] Thus, the essential undergirding impulses of caste – the dependence of duty and privilege on birth, the sacredness of the social order, and the preservation of solidarity and purity – blossom and find their fullest expression in Christ.[120]

Farquhar rejects the Vedantic conception of Brahman as the spiritual Self of the universe and Brahman's identity with the individual self due to its inherent implication of the identity of man with God.[121] This doctrine, however, has real value in its reflection of truths such as: "...man's dignity and spiritual grandeur; the immensity of his intellectual faculty; the boundlessness of his desires; his passion for immortality; his nearness, likeness, and kinship to God... and lastly, the spontaneous desire of the soul for union with God."[122]

Farquhar speaks positively about the ideals and practices of the Indian ascetic tradition:

> As long as the world lasts, men will look back with wonder upon the ascetics of India. Their quiet surrender of every earthly privilege and pleasure, and their strong endurance of many forms of suffering will be an inspiration to all generations of thinking Indians. For nearly three thousand years the ascetics of India have stood forth, a speaking testimony to the supremacy of the spiritual.[123]

A fatal weakness of the ancient Hindu ascetic ideal, according to Farquhar, is that it fosters a world-denying passivity while modern India requires inspiration for self-sacrificing service. Christ's call to discipleship brings the Hindu ascetic ideal to its true fulfilment by insisting on self-sacrificial love and service instead of self-torture leading to passivity and inaction. The Hindu convert is thus "the true modern sanyasi", and by making his followers servants of humanity, Christ "...completes and consummates the ideal of the Hindu monk."[124]

In Farquhar's view, those who worship images regard each idol as "a living personal god."[125] Image worship is "one of the chief hindrances to the progress of India" and "the chief source of the limitless mass of superstitions..."

---

[117] Farquhar, *ibid.*, 177.
[118] Farquhar, *ibid.*, 197-202.
[119] Farquhar, *ibid.*, 202.
[120] Farquhar, *ibid.*, 203-210.
[121] Farquhar, *ibid.*, 226.
[122] Farquhar, *ibid.*, 226.
[123] Farquhar, *ibid.*, 273.
[124] Farquhar, *ibid.*, 295-296.
[125] Farquhar, *ibid.*, 317.

enslaving Hindus. On the other hand, it is "...completely justified in the case of men who really believe in them", and ministers to some strong and valuable religious instincts, such as the desire to have an intimate relationship with a personal God.[126] These religious instincts find their fullest satisfaction in Christ, who reveals and enables pure spiritual worship of God the Father.[127]

The threads of Farquhar's discussion come together in the penultimate chapter, in the central theme of Christian faith, the incarnation. The God of the Bible and the Brahman of Hinduism both share a "transcendent, spiritual and absolute" quality. But in contrast to Brahman, the God of Christian faith is also the source and ground of morality, supremely personal, the creator, vitally related to humanity and the universe.[128] A problem confounding Hindu philosophers and theologians for many centuries, which "...deprived God of a living, active character... [and] set an impassable barrier between the ardent worshipper and Brahman..." finds resolution and fulfilment in the God revealed as the Father of Jesus Christ.[129]

Likewise, although the Vedanta concurs with the Christian view of the divine aspect of human nature, it is at odds with the Christian understanding of human personhood, man's self-consciousness, his moral freedom, and his capacity for devotional intimacy with God.[130] The Christian doctrine of man is thus "...the final truth of which the strict Vedanta and Hindu theism offer each a partial adumbration."[131]

Farquhar regards the Hindu incarnation stories as historically baseless, but sees value in their witness to the Hindu aspiration for God to manifest himself in human form.[132] Christ "crowns" the Hindu idea of the incarnation in four ways: (1) in Christ, God actually becomes man and enters fully into human experience;[133] (2) Christ reflects the perfect divine character and the *sadhu* ideal of self-sacrificial service;[134] (3) Christ's teaching ministry fulfils the Hindu and Buddhist ideal of the incarnate God as teacher;[135] and (4) the idea of vicarious suffering cherished by some Hindu saints is fulfilled in Christ's redemptive death.[136]

In considering the Hindu religious organism, consisting of the social and family organisation, system of morality, various cultic rites and cultural practices, Farquhar sees gleams of spiritual light reflected through the most

---

[126] Farquhar, *ibid.*, 341.
[127] Farquhar, *ibid.*, 343-350.
[128] Farquhar, *ibid.*, 408-421.
[129] Farquhar, *ibid.*, 419.
[130] Farquhar, *ibid.*, 420.
[131] Farquhar, *ibid.*, 421.
[132] Farquhar, *ibid.*, 423-425.
[133] Farquhar, *ibid.*, 433.
[134] Farquhar, *ibid.*, 433-438.
[135] Farquhar, *ibid.*, 438-441.
[136] Farquhar, *ibid.*, 444.

crude of Hindu superstitions, all of which may reappear in Christ in healthy spiritual practices.[137] Farquhar's concluding proposal is thus bold and radical: the Hindu religious organism is fatally flawed; hence, the patriotic Hindu must be willing to throw off its oppressive traditions and degrading superstitions, for the future health and progress of India. His final word is a summary statement of his principal thesis:

> We have already seen how Christ provides the fulfilment of each of the highest aspirations and aims of Hinduism. ...every line of light which is visible in the grossest parts of the religion reappears in Him set in healthy institutions and spiritual worship.... In Him is focused every ray of light that shines in Hinduism. He is the Crown of the faith of India.[138]

A Critical Analysis of Farquhar's Fulfilment Approach

Farquhar's Conception of Fulfilment

Before we respond to criticisms of Farquhar's approach, we need to clarify his use of the term fulfilment and understand the distinctiveness of his approach as a leading illustration of nineteenth century evolutionary fulfilment. Farquhar does not offer a clear definition of fulfilment in any of his writings, but uses the term in at least three complementary senses.

First, fulfilment denotes the completion of incomplete truth or partial light in other religions. This is derived from the empirical observation of elements of beauty, goodness, and truth in other religions arranged on an evolutionary scale.[139] These fragments of truth and light are fulfilled as they are completed, their meaning clarified, and as they reappear in a higher form in Christianity.[140] Second, fulfilment also signifies the satisfaction of basic human religious needs and instincts in Christ. Farquhar sought to discern the religious yearnings and impulses behind every expression of Hindu belief and practice.[141] Third, fulfilment involves replacement of imperfect truths by complete truths, of the lower religion by the higher, of partial revelation by the full light of the incarnation. Fulfilment is not destruction of the old, but its transfiguration and replacement by the new. This replacement also involves mutuality of fulfilment with the new being enriched and complemented by elements of the old.

Christ thus fulfils Hinduism by (1) clarifying, correcting, supplementing and transforming elements of truth it legitimately affirms; (2) satisfying every valid religious aspiration and instinct expressed in it; and (3) inviting the Hindu to

---

[137] Farquhar, *ibid.*, 446-452.

[138] Farquhar, *ibid.*, 457-458.

[139] Farquhar, 'The Relation of Christianity to Hinduism', 420.

[140] Farquhar, 'Christ and the Religions of the World', 197.

[141] Farquhar, *ibid.*, 195.

allow a reborn, Christ-centred Hinduism to replace ancestral faith. Farquhar uses fulfilment in all these senses, both concurrently and separately, and failure to note these distinctions often led to a misunderstanding of his views.[142]

There is an implicit commitment to the New Testament promise-fulfilment model in Farquhar's fulfilment approach. His view is, however, primarily an illustration of the nineteenth century evolutionary fulfilment model. The features which place Farquhar's approach within this historically unique category of fulfilment include its dependence on the scientific study of religion, on the basis of which it recognizes the presence of fragments of truth in all religions, and its employment of the evolutionary hypothesis for affirming continuity between Christianity and other religions.

Although Farquhar's approach falls broadly within this category, it must be distinguished from other forms of evolutionary fulfilment. In contrast to Muller, who sees Christ as representing a higher but penultimate stage of religious evolution, Farquhar follows Monier-Williams and Slater, in affirming the absolute supremacy of Christ. Whereas Muller regards the ultimate fulfilment of religious evolution as going beyond Christianity and including elements of truth from other religions in a syncretistic consummation, Farquhar like Westcott, insists on the finality of the incarnation. On the other hand, Farquhar's insistence on the absolute supremacy of Christ does not cause him to preclude the possibility of non-Christian elements enriching, even unveiling aspects of truth previously latent within the gospel. At this point, Farquhar's approach is more in line with the dual consummation theory of Westcott than the more closed views of Monier-Williams and Slater.

This observation is critical in view of Maw's summary conclusion regarding Westcott and Slater's fulfilment views.[143] According to Maw, a significant point of contrast was that whereas the Western theological formulation of Christianity represented an absolute given for Slater, Westcott's ideal of dual consummation and mutual enrichment saw the Church as being incomplete until every race and culture had contributed their distinctive interpretations of the Christ-event. Maw summarily extends the contrast between Westcott and Slater to Westcott and Farquhar, although as we have seen, Farquhar's view is closer to Westcott than Slater at this point.[144]

This point is also overlooked in Hedges' study, leading him to conclude that Farquhar's framework was not favourable to the development of an indigenous

---

[142] For instance, Hogg focussed primarily on the subjective sense of fulfilment as the satisfaction of a need, and the replacement idea in Farquhar's fulfilment view escaped some of his conservative critics.

[143] M. Maw *Visions of India: Fulfilment Theology, the Aryan Race Theory, and the Work of British Protestant Missionaries in Victorian India* (Frankfurt: Peter Lang, 1990), 342-348.

[144] Although Maw does refer to *The Crown of Hinduism,* his assessment is based almost exclusively on the Edinburgh Missionary Conference Commission IV papers; Maw, *Visions of India*, 344-347.

Indian Christian theology: "Farquhar was vehemently opposed to any influence of Indian thought on Christianity," and "Farquhar has no place for any inkling of Hindu thought at all to enter the arena of Christian teachings."[145] He, consequently, sees little positive content in Farquhar's life through death principle, or in his metaphor of Christianity as "crowning" Hinduism.[146]

Hedges' criticism focuses on Farquhar's resistance to Hindu "doctrine", which is misleading because, to Farquhar, the term doctrine would clearly have implied a core affirmation of Christian faith, which most missionary fulfilment thinkers would have regarded as compromise.[147] However, Farquhar's vision of the regeneration of Hinduism envisaged the preservation of its "spiritual treasures" – its art, literature, philosophy, and other aspects of its culture – which he tries to distinguish from allegiance to the person and principles of Christ.[148] Beyond that, echoing Westcott's dual fulfilment conception, he also believed that the "wonderful religious genius of India" would illuminate aspects of Christ's person and message hitherto undiscovered.[149]

Hedges also misinterprets Farquhar's view of the revelatory value of non-Christian religious experience. In highlighting the need for a *Logos* theology to undergird a viable fulfilment approach, he offers the following summary assessment of Farquhar's approach: "...he [Farquhar] sees the non-Christian religions as being human, and does not develop a Logos theology...."[150] Earlier he asserts that Farquhar views non-Christian religions as purely human creations, with no notion of a divine element underlying them, no direct knowledge of or communion with God, and no salvific value.[151]

Farquhar does speak of the religious impulse within non-Christian religions as springing from "natural religious instincts" or "human religious consciousness".[152] However, these expressions should not be interpreted in terms of natural as opposed to supernatural or human as opposed to divine; the emphasis rather is on natural and human as meaning "built-in, intuitive and common to humanity" – taken in an ontological rather than epistemological sense. The textual evidence, moreover, plainly contradicts Hedges' conclusions.

Farquhar had maintained that there was divine revelation in other religions since the earliest years of his theological development. He argues subsequently

---

145 Hedges, *Preparation and Fulfilment*, 299, 338.

146 Hedges, *ibid.*, 334-340.

147 Cracknell's evaluation of responses to the Commission IV questionnaire highlights the missionary fulfilment thinkers' firm commitment to the decisiveness of Christ; Cracknell, *Justice, Courtesy and Love*, 219f.

148 Farquhar, 'The Greatness of Hinduism', 57-58; Farguhar, *The Crown of Hinduism*, 54.

149 Farguhar, *The Crown of Hinduism*, 64.

150 Hedges, *Preparation and Fulfilment*, 341-342.

151 Hedges, *ibid.*, 290, 332-333.

152 Farquhar, 'Christ and the Religions of the World', 196-197.

for the preservation of the literary tradition of India, claiming that it contains the record of God's word to humanity. Farquhar's fulfilment approach has its origins empirically in the recognition of the presence of the light of revelation in non-Christian religious systems. He acknowledges his dependence on the early church fathers for this insight. In later years we observe intimations of a *Logos* theology and belief in the universality of divine revelation as he seeks to explain the presence of light in other religions. He sees every element of religion as deriving from "some genuine instinct, deep seated in the mystery of our common religious nature" to which Christ has a direct mystical relationship.[153] In *Crown,* he reiterates that Christ is the universal light who enlightens every human being.[154]

He reasserts Christ's mystical relation to every member of the human family in a later response to criticisms of his fulfilment view: he is "the Light of all the nations... [who] sends His rays into every human spirit...." This is part of the rationale for exploring the relationship between religions: "...since He [Christ] is so sensitive to all that man experiences, we are driven to ask how the light in Hinduism is related to the infinitely brighter light which streamed from Him in the incarnation."[155]

No further explanation of this theme is offered possibly due to Farquhar's own inadequate theological apparatus. The closest Farquhar comes to suggesting a solution is his concluding assertion in *Crown*: "...every line of light which is visible in the grossest parts of the religion reappears in Him.... In Him [Christ] is focused every ray of light that shines in Hinduism."[156] Thus, although Farquhar does not have a clearly formulated *Logos* Christology, elements of the *Logos* fulfilment model are implicit and integral to his thought. The evidence thus contradicts Hedges' claim that Farquhar saw no divine element or knowledge of God in non-Christian religions. As a further counterpoint to Hedges' criticism, Farquhar also ascribed provisional salvific value to Hinduism.[157]

Farquhar's view met with a mixed response in India.[158] The most trenchant theological criticism came from the philosopher-theologian, A.G. Hogg.[159] Hogg was a missionary contemporary of Farquhar and an original thinker who made an important contribution to missionary theology in the first half of the

---

[153] Farquhar, 'Christ and the Religions of the World', 196-197.
[154] Farguhar, *The Crown of Hinduism*, 27.
[155] Farquhar, 'The Relation of Christianity to Hinduism', 422.
[156] Farguhar, *The Crown of Hinduism*, 458.
[157] See p.84-5.
[158] The criticism was especially strong from conservative missionary quarters, which came in two phases; see Sharpe, *Not to Destroy*, 309-323; 345-357; also Hedges' discussion; Hedges, *Preparation and Fulfilment*, 361-377. We consider the key issues later in this section.
[159] Sharpe, *Faith Meets Faith*, 34, 37-44; Hedges' evaluation of Hogg's criticisms; Hedges, *Preparation and Fulfilment*, 347-360.

twentieth century.[160] Hogg made his theological opposition to the fulfilment approach evident in his submission to Commission IV of the Edinburgh World Missionary Conference in 1910. His criticisms of Farquhar's fulfilment view were, however, expressed more pointedly in a review of Farquhar's *Crown.*[161]

Of the many objections directed against Farquhar's fulfilment view, five warrant serious consideration. We will take up each of these, in turn, at relevant stages of our theological assessment. We begin by evaluating the pedagogical value of Hinduism in Farquhar's approach; we then examine his scheme for affirming continuity between Christianity and Hinduism; and, third, assess the manner in which the decisiveness of Christ is affirmed within his view.

The Pedagogical Value of Hinduism

Farquhar's apologetic approach attempted to remove the misconception that the Christian gospel was anti-national and destructive of the Indian religious and cultural heritage. His method was designed to demonstrate that far from being foreign to the Indian culture, Christ represented the true fulfilment of the instincts underlying various elements of Hindu belief and practice.

Two important objections were raised against Farquhar's thesis in this regard. First, Hogg criticised Farquhar's theory as lacking in content and empirically unsustainable in the light of actual Hindu religious experience. Closely linked to this was the perception, even among those who agreed with the broad thrust of his thesis, that his arguments stretched the limits of the evidence.

OBJECTION 1: CHRIST OFFERS THE SOLUTION TO A NEED WHICH HINDUISM DOES NOT FEEL.

Hogg's review of Farquhar's work commends its scholarly quality while lamenting its lack of theological sophistication. His main criticism is that the need which Farquhar's approach shows Christ as satisfying within Hinduism is an artificial need created by and resulting from its encounter with Christianity: "What Christ directly fulfils is not Hinduism but the need of which India has begun to be conscious… the need, by making her feel conscious of which, He

---

[160] For a semi-biographical outline of the development of Hogg's thought, see E.J. Sharpe, *The Theology of Hogg* (Bangalore/Madras, 1971); cf. Sharpe, *Not to Destroy*, 273-274, 284-291, 350-352. Jathanna, *The Decisiveness of the Christ-event and the Universality of Christianity in a World of Religious Plurality: With Special Reference to Hendrik Kraemer and Alfred George Hogg as well as to William Ernest Hocking and Pandipeddi Chenchiah* (Berne: Peter Lang, 1981), 145-244 offers a thorough analysis of Hogg's distinctive view of the relation of Christianity to other religions.

[161] Hogg reviewed Farquhar's book twice: A.G. Hogg, 'The Crown of Hinduism and other Volumes', *Madras Christian College Magazine* 13 (1914), 423ff; A.G. Hogg, 'The Crown of Hinduism and other Volumes', *International Review of Mission* 3:9 (1914), 171-173. I refer here to the second.

has made her no longer quite Hindu."[162] He further maintains that Hinduism represents not just a quest for fulfilment, but "...a finding as well as a seeking".[163]

In his submission to Commission IV of the Edinburgh World Conference, Hogg had earlier raised essentially the same question. He argued that although Christian beliefs are able to arouse a yearning in some Hindus which then only Christ is able to satisfy, the undisturbed Hindu consciousness does not point to fulfilment in Christ or Christianity: "Christianity is the solution of a religious problem which the typical Hindu does not feel but which, under favourable conditions, he can be made to feel."[164] He adds that Farquhar's view is contradicted by the evident lack of a hunger for Christ in India and makes Christian proclamation vulnerable to the charge of condescension.[165]

Hogg's criticism goes to the root of the fulfilment approach.[166] It must be examined, first, in the context of the fundamental divergence in his approach from that of Farquhar on the question of Christian-Hindu relations. Second, the charge that Christianity offers the solution to a need that the typical Hindu does not really feel must be tested ultimately on empirical grounds. Evaluation of the empirical evidence is an important issue and will be treated in some detail in chapter five. Our present concern is with a theological assessment of Hogg's objection.

A critical component of Hogg's view was his distinction between faith and faiths, and between faith in God and beliefs about God. Faith is the existential aspect of religion, an immediate living trust in God, the common inner core of religious life, and is the same in all religions.[167] Beliefs are the intellectual expressions used to articulate and communicate the implications and consequences of faith, distinctive to each religion.[168] Faiths describe various systems of life and thought, which include beliefs.[169]

---

[162] A.G. Hogg, 'The Crown of Hinduism, and Other Volumes', *International Review of Mission* 3, 9 (1914): 172-173.

[163] A.G. Hogg, 'The Christian Attitude to Hinduism', in *The Theology of A.G. Hogg*, ed. E.J. Sharpe (Bangalore/Madras: CISRS/CLS, 1971), 106.

[164] A.G. Hogg, 'Hinduism', in *The Theology of A.G. Hogg*, ed. E.J. Sharpe (Bangalore/Madras: CISRS/CLS, 1971), 107.

[165] Hogg, 'The Crown of Hinduism, and Other Volumes', 173.

[166] Hedges' different approach sees Hogg's principal criticism as directed towards the lack of consciousness of sin within Hinduism; Hedges, 'A History and Study of Fulfilment Theology', 367-381.

[167] A.G. Hogg, *Karma and Redemption: An Essay Toward the Interpretation of Hinduism and the Restatement of Christianity* (1909; repr., Madras: CLS, 1970), xix; O.V. Jathanna, *The Decisiveness of the Christ-event*, 209 clarifies that this affirms continuity between rather than a strict identity of the "faith" at the core of all religions.

[168] E.J. Sharpe, 'Introduction' in *Karma and Redemption*, A.G. Hogg (Madras: CLS, (1909), 1970), xiv.

[169] A.G. Hogg, 'The Christian Attitude to Non-Christian Faith', in *The Theology of A.G. Hogg*, E.J. Sharpe (Bangalore/Madras: CISRS/CLS, 1971), 206.

Hogg was convinced that in the encounter between Christian and non-Christian faiths, "points of contact in the real, deep sense of the word, can only be found by antithesis".[170] The Christian approach to Hinduism must focus on neither points of continuity nor diverse conflicting beliefs, but instead locate as its point of departure one fundamental contrast of principle that would illuminate all other differences.[171] The distinction between faith and faiths/beliefs, in Hogg's scheme, was thus designed to demonstrate the fundamental antithesis between Christian and non-Christian faiths, and affirm the essential continuity between Christian and non-Christian faith.[172] He insists, however, that Christian allegiance to the absolute Lordship of Christ marks the qualitative uniqueness of Christian faith.[173]

A critical question that arises in evaluating Hogg's objection is whether or not he regards Hinduism as having any value as a pedagogy to Christ, and if so, how does he understand its function?

In answering the first part of this question, we must begin by drawing attention to the continuity that Hogg seems to affirm on the one hand, between the faith, which is at the core of all religions, including Hinduism and Christianity,[174] and on the other hand, between revelation in Christianity and non-Christian religions. Jathanna's study clearly shows that in Hogg's theological framework every religion is founded on revelation.[175] However, Hogg regards the revelation in Christ as unique and decisive, and if God is the source of all revelation, his theological framework should allow for continuity between revelation in Christ and non-Christian religions.[176]

He thus does not confine God's revelatory and saving activity to the Incarnation, and accepts the role of non-Christian religions in preparing the way for God's perfect revelation of himself in Christ.[177] The God who is the

---

[170] Hogg, 'Non-Christian Faith', in *The Theology of A.G. Hogg*, ed. E.J. Sharpe (Bangalore/Madras: CISRS/CLS, 1971), 210-211.

[171] Hogg's key illustration of this is the idea of *karma* as contrasted with the Christian idea of redemption; Hogg, *Karma and Redemption*.

[172] Jathanna, *The Decisiveness of the Christ-event*, 209, 271-273; Jathanna, however, demonstrates the inadequacy of this distinction between "faiths" and "faith", based on Hogg's own inconsistent use of these terms, as well as logical and theological grounds.

[173] A.G. Hogg, *The Christian Message to the Hindu* (London: SCM Press, 1947), 28.

[174] Jathanna, *The Decisiveness of the Christ-event*, 197, 209.

[175] Jathanna, *ibid.*, 170, 195, 202, 268; Hogg states this most explicitly in opposition to Kraemer's discontinuity thesis at the Tambaram Conference in 1938: "...is not every religion founded on what is, in some sense, revelation on a.. Divine effort of self disclosure?", 'Non-Christian Faith', in Sharpe, *The Theology of A.G. Hogg*, 209.

[176] Hogg tries to differentiate between revelation in Christian faith and other religions by drawing a tenuous distinction between the "occurrence" and "content" of revelation. But, as Jathanna, in *The Decisiveness of the Christ-event*, 202, 264, points out, this distinction, designed to affirm the *sui generis* quality of the "content" of revelation in Christ is artificial and forced.

[177] Jathanna, *ibid.*, 242-243.

source of revelation in non-Christian religions is the same God who offers a decisive self-disclosure of himself in Christ. Conflict or contradiction between the two modes of revelation is thus inconceivable. We are thus justified in concluding that a non-Christian who rejects God's revelation in Christ does so in contradiction to the real intent of the revelation within his religion, whereas a positive response to God's self-disclosure in Christ would be in actual continuity with the pre-Christian revelation received.[178]

For a clearer understanding of how this pedagogy works as a preparation for Christ in Hogg's framework, we need to examine his analysis of the Christian encounter with the Hindu religious consciousness. According to Hogg, prior to Christian influence, the Hindu lives in a state of equilibrium, satisfied by the experience of the transcendent provided within his ancestral tradition. The presentation of Christ disturbs this equilibrium, creating a spiritual dissatisfaction and consciousness of new problems. To these elements thus thrown into discord and imbalance "...only beliefs of a Christian type can restore equilibrium." Hogg concedes that whilst it may be permissible to characterize this as fulfilment, it "...obscures the fact that it fulfils by, at least partially, destroying."[179]

Farquhar does not deny Hogg's assertion that the presentation of Christ disturbs the Hindu consciousness and creates a sense of need for Christ. This is, in fact, a critical component of his own case in *Crown*, closely linked to his argument for the replacement of Hinduism with a system more appropriate to the demands of modernity. He reasserts this in his later response, reacting explicitly to one of Hogg's arguments cited earlier:

> He [Christ] brings the final truth of God... only in the revealing light of His person, life and atoning death do men begin to see that their old religion is very imperfect, and that it can find completion only in Him. Therefore, we need not conclude that, if Christ fulfils Hinduism, 'then India ought to have been always hungry for Christ.' Do the life and death of Christ suggest that the Jews were hungry for Him when He came?[180]

Farquhar then employs the metaphor of "a great search-light flung across Hinduism" which lights up all its weaknesses and corruptions and uncovers its best parts. The positive aspects are thrust into the foreground, and the negative elements "destroyed or driven underground".[181] Although the metaphor is different, Farquhar's fulfilment approach does seem to take Hogg's main point into account. The difference is that Hogg sees Hinduism as a coherent system

---

[178] Jathanna, *ibid.*, 269-270.

[179] Hogg, 'Hinduism', in *The Theology of A.G. Hogg*, ed. E.J. Sharpe (Bangalore/Madras: CISRS/CLS, 1971), 107.

[180] Farquhar, 'The Relation of Christianity to Hinduism', 427.

[181] Farquhar, *ibid.*, 427.

of beliefs with an inner equilibrium of its own, whereas Farquhar views Hinduism as consisting of a body of doctrines or truths.

There is, however, an important point of concurrence. Both agree that Christ does not act upon a religious vacuum when he encounters the Hindu religious consciousness. Rather, his engagement of the religious resources of Hinduism produces some amount of tension, conflict and transformation. Whereas Hogg regards "the original disturbance of equilibrium" as being of critical significance, Farquhar regards the affirmation of continuity or, in Hogg's terms – the restoration of equilibrium by Christ – as the decisive point in the Christian-Hindu encounter.

The differences between the approaches of Hogg and Farquhar thus appear to be less substantial than formal, and the force of Hogg's criticism diminishes significantly.[182] His objection focuses largely on the appropriateness of the term fulfilment to describe the relation of Christianity to Hinduism. However, he reluctantly concedes the use of the term if it incorporates the idea of the destruction of some old elements. This is an integral component of Farquhar's fulfilment view. Farquhar's choice of the term is justified in the light of his overriding apologetic concern: to affirm Christian continuity rather than dissonance with the Indian tradition.

OBJECTION 2: THE EVIDENCE IS FORCED TO FIT THE THEORY.

A charge frequently levelled against Farquhar's view was that the evidence is forced or "tortured to fit the theory".[183] One of the earliest reviewers of *Crown* claims that rather than allowing the findings of research to shape his hypothesis, Farquhar bases his argument on generalizations through which he filters the empirical data.[184] Tomlinson's otherwise favourable review suggests that Farquhar's insistence that Christ "crowns" every Hindu aspiration could make Hindus feel that Christ is being imposed upon them. He recommends that "a work of destruction" must precede the presentation of Christ as "fulfiller" of India's religious longings.[185]

Hogg concedes that Christ does fulfil "what is good" in Hinduism, but concerning the details of Farquhar's view insists that: "Christ… leaves out so much of what was in Hinduism, and He fulfils so much of what was never in Hinduism, that Mr. Farquhar's tracing out of the aspect of fulfilment

---

[182] Hedges' approach to Hogg's criticism of Farquhar focuses on the lack of consciousness of sin within Hinduism. His conclusion, however, is similar: "I find it difficult to distinguish where the difference, in practical terms, lies between Hogg's contention that Jesus provides the answer to the need felt by the Hindu for a divine saviour to release him from sin. … Thus even this critic of fulfilment theology uses similar patterns of thought and language to the fulfilment theologians themselves; Hedges, *Preparation and Fulfilment*, 347ff; 359-360.

[183] A. Race, *Christians and Religious Pluralism* (New York: Orbis, 1982), 58.

[184] V.A. Sukhtankar, 'The Crown of Hinduism', *The Indian Interpreter* 8, 4 (1914): 172.

[185] W.E. Tomlinson, 'The Crown of Hinduism' *Harvest Field* 34, 1 (1914): 7-8, 11.

sometimes seems far-fetched."[186] Gulliford affirms the fulfilment approach in principle, but objects to Farquhar glossing over aspects of Hindu teaching and practice that are incompatible with Christian faith:

> God has not left Himself without witness among Hindus; everywhere there are broken and scattered fragments of pure desire and earnest seeking. Of these Christ is the fulfiller... but in what we regard as the essentials of Hinduism – pure pantheism, *karma* and transmigration, caste, and idolatry – Jesus Christ has neither part nor lot.[187]

Thus, many of Farquhar's conservative opponents were willing to acknowledge that Christianity fulfilled the positive aspects of Hinduism, but could not see how Christ could fulfil elements that seemed to contradict corresponding Christian affirmations.

Two factors need to be considered in evaluating this criticism. The first is the differing conceptions of fulfilment of Farquhar and his interlocutors. Most of those who criticized Farquhar's view at this point interpreted fulfilment as excluding antithesis.[188] Farquhar, however, understood fulfilment to include antithesis and the idea of replacement. Although Farquhar did not ignore antithetical elements, his project was ambitious in its comprehensive attempt to explore multiple points of contact with Hinduism. His detractors' charge that his view is at times forced may thus be justified.

Second, Farquhar is able to affirm the reality of access to God by people of all faiths based on his conviction regarding the universal Fatherhood of God.[189] Convinced that there was a religious consciousness common to all human life underlying every religious belief, rite, and institution, he sees gleams of spiritual light reflected through gross Hindu superstitions and debasing practices. God accepts a person not so much on the basis of accuracy of beliefs or sophistication of practices as on his sincere response to the highest and fullest truth he has received. The instincts underlying diverse forms of religious expression are more important than the forms themselves. Hence, Farquhar's approach sought to uncover the religious instincts and ethical sentiments underlying various aspects of Hindu faith and practice, showing how they can be fulfilled in Christ.

---

[186] Hogg, 'The Crown of Hinduism', 173.

[187] H. Gulliford, 'Christ the Fulfiller of Hinduism', *Harvest Field* 34 (1914): 368-369.

[188] See Blanchard's characterization: "...the truth of the matter lies in a tension between 'fulfilment' and 'antithesis'. ... In this sense Christianity becomes a replacement for Hinduism, not exactly a fulfilment..." M. Blanchard, 'Christianity as Fulfilment and Antithesis', *The Indian Journal of Theology* 17 (1968): 13-14.

[189] *Inquirer* 4, 8 (April 1903): 3.

Farquhar's position did not imply a simple sanction or justification of the grosser aspects of Hindu tradition.[190] For instance, he denounces the evils of image worship, but in keeping with his method, attempts to identify the religious instinct underlying the practice: "… the truth that at any moment, at any place, we may have access to the Father's heart".[191] By revealing the true nature of the Father, Christ leads this legitimate religious sentiment to its fulfilment in the true worship of the Father.[192]

The impulse of preservation in Farquhar's view is thus balanced by an impulse for correction and completion. However, it is not Hinduism as a system that must be preserved. His view of the Hindu tradition as a pedagogy to Christ implies that the baser elements of Hinduism must give way to the fuller revelation of God in Christ.

Evolutionary Continuity and Progressive Revelation

Farquhar's quest for a unifying theory of religion was motivated by the following conviction: "The Universe is one, and humanity is one; religious truth must therefore be one all over the world, and must be held to be discoverable by the human conscience and mind."[193] From an early stage of his theological development, he was increasingly drawn to the evolutionary theory. The relation between Christianity and Hinduism is first described explicitly in evolutionary terms in the 'Crown of Hinduism',[194] and thereafter continued to condition his fulfilment approach. This dependence on evolutionary philosophy became another major point of contention since it seemed to undermine the Christian doctrine of revelation.

OBJECTION 3: OPPOSITION TO THE USE OF EVOLUTIONARY THEORY.

Farquhar's description of Christianity as the "evolutionary crown" of Hinduism seemed to suggest that Hinduism would automatically evolve into Christianity thus reducing religion to a purely natural process.[195] Sharpe highlights the significance of this conservative objection as advanced by Mackichan:

> The necessity of a sympathetic approach to Hinduism; a conviction of the unconditional superiority... of Christianity over Hinduism; the awareness that replacement of Hinduism by Christianity was the goal of missionary work: on all these points Mackichan and Farquhar shared substantially the same position. But

[190] See Gulliford, 'Christ the Fulfiller of Hinduism', 367-368; Tomlinson, 'The Crown of Hinduism', 10-11 in contrast, regards those who see Farquhar as simply defending idolatry, as misinterpreting his viewpoint.
[191] Farquhar, *The Crown of Hinduism*, 341-342.
[192] Farquhar, *The Crown of Hinduism*, 350.
[193] *Inquirer* 4:2 (October 1902): 8.
[194] Farquhar, 'The Crown of Hinduism', 67.
[195] Sharpe, *Not to Destroy*, 316-317.

> the use of the term "evolution" was a different matter. The evolutionary position was anathema to the conservative Evangelical mind *a priori*: hence Mackichan's attack.[196]

To Farquhar's conservative detractors, the evolutionary continuum seemed to ignore a deep theological gulf between the Christian gospel and Hinduism. Some regarded Farquhar's use of the evolutionary framework to posit a qualitative connection between Christian faith and even the gross aspects of non-Christian religion as compromise bordering on blasphemy. Even his sympathisers found it difficult to support his uncritical appreciation of Hindu religious phenomena and practice. They insisted that at some points the only appropriate attitude to other religions was one of confrontation.[197]

Two points of clarification are in order in Farquhar's defence. First, Farquhar adopted the evolutionary framework desiring to base his apologetic on the neutral common ground of the science of religion. Second, he does not apply the evolutionary theory uncritically. He does not accept the idea implicit in the evolutionary hypothesis that the lower religions automatically evolve into Christianity. There is no question of Hinduism developing into Christianity of its own accord. His employment of the "life through death" metaphor in *Crown* clarifies that in his view Hinduism does not automatically develop into Christianity, but must be consciously replaced by it.

Sharpe suggests that in this respect the idea of evolution may not have been essential to Farquhar's fulfilment framework.[198] At least two factors lend credence to this suggestion. First, Farquhar's view is inconsistent with the evolutionary hypothesis at one vital point. According to the evolutionary framework, more recent forms of Hinduism should occupy a higher place on the evolutionary continuum, and thus be closer to Christian faith than the older Vedic Hinduism. Farquhar, like Banerjea before him, regarded Vedic Hinduism as closer to Christianity than the later corrupted forms of Hinduism.[199] Second, although the concept of evolution was fairly important in his earlier writings, in *Crown*, it is referred to in the opening paragraphs, and thereafter hardly finds mention.

Thus, although the motivation to adopt the evolutionary framework formally was to base his approach on the neutral common ground of a scientific theory, the concept of progressive revelation as observed in the New Testament promise-fulfilment model provided the more fundamental orientation. Nevertheless, his formal appropriation of the evolutionary theory resulted in

---

[196] Sharpe, *ibid.*, 348.
[197] Sharpe, *ibid.*, 317-320.
[198] Sharpe, *Faith Meets Faith*, 29.
[199] Farquhar, *The Crown of Hinduism*, 75-77; cf. 142.

the credibility of his view being weakened with the decline in influence of the evolutionary theory.[200]

Farquhar's understanding of progressive revelation as a theological device for affirming continuity was more critical to his fulfilment approach than the evolutionary theory, despite the attention his critics gave to the latter. He was also convinced that Jesus' attitude to Judaism as recorded in the New Testament offered the most appropriate illustration of how progressive revelation should be applied in the fulfilment approach.

Two important questions arise in relation to his understanding of progressive revelation: (1) What kind of differentiation does he draw between divine revelation through Old Testament prophetic inspiration, in other religions, and in Christ? (2) What qualitative distinction does his characterization of Christ as the "evolutionary crown" of Hinduism enable him to affirm between Christ and Hinduism, and the other religions located along the evolutionary continuum? We will address the first question here and consider the second under the following point in our analysis.

In an early exposition of Hebrews 1:1-2 in *The Inquirer*, Farquhar explains his view of the Christian attitude to the Jewish scriptures, at the same time clarifying his understanding of how the revelation in Christ is related to the non-Christian scriptures. The Old Testament writings are regarded as "fragmentary and occasional" as compared to "the full and final revelation" made through Christ. Although the whole Bible is God's word, the Old Testament must be read in the light of the teaching of Christ.[201] God has spoken to the writers of the sacred books of Hinduism and Islam as well, but the divine message in them is mixed with their own thoughts.[202] The light of revelation in these scriptures is likened to the light of the "stars" and contrasted with the light of the "Sun" in Christ.[203]

In a later article, he asserts that the Old Testament prophetic utterances did not necessarily involve detailed verbal inspiration; the prophets rather were only "... giving expression to natural longings of the human religious consciousness." Fulfilment of these prophecies in Christ, thus, does not necessitate a detailed fulfilment of the words of Old Testament prophecy; it signifies instead fulfilment of "... every natural religious instinct and aspiration of the human spirit" of which these prophecies are but imperfect intimations.[204]

---

[200] This weakness marked not just Farquhar's view, but much of the nineteenth century Protestant fulfilment tradition as well. In the post-war years the hypothesis of a unilinear evolution of religion was displaced by a phenomenological approach to the study of religion, enabling a more objective and value-free assessment of religious phenomena; E.J. Sharpe, *Comparative Religion: A History*, (London, Gerald Duckworth, 1975), 220; cf. Race, *Christians and Religious Pluralism* (New York: Orbis, 1983), 57-58.

[201] *Inquirer* 4:7 (March 1903): 3-4.

[202] Farquhar, 'The Greatness of Hinduism', 57.

[203] *Inquirer* 4:7 (March 1903): 4; cf. Farquhar, 'Greatness of Hinduism', 68.

[204] Farquhar, *A Primer of Hinduism*, 196-197.

Farquhar's application to other faiths of his understanding of how Christ fulfils Old Testament prophecy indicates that he regards the revelation in other religions as qualitatively the same as that in Old Testament Judaism. Revelation consists essentially of "the natural longings of the human religious consciousness", expressed simply in earlier forms of religion, and with greater clarity and sophistication in later forms. Farquhar thus seems to draw a quantitative rather than qualitative differentiation between divine revelation in Old Testament and the Hindu tradition.

How does Farquhar then view the relation between the revelation of God in Christ and the light in other religions? In his view of progressive revelation as a gradual historical process, Christ is the climax and culmination, "the full and final revelation". In 'Crown' he affirms the supreme authority of Christ as mediated through the New Testament, "...the focus of all Revelation, the central sun in the light of which everything must be read and estimated."[205]

In Farquhar's scheme, however, the revelation in Christ can only be quantitatively greater than that in the other religions. Thus, within his framework of evolutionary continuity, he is unable to emphasise adequately the transcendence of Christ and the newness of what fulfilment in Him brings. We will subsequently examine the implications of this observation for the affirmation of Christ's decisiveness within his fulfilment framework.

OBJECTION 4: THE JEWISH-CHRISTIAN FULFILMENT MODEL CANNOT BE APPLIED TO THE HINDU-CHRISTIAN RELATIONSHIP.

Farquhar's use of the concept of progressive revelation in his fulfilment approach is patterned after Jesus' application of it to his fulfilment of the Jewish scriptures as recorded in the New Testament. Mackichan, who led the conservative protest at this point, was not entirely negative toward other religions but insisted that the Jewish-Christian fulfilment model could not be applied to Christianity and Hinduism or any other ethnic faith. He held that Christ's statement concerning fulfilment was context-specific.[206] Christians must thus affirm the grandeur and nobility of India's religious efforts, but recognize that in the final analysis these have failed to lead India to the true knowledge of God.[207]

Farquhar acknowledges the force of this objection in his own response to some of the criticisms of his view, but advances several counter-arguments.[208] First, certain features of Christ's life and teaching, such as divine Sonship and Christ's resurrection, do not seem to connect with anything in the Old Testament. In fact, the Hindu teaching concerning incarnation, immortality and

---

[205] Farquhar, 'The Greatness of Hinduism', 68.

[206] D. Mackichan, 'A Present-Day Phase of Missionary Theology', *International Review of Mission* 3 (1914): 246, 248.

[207] Mackichan, 'A Present Day Phase of Missionary Theology', 251, 253.

[208] Farquhar, 'The Relation of Christianity to Hinduism'.

attitude to the sensory world suggest some points at which Hinduism may present "a richer *preparatio* for Christ than Judaism." Second, he suggests that there are some elements in Judaism that are at least as antagonistic to Christianity as certain aspects of Hinduism are, such as the concept of a political messiah and the ethical legalism of the Jews.[209] Third, several features of Old Testament religion do not appear in Christianity. The validity of the fulfilment approach is thus not contingent on every element of the old religion reappearing in the new.[210]

He argues that there were various ways in which Jesus saw himself as fulfilling the Old Testament law and prophecies. Thus, whereas some prophecies were fulfilled in his personality, others were actualised in his work. Likewise, fulfilment of the law could involve: "...universalising a narrow precept, or moralizing an external command... [or] the dissolution of an old institution."[211] The "limitations and variations" of Christ's use of fulfilment thus suggest that the concept may be freely applied to Hinduism as well.[212]

Bernard Lucas advances a compelling argument in support of Farquhar's approach: if critics of the fulfilment view are prepared to recognise the genuine strivings reflected in the Hindu tradition and experience as evidence of divine revelation at work, then, "...to repudiate the connection [of fulfilment continuity between Christ and Hinduism] is not only to be inconsistent in thought, but it is also to represent the acceptance of Christ as a national and religious apostacy [*sic.*] from which every true Hindu must naturally and rightly recoil."[213] Lucas' point is important for the Christian witness in India because it brings us back to the original impulse of Farquhar's fulfilment quest – for a way of presenting Christ not as an alien, but a kinsman of the Hindu community.

Within this continuity affirmed through progressive revelation, Farquhar was able to maintain that elements of the Hindu literary tradition compatible with Christological truth should continue to nourish Indian society even after the demise of Hinduism as a system. This understanding also enabled him to recognise that aspects of truth latent within the gospel may be uncovered in its encounter with the rich religious tradition of India.

---

[209] Farquhar, *ibid.*, 425-26.
[210] Farquhar, *ibid.*, 428.
[211] Farquhar, *ibid.*, 426.
[212] Farquhar, *ibid.*, 427. The debate continued in the *Harvest Field*, the chief participants being Gulliford, Wohlenberg, and Lucas; see Gulliford, 'Christ the Fulfiler of Hinduism', 365; B. Lucas, 'Not to Destroy, but to Fulfil', *Harvest Field* 34 (1914): 422-424; B. Lucas, C. Wohlenberg, and H. Gulliford, 'Not to Destroy but to Fulfil', I, II, III, in *Harvest Field* 34:12 (1914): 451-464; cf. Sharpe, *Not to Destroy*, 355-357.
[213] Lucas, Wohlenberg, and Gulliford, 'Not to Destroy but to Fulfil', I, 455-56.

Christ, the Crown of Hinduism

Farquhar's apologetic was concerned with affirming the supremacy of Christ based on his thesis that Christ is the "consummator" of all the world's religions and the "spiritual crown" of Hinduism.[214] To what extent does he succeed in affirming the decisiveness of Christ in relation to Hinduism and the other religions?

Farquhar's Christology was cast in the straightforward categories of nineteenth century evangelical orthodoxy. His entire discussion of the Hindu teaching on incarnation and its fulfilment in Christ rests on an orthodox understanding of the deity of Christ: "In relation to God the Father, Jesus called Himself the Son, and He affirmed that He alone could reveal the Father."[215] The essence of the Hindu doctrine of the incarnation "...that God became a man, was born, lived, and died a man", is fulfilled in the Christian conviction that "Jesus is the incarnate Son of God" and "the revelation of God."[216]

Likewise, in his treatment of the work of Christ, we find as much discussion on the themes of atonement and redemption as the context warrants.[217] For instance, in concluding his discussion of how Christ fulfils the Hindu concept of incarnation, he affirms the orthodox doctrine of the substitutionary atoning death of Christ:

> Jesus came into the world to save men from sin... and the greatest of His acts was His redemptive death. ...in His death Jesus laid down his life deliberately, voluntarily, in full obedience to His Father's will, realizing that the Cross was needed to secure our emancipation from the chains of sin. His blood was the only possible ransom. It was shed for us.[218]

We have earlier noted that there are intimations of a *Logos* theology in Farquhar's thought that remain largely undeveloped.[219] His Christological framework is, however, inadequate for sustaining his fulfilment view. The main question left unaddressed is whether there is anything transcendent or new in the fuller and brighter light that Christ brings. Is Christ then the crown of Hinduism only in a quantitative sense? If so, what does this indicate regarding his view of Christ's decisiveness? Farquhar does not appear to have seen the need for providing an original Christological framework for his fulfilment approach. His intention rather seems to have been to reinterpret the

[214] Farquhar, 'Christ and the Religions of the World', 196; Farquhar, 'The Greatness of Hinduism', 67; Farquhar, *The Crown of Hinduism*, 77.
[215] Farquhar, *The Crown of Hinduism*, 428-429.
[216] Farquhar, *ibid.*, 437.
[217] Inadequate treatment of the atonement and redemption is one of Sharpe's arguments for the influence of a liberal view of Christ upon Farquhar, a case that seems overstated; Sharpe, *Not to Destroy,* 339-345.
[218] Farquhar, *The Crown of Hinduism*, 444.
[219] See pp.70-71.

data of the Hindu tradition within a scheme that pointed to fulfilment in Christ as described in the Gospels and interpreted in the categories of nineteenth century evangelical faith.

We are thus compelled to explore Farquhar's earlier writings for light on certain questions unclarified in the later exposition of his fulfilment view. The most critical is whether the light that shines outside of Christ is adequate for salvation.

In response to a question, "Is Christ the only means of salvation?" in *The Inquirer* in 1903, Farquhar asserts that if there were different ways of salvation, then we should not be concerned about spreading Christianity. However, if Christ did indeed speak the truth, then salvation is only in him, and He must be proclaimed: the entire issue focuses on Christ.[220] This dogmatic assertion is, however, balanced by a reasonable explanation of how those who have never heard of Christ will be judged:

> Will then no one be saved except such as have definitely accepted Christ? Far from it. Many millions have never heard of Christ at all; and amongst them there must be large numbers who have lived in accordance with all the moral and spiritual light they had; such men will undoubtedly be saved; for they have done the will of our Father in heaven as for [sic.] as they knew it.[221]

In response to another question, he insists that the Bible does not automatically condemn those who have not heard of Christ. The person who is sincere in following all the light he possesses will be saved, whether he is a Hindu or a Christian.[222] But God accepts whoever is saved only through Christ, even if they have never heard of him:

> He is the sacrifice for the sins of the whole world; and the man who, not having heard of Christ, repents of his sins in all sincerity, and cries to God for pardon, is by God forgiven for Christ's sake. He is the Life of men; and the man who in all sincerity, not knowing Christ, cries to God for strength and purity, is filled with the life that is in Christ. But such men, if Christ were presented to them would at once recognise Him as the Image of God, and would accept Him publicly as their Saviour and Lord.[223]

How is the man who does not know Christ "filled with the life that is in Christ"? What about those who live true to all the moral and spiritual light they have, but yet do not accept the Lordship of Christ when they have the opportunity? These questions expose the inherent problem for Farquhar's Christology when he tries to assert the decisiveness of Christ within the

---

220 *Inquirer* 4:12 (August 1903): 5.
221 *Inquirer* 4:5 (January 1903): 2.
222 *Inquirer* 4:9 (May 1903): 7; *Inquirer* 4:5 (January 1903): 3.
223 *Inquirer* 4:5 (January 1903], 3.

framework of his view of evolutionary continuity between Christ and other faiths.

OBJECTION 5: THE FULFILMENT APPROACH REFLECTS AN ATTITUDE OF CONDESCENSION.

Farquhar's view of how those ignorant of Christ may yet be saved by Him has been described as a form of inclusivism,[224] and exposed it to the criticism of condescension and triumphalism. The condescension charge was addressed originally by Hogg, described by Kraemer as "benevolent superiority intending to be gracious modesty", and censured by Radhakrishnan for its "imperialistic chauvinism".[225] Describing condescension as "the most damning criticism of fulfilment", Richard defines it as a posture that assumes the superiority of the Christian system and "...defines and passes judgment on Hinduism as inferior and preparatory at best."[226]

As Richard points out, this charge is to some extent unavoidable for any position seeking to affirm the decisiveness of Christ. In fact, the claim of Christianity or any other faith or ideology to have access to a universal key which enables the rest of humankind to understand our universe better would inevitably expose it to the charge of condescension.

The dominant nineteenth century missionary approach asserted the supremacy of Christ in terms that were extremely critical and denunciatory of the Hindu tradition. Farquhar's approach was an attempt to articulate essentially the same Christological conviction in more irenic terms, which gave serious consideration to the phenomenological data of other religions. The condescension implicit in his fulfilment approach is at least an advance from the cultural imperialism that dominated nineteenth century missionary theology up to his time. Farquhar himself would appeal to the historical precedent of Christ's approach to Judaism in the New Testament. His assertion that Christ fulfils Hinduism is no more condescending than the New Testament testimony to Christ's claim that he had come to fulfil the Jewish religious tradition.

Summary Evaluation

According to his chief commentator and critic, Farquhar was the one individual most responsible for "...bringing about a decisive change in the thinking of Christians over against the phenomena of other faiths" in the first quarter of the

[224] Race, *Christians and Religious Pluralism*, 57-58, 68 treats Farquhar as a leading illustration of the inclusivist model.

[225] Hogg, 'The Crown of Hinduism', 173; H. Kraemer, *Religion and the Christian Faith* (London: Letterworth, 1956), 215; S. Radhakrishnan, *East and West in Religion* (London, 1933), 21-24.

[226] H.L. Richard, 'A Survey of Protestant Evangelistic Efforts among High Caste Hindus in the Twentieth Century', *Missiology: An International Review* 25:4: (1997), 422; cf. E.J. Sharpe, 'Christ the Fulfiller', *Bangalore Theological Forum* 3:1 (1969), 9.

twentieth century.[227] Frequent references in the last two decades to Farquhar's role as a leading proponent of Protestant fulfilment thought acknowledge his key role in inaugurating a new era in the Christian approach to other religions.[228] The significance accorded to Farquhar in this regard has been questioned in Hedges' recent evaluation of his contribution. Essentially following Cracknell's assessment in this regard, he asserts that:

> Farquhar was far from being an original or exemplary exponent of fulfilment theology. ...he adds nothing new to the theory of fulfilment theology. His association with the idea may therefore be surprising except in as far as he can be seen to have been the right man, in the right place, at the right time.[229]

Cracknell and Hedges' judgments are based on detailed examinations of the development of nineteenth century Protestant theology of religion, and certainly reinforce what most informed commentators of Farquhar since Sharpe have been careful to note: that the groundwork for Farquhar's fulfilment view had already been laid in preceding years.[230] Hedges rightly calls our attention to the multiple sources of fulfilment reflection from which Farquhar could have drawn, but seems to overstate his case.

One of Hedges' crucial arguments is the supposed close relationship between Farquhar's and Slater's work.[231] But the points of contrast between the approaches of Slater and Farquhar are at least as significant as the common elements:[232] (1) Whereas Slater followed Monier-Williams in speaking of fulfilment in Christianity, Farquhar, like Muller, emphasised fulfilment in Christ; (2) Farquhar's neglect of Slater's emphasis on the motif of sacrifice is a significant point of contrast; (3) Farquhar's notion of mutual fulfilment is absent in Slater's view; (4) Slater freely quotes and explicitly draws from other scholars of religion, such as Muller, Monier-Williams and Banerjea; Farquhar – a more thorough scholar of religions in Hedges' view – preferred to base his views on independent and original research of texts. Consequently, apart from a single footnote reference in one paper, Farquhar does not acknowledge

---

227 Sharpe, *Faith Meets Faith*, 20.

228 G. Studdert-Kennedy, *British Christians, Indian Nationalists and the Raj* (Delhi: Oxford University Press, 1991), 70-77; G. D'Costa, *John Hick's Theology of Religions: A Critical Evaluation* (Lanham: University Press of America, 1987), 18-19; J. Dupuis, *Toward a Christian Theology of Religious Pluralism* (New York: Orbis, 1997), 133; see p.7, n.21.

229 Hedges, *Preparation and Fulfilment*, 340-341, also n. 355; cf. Cracknell, *Justice, Courtesy and Love*, 172-173.

230 This is in fact assumed in the plan of Sharpe's study and explicitly stated; Sharpe, *Not to Destroy*, 23.

231 Hedges, *Preparation and Fulfilment*, 161-163, 284.

232 Hedges, *Preparation and Fulfilment*, 170, 295.

Slater's influence on any aspect of his work, which is striking, given the depth and quality of his scholarship.[233]

Hedges' comment is also accurate in that Farquhar was clearly not the originator of the nineteenth century Protestant fulfilment tradition. The origins of his sympathetic attitude towards other faiths may go back to the influence of Fairbairn, and through him, to a variety of other influences. Our survey of his early writings indicates that he had a basic irenic posture towards other religions since his earliest years as a missionary.[234] There were, moreover, various versions of the fulfilment approach in circulation from at least the middle of the nineteenth century. Was Farquhar's role then merely accidental, as suggested by Hedges, or does the nature of his contribution justify his widespread recognition as a leading advocate of fulfilment theology in the modern period?

A major factor that neither Hedges nor Cracknell explain is the recognition accorded to Farquhar by his contemporaries for his creative contribution. Sharpe records some of these acknowledgments: he "led the way in building up a new [missionary] apologetic"; he inaugurated "a new attitude towards Indian culture"; he was "a pioneer in a new approach to the great religions of India".[235] In summarising the significance of Farquhar's work, Nicol Macnicol, himself an exponent of the fulfilment school, claimed that Farquhar: "...more than any other individual, brought about a new orientation of the whole missionary outlook towards the non-Christian religions."[236] Elsewhere, Macnicol offered the following explanation regarding the significance of Farquhar's work:

> Others may have discovered simultaneously with him, or even before him, the implications for missionary method of the facts that 'comparative religion' was disclosing; the significance of his name and work consists in the fact that he translated this discovery into action and summoned others to unite with him in a new adventure of the mind.[237]

Farquhar thus deserves credit not as originator of the fulfilment approach, but for developing it into a tradition of encounter. Two factors facilitated his contribution in this regard. First, Farquhar's scholarship was persuasive,

---

[233] See p.54 n.48.

[234] Hedges' deduction that Farquhar "made many harsh attacks upon Hinduism in his early days", based on Farquhar's admission of having used "unguarded expressions" in the course of his teaching has little merit; Hedges, *Preparation and Fulfilment*, 278, n. 3

[235] *The Scotsman* [19.7.1929]; A.J. Appasamy to Mrs. E.N.M. Farquhar [7.8.1929]; H.A. Popley to Mrs. E.N.M. Farquhar [undated], all quoted in Sharpe, *Not to Destroy*, 9-10.

[236] N. Macnicol, 'Farquhar, John Nicol', in *Dictionary of National Biography 1922-193*, ed. by J.R.H. Weaver (London: Oxford University Press, 1937), 296.

[237] 'Dr. J.N. Farquhar', *Young Men of India* 41:9: 681; quoted in Sharpe, *Not to Destroy*, 10.

combining sympathy and scholarly depth. Prior to Farquhar, fulfilment approaches emerged either as the fruits of the research of outstanding scholars of religion, or missionary practitioners whose field experience made them sympathetic to other religions. Farquhar was the first missionary to expound the fulfilment approach at length based on both detailed textual and field research of non-Christian sources of tradition. Emilsen observes that for the next twenty years after the publication of *Crown*, "...the correlation that he [Farquhar] made between sympathy and knowledge was to be almost the norm of the missionary point of view."[238] Farquhar's unique influence as a fulfilment advocate was thus due to the fact that his work combined the in-depth study of religions with sensitivity derived from his practical experience as a missionary.

Second, Farquhar's editorship of *The Inquirer* and subsequent publications gave him privileged access to communication and the opportunity to influence scholarly opinion. But the quality of his work earned him credibility and editorship of a number of series on the fulfilment theme, eventually leading to his recognition as a spokesman and leader of the fulfilment school. There are thus adequate grounds for assigning Farquhar a leading role in the development of the Protestant fulfilment tradition in the modern period.

The greatest strength of Farquhar's approach is that it was grounded in the serious and sympathetic evaluation of the data of non-Christian religions, and Hinduism in particular. Race thus cites Farquhar's work as an outstanding illustration of a fulfilment view based on a rigorous and detailed study of the Hindu tradition, rather than an *a priori* imposition of Christian categories upon the Hindu religious system.[239] The detailed breadth of scholarship evinced by a work like the *Crown* gave his view considerable validity.[240]

A second strength of Farquhar's approach was that it provided an empirical and theological basis for a positive appreciation of Hinduism and other religions. He not only pointed out elements of objective truth in other religions which Christians could celebrate, he also defined continuity between religions formally in terms of the evolutionary framework, and by his identification of a fundamental religious consciousness common to all religions.

Third, Farquhar's approach was based upon the New Testament fulfilment model of Jesus, the biblical concept of progressive revelation, and, to a lesser extent, on the approach of the early Church Fathers. This helped compensate for his lack of a proper theological apparatus. The New Testament antecedents

---

[238] W.W. Emilsen, *Violence and Atonement: The Missionary Experiences of Mohandas Gandhi, Samuel Stokes and Verrier Elwin in India before 1935* (Frankfurt: Peter Lang, 1994), 32.

[239] Race, *Christians and Religious Pluralism*, 57.

[240] E.J. Sharpe 'J.N. Farquhar 1861-1929: Presenting Christ as the Crown of Hinduism' in *Mission Legacies: Biographical Studies of Leaders of the Modern Missionary Movement*, ed. G.H. Anderson, et al. (New York: Orbis, 1995), 294. Sharpe, in fact, regards Farquhar's "solid scholarship" more than his theology of encounter as the true measure of his missionary achievement.

of fulfilment were, consequently, Farquhar's primary source of appeal in responding to criticisms of his view.

Two significant weaknesses remain to be mentioned. First, there is no meaningful reference to indigenous fulfilment thought. K.C. Sen, Nehemiah Goreh, and K.M. Banerjea had already articulated their own versions of fulfilment theology to the previous generation, and the absence of any interaction with their thought is a serious lapse. This is a striking omission in the case of Banerjea, considering the resonance of several ideas in chapter one of *Crown* with Banerjea's main thesis, and Farquhar's passing reference to Banerjea's work in a later article.[241]

A second problem in Farquhar's view is its overly pessimistic view of the future of Hinduism, leading to an overt triumphalism in some of his writings. He saw no future for Hinduism, anticipating its disintegration, eventual demise, and replacement by Christianity in India. Although Farquhar, in fact, envisions a Christ-centred rebirth of Hinduism rather than its total destruction or eradication, his prediction seems way off the mark in the light of what we witness of the strength and vibrancy of Hinduism in the twenty-first century.

Our principal interest in examining Farquhar's fulfilment view is to provide a framework for interpreting and interrogating two Indian Christian fulfilment approaches. We need to highlight three crucial issues in this regard that have emerged in our study of Farquhar's view, corresponding to three components of our definition of fulfilment. Hogg's criticism that Christianity does not fulfil any real need intrinsic to Hinduism strikes at the root of the fulfilment approach. Hence, the first question we need to pose to Indian fulfilment approaches in subsequent chapters is: What resources are there, if any, in the Hindu tradition and religious experience that witness to the presence of a real hunger for what is found eventually in Christ?

A second question pinpoints the need for a way of affirming continuity that does not compromise the distinctiveness of the revelation in Christ. Farquhar employed the device of evolutionary theory, which he tried to ground in an appropriation of the theological notion of progressive revelation. Is the idea of progressive revelation the best available theological device for affirming continuity as well as transcendence? Closely linked to this is the need for an adequate Christology that would sustain the fulfilment approach: Are there Christological resources for grounding the central fact of the Christian faith, the incarnation, in the Hindu tradition in a way that responds to some of its deepest aspirations, and yet affirms the decisiveness of the Christ-event?

We conclude this assessment of Farquhar's fulfilment approach by reviewing its foundational premise: the fundamental religious question of the meaning of life receives its decisive answer in Christ. Farquhar's work was devoted to the application of this premise to the vast data of Hindu religious tradition and experience. He described his work in this regard as "the work of a

---

[241] Farquhar, *The Crown of Hinduism*, 66-77; see p.65.

poorly equipped pioneer in a vast unexplored country."[242] In the rest of this study we attempt to build upon Farquhar's discoveries by drawing from the exploratory insights of two Indian converts.

[242]Farquhar, 'The Relation of Christianity to Hinduism', 430.

Fulfilment in Krishna Mohan Banerjea's Vedic Theology

Our analysis of Farquhar's fulfilment view as a typical model of the nineteenth century fulfilment tradition provides the necessary framework for our examination of the fulfilment approaches of two representative Indian fulfilment thinkers. The first of these, Krishna Mohan Banerjea, was a pioneer of indigenous theology and one of the earliest proponents of the fulfilment approach in India.[1]

The first half of the nineteenth century witnessed a critical encounter between alien western ideas and the traditions of India, resulting from the introduction of English education and the contact of British officials and missionaries with the educated Hindu class in Bengal. This gave rise to a vigorous movement for social, cultural and intellectual change commonly

---

[1] There are only two full-length treatments of the life and thought of Krishna Mohan Banerjea: R. Ghosha, *A Biographical Sketch of the Rev. K .M. Banerjea* (1893. repr., Calcutta,1980); and T.V. Philip, *Krishna Mohan Banerjea: Christian Apologist* (Madras: CLS, 1982). The first of these is a personal biography by a close friend; the second is an examination of his life and contribution. Other shorter but fairly original treatments include: R.D. Paul, *Chosen Vessels: Lives of Ten Indian Christian Pastors of the Eighteenth and Nineteenth Centuries* (Madras: CLS,1961), 138-167; K. Baago, *Pioneers of Indigenous Christianity* (Madras: CLS, 1969), 12-17, 89-103; H. Das, 'The Rev. K.M. Banerjea', *Bengal Past and Present* 37, 73 (1929): 133-144; H. Mitra, 'Banerjee, Krishnamohun', in *Dictionary of National Biography, 1922-1930*, ed. S.P. Sen (Calcutta: Institute of Historical Studies, 1972), 118-120. Serious assessments of Banerjea's thought have been hard to come by in recent decades. The only exception is a brief but incisive two-part critique of Banerjea's fulfilment theory by H.L. Richard, 'The Aryan Witness Recalled: Vedic Sacrifice and Fulfilment Theology', *To All Men All Things* 3, 3 (1993): 1-7; and H.L. Richard, 'The Aryan Witness Recalled: Vedic Sacrifice and Fulfilment Theology', *To All Men All Things* 4, 1 (1994): 1-5; Aleaz and Hedges offer brief and somewhat cursory treatments of his thought, Aleaz, K.P. Aleaz, 'The Theological Contributions of Krishna Mohun Banerjea', *National Council of Churches Review* 117 (1997): 41-56; Hedges, *Preparation and Fulfilment: A History and Study of Fulfilment Theology in Modern British Thought in the Indian Context* (Bern, Peter Lang, 2001), 144-149. A reprint of Aleaz' article with expanded references is included as an "Introduction" to his published compilation of Banerjea's major writings; K.P. Aleaz, *From Exclusivism to Inclusivism: The Theological Writings of Krishna Mohan Banerjea (1813-1885)* (Delhi: ISPCK, 1998).

characterized as the Bengal renaissance, in which Banerjea was a leading figure.[2]

The Man and His Background (1813-1885)

Krishna Mohan Banerjea was born to a poor *kulin* Brahmin family, and was brought up in an atmosphere of strict religious orthodoxy fostered by his pious mother and his maternal grandfather, a Sanskrit scholar of some standing.[3] Banerjea was an early representative of a progressive class of high-caste Bengalis called the *bhadralok*, who attempted to accommodate their traditional Hindu culture to the western life-style of the British, thus setting in motion a process of cultural transformation with far-reaching consequences for Indian society as a whole.[4]

A critical feature in the *bhadralok* appropriation of the British life-style was learning the English language, in keeping with which Banerjea received a quality English education under the patronage of the famous philanthropist, David Hare. His love for learning led him to pursue a course of studies in Sanskrit at Sanskrit College, enabling him to excel as a Sanskrit scholar in later years.[5]

In 1824, Banerjea entered Hindu College where he came under the influence of the controversial Eurasian teacher, Derozio, and became a leader in the

---

[2] J. Lipner, 'A Modern Indian Christian Response' in *Modern Indian Responses to Religious Pluralism*, ed., H.G. Coward (Albany: State University of New York, 1987), 292-295. There is a substantial body of literature which deals with the nineteenth century renaissance in Bengal, including: S.N. Banerjea, *A Nation in Making* (London, 1925); D. Kopf, *British Orientalism and the Bengal Renaissance: The Dynamics of Indian Modernization:1773-1835* (Berkeley: University of California, 1969); A. Poddar, *Renaissance in Bengal: Quests and Confrontations:1800-1860* (Shimla: Indian Institute of Advanced Study, 1970); Sarkar, *Bengal Renaissance and other Essays* (New Delhi, 1970); S.K. Das, *The Shadow of the* Cross (New Delhi: Munshiram Manoharlal, 1974).

[3] Mitra, 'Banerjee, Krishnamohun', 118; Philip, *Krishna Mohan Banerjea*, 2. Copley mistakenly describes Banerjea's father as having been an Assistant Abkari Superintendent, a description that applies to Banerjea's brother; A. Copley, 'The Conversion Experience of India's Christian Elite in the Mid-Nineteenth Century', *The Journal of Religious History* 18, 1 (1994): 66; cf. Ghosha, *A Biographical Sketch*, 2.

[4] The *bhadralok* (the cultured folk) phenomenon arose in the wake of Lord Cornwallis' Permanent Settlement of 1793, which compelled a growing number of upper-caste Bengalis to seek non-traditional occupations and alternative life-styles. Lipner describes them as functioning in effect as "cultural middlemen/ brokers", mediating British ideas and way of life to fellow-Indians; J. Lipner, 'A Modern Indian Christian Response' in *Modern Indian Responses to Religious Pluralism*, ed. H.G. Coward (Albany: State University of New York, 1987), 292-293; for details, see D. Kopf, *The Brahmo Samaj and the Shaping of the Modern Indian Mind* (Princeton: Princeton University Press, 1979), 86-128.

[5] Ghosha, *A Biographical Sketch*, 3-5; Mitra, 'Banerjee, Krishnamohun', 118.

radical youth movement later known as Young Bengal.[6] An active member of Derozio's Academic Association, Banerjea served as editor of the *Enquirer*, one of Young Bengal's many periodicals, and was at the forefront of a virulent campaign against Hindu orthodoxy launched through its pages.[7] His association with this movement's critical rejection of Hindu orthodoxy resulted in him eventually having to leave home.[8]

During this period of emotional stress and spiritual turmoil, Banerjea came under the influence of the Scottish Presbyterian missionary educator, Alexander Duff, and became convinced of the truth of Christianity.[9] His subsequent conversion and baptism in 1832 caused a great stir within the high caste Hindu community of Calcutta.[10] Banerjea described his conversion experience as follows:

> ...I remained in a state of doubt and perplexity for a long time; till God, by the influence of His Holy Spirit, was graciously pleased to open my soul to discern its sinfulness and guilt, and the suitableness of the great salvation which centred in the atoning death of a Divine Redeemer.[11]

Banerjea's conversion was variously interpreted. Some ascribed grossly carnal motives to it.[12] Others felt Christianity offered him a platform for retaliating against his ostracization by the orthodox Hindu community.[13]

---

[6] Henry Louis Vivian Derozio, a young but brilliant teacher of English Literature and History, became the focus of a movement of radical intellectualism and liberalism amongst the student community at Hindu College. The Derozians, pioneers of the movement called 'Young Bengal', encouraged the spirit of rationalism and free thinking which undergirded western secular education. The resulting skepticism towards traditional culture, religion, and values among English-educated youth eventually caused a storm of dissent within the orthodox Hindu community. The movement contributed greatly to intellectual and social reform, significantly influencing the Bengal renaissance. On Derozio and Young Bengal, see Poddar, *Renaissance in Bengal*, 113-145 and Das, *Shadow of the Cross*, 43-58.

[7] Poddar, *Renaissance in Bengal*, 123; for Derozio's influence on Banerjea, see Ghosha, *Biographical Sketch*, 7-13. The Derozians were in general equally opposed to Christian faith, but Copley and Das believe that Derozio may have laid the foundation for Banerjea's conversion by leading his followers to recognize a rationalism in Christianity and to attend Alexander Duff's lectures on Christian faith; Copley, 'The Conversion Experience', 67, n. 61; cf. Das, *Shadow of the Cross*, 50.

[8] The incident which led to this became well-publicized: his friends rashly provoked his orthodox Brahmin neighbours by throwing beef into their compound, causing considerable indignation within the Hindu community of Calcutta; Ghosha, *A Biographical Sketch*, 15-16.

[9] Poddar, *Renaissance in Bengal*, 124; cf. Paul, *Chosen Vessels*, 148.

[10] Ghosha, *A Biographical Sketch*, 19-20; cf. Philip, 'Krishna Mohan Banerjea', 6-8.

[11] G. Smith, *The Life of Alexander Duff* (London, 1853), 61-62.

[12] Dwarkanath Tagore attributed his baptism to "beef and brandy", Ghosha, *A Biographical Sketch*, 20.

[13] Das, *Shadow of the Cross*, 51, 53.

Another view regarded it as reflecting the common identity crisis of anglicised Bengali intellectuals, alienated from traditional beliefs and values, but yet not fully European.[14] However, in questioning the plausibility of these explanations, Philip points out that these interests would have been better served had Banerjea followed the lead of some of his friends and joined the Brahmo Samaj.[15]

Copley and Philip concur in their assessment that Banerjea's conversion was fundamentally the culmination of a spiritual quest grounded in reason.[16] Das, too, believes that it was a carefully reasoned spiritual response to the claims of Christian faith involving an intense process of intellectual doubt and emotional struggle.[17] In analysing Banerjea's conversion, Philip observes that he experienced the Christian gospel as a message of both social and personal redemption, and was thus convinced that Christian faith alone could ultimately regenerate Indian Society. Philip concludes that: "It was this experience and conviction... that made him a Christian, a Pastor, a theological teacher, a social reformer and above all, a Christian apologist."[18]

Banerjea was baptized in the Scottish Presbyterian Church, but convinced by the Episcopal form of Church government, soon transferred allegiance to the Anglican Church.[19] After a short period of theological study and preparation at Bishop's College, he was ordained in 1839,[20] and appointed priest of Christ Church, Cornwallis Square, becoming the first Indian to be given charge of an Episcopal Church in Bengal.[21] Banerjea was a competent preacher both in English and Bengali, and an effective Pastor and evangelist. He led large

---

[14] Poddar, *Renaissance in Bengal*, 40-41, 128.

[15] Philip, *Krishna Mohan Banerjea*, 10-11.

[16] Copley, 'The Conversion Experience', 67-68; cf. Philip, *Krishan Mohan Banerjea*, 11.

[17] Das, *Shadow of the Cross*, 52. Maw represents Banerjea as "begging" a reluctant Duff to admit him to the Church following his rejection from home and the Hindu community; this is without support even in the source Maw cites; M. Maw, *Visions of India: Fulfilment Theology, the Aryan Race Theory, and the Work of British Protestant Missionaries in Victorian India* (Frankfurt: Peter Lang, 1990), 45; cf. Das, 'The Rev. K.M. Banerjea', 138-141.

[18] Philip, *Krishna Mohan Banerjea*, 11.

[19] Ghosha, *Biographical Sketch*, 21.

[20] According to Poddar, *Renaissance in Bengal*, 125; Philip, *Krishna Mohan Banerjea*, 14; Aleaz, *From Exclusivism to Inclusivism*, xxxi; and Lipner, 'A Modern Indian Christian Response', 303. Ghosha, *A Biographical Sketch*, 22 and Paul, *Chosen Vessels*, 153 give 1836 as the year of his ordination.

[21] Specially built for him, the church was closely associated with his name for years to come as *Kristobando's Girija;* Philip, *Krishna Mohan Banerjea*, 13-14.

numbers of Hindus to Christian faith, including several who subsequently came to occupy responsible positions in society.[22]

In 1852, Banerjea accepted appointment as a professor at Bishop's College, Calcutta, where he served until 1867.[23] Banerjea combined his scholarly pursuits with growing involvement in civic affairs and socio-political issues.[24] Following his retirement from Bishop's College, he was drawn to the forefront of several civil rights movements. In 1876, he was elected a municipal commissioner for Calcutta, and was awarded the honorary degree of Doctor of Law by the Calcutta University for his contribution to oriental literature and higher education. In 1885, the year of his death, the British Government conferred on him the rank of Companion of the Indian Empire.[25]

Banerjea was a Christian statesman, linguist, historian, social reformer, and national civil rights leader. He knew at least ten languages: Bengali, Sanskrit, Hindi, Oriya, Persian, Urdu, English, Latin, Greek, and Hebrew, and his great intellect and breadth of learning enabled him to engage in a wide variety of scholarly pursuits.[26] He wrote, edited, and translated a number of books and articles on different subjects, and contributed regularly to a wide range of periodicals.[27] This study examines Banerjea as a leading figure amongst a special class of pioneers of indigenous Christian thought – educated Hindu converts who struggled to shape their Christian identity in a way that affirmed their cultural and national heritage and remained faithful to their experience of Christ.

---

[22] These included "several hundred" Hindus in Krishnagar in 1839, Das, *Shadow of the Cross*, 52. One of the most notable of Banerjea's converts, Madhusudan Dutta, was a renowned 19th century Bengali poet; Philip, *Krishna Mohan Banerjea*, 15-17.

[23] The majority of sources confirm that he retired from Bishop's in 1867: Ghosha *A Biographical Sketch*, 36; Paul, *Chosen Vessels*, 161, 165; Baago, *Pioneers of Indigenous Christianity*, 13; R. Boyd, *An Introduction to Indian Christian Theology* (1969; repr., Delhi: ISPCK, 1991), 280; and Aleaz, *From Exclusivism to Inclusivism*, xxi, xxxi-xxxii. M.M. Thomas and P.T. Thomas, *Towards an Indian Christian Theology: Life and Thought of Some Pioneers* (Tiruvalla: New Day Publications of India, 1992), 23; Mitra, 'Banerjee, Krishnamohun', 119; and Maw, *Visions of India*, 45 regard 1868 as the year of his retirement from Bishop's College, whereas Philip, *Krishna Mohan Banerjea*, 18; and Lipner, 'A Modern Indian Christian Response', 303 date his tenure there as commencing from 1868.

[24] Lipner, 'A Modern Indian Christian Response', 303.

[25] Mitra, 'Banerjee, Krishnamohun', 119. Banerjea's various literary and socio-political affiliations and memberships are too numerous to list; for sample listings, see Poddar, *Renaissance in Bengal*, 126-127, and Aleaz, *From Exclusivism to Inclusivism*, xxxii.

[26] Mitra, 'Banerjee, Krishnamohun', 119; Philip, *Krishna Mohan Banerjea*, 55.

[27] Banerjea edited and published *Vidyakalapadrum* or *Encyclopaedia Bengalensis* in thirteen volumes. For other works and periodicals he edited or contributed to regularly, see Aleaz, *From Exclusivism to Inclusivism*, xxxii. Philip lists forty-one of Banerjea's published English works in chronological order Most of these are difficult to locate, but the maximum number of titles are available in the National Library in Calcutta; Philip, *Krishna Mohan Banerjea*, 126-128.

His Theological Development

The Christian encounter with Hinduism in the nineteenth century caused a large number of Christian apologetic writings to emerge, marking the beginning of indigenous theological thinking in India. Banerjea is widely regarded as "the foremost Indian Christian apologist" of this period, and the following assessment focuses upon this aspect of his work.[28]

Banerjea made his theological contribution at the most intense period of the religious confrontation between Christianity and Hinduism. Four main groups were involved in the controversies that arose during this period: the Young Bengal liberals, the orthodox Hindu party, the Brahmo Samaj, and the Christian missionaries. In a somewhat superficial assessment, Philip identifies Banerjea's approach with the confrontational missionary posture of this period.[29] Although the approach of the class of early Christian apologists that Banerjea represented bore some correspondence with this missionary posture, it was distinctive in its attempt to preserve both indigenous cultural roots and national identity.[30]

However, deriving from this identification of Banerjea's approach with the dominant missionary attitude of this period, most analyses of Banerjea's apologetic approach distinguish two stages in his theological development.[31] The basis for this two-stage view is the following perception:

> Till about 1870 his position had been that which he expressed in his *Dialogues* in which by implication he discarded the whole religious heritage of his country. In 1875, however, he published a little book [*Arian Witness*] which revealed a completely different attitude to Hinduism...[32]

This scheme distinguishes a first stage in which, like the missionary writings of the period, Banerjea's earlier apologetic speeches and writings sought to expose the errors and weaknesses of Hinduism, setting forth Christian claims against Hindu criticisms of Christianity. In the second stage, Banerjea is thought to have moved away from this negative posture in pursuit of a more positive relationship between Christianity and Hinduism, emphasizing continuity and fulfilment rather than points of contrast.

There is no consensus regarding the precise date of the supposed transition between the two stages in Banerjea's apologetic approach. According to Baago, the transition took place by 1870, sometime after his retirement from Bishop's

---

[28] Philip, *Krishna Mohan Banerjea*, 2, 94.

[29] Philip, *Krishna Mohan Banerjea*, 72-75.

[30] Copley, 'The Conversion Experience', 68 observes that Banerjea's relationship with the CMS missionaries was often contentious.

[31] Baago, *Pioneers of Indigenous Christianity*, 13; Philip, *Krishna Mohan Banerjea*, 77, 88-89, 94; Boyd, *An Introduction*, 280-281; Thomas and Thomas, *Towards and Indian Christian Theology*, 25; Aleaz, *From Exclusivism to Inclusivism*, xxi, xxxiii; Copley, 'The Conversion Experience', 68.

[32] Baago, *Pioneers of Indigenous Christianity*, 13.

College, with "a completely different attitude to Hinduism" reflected in his *Arian Witness*, published in 1875.[33] Philip detects a "marked change" in Banerjea's approach to Hinduism from about 1865, although the reasons for this view are not convincing.[34] Aleaz perceives this "marked change" as having occurred as early as 1861, the year when he published his *Dialogues*.[35]

The period between the publication of *Claims* in 1864 and *Arian Witness* in 1875 was clearly a significant period of transition in the apologetic approach of Banerjea.[36] However, suggesting a particular year as marking the point of transition between two stages is to go beyond the purview of the evidence. The lack of consensus on this issue suggests that the transition in Banerjea's apologetic approach was not as sharp or sudden as expressions like "completely different attitude" and "marked change" seem to suggest. The movement of thought in Banerjea was thus more gradual and progressive than the two-stage theory seems to imply.

On one hand, as Copley points out, there is evidence that Banerjea's conversion was marked by continuities from his earliest days as a Christian; for instance, seeing no need for converts to adopt a European way of life.[37] Lipner observes that from the earliest years following his conversion, Banerjea's rationalist *bhadralok* background caused him to ascribe a considerable amount of value to his Hindu past while remaining critical of its weaknesses.[38] Thus, even Sisir Kumar Das, who viewed Banerjea as having "nothing but hatred for Hinduism", regarded him as an exception to the general tendency among early converts to become Westernised, and was convinced that he succeeded in demonstrating that it was possible to be a Christian and an Indian at the same time.[39]

---

[33] Baago, *ibid.*, 13; Boyd, *An Introduction*, 281, too, sees a significant shift in Banerjea's views following his retirement.

[34] Philip, *Krishna Mohan Banerjea*, 88-89, 94; accepted by Thomas and Thomas and implicitly by Copley as well; Thomas and Thomas, *Towards an Indian Christian Theology*, 25; Copley, 'The Conversion Experience', 68. Philip's suggestion is based on a tenuous link which he sees between the sentiments expressed by Banerjea in a pamphlet published in 1865, entitled *Sanctity of Conjugal Relations*, and his overthrowing of the missionary yoke and awakening of national consciousness. Hedges follows Maw in seeing this positive attitude to Hinduism even earlier, in 1863; Hedges, *Preparation and Fulfilment*, 145; cf. Maw, *Visions of India*, 49.

[35] Aleaz, *From Exclusivism to Inclusivism*, xxi. In an earlier article Aleaz suggests that Banerjea "crossed over from exclusivism to inclusivism" in 1857; K.P. Aleaz, 'Bishop's College and the Propagation of the Gospel: Origin and Growth of a Vision', *National Council of Churches Review* 115 (1995): 919.

[36] *Claims* representing the last in an earlier series (between 1841 and 1865), and *Arian Witness*, the first in a later series of publications (between 1875 and 1881), Philip, *Krishna Mohan Banerjea*, 94f, 112f.

[37] Copley, 'The Conversion Experience', 68.

[38] Lipner, 'A Modern Indian Christian Response, 304.

[39] Das, *Shadow of the Cross*, 52.

A more careful appraisal of the evidence suggests that Baago's assessment may be an overstatement. Some basic continuities which seem to run through Banerjea's thought since the earliest years contradict the claim that Banerjea summarily rejected the Hindu tradition in his earlier writings and displayed a more irenic attitude only in later years. For instance, in Banerjea's most significant early work, *Dialogues*, he finds support in the Hindu texts for the Christian doctrines of revelation, the incarnation, and the atoning sacrifice of Christ. Thus, conceptions integral to Banerjea's thought in later years, such as primeval revelation and sacrifice as a means of redemption from sin, were first articulated in the *Dialogues*. This is a fact acknowledged even within the two-stage chronological scheme of Aleaz.[40]

On the other hand, although Banerjea's later writings do reflect a more irenic apologetic posture, there is no reason to believe that he ever diluted or abandoned his firm commitment to the decisiveness of Christ. His basic apologetic concern remained largely unchanged with the passage of time, even as his quest for continuity between Christian faith and his ancestral religion directed him towards more positive lines of research and enquiry. There are, however, grounds for distinguishing an earlier and later period of development in Banerjea's thought, if we treat the years between 1864 and 1875 as a period of significant transition. The classification of his literary contribution into these two periods provides an appropriate chronological framework for examining the development of his fulfilment view.

The Emergence of Fulfilment in Banerjea's Early Thought

Banerjea's early apologies were essentially historical and philosophical enquiries in which he sought to challenge the rational tenability of Hinduism, and correspondingly, to affirm the reasonable basis of the Christian faith. His purpose was to defend Christianity against the criticism of its opponents and, at the same time, convince his fellow-countrymen to accept Christianity. We focus our attention in this section on the most important of his apologetic writings prior to 1865, *Dialogues on Hindu Philosophy*.[41] This was Banerjea's first full-length and detailed treatment of any subject, on the occasion of a competition in which John Muir offered a prize of three hundred pounds for the

---

[40] Thus based on his observation of such "positive acknowledgements" regarding Hinduism in *Dialogues*, Aleaz dates the second phase of Banerjea's thought from the year of its publication; Aleaz, *From Exclusivism to Inclusivism*, xxi-xxii.

[41] His other writings of this period were *Truth Defended and Error Exposed* (1841), 'The Transition States of Hindu Mind', in *Calcutta Review* 11:5 (1845) and *The Claims of Christianity in British India* (Calcutta, 1864), reprint in T.V. Philip, *Krishna Mohan Banerjea: Christian Apologist* (Madras: CLS, 1982). Appropriate reference will be made to *Claims of Christianity*, but the two other articles are unavailable; for the context of these articles, see Ghosha, *A Biographical Sketch*, 29, 32-33, 39-40; Philip, *Krishna Mohan Banerjea*, 94.

best English essay exposing and refuting the fundamental errors of the Nyaya, Sankhya, and Vedanta philosophies.[42]

In the preface to *Dialogues*, Banerjea states his twofold purpose as: "*first*, to give a correct and authentic statement of the doctrines of Hindu philosophy, and, *secondly*, to suggest such modes of dealing with them as may prove most effective to the Hindu mind."[43] His approach, in his own words, will be, "to recognize what we have found to be true, and courageously to condemn what we have discovered to be false."[44]

Banerjea makes it clear that he will not be appealing to "the primary standard of truth" for Christians, the Bible, in his apologetic argument. Rather, the criterion of truth would be "the work of the Law written in the hearts of men", the intuitive sense of right and wrong determined by the authoritative voice of conscience. Thus, the common ground of appeal between him and his dialogical opponents is reason:

> Our test of truth and error in these discussions is accordingly the same which writers on moral philosophy and natural theology are in the habit of observing. It is substantially the very test to which the founders of the Hindu philosophy themselves appeal.[45]

In this fairly extended treatise, Banerjea deals with a broad gamut of issues, including the authority of the Vedas; the six Hindu philosophical systems, in terms of their origin, doctrine of God, creation and salvation;[46] and the evidences for the truth of Christianity. Presented as a series of ten imaginary dialogues between three Hindu friends, one of who, Satyakama, is a convert to Christianity, Banerjea pits the arguments of the contending schools of Hindu philosophy against one another, in refuting all of them in favour of Christianity. Consistent with the tone of his writings during this period, the author's style of argument is rationalistic and his attitude to Hindu philosophy essentially negative.[47] His arguments focus around the following issues in the Christian-Hindu encounter.

In the first place, Banerjea defends Christian evangelistic activity against Hindu criticism of Christianity as a foreign religion, destructive of the Indian

---

[42] Ghosha, *A Biographical Sketch,* 37-38; Paul, *Chosen Vessels*, 162; Philip, *Krishna Mohan Banerjea,* 98.

[43] K.M. Banerjea, *Dialogues on Hindu Philosophy Comprising the Nyaya, Sankhya and Vedant: to which is added a discussion of the authority of the Vedas* (1861; repr., London and Madras: CLS, 1903), v.

[44] Banerjea, *Dialogues on Hindu Philosophy*, vi.

[45] Banerjea, *ibid.*, vi.

[46] Banerjea treats the six Hindu philosophical systems in pairs, and in his discussion often regards them in effect as three main systems: Nyaya (and Vaiseshika), Sankhya (and Yoga), Vedanta (and Mimamsa); Banerjea, *Dialogues on Hindu Philosophy*, vii-viii.

[47] Philip, *Krishna Mohan Banerjea*, 96.

way of life.[48] At the outset, he points out that Hindu tradition itself upholds the idea that truth should be judged on its own merit regardless of the place of its origin.[49] It was a fallacy to speak of Hinduism as the only religion meant for the inhabitants of India, since the notion of a unified system as the common religion of all Hindus had no basis either in the historical tradition or the ancient Scriptures of India.[50] He argues, furthermore, that there was no "eternal dharma" prescribed by the Hindu scriptures except caste *dharma*, and that Hinduism in fact provided for individuals and groups to pledge allegiance to any deity of their choice [*Ishtadevata*] and yet remain within the Hindu fold socio-culturally.[51]

A major issue Banerjea addresses is the divine authority of the Vedas.[52] He draws attention to the inherent inconsistency in some orthodox schools of Hindu philosophy, which regard the Vedas as divine revelation and yet reject some vedic teachings as impure, thus challenging their absolute authority.[53] Second, the Vedas themselves testify against their eternity in that they contain the names of persons and places not eternal.[54] Furthermore, the belief that the Veda is authoritative because it is God's word cannot be sustained by most of the philosophies that deny the existence of a Supreme Being.[55] His main argument against the authority of the Vedas, however, is the absence of external historical evidence to substantiate its authenticity.[56] He contrasts this with what he regards as convincing external evidence for the reliability of the Bible and truth of Christianity: the fulfilment of biblical prophecy, the miracles of Christ, and the rapid spread of Christianity.[57]

A substantial portion of Banerjea's argument is directed towards exposing the Buddhist influence upon Brahmanical Hinduism. He concludes a careful historical and philosophical analysis by arguing that the essential teachings of the Hindu philosophies are not derived from the Vedas or any pre-Buddhist writings, but have been borrowed from Buddhism. The Buddhists made the first attempts at philosophical speculation in India, and employed reason and argument in religion in challenging vedic and Brahmanical authority.

---

[48] Banerjea, *Dialogues on Hindu Philosophy*, 3-27.
[49] Banerjea, *ibid.*, 12-13.
[50] Banerjea, *ibid.*, 21f.
[51] Banerjea, *ibid.*, 25-27.
[52] Banerjea, *ibid.*, 351-385.
[53] Banerjea, *ibid.*, 8, 38-42.
[54] Banerjea, *ibid.*, 359-361, 364-366.
[55] Banerjea, *ibid.*, 368-369.
[56] Banerjea, *ibid.*, 366-376, 385-386.
[57] Banerjea, *ibid.*, 386-398, 406-407; he regards the miracles in Hinduism as qualitatively different from those in Christianity, being morally imperfect with inadequate supporting evidence, Banerjea, *Dialogues on Hindu Philosophy*, 396; cf. Das, *Shadow of the Cross*, 53.

Brahmanical philosophy has been taken captive from within by Buddhist logic and metaphysics.[58]

Banerjea also examines the doctrines of God, creation, and salvation in the six Hindu philosophical systems. His assessment concludes that the various schools of Hindu philosophy had capitulated to the Buddhist intellectual assault, with an inadequate doctrine of creation and an essentially atheistic rather than theistic framework. His main criticism of the doctrine of God and creation in Hindu philosophy is its failure to postulate the existence of a supreme and sovereign being as the creator and sustainer of the universe. He thus skilfully employs the arguments of the various schools against one another, pointing out logical inconsistencies in all of them.[59]

Banerjea was one of the first few Indians in the nineteenth century to address an apologetic against Hindu philosophy based on a combination of an intimate knowledge of Hinduism and rationalist and evidential criteria. His apologetic approach was in formal continuity with that of the missionary apologists, but there are some vital points of difference often overlooked by critics.[60]

To begin with, although Banerjea's approach at this stage is decidedly negative, and at times aggressive, the terms of his discourse are largely academic and he remains respectful towards his partners in dialogue. This is in contrast to the harsh and virulent rhetoric that characterised much of the missionary apologetic of this period.[61]

Second, overtones of cultural imperialism tainted the missionary approaches,[62] while Banerjea addresses his interlocutors as one within the Hindu fold. Although he rejects some aspects of his ancestral religion, he identifies closely with his cultural heritage. Unlike most of the missionaries who possessed, at best, a superficial grasp of Hinduism, Banerjea was a skilled Sanskritist, whose arguments were based on a first-hand, in-depth knowledge of the Hindu scriptures, philosophy, and tradition.

The third and most critical contrast with respect to our present study is the evidence of Banerjea's quest for a bridge of continuity between Christian faith and Hinduism even in this early stage of his thought. Thus, although *Dialogues*

---

[58] Banerjea, *Dialogues on Hindu Philosophy*, 36-40, 150-167, 199-204, 207-210, 225-249. Banerjea sets forth essentially the same case in another article devoted to this theme. K.M. Banerjea, *On the Relation between the Hindu and Buddhistic Systems of Philosophy and the Light which the History of One Throws on the Other* (Calcutta, 1861), reprint in T.V. Philip, *Krishna Mohan Banerjea: Christian Apologist* (Madras: CLS): 131-158.

[59] Banerjea, *Dialogues on Hindu Philosophy*, 39-65, 89-113, 299-308.

[60] Philip, *Krishna Mohan Banerjea*, 72-74, 88-89; cf. Baago, *Pioneers of Indigenous Christianity*, 13.

[61] See pp.16-17.

[62] See p.18.

is essentially negative in its attitude to Hinduism, it has positive acknowledgments of points of contact between Christianity and Hinduism.

The first point of contact Banerjea discerns is the idea of a divine revelation. God has made something of himself known through "the light of nature" or "the book of nature" – facts accessible to natural reason.[63] Some aspects of this knowledge of God may be found in Hindu philosophy, as reflections of a "religious sentiment",[64] which God has implanted in human nature: "The minds of our ancestors were universally imbued with notions of a Revelation or supernatural communication to man, but they could not explain what that Revelation was, or how it was given."[65]

He further sees the philosophical systems implicitly affirming the fact of an original primitive revelation from God,[66] a pivotal component of his fulfilment view in later writings. He sees the validity of this conception confirmed by the continuity observed between certain teachings in the Hindu scriptures and their fuller and clearer illumination in biblical revelation.[67]

Banerjea also finds points of contact in the Hindu texts for the Christian doctrines of the incarnation and the atoning work of Christ. He was thus convinced that the *avatara* idea in the *Bhagvadgita* was derived from a primitive revelation of a future saviour:

> The doctrine of Christ's incarnation for the redemption of the world, involved in the primitive revelation of a future Saviour, receives some confirmation from detached expressions in several portions of the Brahminical sastras. The idea propounded in the Bhagavadgita and other works that Vishnu descended in human form for the relief of the world, whenever it is opposed with sin and wickedness... was apparently derived by tradition from the primitive revelation of a future Saviour...[68]

Likewise, the ancient vedic conception of sacrifice is also a survival of the primitive revelation given by God to all mankind. The offering of sacrifice for redemption from sin was an ancient institution originally ordained by God to represent the future sacrifice of Christ.[69] The Vedas record this primitive practice without explanation: the fuller explanation is offered only in the biblical account of the universal sacrificial atonement of Christ.[70]

---

[63] Banerjea, *Dialogues on Hindu Philosophy*, 15.
[64] Banerjea, *ibid.*, 52-53.
[65] K.M. Banerjea, *The Claims of Christianity on British India*, Calcutta 1864., repr. in T.V. Philip, *Krishna Mohan Banerjea: Christian Apologist* (Madras: CLS, 1982), 175.
[66] Banerjea, *Dialogues on Hindu Philosophy*, 382-385.
[67] For illustrations, see Banerjea, *ibid.*, 396-397.
[68] Banerjea, *ibid.*, 405-406.
[69] Banerjea, *ibid.*, 397-398; cf. Banerjea, *Claims of Christianity*, 174-175.
[70] Banerjea, *Dialogues on Hindu Philosophy*, 398.

These ideas seem to represent an incipient form of fulfilment during this early period of Banerjea's theological development. Lipner provides the only evidence available regarding Banerjea's approach to Hinduism from the years between 1864 and 1875, an ordination sermon in Bengali delivered in 1870.[71] In this sermon, Banerjea refers to a number of Hindu themes and characters as prefiguring Christ, the true sacrifice, of which the vedic offerings and sacrifices are only a copy, and the true *Hari*, the only one who removes our sins.[72]

In succeeding years, Banerjea applied his scholarship to the exploration and development of a clearer basis for continuity between Christian faith and Hinduism. Banerjea's understanding of the relationship between Christian faith and Hinduism in terms of the fulfilment approach is expounded more clearly in his later writings.

Christianity as the Fulfilment of Hinduism in Banerjea's Later Thought

In 1875, Banerjea published *Arian Witness*,[73] the first in a later series of writings, which seek to explore a more positive relationship between Hinduism and Christianity. The other important writings of this period, *Two Essays as Supplements to the Arian Witness*[74] and *Relation between Christianity and Hinduism*,[75] essentially build upon the central argument of *Arian Witness*. Consequently, there is repetition, continuity, and some progression of thought in these later writings. Philip summarises the shift in outlook in Banerjea's post-1875 writings as follows:

> In his *Dialogues on Hindu Philosophy*, he acknowledged the existence of a rudiment of primitive revelation in Hinduism. Krishna Mohan developed this idea further in his later writings and endeavoured to show that Christianity was the

---

[71] On June 9, 1870 at Trinity Church, Amherst St., Calcutta; pamphlet, printed at Chinsurah by D.E. Rodrigues, 1870, quoted in Lipner, 'A Modern Christian Response', 305, 314, n. 26.

[72] Lipner, 'A Modern Christian Response', 305.

[73] "Arian" here is the antiquated spelling for what we designate as "Aryan" in modern times. The preface indicates that the book is in two parts: historical – "an inquiry after the original settlement of the Asiatic Arians, and the early adventures of the Indo-Arians", and, theological – "an investigation of their ancient legends, traditions, and institutions in the light of corroborative evidences of Sacred history and of some of the fundamental principles of Christian Doctrine"; K.M. Banerjea, *The Arian Witness: or Testimony of Arian Scriptures in Corroboration of Biblical History and the Rudiments of Christian Doctrine, Including Dissertations on the Original Home and Early Adventures of Indo-Arians* (Calcutta: Thacker, Spink, 1875), iii.

[74] K.M. Banerjea, *Two Essays as Supplements to the Arian Witness* (Calcutta: Thacker, Spink, 1880).

[75] K.M. Banerjea, *The Relation between Christianity and Hinduism* (Calcutta: Oxford Mission Press, 1881), reprint in T.V. Philip, *Krishna Mohan Banerjea: Christian Apologist* (Madras: CLS, 1982), 181-201.

fulfilment of Vedic religion. It was no longer Christianity and Hinduism contrasted, but Christianity as fulfilment of Hinduism. For him, no one could be a true Hindu without being a true Christian.[76]

Rather than try to undermine Hinduism rationally, Banerjea now sought meaningful continuity between Hinduism and Christian faith. He did this by discovering striking parallels between the Old Testament and the Vedas. Banerjea's innovative thesis was first stated in *Arian Witness*, and remained substantially intact through his subsequent writings, but our analysis of his thought will focus primarily on the final concise statement of his view of fulfilment in *Christianity and Hinduism*. We will, however, first discuss the contribution of the other two writings to the development of his thesis.

In setting forth his objectives in *Arian Witness*, Banerjea lists various points at which he expects his vedic Arian Witness to confirm different aspects of the biblical worldview. Several of these either explicitly mention or imply the concept of sacrifice: that sacrifice is the divinely-sanctioned means for the remission of sins; that the seed of the woman will bruise the serpent's head; that *Prajapati*, the Lord and Preserver of Creation, offered himself as a sacrifice for the welfare of mortal souls which had attained immortality.[77]

The Christian apologetic of this period was obliged to respond to an important challenge, the common rejection of Christianity on nationalist grounds. Banerjea's second main objective addresses this concern: to refute the charge that Christianity was a foreign religion by demonstrating its direct continuity with the cardinal teachings of the Vedas:

> We look to our Witness also for the disproof of an idea often broached against Hindoo Christians that they are rebels against the *sanatana dharma* of the country, and apostates from the faith that has animated the Hindoo mind, and the rule of life that has governed Hindoo practice, from time immemorial… [and to prove that] …Hindoo Christians can alone have the satisfaction of knowing that the fundamental principles of the Gospel were recognized, and acknowledged, both in theory and practice, by their primitive ancestors, the Brahminical Arians of India, and that if the authors of the Vedas could by any possibility now return to the world, they would at once recognise the Indian Christians far more complacently as their own descendants, than any other body of educated natives.[78]

---

[76] Philip, *Krishna Mohan Banerjea*, 113.

[77] Banerjea, *Arian Witness*, 8-9, 144-150, 194, 200-205, 210-213, in which the texts he cites include *RV* i.59,21, i.90,6, i.164,35, x.121,2; *Tandya Maha Brahmana* i.55,332,410; *Satapatha Brahmana*, 828, 836; *Taittiriya Sanhita* vi.3.4, vii.4.2.1. He sees the *Arian Witness* as also confirming two other biblical ideas: social equality and the Mosaic account of Creation.

[78] Banerjea, *Arian Witness*, 10; cf. Richard's summary of Banerjea's thesis; Richard, 'Aryan Witness Recalled', 1.

In the first part of the book (chapters 1-3) Banerjea compares a number of vedic and Assyrian texts, and discusses points of similarity between the Hebrew and Sanskrit languages, in an attempt to prove that the original home of the Aryans was Media. In a significant shift from his earlier position, Banerjea now seems convinced of the historical authenticity of some vedic texts.[79] In chapters 4-6, he observes striking parallels in the Vedas to the biblical accounts of the Creation, the Fall, and the Flood, and indicates the common etymological roots of Noah and Manu, seeking to demonstrate that these Old Testament accounts are "abundantly confirmed by Arian records".[80]

In the last two chapters, Banerjea examines what is for him the central theological issue – the theme of sacrifice in the Vedas and its relation to the biblical teaching of Christ's sacrificial death. He affirms as a basic premise, that the Christian worldview "has for its cornerstone the Sacrifice of the Lamb slain from the foundation of the world", based on a key principle that "without shedding of blood there is no remission" of sin.[81] Having its primeval origins in the antediluvian period, the offering of sacrifices was a recognized institution throughout the Old Testament, foreshadowing the sacrifice of Christ on the cross of Calvary.[82]

He finds the perpetuation of the practice of sacrifice through successive generations, and the tradition of its efficacy to abolish sin and overcome death, convincing proof of its divine origin.[83] His apologetic purpose is thus to justify the truth of the Christian claim concerning "the Sacrifice *of the Lamb of God which taketh away the sin of the world*".[84]

The importance of the concept of sacrifice alluded to earlier in *Dialogues*, emerges here as the theological pivot of Banerjea's thesis regarding the relation between Hinduism and Christianity. He now regards sacrifice as the most important element common to both the Christian scriptures and the vedic witness, and he regards Christ as the fulfilment of the vedic religion based on this conviction. We will return to this issue at appropriate points in our subsequent exposition of Banerjea's fulfilment approach.[85]

In the first of his *Two Essays*, Banerjea attempts to substantiate further the historical and etymological argument of his earlier treatise.[86] The second is a theological justification of the claim of *Arian Witness* against the objection that: "...it would be contrary to Scripture to hold that any heathen Sastra could have inculcated doctrines which composed the sacred mysteries of the

---

[79] Banerjea, *ibid.*, 13-112; see especially pp.111-112.
[80] Banerjea, *ibid.*, 113-193.
[81] Banerjea, *ibid.*, 2.
[82] Banerjea, *ibid.*, 2-4.
[83] Banerjea, *ibid.*, 4-5, 7.
[84] Banerjea, *ibid.*, 7-8.
[85] Richard notes that sacrifice is the only aspect of Banerjea's argument that he develops at length after *Arian Witness*; Richard, 'Aryan Witness Recalled', 2.
[86] Banerjea, *Two Essays*, v.

Christian Faith."[87] Here again Banerjea makes a strong case for the "decidedly theistic" tone of the Rg Veda. Further elaborating the vedic idea of the self-sacrifice of the *Prajapati*, he concludes that Christianity "fills up... a most important vacuum – in the vedic account of sacrifices, by exhibiting the true Prajapati – the *Lamb slain from the foundation of the World*."[88] We are concerned with the central thread of the argument of these essays, and will return to it later in our discussion.

We find Banerjea's most succinct and systematic statement of his fulfilment approach in the last of his published addresses on the subject, *Christianity and Hinduism*.[89] His position is set forth clearly in the form of two propositions:

> 1st. That the fundamental principles of Christian doctrine in relation to the salvation of the world find a remarkable counterpart in the Vedic principles of primitive Hinduism in relation to the destruction of sin, and the redemption of the sinner by the efficacy of Sacrifice, itself a figure of *Prajapati*, the Lord and Saviour of the Creation, who had given himself up as an offering for that purpose.
>
> 2ndly. That the meaning of *Prajapati*, an appellative, variously described as a *Purusha* begotten in the beginning, as *Viswakarma* the creator of all, singularly coincides with the meaning of the name and offices of the historical reality Jesus Christ, and that no other person than Jesus of Nazareth has ever appeared in the world claiming the character and position of the self-sacrificing *Prajapati*, at the same time both mortal and immortal.[90]

Banerjea clarifies his apologetic purpose in the opening paragraphs of his address: to lead to a better understanding between the rulers and the ruled, between the West and East, and to prove that the "Defender of the [Christian] Faith", the Queen of England, is in effect the protector of the ancient principles of Hinduism as well.[91]

Banerjea defines Christianity as "a scheme of reconciliation of man with God" through the sacrifice of Christ. It is also critically important for him to consider Hinduism in its original form, as "the religion of the Vedas", since all the different Hindu schools and sects refer to the ancient Vedas as the sacred

---

[87] Banerjea, *ibid.*, vi; this was not an objection addressed directly against Banerjea, but the substance of a newspaper controversy aroused by a preacher who shared Banerjea's ideas with a group of educated Hindus; Banerjea's response was essentially an invitation to seriously consider the evidence, Banerjea, *Two Essays*, 74-76.

[88] Banerjea, *ibid.*, 79.

[89] Delivered at Christ Church in Cornwallis Square, Calcutta, and published as a contribution to the Oxford Mission Occasional Papers, Ghosha, *Biographical Sketch*, 49.

[90] Banerjea, *Christianity and Hinduism*, 181-182.

[91] Banerjea, *ibid.*, 182. This irenic political view must be set in the context of the favourable attitude towards British rule within some quarters of the Indian intelligensia; see Sen's similar posture, 26.

oracles of their religion.[92] Christianity is, hence, compared with the earliest form of Hinduism as found in the Vedas.

Banerjea begins the defence of his first proposition with a discussion of the vedic view of God and creation. Contrary to popular missionary opinion, and in agreement with his reformed Hindu dialogical opponents, Banerjea's study had convinced him that vedic Hinduism is not polytheistic, but theistic.[93] In his earlier discussion of the issue, which includes a brief review of the cosmological and teleological arguments as they occur in ancient Indo-Aryan and Iranian texts, he arrives at a similar conclusion, but asserts further that: "The Rig-veda *does* appear to have arisen in a state of Society where monotheism may be said to have prevailed.... That was certainly a system of monotheism."[94] In this later work he is more cautious:

> ...in the earliest period of our history, as disclosed in the Rig Veda, our primitive ancestors had clear and decided conceptions of Deity.... It is, however, difficult to say that the Vedic dogma was pure monotheism, untainted by polytheism.[95]

However, he offers summary evidence for the view that vedic Hinduism acknowledged the existence of a supreme, unborn, eternal being who is far above heaven and earth, although designated by various names.[96]

Banerjea next considers vedic rituals, more specifically *yagna*, sacrificial rites, "the first and foremost rites of religion", the panacea for all evil and the secret of all success in the ancient world.[97] He cites three lines of evidence that indicate the importance of the rite of sacrifice in the Vedas. To begin with, "Creation's Lord" himself is regarded as the originator of the sacrificial

---

[92] Banerjea, *ibid.*, 182-184. The term 'Vedas' can: (1) refer to the four collections of hymns – Rgveda, Samaveda, Atharvaveda and Yajurveda; or, (2) include the Brahmanas and Upanishads along with these four hymns. From the citations in Banerjea's texts it seems evident that he included at least the Brahmanas in his use of the term. This raises a critical issue regarding the extent to which the religion of the Rgvedic period can be clearly distinguished from that of the Brahmanas. Banerjea's understanding of vedic religion assumes a unity supported by A.A. Macdonell, 'Vedic Religion', in *Encyclopedia of Religion and Ethics*, vol. 12, ed. J. Hastings (Edinburgh: T & T Clark, 1921), 613; P.S. Deshmukh, *The Origin and Development of Religion in Vedic Literature* (London: Oxford University Press, 1933), 339 and I. Selvanayagam, *Vedic Sacrifice: Challenge and Response* (New Delhi: Manohar, 1996), 54, 60, 65, while K.R. Potdar, *Sacrifice in the Rgveda: Its Nature, Influence, Origin and Growth* (Bombay: Bharatiya Vidya Bhavan, 1953), 2-3, 11-12 draws a clear distinction between the two periods.

[93] Banerjea, *Christianity and Hinduism*, 183-185.

[94] Banerjea, *Two Essays as Supplements to the Arian Witness* (Calcutta: Thacker, Spink, 1880), 45ff, 52, 78.

[95] Banerjea, *Christianity and Hinduism*, 185.

[96] Banerjea, *ibid.*, 184-186.

[97] Banerjea, *ibid.*, 186.

institution. The institution of sacrifice thus existed from time immemorial, since the Vedas knew of no time when it was not practised.[98]

Banerjea shows, secondly, that great virtues are attributed to the sacrificial institution. In vedic times a wide variety of material and spiritual benefits were ascribed to the institution of sacrifice: by virtue of sacrifice the world was created and sustained, it provides strength against enemies, and, most importantly, it was "the great means of escape from the pernicious effects of sin".[99] In *Arian Witness* he had pinpointed three ways in which the Vedas relate the benefits of sacrifice to human life:

> (1) The mystical identification of the sacrificer with the victim, which is the ransom for sin; (2) Sacrifice the great remedy for the ills of life – the ship or ark by which we escape sin and all worldly perils. (3) Sacrifice the instrument by which Sin and Death are annulled and abolished.[100]

The first of these is part of the climax of Banerjea's argument and comes up later in this article. He treats the other two features together here, dwelling especially on the value the Vedas place upon sacrifice for the remission and annulment of sin, using the recurring vedic imagery of sacrifice as the "good ferrying boat" by which humanity may escape sin.[101]

Third, sacrifice was the means by which the *Devas*, originally mere mortals, were promoted to heaven and attained their present status as gods. The way is thus indicated for humanity in general to become glorified and attain to heaven through right performance of sacrifices.[102]

Banerjea presents the heart of his argument in his explanation of the high degree of importance accorded to sacrifice in the Vedas:

> ...the key to the proper understanding of the whole subject was the self-sacrifice of *Prajapati*, the Lord or supporter of the Creation, the "*Purusha* begotten before the world", "the *Viswakarma*, the Author of the universe". The idea is found in all the three great Vedas – Rig, Yajur, and Sama – in Sanhitas, Brahmanas, Aranyakas and Upanishads. The Divine *Purusha* who gave himself up as a sacrifice for the *Devas*, i.e., *emancipated mortals*, had, it is said, desired and got a mortal body *fit for sacrifice*, and himself became *half mortal* and *half immortal*. …he made sacrifice a reflection or figure of himself….[103]

---

[98] Banerjea, *ibid.*, 187; the point is established in detail in Banerjea, *Arian Witness*, 195-197.

[99] Banerjea, *Christianity and Hinduism*, 187-188; cf. Banerjea, *Arian Witness*, 200.

[100] Banerjea, *Arian Witness*, 206.

[101] Banerjea, *Christianity and Hinduism*, 188-189; cf. Banerjea, *Arian Witness*, 202, 208, 210-211.

[102] Banerjea, *Christianity and Hinduism*, 189-190; cf. Banerjea, *Arian Witness*, 201-202.

[103] Banerjea, *Christianity and Hinduism*, 190.

Having thus presented his main hypothesis, he explains that his case is not based on an isolated passage, but that various expressions of the concept of divine sacrifice in the Vedas considered cumulatively, gives it the status of a prominent doctrine.[104] This concept of the divine self-sacrifice of *Prajapati* or *Purusha* constitutes the central motif of the theme of sacrifice in the Vedas, and throws light on other texts relating to the subject.[105]

For instance, the somewhat obscure passage in the Rg Veda which says, "*Viswakarma* had in a universal sacrifice offered all creatures, and then eventually offered Himself also", can be understood on the basis of the biblical teaching that "If one [Christ] died for all, then were all dead" (2 Cor. 5:14, KJV). In Banerjea's explanation: "...the world was condemned, and offered for sacrifice... devoted to destruction, for sin; and the Divine Saviour then offered himself for its deliverance." The biblical doctrine of redemption through the vicarious death of Christ thus finds a remarkable counterpart in the vedic understanding of salvation by the self-sacrifice of *Prajapati*.[106]

For Banerjea, this concurrence of vedic ideas with biblical teaching confirms the truth of Christianity, and is of vital significance for the Christian evangelistic appeal:

> Christian evangelists when they draw our attention to the claims of Gospel truth do not utter things which can be called *strange* to Indian ears. Salvation from sin by the death of a Saviour, who was God and man himself, was a conception which had administered consolation to our ancient *Rishis*, and may yet, in a higher form, and to a greater degree, do the same to all India.[107]

Banerjea believed that the only way to explain the existence of this tradition of a self-sacrificing Saviour in vedic Hindu thought was by assuming its origin in some primeval revelation. The Old Testament figures Abel and Noah must have received true knowledge concerning the meaning and value of sacrifices through divine revelation. Like the pre-Mosaic patriarchs, the ancient Brahmins of India had received them as *Smriti*, or recollections of the original *Sruti*, primitive unwritten revelation, the common inheritance of all mankind.[108] But what was transmitted to these vedic sages through succeeding generations was subject to human error and, hence, inaccurate and distorted.

Consequently, whilst the details of the sacrificial ritual were successfully perpetuated from one generation to the next, the underlying theological

---

[104] Banerjea carefully refutes a prevailing misconception that the self-sacrifice of *Purusha* is a reference to "the barbarous practice of human sacrifices", comparing it to the charge of cannibalism directed against the early church's celebration of the Lord's supper; Banerjea, *Arian Witness*, 204-206.

[105] Banerjea, *Christianity and Hinduism*, 191.

[106] Banerjea, *ibid.*, 191-193.

[107] Banerjea, *ibid.*, 193.

[108] Banerjea, *Arian Witness*, 204, 228.

doctrine could not be accurately preserved and transmitted by means of unwritten tradition.[109] However, although the true significance of sacrifice was lost by the time of the Vedas, the vedic practitioners of sacrifice seem to have recognised its ultimate mysterious and transcendent quality:

> To what extent the Indo-Arians had correctly comprehended the doctrine on which sacrificial ceremonies were founded, we cannot easily guess. But we find they considered it a *mystery*.... They seem to have had an idea that there must be a *really saving Sacrifice*, and that their own ritual was its distant *reflection*.[110]

Banerjea remained convinced that the vedic testimony to the primeval institution of sacrifice had value as a genuine reflection of the Christian doctrine of the vicarious sacrifice of Christ.[111]

In his second proposition, Banerjea points out that the name *Prajapati* not only means the Lord of the creatures, but also supporter, feeder, and deliverer of his creatures, corresponding to the meaning of the name Jesus in the Hebrew, which signifies help, deliverance, and salvation.[112] He draws attention here to the true significance of the practice of sacrifice, which had been lost to the Hindu tradition:

> ...the doctrine of Sacrifice, as a figure of *Prajapati*, ... did not long continue in its integrity among our forefathers; but had fallen into oblivion even before the age of Buddha. The practice of sacrifice continued indeed, but its origin and object... as a figure or type of a self-sacrificing Saviour, had long vanished from the conceptions of our countrymen...[113]

Thus, although the title *Prajapati* has been applied to several characters in the Hindu scriptures, none of them corresponds to the ideal of a self-sacrificing Saviour of the world. Jesus alone fulfils what *Prajapati* stood for in the primitive vedic tradition: he is the true *Prajapati*, the true Saviour of the world, and his Church, the true Ark of salvation.[114]

Banerjea then presents his broader thesis regarding the relation between Christianity and Hinduism "to all who are friends of truth", Christian and Hindu alike, as a means of bridging the gulf which separates them. He believes the Vedas predict the coming of Christ, but compares their testimony to the truth revealed in Jesus as a fragment to the whole: whereas Jesus is the true *Prajapati* or the diamond, the doctrines of the Vedas are only fragments of the

---

[109] Banerjea, *ibid.*, 212.
[110] Banerjea, *ibid.*, 212-213; cf. Banerjea, *Christianity and Hinduism*, 189.
[111] Banerjea, *Arian Witness*, 215-217.
[112] Banerjea, *Christianity and Hinduism*, 194.
[113] Banerjea, *ibid.*, 194-195.
[114] Banerjea, *ibid.*, 195.

diamond sparkling amidst dust. Jesus is the true sun and the true light; the vedic doctrines are planets reflecting the light of the sun feebly.[115]

Banerjea's comments in this regard represent the earliest attempt by an Indian Christian to relate Christian truth to the testimony of the Vedas. However, even at this later stage, Banerjea does not appear to hold a very high view of the Vedas. They possess little light of their own: the "fragments of diamond" in them are partial and derived reflections of truth, the greater portion being likened to dust.

But how does Banerjea distinguish "diamond" from "dust" in his reading of the Vedas? His criterion for discerning truth is clearly Christological: Christ is the standard by which light and truth are identified in the Vedas. This discerning of truth in the Vedas would appear to be an epistemological possibility only for the Christian. He seems to suggest, however, that based on the common faculty of reason, the presence of prefiguring pointers to Christ in the Vedas may be observed by both Christians and Hindus alike.[116]

He appeals to Christians not to allow traditional prejudices to blind their eyes to the evidence of divine light and grace in the Hindu tradition.[117] Likewise, the tolerant Hindu who is open to truth regardless of the source should not have any sense of national humiliation in acknowledging that the Jesus of the New Testament corresponds to the *Prajapati* of the Vedas.[118] Banerjea thus reiterates the basis for his claim that Jesus alone fulfils the ideal of the vedic *Prajapati*:

> The position of *Prajapati*, himself the priest and himself the victim, no member of that [Hindu] Pantheon has dared to occupy. His throne is vacant, and his crown without an owner. No one now can claim that crown and that throne in the hearts of Hindus, who are true to the original teaching of the Vedas, so rightfully as the historical Jesus, Who in name and character, as we have seen, closely resembles our primitive "*Prajapati*".[119]

In the closing paragraphs of his address, Banerjea calls his Hindu brothers to account for the insight that the widespread availability of the Vedas has given them into the purpose of God.[120] He draws analogies from the world of astronomy and medical science, in showing how the Hindu mind has had no difficulty accepting the great improvements of modern science as the fulfilment of principles recorded in the ancient religious texts. In seeking to repudiate the charge of cultural imperialism against Christianity he emphasises the cultural

---

115 Banerjea, *ibid.*, 196.
116 Banerjea, *ibid.*, 196-197, 199.
117 Banerjea, *ibid.*, 196.
118 Banerjea, *ibid.*, 197.
119 Banerjea, *ibid.*, 197; cf. 195f.
120 Banerjea, *ibid.*, 198.

neutrality of Christian faith, which requires only purity of heart, mind, and actions.[121]

Banerjea concludes with the assertion that since Christianity is essentially "Vedic doctrine in its legitimately developed form…", no person can be a true Hindu without being a true Christian. A final impassioned appeal boldly and imaginatively invites Hindu readers to consider his message as the "voice" of their ancestors, the vedic seers:

> ...it is the voice also of your primitive ancestors calling upon you in the voice of their Vedas... not to waver in your duty to acknowledge and embrace the true *Prajapati*, the true *Purusha* begotten before the worlds, who died that you might live, who by death hath vanquished death, and brought life and immortality to light through the Gospel. …You will find in Him everything worthy of your lineage, worthy of your antiquity, worthy of your traditions...[122]

A Critical Analysis of Banerjea's Fulfilment Approach

Banerjea's fulfilment approach is of special importance in the history of Indian Christian thought, since it was one of the earliest attempts by a Hindu convert to relate his Christian faith to his ancestral religion on this basis.[123] In this analysis, we first comment on the distinct impulses which Banerjea's fulfilment approach represented and summarise the distinctive features of his view. Secondly, we need to assess briefly the integrity of Banerjea's interpretation of the vedic sources in the light of recent criticisms concerning his use of vedic texts. Finally, we will apply the fulfilment grid outlined in chapter one in a theological assessment of his view.

A critical impulse shaping Banerjea's approach was his concern to redeem the Christian faith from the charge of foreignness by demonstrating that Hindu converts could pledge allegiance to Christ and remain loyal to their ancestral culture.[124] Thus, despite some formal similarities his earlier apologies bore to those of the missionary apologists, Banerjea's approach was sensitive and reflected a sympathetic and sophisticated grasp of the Hindu religious tradition.

Banerjea devoted his apologetic endeavours to finding points of continuity between Christian faith and the Hindu religious tradition, eventually finding a basis in the Vedas for an evangelistic appeal to Hindus. Philip describes him as

---

[121] Banerjea, *ibid.*, 199-200.

[122] Banerjea, *ibid.*, 200.

[123] T.V. Philip, 'Krishna Mohan Banerjea and Arian Witness to Christ: Jesus Christ the True Prajapati', *Indian Journal of Theology* 29, 2 (1980): 74.

[124] Hedges, too, sees the emerging nationalist spirit as an important impulse in Banerjea's apologetic framework, designed to show that Christianity was not an alien religion to India; Hedges, 'A History and Study', 145-146. This issue was to take on greater importance in subsequent years, and was, in fact, the starting point of Farquhar's apologetic in *Crown of Hinduism*, see p.59.

one of the first Indian Christian thinkers who demonstrated "a clear recognition of the importance of the spiritual heritage of India for the understanding of the Christian Gospel."[125] He was, also the first to refer to converts as "Hindoo Christians", a characterization popularised by Upadhyay in later years.[126]

Banerjea saw a key to his quest for a bridge of continuity between Christianity and Hinduism in the thesis that the Vedas prophetically affirm the fundamental principles of Christian faith in their teaching regarding the self-sacrifice of *Prajapati*, historically fulfilled only in Jesus Christ. This places his notion of fulfilment most naturally within the category we have described earlier as prophetic or promise-fulfilment. The vedic *Prajapati* as a prefigurement of Jesus here corresponds to the Old Testament conception of a promised Messiah, which Jewish Christians saw fulfilled in the person of Jesus of Nazareth. We need, however, to highlight some of the distinctives of Banerjea's prophetic fulfilment view.

First, although there is some formal similarity between Banerjea's manner of citing the Vedas and the New Testament writers' use of the Old Testament, there is a significant theological difference in the two strategies. Banerjea's approach to the Vedas was more analogous to the early fathers' approach to Greek philosophy, and consequently bears some resemblance to their logos-historical fulfilment approach. Just as the fathers discerned certain "fragments of truth" in Greek philosophy, in Banerjea's reading of the Vedas, he perceives "fragments of diamonds sparkling amid dust and mud", which served as preparation for the Christian gospel. Banerjea thus maintains a dialectical attitude to the Vedas, both affirming elements of continuity and distinguishing elements of discontinuity between Christian faith and the vedic tradition.

A second distinctive of Banerjea's approach is an important point of contrast with the views of the early fathers. Whereas the fathers grounded their view in a Logos salvation-history framework, Banerjea based his fulfilment notion on his theory of a primeval revelation. This theory was a distinctive device to establish the theological and historical continuity of Christianity with vedic Hinduism in a universal salvation-history trajectory which culminated in Christ.

Third, Banerjea's fulfilment approach was based on an understanding of the development of Hinduism clearly at odds with that of Max Muller, and developed in a direction quite different from Muller's influential evolutionary fulfilment view. According to Muller's history of religions school, the more recent forms of Hinduism occupied a higher place on the evolutionary continuum, and were thus closer to Christian faith than the older vedic Hinduism. Farquhar's view of fulfilment was also partly conditioned by this theory of the development of religions. Banerjea's view, in contrast, considered earlier vedic Hinduism closer to Judeo-Christian monotheistic religion than

---

[125] Philip, 'Krisna Mohan Banerjea', 125.
[126] Banerjea, *Arian Witness*, 10; see p.30, n. 164.

later Hinduism, and hence did not share the liability of Farquhar's approach in this regard.

Banerjea's work seems to have been received enthusiastically by his contemporaries. According to Maw, this "...reveals as much about the Protestant Church in India as it does about Banerjea's own abilities and reputation. He baffled no one; commendation was mixed with neither confusion nor surprise."[127] Maw, who interprets Banerjea's thought in terms of the Aryan race theory, sees the widespread popularity of Muller's Aryan Race theory and Banerjea's "ingenious erudition", without precedent in the Indian missionary field, as the main reasons for this enthusiastic response.[128] The evidence suggests that, for the most part, Banerjea's view went unchallenged by Christian missionaries within and the Hindu scholarly community without.[129]

H.L. Richard's suggestion that the response to Banerjea's thesis must have been negligible from the scholarly world and the Hindus whom he sought most to convince, is thus misplaced on at least two counts.[130] On one hand, Banerjea's lectures and writings were difficult to ignore, given his stature as a public figure and scholar of considerable repute.[131] Renascent Hindu movements such as the Brahmo Samaj and Arya Samaj, amongst which were some of Banerjea's friends and interlocutors, would have had both reason and the expertise to respond to such a provocative thesis from a man of his influence. Rather than proving that Banerjea's work was not noticed or his voice not heard, the "negligible" response in this case may indicate that Banerjea's thesis was convincing and not easily refuted.

Second, there is evidence that Banerjea's writings were not only widely known, but also met with favourable acceptance in some scholarly circles. In a Christian evaluation of the religion of the Rg Veda published in the same year as Banerjea's *Christianity and Hinduism*, K.S. Macdonald concurs with Banerjea's central thesis, citing his *Arian Witness* in support at several significant points.[132] Macdonald offers the following significant comment towards the end of his discussion:

---

[127] Maw, *Visions of India*, 45, 48-49.

[128] Maw, *ibid.*, 48, 46-49; Hedges is right to disagree with Maw in seeing the basic impulse for Banerjea's thought in his evangelical Christian influence rather than the Aryan race theory, Hedges: *Preparation and Fulfilment*, 144; for Muller's 'Aryan race' theory.

[129] The historical portion of *Arian Witness* met with some objections from "one hostile critic", but none seemed to take issue with Banerjea's theological arguments within the first four years of its publication; Banerjea, *Two Essays*, iii, vi.

[130] Richard, *The Aryan Witness*, 1.

[131] A renowned scholar like Monier-Williams quotes Banerjea in support of some of his views Monier-Williams, *Indian Wisdom* (London: William H. Allen, 1875), xxxvii.

[132] Macdonald makes at least ten references to Banerjea's writings, K.S. Macdonald, *The Vedic Religion or the Creed and Practice of the Indo-Aryans three thousand years*

> In the absence of any other more reasonable explanation of the Vedic sacrifices generally, and of the Purusha or Prajapati sacrifice in particular, I conclude, with the learned and venerable Dr. K.M. Banerjea, that in these sacrifices we find traces of a 'primitive tradition of the Lamb slain from the foundation of the world'.[133]

There is thus some evidence to indicate a positive response to Banerjea's fulfilment approach during his lifetime. The most serious critiques of Banerjea's fulfilment view have not come from any of his contemporaries, but emerged in more recent discussions of his thought. We will consider the more significant of these criticisms as a prelude to our analysis of his fulfilment approach.

H.L. Richard's two-part article, 'The Aryan Witness Recalled: Vedic Sacrifice and Fulfilment Theology', contains the most rigorous critical analysis of Banerjea's view to date.[134] Richard's objections focus on three points: (1) Banerjea's application of a view of myth called "euhemerism"[135] to vedic myths; (2) his method of selective proof-texting to prove a point without regard to the wider context; and, (3) his misinterpretation of the data relating to the vedic teaching on sacrifice.[136]

The first two of these objections do not warrant much discussion, since they are features that mark not only Banerjea's writings, but characterise the broad approach to the study of ancient scriptures in the nineteenth century. Richard himself admits that, in principle, Banerjea follows Max Muller in his adoption of the euhemerist analysis of mythology.[137] Likewise, in the matter of "selective proof-texting", Banerjea's approach had much in common with others engaged in the work of comparative religion, such as Muller, Monier-Williams, or Sen.[138]

---

ago (London: James Nisbet, 1881), 76, 86, 87, 105-106, 220, 243, 244; 73, 88, 216-217; seven of these are to *Arian Witness*, and the others unspecified.

[133]Macdonald, *Vedic Religion*, 243.

[134] Richard, 'The Aryan Witness Recalled'(1993) and Richard, 'The Aryan Witness Recalled (1994); Richard's assessment is based entirely on Banerjea's *Arian Witness*, the theological thesis of which is argued more closely and clearly in Banerjea's later more concise article, *Christianity and Hinduism*.

[135] Named after its founder, the Greek mythographer, Euhemerus, this approach to the interpretation of primitive myths attempts to provide a historical basis for mythical beings and events, by asserting that the gods were originally human heroes and conquerors who were subsequently divinized, *Encyclopaedia Britannica*, s.v."Euhemerism," Encyclopaedia Britannica Online, http://www.britannica.com/EBchecked/topic/195140/Euhemerism (accessed October 14, 2009)

[136] Richard, 'Aryan Witness Recalled', 2-3.

[137] Richard, *ibid.*, 6, n. 8.

[138] In fact, in accordance with his prophetic fulfilment approach, Banerjea's manner of quoting the Vedas is similar to a form of "proof-texting" observed in some New Testament citations of the Old Testament; see R.T. Mead, 'A Dissenting Opinion about Respect for Context in Old Testament Quotations' in *The Right Doctrine from the*

A typical illustration from Muller is his attempt to show that the "highest truth of Christianity" – loving one's enemies and overcoming evil with good – was present in many of the non-Christian religions of the world. He quotes texts which seem to echo this teaching of Christ, from Lao-tze, Confucius, the Buddha, the *Hitopadesa*,[139] and a Persian poet named Hafiz, without regard to their broader historical or literary context.[140] Similarly, Sen often cites Christian texts to establish a point without regard to their wider context. Christ's words, "I and my Father are one", are thus used to justify an essentially Hindu understanding of self-abnegation and the eradication of the self as the basis of Christ's experience of identity with the Godhead.[141] The "proof-texting" method is also applied as Sen sees the Vedantic idea of absorption and immersion in the deity in Christ's prayer, "As Thou Father art in me, and I in Thee, that they also may be one in us".[142]

Thus, the worst that can be said about Banerjea with regard to the charge of "euhemerism" and "proof-texting", is that both his method and insights were constrained by the existing horizons of knowledge and the tools of critical study available in his time.

Richard's most serious criticism addresses Banerjea's interpretation of the vedic teaching regarding sacrifice. He summarises the foundation for Banerjea's 'fulfilment' claims in relation to sacrifice in terms of five points:

> 1. Sacrifice was an essential part of Vedic worship. 2. Every variety of blessing was considered to be available through sacrifice. 3. The gods themselves attained heaven by sacrifice. 4. Sacrifice is sometimes associated with sin. 5. The sacrifice of God himself is a fairly common theme.[143]

The centrality of sacrifice to vedic life is, of course, impossible to contest. According to Walker: "Sacrifice was one of the main pillars of the Vedic religious system, and... sacrifice an essential condition of salvation.... "[144] Aguilar describes it as, "the origin of everything... the principle *par excellence*... the navel of the world", and "...not only the central act of religion,

---

Wrong Texts? Essays on the Use of the Old Testament in the New, ed. G.K. Beale (Grand Rapids: Baker, 1994).

[139] Sanskrit collection of fables.

[140] F.M. Muller, *Physical Religion* (New Delhi: Asian Educational Services, 1979), 359-363.

[141] D.C. Scott, ed. 'Who is Christ?' in *Keshub Chunder Sen* (Madras: CLS, 1979), 203-205.

[142] Scott, 'Who is Christ?' 211-214.

[143] Richard, 'Aryan Witness Recalled', 3.

[144] B. Walker, *Hindu World: An Encyclopedic Survey of Hinduism*, vol. 2 (New Delhi: Munshiram Manoharlal Publishers, 1983), 316.

but also the supreme principle of all things.... "[145] Richard thus has no difficulty with the first two assertions.[146]

Richard's objections to Banerjea's argument begin with the third point, in which he seems to treat literally and euhemeristically the vedic account of gods who were previously men, attaining deity through sacrifices.[147] His real contention with Banerjea's thesis, however, is expressed in the fourth and fifth points. In the fourth point, he concedes that "The Vedas and Brahmanas have a significant number of references to sin and cleansing from sin", but then observes that sacrifice and cleansing of sin are not related often enough to justify Banerjea's claim "...that sacrifice is the means for cleansing sin.... He is clearly here reading Biblical meaning into non-Biblical texts."[148]

The reading of "biblical meaning into non-biblical texts" integral to Banerjea's approach raises a theological question that we will address subsequently. The immediate context, however, suggests that Richard's objection is that Banerjea's association of sacrifice with cleansing or forgiveness of sin does not have adequate basis in the vedic texts. Richard indicates that in the examples Banerjea cites, the term *durita* which he renders "sin" has a much wider range of meaning.[149]

In response, it must be pointed out that Banerjea does not limit the benefits of sacrifice only to cleansing from sin. The broader benefits of sacrifice are usually mentioned in his discussions before he highlights its efficacy for the annulment of sins, an emphasis natural and necessary to the overall direction of his argument.[150] The question is whether there is adequate textual basis for Banerjea's claim that cleansing from sin is also one of the benefits of sacrifice.[151]

---

[145] H. Aguilar, *The Sacrifice in the Rgveda (Doctrinal Aspects)* (Delhi: Bharatiya Vidya Prakashan, 1976), 18, 57, 195.

[146] Richard acknowledges the centrality of sacrifice in vedic theology, life and worship, citing Raimundo Panikkar's assessment that the word *Yagna*, sacrifice, most adequately expresses "the quintessence of the Vedic Revelation" in a single word, Richard, 'Aryan Witness Recalled', 3; cf. R. Panikkar, *The Vedic Experience: Mantramanjali* (Pondicherry: All India Books, 1989), 347.

[147] Banerjea's argument is not undermined even if this point is conceded: his real concern is to emphasise the value of sacrifice in promoting men to heaven and immortality, Banerjea, *Arian Witness*, 201; Banerjea, *Christianity and Hinduism*, 190; cf. Panikkar, *Vedic Experience*, 380-381.

[148] Richard, 'Aryan Witness Recalled', 4.

[149] Richard thus rightly observes that Griffith's translation of the Rg Veda does not render *durita* as sin in any of Banerjea's examples, Richard, 'Aryan Witness Recalled, (1993), 4.

[150] Banerjea, *Arian Witness*, 200-203; Banerjea, *Christianity and Hinduism*, 187-188; Banerjea, *Two Essays*, 57, 59.

[151] Studies in the last couple of decades have not only tried to recover the importance of the vedic concept of *yajna* (sacrifice) as a central category for understanding the development of Hinduism, they have also highlighted the complexity of issues involved

The idea that sin brings discord to the divinely established cosmic order, the belief that retribution follows sin, and that the divinity can be propitiated, may all be legitimately inferred from the vedic texts.[152] The desire to be freed from sin and prayers for forgiveness are expressed in a significant number of Rg vedic hymns.[153] In several places, cleansing from sin is explicitly stated to be a benefit of sacrifice or implied by the context.[154] Several scholars clearly see expiation and the forgiveness of sins, as one of the impulses of the vedic *yajna*: "...if the sin is violation of divine will and thereby provocation of divine wrath, the act of expiation is addressed to the god; he is gratified and pacified through gifts...."[155]

Zaehner lists the removal of "'sin' incurred by contact with taboo objects or by incorrect performance of the ritual", as one of the three purposes of sacrifice.[156] Against the criticism that the consciousness of sin was absent from vedic religion, Radhakrishnan argues that:

> The Vedic conception of sin is analogous to the Hebrew theory.... We sin when we transgress the commands of God. The gods are the upholders of the Rta, the moral order of the world. They protect the good and punish the wicked. Sin is not merely the omission of the external duties. There are moral sins as well as ritual sins. It is a consciousness of sin that calls for propitiatory sacrifices.[157]

Jose Thachil's study delineates the efficacy of sacrifice to remit sins as one of the four similarities between the concept of sacrifice in Vedic Hinduism and Christianity:

> In the Vedic Religion as well as in Christianity, sacrifice is regarded as a means for remission of sins though there is difference with regard to emphasis... we find

---

in arriving at a precise understanding of the vedic *yajna*. Our intent is simply to indicate that Banerjea's perspective on this issue is at least a valid alternative which finds some support in modern scholarship, see David Scott's "Foreword" in Selvanayagam, *Vedic Sacrifice*, 11-20, 29-50, 81.

[152] See Miller, *The Vision of Cosmic Order in the Vedas* (London: Routledge & Kegan Paul, 1985), 141-150, 161-170; Potdar, *Sacrifice in the Rgveda*, 280.

[153] For instance: *RV* I.31.15-16; 157.4; 189.1,5; II.28.3-5,9; 29.1,5-6; IV.12.4-5; 54.3; V.85.7-8; VII.86.2-7; X.63.6-8; cf. Miller, *Vision of Cosmic Order*, 171-182.

[154] For instance: *RV* I.23.17-22; 24.9-15; 34.9-11; 114.4; 162.22; VI.74.1-3; VII.51.1; 93.7-8; X.105.8-9.

[155] Oldenberg, *The Religion of the Veda*, trans. S.B. Shrotri (Delhi: Motilal Banarsidass, 1988), 182-187; cf. Potdar, *Sacrifice in the Rgveda*, 281.

[156] R.C. Zaehner, *At Sundry Times: An Essay in the Comparison of Religions* (London: Faber and Faber, 1985), 44-45.

[157] S. Radhakrishnan, *Indian Philosophy* (London: George Allen & Unwin Limited, 1962), 108-109.

a similarity between the Vedic and the Christian concepts of sacrifice, on the basis of the efficacy of sacrifice to remit sins.[158]

Richard's fifth point brings us to the climax of Banerjea's argument and the most controversial aspect of his thesis. Richard has no difficulty with Banerjea's identification of the self-sacrifice of *Prajapati* as a key motif for understanding vedic sacrifice.[159] What he objects to is Banerjea's inference that the vedic figure of the self-sacrificing *Prajapati* reflects an ancient revealed truth that points to Christ.

In the first of three arguments, Richard accepts Banerjea's employment of the *purusha-sukta* text[160] as a *locus classicus* for affirming the sacrifice of God himself as a key to understanding vedic sacrifice. However, based on its late dating insists that: "...it is far better to see this as a myth developed to justify the practice of sacrifice rather than Banerjea's reading of it as a foundational theory underlying all sacrificial practices."[161]

Although the *purusha-sukta* text represents one of the latest hymns of the Rg Veda, it is also regarded as preserving a very primitive belief regarding the origin of the world from the body of a primeval giant.[162] Thus within the tradition as recorded, is a myth which antedates the text itself. Although this by no means confirms Banerjea's hypothesis, it does indicate that his interpretation need not be excluded on grounds of the late dating of the text. Furthermore, it suggests that the complex process by which tradition is transmitted and recorded does not preclude the possibility of several layers of tradition being recorded within the final form of a given text.

Richard's second, more critical argument is stated as follows:

> The *purusha-sukta* is a rich mine for all kinds of ideas, and only the bravest interpreter would dare to claim to have adequately and truly analysed it. But on one broad point there is no room for debate, and that point alone explodes Banerjea's interpretation. *The cosmic sacrifice of the Deity presented in Vedic texts and hymns is an account of creation and is never associated with redemption.*[163]

---

[158] J. Thachil, *The Vedic and the Christian Concept of Sacrifice* (Alwaye: Pontifical Institute of Theology and Philosophy, 1985), 335, 337-350 also indicates several points of difference between the vedic and Christian conceptions of sacrifice.

[159] Banerjea is clearly within the bounds of textual evidence at this point since *Purusa/Prajapati*, the highest principle, is constantly identified with sacrifice in the Vedas: Aguilar, *Sacrifice in the Rgveda*, 199; cf. Panikkar, *The Vedic Experience*, 348f, 381f; Thachil, *Vedic and the Christian Concept of Sacrifice*, 44-45.

[160] *RV* x.90.

[161] Richard, 'Aryan Witness Recalled', (1993), 5.

[162] Macdonell, 'Vedic Religion', 602; Deshmukh, *Origin and Development of Religion*, 327, 329.

[163] Richard, 'Aryan Witness Recalled', 5.

In the vedic scheme of things, however, the theme of redemption is closely interwoven with the fact of creation. Panikkar's commentary clarifies that not only is *Prajapati* the primordial being through whose self-sacrifice creation comes into being, but the created order thus brought into being, one with although distinct from *Prajapati*, "...must attempt by means of sacrifice to recover its true status, to return to its source, retrieve its unity, that is, to become immortal, divinized."[164] Thus, if immortality is the ultimate goal of "redemption", then sacrifice is the way to immortality, and the self-sacrifice of *Prajapati*, the original primordial life-giving act: "...all sacrifice involves a dying. But this immolation is a dying-for-life, for the sacrifice in the very act of dying renews itself within the universe; it is thus a universal principle of life, everywhere in operation."[165]

Essentially the same insight emerges more explicitly from Malieckal's study on the theology of sacrifice. Describing the creative and redemptive aspects of the vedic teaching in terms of a "sacrificial trajectory" which begins in the highest heaven, passes through the earth and again ends in the highest heaven, he makes the observation that "...viewed from the sacrificial perspective, creation in its integral sense includes also re-integration, redemption."[166] He then uses this basic insight to analyse the vedic texts relating to sacrifice. Malieckal traces this trajectory in the *Purusa-sukta* and confirms the essential continuity between the creative and redemptive aspects of vedic sacrifice in the following comment:

> There is a continuity and unity of what may be called the creative and redemptive dimensions of sacrifice in the Vedic sense; the sacrifice of man on earth has a special 'redemptive' character; it is his *sahakarma* (co-operation) with the *karma* (sacrifice) of Prajapati.... Thus in a way the symbolism of the sacrificial post, its double aspect of manifestation and re-unification – Vedic idea of creation and redemption – approximates the symbolism of the Cross of Jesus Christ.[167]

Aguilar's interpretation of the Rg vedic conception of sacrifice, likewise, also affirms the continuity and unity of the creative and redemptive aspects of sacrifice:

> In relation to the Vedic image of the World... the myth of Purusa/Prajapati reveals to us in an authentic way that the cosmic processes of separation and reunion which constitute the creation and redemption of the world... are not merely

---

[164] Panikkar, *Vedic Experience*, 381.
[165] Panikkar, *ibid.*, 387.
[166] L. Malieckal, *Yajna and Sacrifice: An Inter-religious Approach to the Theology of Sacrifice* (Bangalore: Dharmaram Publications, 1989), 22-23.
[167] Malieckal, *Yajna and Sacrifice*, 130.

> mechanical, unconscious processes, but they are dominated by a spiritual law of perfect altruism leading to a self immolation, full of understanding and love.[168]

He sees the relation between the older myth of the Lord of trees and that of *Purusa/Prajapati* expressed in terms that closely parallel the Christian account of the crucifixion, with the symbolism of the cosmic tree as the sacrificial post for the sacrifice of *Prajapati* bearing close resemblance to the Christian symbolism of the cross.[169] He thus concludes that: "...the interchange which takes place between the divine and human planes by means of the sacrifice is... something touching the entire economy of the creation and redemption according to the Vedas."[170]

Third, Richard objects to Banerjea's application to Christ of the representation of *Prajapati* as half mortal and half immortal in the *Satapatha Brahmana.*[171] Richard regards this as inappropriate since the worldview of the *Satapatha Brahmana* is far removed from that of the Bible, and the orientation of the *Prajapati* myth incompatible with Banerjea's application of it to Christ. This leads to a critical issue at the heart of fulfilment theology: the legitimacy of a Christian reading of non-Christian texts. We will address this question at various points in our study, but note now that the strategy that Banerjea employed in reorienting a concept having connotations originally foreign to the Christian framework in accordance with Christological truth, is not peculiar to Banerjea, but common to many expressions of fulfilment theology.

The support we have drawn from various scholars in responding to objections to Banerjea's case does not imply that they all share the same framework of interpretation with respect to the Vedas or the Bible and Christian faith. The aspects of broad concurrence have been drawn upon to counter objections to Banerjea's reading of the vedic texts. Although Banerjea's original interpretation of the vedic teaching on sacrifice may seem eccentric at some points due to its fulfilment orientation, we have reasonable grounds for inferring that sacrifice was an essential part of vedic worship; that it was considered a means of obtaining a variety of material and spiritual blessings; that it was associated with the annulment and cleansing of sin; and, that the self-sacrifice of *Prajapati* is an important interpretive key for understanding the vedic teaching on sacrifice. Thus, the only point at dispute in Banerjea's argument is his incorporation of the primordial self-sacrifice of the vedic *Prajapati* figure within a prophetic fulfilment scheme in which Christ is identified as the true *Prajapati*, who sacrificed his life for all humanity.

We will discuss this further after addressing three important issues in Banerjea's approach: the pedagogical use of the Vedas; his employment of the

---

[168] Aguilar, *Sacrifice in the Rgveda*, 143-144.
[169] Aguilar, *ibid.*, 145-147.
[170] Aguilar, *ibid.*, 150-151.
[171] *SB Satapatha Brahmana* X.1.3-4; Banerjea, *Christianity and Hinduism*, 182, 190.

concept of a universal primeval revelation as a device for establishing theological continuity between Christianity and Hinduism; and the claim that the concept of *Prajapati* is a prophetic prefigurement fulfilled in Jesus Christ.

Use of the Vedas

An important presupposition of Banerjea's fulfilment approach was his definition of Hinduism as "the religion of the Vedas".[172] Muller's Aryan race theory based on the Vedas, and the growth in influence of the Arya Samaj had greatly enhanced the authority of the Vedas among the educated classes in India.[173] Banerjea realised that to convince the educated Hindu community of the relevance of the Christian gospel, he would have to show its relation to the ancient religion and culture of India. He saw more hope for such a meeting point in the Vedas than in the philosophical schools that developed later.[174]

The dependence of Banerjea's apologetic method upon the Vedas raises two questions: (1) How did he view the inspiration and authority of the Vedas in relation to that of the Bible? (2) How legitimate is his approach in drawing support for a Christian doctrine from Hindu religious texts? The importance of these questions is highlighted by the fact that the only serious and immediate controversy seemingly raised by Banerjea's work challenged his claim that pointers to the "sacred mysteries" of the Christian faith could be found in a "heathen Sastra".[175]

The publication of *Arian Witness* marked a distinct shift in Banerjea's attitude to the authority of the Vedas. In contrast to the earlier largely subversive attitude reflected in *Dialogues*, he was now prepared to grant the Vedas some degree of historical authenticity as authoritative accounts of the original Hinduism in its purest form. This is made explicit in his claim that he did not know of any people, apart from the Jewish nation, who possessed "...such an approximation to the Scriptural teaching... as is found in the ancient Arian records."[176]

---

[172] See p.107.

[173] Baago's suggestion that Banerjea's regard for the Vedas was inspired by the Arya Samaj leader, Dayanand Saraswati, seems unlikely. His more ambivalent attitude to the Vedas is better explained by the rationalistic Derozian influences of the earlier years; Baago, *Pioneers of Indigenous Christianity*, 12; Maw, *Visions of India*, 46.

[174] Banerjea's favourable attitude was primarily towards vedic religion; there is no indication of any significant change in later years in the negative attitude towards philosophical Hinduism reflected in his *Dialogues*.

[175] See p.106.

[176] Banerjea, *Arian Witness*, 194; cf. Goreh's similar conviction, N. Goreh, *A Rational Refutation of the Hindu Philosophical Systems* (Calcutta: Bishop's College Press; original Hindi title *Shaddarshana Darpana*, 1860), 40.

A cursory reading of his later writings suggests that Banerjea was trying to make the Vedas serve as the functional equivalent of the Old Testament for the Hindu-Christian, quoting vedic texts in much the same manner as the New Testament writers use the Old Testament. The Vedas are frequently cited with introductory phrases like "the Rig Veda declares…", and "the Vedas say…", but most often quotations from the Vedas as well as references to vedic teaching occur in the text – usually with annotation in a foot-note – as a matter of course, to illustrate correspondence with Christian teaching. For instance:

> The Vedic writers say distinctly that the Lord of the Creation, himself a Purusha begotten in the beginning (or before the worlds) offered himself a sacrifice.... Then they say that the Author of the Universe sacrificed all creatures to Himself and eventually sacrificed himself for them. The meaning of this is doubtless obscure, but it conversely fits in the apostolical idea that 'if Christ died for all, then were all dead.'[177]

The quotation or reference is usually made to demonstrate that a particular aspect of Christian teaching has been foreshadowed in the Vedas. His conclusion is stated quite simply as follows: "The Vedas foreshew the Epiphany of Christ. The Vedas shed a peculiar light upon that dispensation of Providence which brought Eastern sages to worship Christ long before the Westerns had even heard of Him."[178] The "foreshewing" here refers primarily, of course, to the vedic ideal of *Prajapati* as a self-sacrificing divine figure, fulfilled in the life and ministry of Christ.

Did Banerjea then regard the Vedas as having a place on par with the Old Testament in the economy of divine revelation? Banerjea seems to acknowledge the presence of light or revealed truth in some portions of the Vedas. He briefly alludes to this in *Arian Witness*,[179] but the second of his *Two Essays* was written expressly to defend the claim that the Vedas could have references to the truths of Christian faith. The significance of this is clarified in *The Relation between Christianity and Hinduism*: the discovery of certain "germs of *Christian* mysteries in the *Heathen* Vedas" indicates that God has given some light to certain Indian *Rishis*, the authors of the Vedas.[180]

In explaining the presence of certain Christian doctrines in the Vedas, Banerjea clarifies that this does not equate their authority with that of the Old or New Testaments:

> ...these doctrines, I say, which had appeared in our Vedas amid much rubbish, and things worse than rubbish, may be viewed as fragments of diamonds sparkling amid dust and mud, testifying to some invisible fabric of which they were

[177] Banerjca, *Two Essays*, 70.
[178] Banerjea, *Christianity and Hinduism*, 196.
[179] Banerjea, *Arian Witness*, 228.
[180] Banerjea, *Christianity and Hinduism*, 198.

> component parts, and bearing witness like planets over a dark horizon to the absent sun of whom their refulgence was but a feeble reflection.[181]

Thus, although he took the light in the Vedas very seriously, Banerjea clearly did not treat the Vedas on par with the Christian scriptures. The "germs" or "fragments" of truth in the Vedas were identified as such based on the criterion of concurrence with Christian doctrine. The Christian scriptures clearly seem to serve a normative function in a summary comparison of the vedic and biblical accounts of sacrifice in *Two Essays*:

> In the whole description of the patriarchal dispensation, the Veda seems to follow the lines of the Bible – the only difference being in the greater clearness and the still greater firmness and certainty of decision with which monotheism is upheld in the Jewish Scriptures....[182]

The point is made more explicit in a subsequent exposition regarding the significance of the vedic teaching on sacrifice:

> Here then we have a teaching the rudiments of which are scarcely different from the rudiments of Christianity, and which can receive its accomplishment from Christianity alone. But the rudiments were never set together to form a practical system in the Veda itself. They remained as scattered fragments indicative of some primeval Revelation.... Those fragments were some of them among the very *arcana* of Gospel Truth, and their embodiment can only be regulated by that Truth.[183]

The New Testament writers accepted the Old Testament in its integrity as divinely inspired and authoritative revelation. Banerjea, in contrast, is eclectic in his use of the Vedas, viewing Christian truths within them as "germs" of truth or "fragments of diamonds sparkling amid dust and mud". Banerjea shares the New Testament writers' experience of Christ, and consequently sees Christ and the Christian gospel in the Vedas, reading them through Christian eyes in much the same way as the New Testament writers read the Old Testament.

In this respect Banerjea's approach is closer to the early fathers' attitude to Greek philosophy. Clement of Alexandria, for instance, clearly perceived certain "fragments of truth" in Greek philosophy as having a pedagogical function for the Greeks similar to that of the Law for the Jews. But while he regarded Greek philosophy as a pedagogy to Christ, he carefully distinguished the action of the *Logos* in Greek philosophy from the inspiration of the Hebrew prophets.[184] Thus, although Banerjea's citation of the vedic texts bears formal

---

[181] Banerjea, *ibid.*, 196.
[182] Banerjea, *Two Essays*, 69-70.
[183] Banerjea, *ibid.*, 72.
[184] Saldanha, *Divine Pedagogy: A Patristic View of Non-Christian Religions* (Rome:

similarities to the New Testament writers' use of the Old Testament, his attitude to the Vedas is theologically more analogous to the early fathers' approach to Greek philosophy.

Banerjea's Christianinterpretation of the Vedas raises a second critical issue: the legitimacy of drawing support for a Christian doctrine through the selective use of Hindu religious texts. This issue relates properly to the broader thesis of fulfilment theology, and will hence be addressed in greater detail towards the end of our study. However, some observations at this stage will help clear the ground for our subsequent discussion.

There are two aspects to the issue. The first is hermeneutical and epistemological: Does a text have only one acceptable meaning, and is this meaning only determined by the rules of historical critical interpretation? Or, can a text also have a derived significance, conditioned by the interpretative rules of a given community? Thus, to what extent is a Christianreading of a non-Christian text an authentic reading? There is, secondly, the broader theological question of how the Christian gospel relates to culture. On what basis do Christians claim the right to interpret a cultural tradition other than their own in terms of their distinctive faith experience?

First, Banerjea's claim to see Christ prefigured in the vedic concept of *Prajapati* must be recognized as an authentic attempt by a Hindu-Christian to relate his experience of Christ to his own ancestral tradition. He was the first to claim that the *Prajapati* concept in the Vedas prefigured Christ, a conclusion he only arrived at several years after his conversion to Christianity. Despite his insistence that his claim is based on objective evidence, so that no person can be a true Hindu without being a true Christian, his is a distinctly Christian interpretation, with which orthodox Hindu scholarship may not necessarily agree.

Christian faith is grounded originally and intrinsically in a claim that parallels Banerjea's Christian interpretation of the Vedas. The primary biblical resources for fulfilment theology are grounded in the historically self-defining claims of Christian faith. The earliest Jewish converts to Christianity reviewed their tradition from the perspective of their experience of Christ and concluded that the coming of Christ fulfilled the messianic expectations of the Jewish scriptures, an interpretation which the Jewish establishment dismissed as heretical. Similarly, the early fathers applied Christological criteria to their interpretation of both the Old Testament and Greek philosophy, and their conclusions, too, were unacceptable to the orthodox. Banerjea's fulfilment approach thus illustrates a straightforward application of the New Testament Jewish-Christian promise-fulfilment model, and confirms our earlier hypothesis

Las), 1984), 132-136; H. de Lubac, *The Church: Paradox and Mystery* (Shannon, Ireland: Ecclesia Press, 1969), 68.

explaining the common appropriation of the fulfilment impulse by Indian converts in the pre-independence period.[185]

When Banerjea interprets his pre-Christian tradition with a Christological grid derived from his experience of Christ, he is only following the lead of his Jewish Christian and patristic theological predecessors. Their universal Christian vision led them to consider a Christological interpretation of creation and culture as a mandatory aspect of their theological task. Banerjea's `Christian' reading of the Vedas was thus an inevitable obligation arising from his understanding of the gospel itself.

We turn then to the second issue of how the gospel relates to culture, a critical component of the Church's theological task arising from the Christian claim to universality. Banerjea was one of the earliest Hindu converts who attempted to demonstrate Christ's universality not by excluding the ancient religious heritage of India, but by penetrating deeply the heart of its sources. As a Hindu-Christian, Banerjea stands on the same ground as the early Jewish Christians or early fathers, who could legitimately claim the ancestral tradition into which they were born as their own. They were entitled to their distinctive interpretation of their personal religious pilgrimage, and also obliged to offer an explanation for their conversion in a way that took account of their pre-Christian experience.

Primeval Revelation

The dependence of Banerjea's fulfilment approach on the Vedas was integrally related to his view of a universal primeval revelation.[186] In *Dialogues*, he cites as evidence the almost universal idea in India of an eternal Veda: "The mystery can only be explained on the supposition of some distorted tradition existing among the Brahmins of a primitive revelation from God."[187]

In his early theological development, Banerjea evidently rejected the possibility that this primitive revelation was contained in the four Vedas: "...no one can pretend that they [the Vedas] are a record of the primeval Sound... there is nothing in the general scope of the Vedas to justify the conclusion that they were revealed in the beginning."[188] The Brahmins may have been aware of

---

[185] See pp.11-12, 44-45.

[186] Banerjea's preferred term, but used interchangeably with "primitive" revelation, and understood as "a body of supernatural truths revealed to man at the beginning of the human race and passed down over the centuries, with remnants of this revelation embedded in primitive religions"; Banerjea uses the term in this sense, but a broader alternative definition is: "all pre-Judaic revelation of God", *New Catholic Encyclopedia*, vol. XII, s.v. "Revelation, Primitive" (New York: McGraw-Hill Book Co., 1957), 440.

[187] The "mystery" refers to the strong tradition of the Vedas' authority, despite what Banerjea regarded as weak rational and philosophical justification, Banerjea, *Dialogues on Hindu Philosophy*, 383.

[188] Banerjea, *Dialogues on Hindu Philosophy*, 385.

the general fact of primitive revelation, but "...their incoherent accounts of the Vedas are but distorted representations of that *fact*..."[189]

The Vedas were thus clearly distinguished from primitive revelation. This primitive revelation is rather identified with *s'abda*, "the primeval Sound", infallible and eternal teaching, an original divine communication given to the first man for the good of all humankind:[190]

> We can have no difficulty in believing that the Almighty made a communication of His will to our first parents when He created them.... That which the first man thus heard from His Maker, was a *s'abda*, an infallible teaching, intended for the benefit of others, *i.e.*, mankind, and coeval with the commencement of human society.[191]

He viewed this primitive revelation in *Dialogues* as the source of the *avatara* idea in the *Bhagvadgita* as well as the vedic conception of sacrifice.[192] In *Arian Witness*, the primitive revelation concept is used to explain how the biblical teaching of Christ's redemptive sacrifice finds such clear resonance with the vedic concept of the self-sacrifice of *Prajapati.*[193] The vedic pointers to biblical teaching are thus "...independent Arian testimonies to facts disclosed by a primeval revelation, the heritage of all mankind alike."[194] Despite their close correspondence with Jewish tradition, there is no evidence that these facts were borrowed, but appear rather to have been preserved within Indian tradition "as a relic of unwritten primitive Revelation".[195]

He concedes that elements of this "unwritten primitive revelation" are contained in the "written" tradition in some portions of the Vedas:

> The Brahmins... used the word "Sruti," or *hearing*, as a general term for such primitive unwritten Revelation. The four Vedas into which the Sruti was afterwards classified, and written down, became the recognized Scriptures of the country. We have no reason to doubt that parts of those Scriptures were the correct *Smriti*, or recollections, of the original *Sruti* or traditional report of a real primitive Revelation - the common inheritance of all mankind...[196]

Thus, whereas in *Dialogues* the Vedas are but "distorted representations" of the fact of primitive revelation, they are here – in portions at least – "...the correct *Smriti*, or recollections" of primitive revelation.

---

[189] Banerjea, *Claims of Christianity*, 175-176.
[190] Banerjea, Dialogues on Hindu Philosophy, 383-385.
[191] Banerjea, *ibid.*, 384.
[192] Banerjea, *ibid.*, 405-406, 397-398.
[193] Banerjea, *Arian Witness*, 203, 214.
[194] Banerjea, *ibid.*, 227-228.
[195] Banerjea, *ibid.*, 228.
[196] Banerjea, *ibid.*, 228; cf. Banerjea, *Two Essays*, 72.

This theory of a primitive revelation is assumed throughout Banerjea's argument in *The Relation between Christianity and Hinduism*, clearly implied in his first proposition, and a critical component of the second. He thus declares that the real significance of the doctrine of sacrifice and of the self-sacrifice of *Prajapati* was "...a fragment of a great scheme of salvation... partially revealed" in the Vedas, subsequently lost in India, but "...has since appeared in its integrity in the Person of Jesus Christ".[197] The main point of this argument, driven home in his subsequent evangelistic appeal, is that the ancient *rishis* who authored the Vedas received and transmitted oral traditions of a primitive revelation, which gave them rudimentary prophetic insight into the saving truth revealed fully in Christ.[198]

According to Richard, Banerjea alone bases his fulfilment approach on a universal primeval revelation.[199] The evidence, however, suggests otherwise. We have observed that a similar conception of an "original" or "primordial" revelation was an important aspect of the fulfilment view of Monier-Williams.[200] Monier-Williams' acquaintance with some of Banerjea's writings makes mutual influence very probable.[201] But Monier-Williams, too, believed that God had made an original revelation to the whole of mankind at the beginning of time that was lost or abandoned, remnants of which continued to persist down through the centuries as truths present in different religions. This thought is echoed in the writings of several other scholars.[202]

Acknowledging his dependence on Monier-Williams, James Vaughan also assumes the theory of a primitive revelation.[203] We see in Frederick Cook's work a similar recognition of the presence of truth in other religions on the basis of a primeval revelation given to the original ancestors of the human race.[204] After evaluating the evidence, Macdonald, too, concurs with Banerjea's position on this issue:

> Consider all these texts together, and you will see the force of Dr. Banerjea's conclusion, – that it is not easy to account for the genesis of the idea underlying Prajapati... offering himself a sacrifice... 'except on the assumption of some primitive tradition of the Lamb slain from the foundation of the world...'[205]

---

[197] Banerjea, *Christianity and Hinduism*, 195.
[198] Banerjea, *ibid.*, 198.
[199] Richard, 'Aryan Witness Recalled (1994), 1.
[200] See p.22.
[201] Monier-Williams, *Indian Wisdom*, xxxvii thus quotes Banerjea favourably in his discussion of the Hindu account of creation as a point of contact with Christianity.
[202] Monier-Williams, *ibid.*, 153f.
[203] J. Vaughan, *The Trident, the Crescent and the Cross* (London: Longmans, Green, 1876), 67-70.
[204] F.C. Cook, *The Origins of Religion and Language* (London, 1884), vi-vii.
[205] Macdonald, *Vedic Religion*, 87.

Maurice Phillips' study of vedic religion concludes with a similar assessment:

> It is difficult to account for the origin of the idea underlying the sacrifice of Prajapati ...except on the supposition of some primitive tradition of Jesus.... The theory of a Primitive Divine Revelation alone is capable of explaining all the religious ideas of the Vedas.[206]

Banerjea's employment of the concept of primeval revelation thus did have a certain measure of acceptance among scholarly circles of his time.[207] It is unfortunate that Banerjea does not clearly explain his understanding of the relationship between natural theology, primitive revelation, and God's revelation in Christ.

Richard fails to do justice to the various nuances in Banerjea's thought when he insists categorically that Banerjea never refers to natural revelation, and that his espousal of the primitive revelation idea prevents him from allowing "...even a hint that there was revelation granted to the ancient sages of Hinduism."[208] This lapse may result from the fact that Richard bases his analysis almost entirely *Arian Witness*, while passages in Banerjea's earlier and later writings clearly contradict Richard's assessment at this point.

Banerjea clearly acknowledges that some measure of the knowledge of God is accessible to natural reason: "Whatever it is within the power of reason to discover, does not need the assistance of revelation. Such questions are left to be determined by the light of nature."[209] The "book of nature" cannot contradict the "book of revelation", hence it is both man's duty and privilege to study this "book of nature", which sets forth fully the power and wisdom of the Creator God.[210]

Banerjea indicates that some intimations of the knowledge of God in Hinduism may be the result of the "light of nature" extending to the human heart. He thus suggests that the references of Patanjali[211] to *Is'wara pranidhana*, or divine contemplation, must be accepted "as a pleasing witness to that religious sentiment, which God has implanted in human nature, and which is indeed the most satisfactory evidence of His existence."[212]

---

206 M. Phillips, *The Teaching of the Vedas* (1894; repr., Delhi: Low Price Publications, 1995), 225, 231-232.

207 This is perhaps why, as Maw notes, Duff seems to have no problems with this theory, which seems to have had fairly widespread acceptance and endorsement even among conservative evangelicals, Maw, *Visions of India*, 42-43, 48-49; see also Hedges, 'History and Study of Fulfilment', 144, 148-149.

208 Richard, 'Aryan Witness Recalled', 1.

209 Banerjea, *Dialogues on Hindu Philosophy*, 15.

210 Banerjea, *ibid.*, 15-16.

211 The founder of the Yoga school of Hindu philosophy.

212 Banerjea, *Dialogues on Hindu Philosophy*, 52-53.

The concept of natural revelation is not prominent in Banerjea's later thought, but there is no reason to presume that he gave up the idea altogether. Writing several years later in *The Relation between Christianity and Hinduism*, he commences his discussion of the concept of God in the Rg Veda with an introduction to natural theology, appealing to the evidence of God in creation, accessible to the human mind.[213] He clearly implies that some elements of a natural theology based on human reason have found their way into the Vedas. Thus, contrary to Richard's assessment, there are allusions to natural theology in Banerjea's thought, although he fails to clarify adequately its relation to his notion of primeval revelation.[214]

Banerjea says significantly more concerning the relation between primeval revelation and the revelation of God in Christ. His earlier view was that the Christian teaching elucidates the nebulous Hindu notion of revelation:

> The minds of our ancestors were universally imbued with notions of a Revelation or supernatural communication to man, but they could not explain what that Revelation was, or how it was given... Christianity steps in and affords an explanation... God did make supernatural communications to man in the infancy of human society.[215]

Subsequently, more content is ascribed to the primitive revelation within Hinduism, and its function as a pedagogy to Christ clearly stated:

> I have shown that your primitive fathers had an insight, doubtless from traditions of some primitive Revelation, into the great mystery of Godliness, which was scarcely less than that of Jewish seers themselves.... You are responsible before God, who caused to be given, and before the spirits of your primitive fathers, who received and transmitted, those rudiments of truth, which, directly or indirectly, lead you to Christ, the Author and Finisher of man's faith, and man's salvation, to whom the *Prajapati* of the Vedas unmistakably refers.[216]

Although Banerjea does not say so explicitly, we can legitimately infer that he views primeval revelation as a form of "supernatural communication", involving more than the knowledge of God mediated through natural revelation or accessible to human reason. He seems to have appropriated an idea current within comparative religion that there was an original and immediate communication of the divine will to all humankind at the time of creation.

Banerjea seems to have regarded this primitive revelation, *s'abda* or *Sruti*, as qualitatively comparable to the revelation given to the authors of the Old

[213] Banerjea, *Christianity and Hinduism*, 184-185.

[214] There is thus little grounds for the vast gulf which Richard draws between Banerjea's fulfilment approach based on primitive revelation and other views based on natural theology; Richard, 'Aryan Witness Recalled' (1994), 2.

[215] Banerjea, *Claims of Christianity*, 175-176.

[216] Banerjea, *Christianity and Hinduism*, 198.

Testament, distinct from natural theology or general revelation. Unwritten in its original form, recollections or fragments of this primitive revelation have been received and transmitted through oral tradition, and recorded by the ancient *rishis* who authored the Vedas. Banerjea's fulfilment approach was grounded in the belief that this primitive revelation was qualitatively continuous with and possessing comparable authority and value as the supernatural truth revealed in Christ.

Christ and Prajapati

Aleaz's evaluation of Banerjea's theological contribution characterizes Banerjea as "the first person to hint at Prajapati as an unknown Christ of Hinduism."[217] Banerjea's fulfilment view has also been described as "an autonomous Indian version of inclusivism",[218] or as marking a "pioneering transition from Exclusivism to Inclusivism".[219] The context and concerns that Banerjea's apologetic seeks to address are remote to the terms and problems of the modern theology of religions debate. If, however, we are to represent his thought accurately in relation to present-day issues, two critical questions need to be posed: How exactly does he view *Prajapati* in relation to Christ? What was his view regarding the salvific value of Hinduism?

The vedic figure of *Prajapati* is crucial to Banerjea's promise-fulfilment scheme. His theory of primitive revelation provides the framework, and the concept of sacrifice the bridge, but *Prajapati* is the figure who strides across the bridge that he tries to erect between Christianity and Hinduism. Banerjea's descriptions of *Prajapati* highlight the close parallels with the pre-existent Christ: "the Lord or supporter of Creation", *Purusha*, "begotten before the world", and *Viswakarma*, "the Author of the universe;[220] half mortal and immortal, he is even identified with "the universal Godhead".[221] The most striking correspondence, however, is in the representation of *Prajapati* as "the Divine Self-sacrificer", and "the Divine Saviour", through whose death, death itself is vanquished.[222]

The Jesus of the New Testament fulfils the ideal of *Prajapati* by the etymological correspondence of the two names, and by his fulfilment of the character and claims of the vedic ideal.[223] *Prajapati* thus prefigures and is fulfilled in the biblical description of Christ as God and man, mortal and immortal, who offered himself as a sacrifice for man's salvation from sin.[224]

---

[217] Aleaz, *From Exclusivism to Inclusivism*, xxi.
[218] Copley, 'The Conversion Experience', 68-69.
[219] Aleaz, *From Exclusivism to Inclusivism*, xxxiv, xxi.
[220] Banerjea, *Christianity and Hinduism*, 190, 196.
[221] Banerjea, *ibid.*, 192, 194.
[222] Banerjea, *ibid.*, 191-192, 196.
[223] Banerjea, *ibid.*, 194-197.
[224] Banerjea, *ibid.*, 193, 198, 200.

Banerjea seems to have tried to get the figure of *Prajapati* to serve in India as a functional equivalent of "the unknown god" in Paul's Athenian address, or the concept of the Logos in John's gospel. In an implicit attestation of Banerjea's claim a contemporary vedic scholar offers the following comment on the relation of the myth of *Purusha/Prajapati* to the broader vedic doctrine of sacrifice:

> Taken in its totality the myth of Purusa/Prajapati is not unworthy of the Christian conception of the redemptive incarnation of the Logos by means of the "kenosis", leaving out the question whether they can be homologated or not.[225]

Banerjea's project succeeded in part, but like most other pioneers his work was limited in theological sophistication and depth.[226] Consequently, although his idea of Christ as the true *Prajapati* was well received by his own generation, the theme was not taken up seriously by mainstream Indian Christian thought in subsequent years. He was, however, the first Indian Christian thinker to suggest the presence of anticipations of Christ in Hindu religious texts. In that sense, his conception of Christ as *Prajapati* may be judged to be a precursor to ideas of the "unknown Christ", "acknowledged Christ", "unbound Christ"[227] and other similar notions that emerged in later Indian Christian thought. How did Banerjea's conviction regarding *Prajapati* as a vedic prefigurement of Christ affect his view of the salvific value of Hinduism? Banerjea does not address the issue directly, hence, we will need to glean his opinion on this question by examining his position on two important issues: his understanding of salvation, and his view of Hinduism as a religious system.

Banerjea's understanding of humankind's sinful condition and salvation through Christ is in line with nineteenth century orthodox Protestantism. Humanity has been created in the likeness of God and for communion with God, but the human soul needs cleansing and purification from sin.[228] By his atoning death, Christ provides redemption from sin and evil, and enables humanity to be restored to communion with God.[229] On this basis, Banerjea

---

[225] Aguilar, *Sacrifice in the Rgveda*, 69.

[226] There is, for instance, no attempt to ascribe revelatory function to the pre-incarnate redemptive ideal of *Prajapati*. Banerjea's view would have been more convincing had his concept of primeval revelation been grounded more clearly in a 'Logos' theology similar to that of the early fathers.

[227] Concepts advanced by Panikkar, *The Vedic experience;* M.M. Thomas, *The Acknowledged Christ of the Indian Renaissance* (Madras: CLS, 1976); and S.J. Samartha, *The Hindu Response to the Unbound Christ* (Bangalore: CISRS, 1974, respectively. Sen, a contemporary of Banerjea, was also around this same time speaking of the presence of a "hidden Christ" in Hinduism based on a *Logos* fulfilment framework.

[228] Banerjea, *Dialogues on Hindu Philosophy*, 397, 407.

[229] Banerjea, *ibid.*, 406.

invites all nations to faith in Jesus Christ, "the self-sacrificing *Prajapati* of the Vedas" and "the true Ark of salvation".[230] But does the presence of the self-sacrificing *Prajapati* ideal within Hinduism make it at least provisionally salvific as a system? Two factors need to be taken into consideration.

First, Banerjea clearly distinguished between Hinduism as an ideal embodied in the Vedas, and the prevailing Hindu social reality, tainted by centuries of corruption and accretion.[231] The essential truths of vedic religion had been lost through the centuries:

> ...the doctrine of sacrifice, as a figure of *Prajapati*, (who had offered himself as a sacrifice for the benefit of the world), did not long continue in its integrity among our forefathers;... its chief characteristic... as a figure or type of a self-sacrificing Saviour, had long vanished from the conceptions of our countrymen....[232]

This vital truth "...had become obsolete and fallen into oblivion by lurking in the sealed manuscripts of the Vedas", and only been brought to the light and restored in the Providence of God with the publication of the Vedas.[233]

It may be reasonably inferred that since Banerjea believed that the Hinduism of his time had lost sight of the essential truth of redemption through sacrifice, he did not regard it as even provisionally salvific. This inference is strengthened by Banerjea's repeated assertion that the "Ark of Salvation" which the Vedas exhort sinners to embark in is not *Prajapati*, nor even Christ, but the Church of Christ: "The ark of salvation, with the *Purusha* begotten in the beginning at its head, can be no other than the Church of Christ...."[234]

What about the ancient vedic religion? There is some ambiguity in Banerjea's thought concerning its salvific value. He seems to suggest that the vedic seers had an incomplete perception of the truth: "They longed for something greater, they panted for something at the same time more convincing to reason and more elevating to the soul..."[235] They were diligent in performing the sacrificial rituals, but were unaware of their actual significance; their true meaning was only disclosed in the Christian revelation.[236] The ancient *Rishis* could not be blamed for their ignorance of later revelation, but would stand in judgment against their Hindu descendants today who reject the teaching of Christ.

On the other hand, Banerjea's representation of the vedic gods as originally mere mortals who "attained heaven" through their sacrifices suggests that the

---

[230] Banerjea, *Christianity and Hinduism*, 196-197.

[231] Banerjea, *Dialogues on Hindu Philosophy*, 36-40, 150-167, 225-249; Banerjea, *Relation between the Hindu and Buddhistic Systems*, 131-158.

[232] Banerjea, *Christianity and Hinduism*, 194.

[233] Banerjea, *ibid.*, 198-199.

[234] Banerjea, *ibid.*, 198-199, 196, 200.

[235] Banerjea, *Claims of Christianity*, 161, 173.

[236] Banerjea, *ibid.*, 174.

vedic religion did have some salvific value.[237] He commends the religious devotion of the ancient *Rishis*,[238] and claims that they were aware of "Salvation from sin by the death of a Saviour..."[239] Furthermore, in indicating points of close correspondence between aspects of vedic and patriarchal religion, he seems to place the vedic seers in the category of Old Testament saints who obtained salvation through their faithful adherence to the sacrificial tradition.[240]

Thus, contrary to some recent characterizations, Banerjea's view of the salvific value of Hinduism does not fit neatly in either exclusivist or inclusivist categories. His understanding of revelation allowed for the presence of truth in Hinduism, but there is no evidence to suggest that he accepted the apostate Hindu system of his time as having even provisional salvific value. He does, however, regard the prospects of salvation in vedic religion more positively in terms corresponding to the faith experience of Old Testament saints.

Summary Evaluation

Philip offers the following summary assessment of Banerjea's theological contribution: "In the depth of his scholarship, the force of arguments and the clarity of his presentation, and in his evangelical purpose Krishna Mohan can be considered the greatest of the Christian apologists of the 19th century."[241]

Banerjea was both a product of his generation and a thinker ahead of his times. His apologetic approach, to some extent, may have been conditioned by Aryan theories that were exciting the intellectual world of his day.[242] The vastly expanded borders of the historiographical and Indological disciplines Banerjea applied in his research make aspects of his method appear somewhat dated a century later. Despite these limitations, however, his view must be commended for its originality and ingenuity. We will first highlight three main weaknesses of Banerjea's approach, before we briefly evaluate its influence and comment on its tenability.

Although Banerjea's prophetic fulfilment approach is patterned after the New Testament model of Jewish-Christian fulfilment, the biblical resources in support of his notion of an original primitive revelation are rather meagre. Although the first few chapters of Genesis suggest some form of supernatural revelation before the patriarchal period and the Old Testament dispensation, little biblical evidence exists on which to base any theories on the mode or

---

[237] Banerjea, *Arian Witness*, 201-202; Banerjea, *Two Essays*, 62.
[238] Banerjea, *Claims of Christianity*, 173.
[239] Banerjea, *Christianity and Hinduism*, 193.
[240] Banerjea, *Two Essays*, 69-70.
[241] Philip, *Krishna Mohan Banerjea*, 125.
[242] Richard, 'Aryan Witness Recalled', (1993), 1.

content of such a revelation.[243] There is thus little biblical or theological justification for Banerjea's primitive revelation theory.

Second, the primeval revelation and *Prajapati* concepts are developed independently in Banerjea's fulfilment approach. As a result, the ideas of revelation and redemption remain mutually detached, a marked weakness when compared with the *Logos* fulfilment view of the early fathers. The fathers' *Logos*-theology recognized the *Logos*, present in the world from the time of creation, as actively illuminating all of humankind and becoming incarnate in the person of Jesus of Nazareth. Banerjea's employment of the primeval revelation theory fails to provide comparable theological coherence and unity to his fulfilment view.

Third, Banerjea's approach provides for fulfilment to proceed in one direction only, without providing for the Christian vision to be enriched by insights from non-Christian religious traditions. There is thus no reverse fulfilment component such as we observed in Farquhar's view. The value of creation, natural revelation and culture is thereby significantly undermined, and the value of inculturation diluted.

In assessing the influence of Banerjea's views on subsequent Indian Christian thought, Richard makes the somewhat tenuous observation that, "Banerjea's position was never widely embraced, yet aspects of it continue to have influence to the present time, especially among evangelical and fundamentalist Christians."[244] Banerjea's fulfilment view was not widely adopted in the form he expounded it, but the basic idea of Christ as the fulfilment of the vedic concept of *Prajapati* continued to be propagated by others within a generation of his life-time.[245] The better known among these are

[243] See *New Catholic Encyclopedia*, vol. XII (New York: McGraw-Hill Book Co., 1957), 440.

[244] Richard, 'Aryan Witness Recalled', (1993), 1.

[245] Boyd points out that echoes of Banerjea's approach may be observed in some of the popular apologetic and evangelistic tracts of the period. Some discerned prophetic pointers to the Christian faith in the writings of many Hindu traditions and sects, such as the Kabir sect, the Lingayats of Mysore and followers of the *Nakalanka Avatara* in Gujarat; Boyd, Indian Christian Thoelogy, 283, 159.

Narayan Vaman Tilak,[246] T.E. Slater,[247] A.S. Appasamy,[248] R.C. Das[249] and D.P. Titus.[250]

There is evidence of Banerjea's direct influence on only two of these figures.[251] However, what is especially striking is that the majority of these were Hindu converts, who seem to have arrived at conclusions corresponding to Banerjea's vedic fulfilment approach independent of his influence. This phenomenon is difficult to explain unless there was some reasonable basis for it. Numerous popular forms of the vedic fulfilment view continue to be published and circulated, finding favourable response in some quarters of the Indian Christian community even today.[252]

Richard's observation that "...the main stream of Indian Christian and missionary thought never accepted the suggestion that Christ is foreshadowed in Prajapati",[253] does, however, rightly reflect an ebb in influence of the vedic fulfilment approach. Reasons for this and for the decline of the Indian fulfilment tradition as a whole had little to do with the quality and depth of Banerjea's pioneering insights. The influence of Banerjea's view declined partly because of the lack of thinkers of comparable calibre who could follow his lead and develop his ideas further. We will need to look at this issue more closely towards the end of our study.

To what extent is Banerjea's fulfilment view defensible? Banerjea discerns the presence of a divine pedagogy in the vedic teaching on sacrifice, and affirms the decisive fulfilment of the vedic concept of *Prajapati* in the historic figure of Christ. He uses the idea of an original universal primeval revelation to

---

246 See pp.39-42; cf. Richard, 'Aryan Witness Recalled' (1994), 2-3.

247 See p.24.

248 A.S. Appasamy, *Fifty Years' Pilgrimage of a Convert* (London, 1924); and A.S. Appasmy, *The Use of Yoga in Prayer* (Madras: CLS, 1926); cf. Baago, *Pioneers of Indigenous Christianity*, 18-25.

249 R.C. Das, *How to Present Christ to a Hindu* (Allahabad: North India Tract & Book Society, 1951); and R.C. Das, *Convictions of an Indian Disciple* (Bangalore: CISRS, 1966); cf. H.L. Richard, *R C. Das: Evangelical Prophet for Contextual Christianity* (Bangalore/Delhi: CISRS/ISPCK, 1995).

250 D.P. Titus, *Fulfilment of the Vedic Quest in the Lord Jesus Christ* (Nainital: Sat Tal Ashram, 1982); and D.P. Titus, *The Concept of Divine Sacrifice in the Bible and Vedic Scriptures* (Nainital: Khristadvaita Ashram, 1993).

251 Two important references confirm Titus' acquaintance with Banerjea's work; Titus, *Concept of Divine Sacrifice*, 7, 17. For Banerjea's influence on Slater, see Maw, *Visions of India*, 55-57, and Richard, 'Aryan Witness Recalled' (1994), 2.

252 It is difficult to document the popular appeal and influence of this view. An unspecified number of Christian *sadhus* presently use some version of the fulfilment approach in their witness to Hindus. Some are mystic-practitioners, who rarely, if ever, put their thoughts in writing; others have a hidden presence, remaining culturally integrated within the Hindu community. Richard admits to the abiding influence of this view, but ascribes its ongoing popularity to "emotional appeal", Richard, 'Aryan Witness Recalled' (1994), 3.

253 Richard, 'Aryan Witness Recalled' (1994), 3.

assert the universal scope of the divine covenant and include vedic religion within the sweep of a cosmic salvation-history scheme. Banerjea's use of the device of primeval revelation was theologically weak, but the main impulse and direction of his fulfilment approach was in essential concurrence with the fulfilment impulse in the New Testament and the early fathers.

With regard to his interpretation of the vedic material, his emphasis on the importance of the theme of sacrifice is in line with mainstream scholarly opinion, but his specific case for treating *Prajapati* as a vedic prefigurement of Christ must be viewed as an alternative Christian reading of the vedic texts. His vedic fulfilment approach may thus be regarded as a valid and credible attempt at discerning a basic underlying continuity in God's dealings with humanity, beneath the various elements of cultic and religious dissonance between Hinduism and Christianity.

The originality of Banerjea's fulfilment approach marks it as a significant milestone in the history of Christian-Hindu encounter. He was, however, representative of a wider group of nineteenth and early twentieth century converts to Christianity, who also tried to reinterpret their pre-Christian tradition from the perspective of their experience of Christ.[254] There were significant differences in each approach, but all viewed their acceptance of Christian faith as in some way a fulfilment of their Hindu religious experience. In the following chapter we consider the approach of another representative of this Indian fulfilment tradition in the pre-independence period, Sadhu Sundar Singh.

---

[254] See pp.25-42

Fulfilment in Sundar Singh's Bhakti Spirituality

We observe a very distinctive expression of the irenic attitude towards Hinduism during our period in an Indian disciple of Christ, Sundar Singh, who embodied the Hindu ideal of the seeker after God while reflecting an authentic Christian life-style.[1] A man of widespread fame and influence, Sundar Singh has sometimes been regarded as the best-known Indian Christian of all time.[2]

The Man and His Background (1889-1929)

Sundar Singh[3] was born in the village of Rampur in the Punjab in a wealthy landowner's family, belonging to the high caste Jat Sikh community.[4] His

---

[1] Several contemporaries of Sundar Singh have furnished accounts of his life and teaching; the more authoritative among these are by R.J. Parker, *Sadhu Sundar Singh: Called of God* (1918; repr., Madras: CLS, 1996) and A.J. Appasamy, *Sundar Signh: A Biography* (1958; repr., London: Lutterworth Press, 1996). The older scholarly accounts of Sundar Singh's life and contribution nclude B.H. Streeter and A.J. Appasamy, *The Sadhu: A Study in Mysticism and Practical Religion* (1921; repr., Delhi: Oxford University Press, 1987) and F. Heiler, *The Gospel of Sadhu Sundar Singh*, trans. Olive Wyon (New Delhi: ISPCK, 1989). In the years after his death a number of popular biographies appeared reflecting the ongoing interest and fascination with his unique person and ministry. Three scholarly works published in recent years are by M. Biehl, *Der Fall Sadhu Sundar Singh – Theologie zwischen den Kulturen* (Frankfurt: Peter Lang, 1990) and P.S. Prakash, *The Preaching of Sadhu Sundar Singh* (Bangalore: Wordmakers, 1991) and E.J. Sharpe, *The Riddle of Sadhu Sundar Singh* (New Delhi: Intercultural Publications, 2004). The first analyses the background and impulses of Sundar Singh's life and contribution, evaluating his thought as an expression of an indigenous "theology between cultures"; the second focuses on the distinctive style and content of his preaching; the third is a critical assessment of the controversy surrounding the life of Sundar Singh, provoked especially by the sceptical responses of some to his claims of ecstatic visions and other unusual mystical experiences. The scope of these studies does not allow them to address in depth the specific question of Sundar Singh's attitude to other faiths. We will refer to other descriptions and analyses of Sundar Singh's life and thought at appropriate points in our assessment.

[2] E.J. Sharpe, 'The Legacy of Sadhu Sundar Signh', *International Bulletin of Missionary Research* 14 (1990) 166. cf. R. Boyd, *An Introduction to Indian Christian Theology* (1960; repr., Delhi: ISPCK, 1991), 92.

[3] The birth centenary of Sundar Singh was marked by a spate of reprints of old works as well as new publications, including T.D. Francis' useful reference work, *The Christian Witness of Sadhu Sundar Singh: A Collection of His Writings* (1989; repr., Madras: CLS, 1993). Francis' work includes a brief introductory essay on Sundar Singh, a

family were nominally followers of the Sikh religion, but the Hindu and Sikh traditions both had a formative influence upon his life.[5] The youngest son in the family, he was brought up in the lap of luxury, and was closely attached to his mother, a refined and deeply pious lady, who exercised the most significant influence upon his early life.[6]

Sundar Singh's mother first instructed him by her own example and religious teaching, and later placed him under the spiritual tutelage of a Hindu *pandit* and an old Sikh *sadhu*, for instruction in the Hindu and Sikh scriptures respectively.[7] Sundar Singh's first contact with Christianity was the daily Bible lessons at the American Presbyterian Mission primary school he attended at Rampur. He later confessed that although his deep prejudices against Christianity caused him to be outwardly resistant to these Bible lessons, the gospel teaching on the love of God had a "wonderful power" and "attraction" for him.[8]

Early in life Sundar Singh's mother ingrained in him the belief that the greatest treasure on earth was peace of heart, which needed earnest seeking. His deep spiritual thirst led him to earnestly search the *Granth*, the Sikh

---

selection of his thoughts as recorded in secondary literature, and a reprint of all nine of his published writings: *At the Master's Feet* (Madras, 1922); *Reality and Religion* (London: Macmillan, 1924); *The Search After Reality* (London, MacMillan, 1925); *The Spiritual World* (London: Macmillan, 1926); *The Real Life* (Madras, 1927); *With and Without Christ* (London: Macmillan, 1929); *The Spiritual Life* (London: Macmillan, 1926), the content of which corresponds very closely to that of *The Real Pearl* (Madras: CLS, 1966); also Sadhu Sundar Singh, *Life in Abundance: Sermons of the Sadhu recorded by Alys Goodwin in Switzerland, March 1922*, ed. A.F. Thyagaraju (Madras: CLS, 1980). Six of these were translated originally from Urdu under his supervision, and the rest published posthumously. Although other sources have been cited, normally references to and quotations from Sundar Singh's writings will be from Francis' work, unless otherwise indicated.

[4] A case for 1888 as the year of his birth has been made largely by German scholars and Prakash, based upon entries in the baptism register of St. Thomas Church, Simla, where Sundar Singh was baptized, 'Certified true copy of baptismal register entry', VPC SSS.1; cf. Prakash, *The Preaching of Sadhu Sundar Singh* (Bangalore: Wordmakers, 1991), 11. Most biographers of Sundar Singh accept 1889 as the year of his birth based on the biography by Rebecca Parker, a close personal friend of Sundar Singh, who scrutinized and approved her manuscript prior to publication; R.J. Parker, *Sadhu Sundar Singh: Called of God* (1918; repr., Madras: CLS 1996), 9; cf. K. Baago, *Pioneers of Indigenous Christianity* (Madras: CLS, 1969), 50; Boyd, *Indian Christian Theology*, 92; F. Heiler, *The Gospel of Sadhu Sundar Sing, trans.* Olive Wyon (1927; repr., London: Allen & Unwin, 1989), 37; A.J. Appasamy, *Sundar Singh: A Biography* (1958; repr., London: Lutterworth Press, 1996), 17; Sharpe, *The Riddle*, 29.

[5] Sadhu Sundar Singh, *With and Without Christ*, in *The Christian Witness of Sadhu Sundar Singh: A Collection of His Writings*, ed. T.D. Francis (Madras: CLS, 1989), 393.

[6] Parker, *Called of God*, 9.

[7] Singh, *With and Without Christ*, in *Christian Witness*, 393-394.

[8] Singh, *ibid.*, 398.

scriptures, the Koran, and the sacred books of the Hindus, often reading the scriptures until midnight, memorizing select portions, and also practising Yoga. The priests, gurus and sadhus, from whom he often sought guidance, even his pious mother, all failed to bring him spiritual solace and satisfaction.[9]

The spiritual crisis in his life intensified with the deaths of his mother and elder brother within the space of a few months. In a subsequent phase of violent opposition to the Christian faith, he publicly burned a portion of the New Testament, arousing the strong disapproval of even his conservative father. Deep spiritual depression and unrest of heart led to thoughts of suicide, culminating in a dramatic experience of Christian conversion three days later.[10]

In Sundar Singh's testimony, on that memorable day he got up at three in the morning, and after bathing, prayed for God to reveal himself and show him the way of salvation, failing which he would commit suicide. He waited till about half-past four, expecting to see Buddha, or Krishna, or some other *avatara*. Instead he suddenly became conscious of a bright radiance, which entered and filled the room, describing what happened subsequently as follows:

> I opened the door to see where it came from, but all was dark outside. I returned inside, and the light increased in intensity and took the form of a globe of light above the ground, and in this light there appeared, not the form I expected, but the Living Christ whom I had counted as dead. To all eternity I shall never forget His glorious and loving face, nor the few words which He spoke: 'Why do you persecute me? See, I have died on the Cross for you and for the whole world.' These words were burned into my heart as by lightning, and I fell on the ground before Him. My heart was filled with inexpressible joy and peace, and my whole life was entirely changed. Then the old Sundar Singh died a new Sundar Singh, to serve the Living Christ, was born.[11]

The precise nature of Sundar Singh's conversion experience has been a source of much controversy.[12] Whatever the precise nature of this experience, without question it constituted a dramatic and decisive turning point in his life.[13] Sundar Singh claimed that from this moment onwards the peace and joy that had been the object of his life-long quest became his most precious possession.

---

[9] Singh, *ibid.*, 393-396; Parker, *Called of God*, 10.

[10] Singh, *ibid.*, 398-399.

[11] Singh, *ibid.*, 399.

[12] Some regarded it as deliberately contrived; others reduced it to a purely subjective psychological experience; but most of those who knew him best accepted his testimony in its integrity. Sundar Singh always distinguished the objectivity of this event from the visions of Christ that accompanied his later experiences of religious ecstasy. For a summary of the discussion, see Prakash, *Preaching of Sadhu Sundar Singh*, 21-23; 128-133; also Sharpe's cautious, if somewhat sceptical assessment, Sharpe, *The Riddle*, 29-37.

[13] Prakash, *Preaching of Sadhu Sundar Singh*, 23.

Sundar Singh faced serious opposition from his immediate family, relatives and the wider Jat Sikh community. After reasonable and loving persuasion had failed, the family and community resorted to severe persecution and attempted abduction and murder.[14] He eventually came under the protection of the Presbyterian missionaries, and after a brief period of Bible study, was sent to the Church Missionary Society station in Simla. He was baptized on September 3, 1905 by the Anglican missionary, J. Redman, and became a communicant member of the Anglican Church.[15]

In December 1909, Sundar Singh entered St. John's Divinity School at Lahore at the behest of the Anglican Bishop Lefroy to prepare for the Anglican ministry, but left within a few months without completing his course.[16] His desire for freedom to speak in churches of various denominations made him reject the offer of a licence to preach in the Anglican churches of the Lahore diocese. Thereafter he continued his ministry as a wandering preacher, but remained a member of the Anglican Church all of his life.[17]

As a result of his devout mother's influence, Sundar Singh had long cherished the sadhu ideal, and within a few weeks of his baptism, decided to express his Christian discipleship by adopting the distinctive life-style of a sadhu.[18] Parker points out that Sundar Singh's adoption of the saffron robe and the sadhu way of life was in fulfilment of a vow made in earlier days, that if God would satisfy his quest for inner peace he would sacrifice all that this world could offer him.[19]

Derived from the root *sadh-* which means "directing to the goal, accomplishing one's aim", the term "sadhu" commonly denotes a Hindu ascetic, holy man or wonder-worker, one who follows a certain *sadhana*, a definite way of life or discipline adopted in order to attain an immediate experience of the divine.[20] This experience may take the form of a vision of a personal God or of absorptive unity with the impersonal *Brahman*. A sadhu devotes himself completely to his *sadhana*, which defines the particular type of

---

[14] Prakash, *ibid.*, 34-37.

[15] Fear of violent opposition from Sundar Singh's relatives and the Sikh community in the immediate vicinity may have prevented the Presbyterian missionaries from baptizing Sundar Singh themselves; Prakash, *Preaching of Sadhu Sundar Singh*, 41.

[16] Prakash, *ibid.*, 62-64; Sharpe, *The Riddle*, 45-47.

[17] For Sundar Singh's ambivalent attitude towards the Church, see D.C. Scott, ed., 'Sadhu Sundar Singh: Church of the Sadhu Ideal', *Jeevadhara* 17 (1987), 267-280.

[18] Singh, *With and Without Christ*, in *Christian Witness*, 400.

[19] Parker, *Called of God*, 19.

[20] Other roughly synonymous terms include *sanyasi*, *yogi*, *vairagi*, and *fakir;* B. Walker, *Hindu World: An Encyclopedic Survey of Hinduism*, vol. 2 (New Delhi: Munshiram Manoharlal Publishers, 1983), 322.

religious life he has chosen and is comprised of a composite of doctrines, rituals, ascetic practices and other prescribed behaviour.[21]

The sadhu ideal in Hinduism is grounded in the scheme of spiritualization envisioned in the four *asramas* (stages in life) characterizing Hindu thought since at least the eighth century BC. According to this scheme, every Hindu male was expected to devote the latter half of his life to religious pursuits culminating in total renunciation.[22] The penultimate stage (*vanaprastha*) involved a qualified asceticism following retirement to a hermitage; in the final stage (*samnyasa*), the individual completely renounces home, family and all other social obligations, adopts the life-style of a wandering mendicant, and gives himself totally to contemplation and self-mortification in quest of spiritual emancipation. Another more ancient ideal of the individual life-long ascetic, found in Vedic and early Upanishadic literature, allowed for the individual to opt directly for *samnyasa*, and a life-long commitment to the ascetic life-style, at any point in his life.[23]

The sadhu ideal is not limited to any one tradition within Hinduism: sadhus may come from any of the classes and castes within Hinduism, hold to a variety of philosophical and religious beliefs, and belong to different sects or religious orders.[24] Many *svatantra* sadhus, however, independent of allegiance to any order, don the saffron robe and adopt a life-style, which fits broadly within the Hindu religious way of life.[25] Sundar Singh's appropriation of the sadhu way of life independent of any existing Hindu religious order was thus an attempt to pursue Christian discipleship in a manner consistent with the *svatantra* sadhu ideal in Hindu tradition.

Sundar Singh was the first Protestant known to have embraced the sadhu lifestyle,[26] a step that aroused misunderstanding and opposition from two quarters.[27] On one hand, Christians doubted whether the Hindu ideal of renunciation it represented was compatible with a Christian world-view that affirmed the material world.[28] Sundar Singh also frequently encountered hostility from the Hindu community, suspicious of what they perceived as

---

[21] K.K. Klostermaier, *A Survey of Hinduism* (New Delhi: Munshiram Manoharlal Publishers, 1990), 329.

[22] The first half consisted of two stages, *brahmacarya* (youthful student years) and *grhastya* (dutiful family life); G.S. Ghurye, *Indian Sadhus* (Bombay: Popular Prakashan, 1964), 2; Klostermaier, *A Survey of Hinduism*, 328.

[23] Klostermaier, *A Survey of Hinduism*, 330; Ghurye, *Indian Sadhus*, 4, 11f.

[24] Dhavamony, 'The Sadhu Ideal as Realized by Hindu Saints', *Studia Missionalia* 35 (1986), 202; for a detailed classification, see Ghurye, *Indian Sadhus*, 70-219.

[25] Klostermaier, *A Survey of Hinduism*, 329-332.

[26] Two prominent Roman Catholic figures who donned the saffron robe before him were Robert de Nobili (1577-1656) and Brahmabandhab Upadhyay (1861-1907); Boyd, *India Christian Theology*, 11f, 63f.

[27] Parker, *Called of God*, 23.

[28] C.F. Andrews, *Sadhu Sundar Singh: A Personal Memoir* (London: Hodder & Stoughton, 1934), 99-100.

fraudulent attempts to camouflage the Christian message by the adoption of Hindu forms.[29] Sundar Singh's adoption of the sadhu way of life remained a life-long commitment, and an integral part of his Christian discipleship and calling as an evangelist.[30] He did not, however, adopt the sadhu life-style uncritically, but gave it his own distinctive interpretation.

Sundar Singh pursued the ministry of an itinerant preacher as a sadhu, travelling across different parts of North India, Tibet, Nepal, and South India. He was forced to endure untold humiliation, hardships, and suffering in the course of his travels. The cumulative record of his missionary adventures includes tales of exceptional courage and heroism, prodigious claims of dramatic supernatural intervention, and several instances when he may have been on the brink of martyrdom.[31]

Sundar Singh's later travels took him to Ceylon and the Far East, and eventually to England, the United States, Australia, the Middle East, and Europe. The extraordinary quality of many of the experiences reported by Sundar Singh became the subject of heated debate, especially following his last visit to the West in 1922. His detractors based their criticisms on alleged discrepancies in Sundar Singh's various testimonies, whereas his supporters attempted to vindicate him by reconciling the supposed discrepancies in his testimony and appealing to the strength and transparency of his character.[32]

His deep distress over the assault on his integrity and his failing health caused him to withdraw to his Subathu[33] retreat, where he gave himself to meditation and to writing his devotional books.[34] In April 1929, he set out on

---

[29] Prakash, *Preaching of Sadhu Sundar Singh*, 46.

[30] Prakash, *ibid.*, 49.

[31] Sundar Singh generally worked independently, except for a brief period when he was associated with the American missionary, Samuel Stokes; Andrews, *A Personal Memoir*, 100-106. Several attempts have been made to reconstruct the itinerary of his various journeys from available sources; Appasamy, *Singh: A Biography*, 26-64, 84-142, 153-174; Heiler, *Gospel of Singh*, 55-93; and Prakash, *Preaching of Sadhu Sundar Singh*, 61, 66-69, 80-124. Sharpe's account of Sundar Singh's travels draws attention to some enigmatic inconsistencies at various points; Sharpe, *The Riddle*, 50-71, 116-121.

[32] His critics, led by Oscar Pfister, a Swiss Reformed Pastor, and Father Hosten, a Belgian Jesuit in Darjeeling, India, denounced him as a pathological liar and imposter. His sympathizers included Friedrich Heiler in Germany, Nathan Soderblom in Sweden, B.H. Streeter in England, and C.F. Andrews, and A.J. Appasamy in India. For details of 'The Sadhu Controversy', see Prakash, *Preaching of Sadhu Sundar Singh*, 128-133; M. Biehl, *Der Fall Sadhu Sundar Singh – Theologie zwischen den Kulturen* (Frankfurt: Peter Lang, 1990), 35-97; E.J. Sharpe, 'Sadhu Sundar Singh and His Critics: An Episode in the Meeting of East and West', *Religion* 6 (1976): 48-66, and Sharpe, *The Riddle*, 122-140.

[33] Sundar Singh owned a small house in this small town close to Simla and Rampur, where he retired for rest and prayer between his tours; Appasamy, *Singh: A Biography*, 178.

[34] E.J. Sharpe, 'The Legacy of Sadhu Sundar Singh', *International Bulletin of Missionary Research* 14 (1991): 163.

what was to be his last missionary journey to Tibet, during which he disappeared in mysterious circumstances, never to be seen again.[35]

Bhakti Mysticism and Sundar Singh's Fulfilment Framework

Sundar Singh's sermons and writings are of great value to us, both for their distinctive theological content as well as their widespread and prolonged influence.[36] His teaching and writings are marked by direct simplicity of insight and vividness of expression. Although his theology is not set forth in a systematic or structured form in any of his writings, the essential elements of his thought seem to fit together into an integrated and coherent pattern.[37]

Sundar Singh's distinctive interpretation of the Christian faith as embodied in his lifestyle and reflected in his sermons and writings raised a number of questions both during his life-time and in the years following his death, many of which were addressed in a substantial body of published writings in Europe.[38] These, for the most part, focused on the "Sadhu controversy" or on his mystical orientation, with little attention being paid to a theological evaluation of his teaching.[39] His contribution to the development of Indian Christianity has thus been largely neglected, and his approach to other religions almost totally ignored.[40]

Our purpose in this study is to examine the fulfilment approach of Sundar Singh, as an Indian convert to Christian faith, whose "access to the innermost chambers of Indian spirituality",[41] resulted in the emergence of an original framework for relating the Christian faith to the *bhakti* tradition. In the first stage of our evaluation, we explore the roots of Sundar Singh's *bhakti*

---

[35] Some believed he had retreated to the Himalayas to spend the rest of his life in prayer and meditation; Andrews, *A Personal Memoir*, 230 investigated the issue in detail, and was convinced that he had died on the way to Tibet.

[36] Sharpe, 'The Legacy of Sadhu Sundar Singh', 165-166; responses to Sundar Singh range from reverence for a modern saint to dismissal as a deluded lunatic or deceiving charlatan; see Sharpe, 'Sadhu Sundar Singh and His Critics', 58-64.

[37] He was, by his own admission, neither a philosopher nor a theologian in the technical sense; see Sadhu Sundar Singh, *Reality and Religion*, in *The Christian Witness of Sadhu Sundar Singh: A Collection of His Writings*, ed. T.D. Francis (Madras: CLS, 1989), 83-86; Streeter and Appasamy, *The Sadhu: A Study in Mysticism and Practical Religion* (1921; repr., London: Macmillan, 1987), 53.

[38] See Prakash's fairly comprehensive bibliography; Prakash, *Preaching of Sadhu Sundar Singh*, 336-339].

[39] D. Bookless, 'The Water of Life in an Indian Cup: Sadhu Sundar Singh and the Indigenisation of Christianity in India' (M.A. dissertation, Cheltenham & Gloucester College of Higher Education, 1990), 5-6; Sharpe, 'The Legacy of Sadhu Sundar Singh', 165.

[40] The issue receives focused treatment only in Gray, 'Sadhu Sundar Singh and the Non-Christian Religions', *International Review of Mission* 60 (1959): 421-426.

[41] Sharpe's expression Sharpe, 'The Legacy of Sadhu Sundar Singh', 161

orientation, and then investigate the nature and extent of *bhakti* influence upon his thought, based on which we propose a framework of continuity between Sundar Singh's *bhakti* and Christian experience.

The Background and Sources of Sundar Singh's Bhakti Mystical Orientation

The outstanding characteristic of Sadhu Sundar Singh's theology is that it is grounded in personal experience: "People do not believe, because they are strangers to the experience.... Faith and experience must come first, and understanding will follow. We cannot understand until we have some spiritual experience, and that comes through prayer..."[42]

This emphasis on spiritual experience in Sundar Singh's religious life and reflection is widely acknowledged by students of his thought.[43] One of the earliest analyses of his life and thought identified him as essentially a mystic, and subsequent studies have tended to regard him primarily as a mystic-saint rather than a philosopher, theologian, or scholar.[44] We will, thus, briefly explore the significance of the term mysticism as it relates to Sundar Singh's distinctive emphasis on spiritual experience.

Earlier definitions tended to describe mysticism in essentialist terms, as a universal phenomenon present in various religious traditions, involving direct, unmediated intuitive experience and non-rational appropriation of the ultimate reality.[45] Critical to this view of mysticism was the epistemological assumption that there was a mystical way of appropriating reality through direct intuitive experience, which bypassed the rational cognitive process.[46]

Recent studies have, however, called into question the inherent reductionism in this view of mysticism, and challenged its underlying universalist axiom, that the unmediated intuitive experience of the transcendent is essentially alike

---

[42] Quoted in Heiler, *Gospel of Singh*, 132-133; cf. Sadhu Sundar Singh, 'Meeting Temptation', in *Life in Abundance*, in *The Christian Witness of Sadhu Sundar Singh: A Collection of His Writing*, ed. T.D. Francis (Madras: CLS, 1989), 496; Sadhu Sundar Singh, *Search After Reality*, in *The Christian Witness of Sadhu Sundar Singh: A Collection of His Writing*, ed. T.D. Francis (Madras: CLS, 1989), 168-170.

[43] "Sundar Singh knows one kind of theology only, the *theologia experimentalis*... only one criterion in religious matters – personal experience of salvation", Heiler, *Gospel of Singh*, 132, 136; cf. Boyd, *Indian Christian Thoelogy*, 94; Prakash, *Preaching of Sadhu Sundar Singh*, 294-295.

[44] Streeter and Appasamy, *The Sadhu*, 143; cf. N. Soderblom, 'Christian Mysticism in an Indian Soul', *International Review of Mission* 11 (1922), 226-238; Sharpe, 'The Legacy of Sadhu Sundar Singh', 163-165.

[45] E. Underhill, *Mysticism: A Study in the Nature and Development of Man's Spiritual Consciousness* (Cleveland: The World Publishing Company, 1970), 71-72.

[46] A. Majumdar, *Bhakti Renaissance* (Bombay: Bharatiya Vidya Bhavan, 1979), vii; S.N. Dasgupta, *Hindu Mysticism* (Delhi: Motilal Banarsidass, 1996), vii-viii.

in all cultures, and that there is a common core to all mystical experiences.[47] Katz thus refutes the notion of pure, unmediated experience implicit in the earlier understanding of mysticism, arguing that phenomenological investigations of mystical experience indicate that: "...the [mystical] experience itself as well as the form in which it is reported is shaped by concepts which the mystic brings to, and which shape, his experience."[48] Arguing along the same lines, Keller in fact suggests that the term mysticism should at best have a tradition specific definition, if not be avoided altogether.[49]

This recognition of the contextuality and plurality of mystical experience makes the traditional generic definitions of mysticism implausible. Hence, the terms mysticism or mystical are used hereafter in this study in a non-technical sense, to denote broadly the inner psychological, devotional, and spiritual dimensions of religious experience, the content of which is context-specific. In Sundar Singh it is expressed in a blend of Hindu and Sikh *bhakti* elements within a framework of Christ-centred devotional experience. At this stage we adopt this only as a hypothesis, which we attempt to verify in the discussion which follows.

We turn, then, to investigate the specific sources of Sundar Singh's mystical orientation. Most commentators locate the original impulse for Sundar Singh's mystical experience in his pre-Christian *bhakti* devotional roots.[50] However, some of the same commentators concur with others in asserting that he frequently disclaimed the influence of any school of Hinduism upon his understanding of the Christian faith.[51] Are there any grounds for suggesting the definitive influence of *bhakti* upon Sundar Singh's mystical orientation?

We first need to offer an explanation for the supposed disclaimer. If Sundar Singh's position in this regard was stated frequently as these commentators maintain, it is hard to explain the lack of evidence of this in any of his published writings. Sundar Singh does seem to include the way of *bhakti* in a general sweeping critique of "the chief doctrines of Hinduism" in which he

---

[47] The case is argued cogently by S.T. Katz, ed., 'Language, Epistemology, and Mysticism' in *Mysticism and Philosophical Analysis* (London: Sheldon Press, 1978), 22-74.

[48] Katz, 'Language, Epistemology, and Mysticism', 23-27, 56-57, 66.

[49] S.T. Katz, ed., "Mystical Literature" in *Mysticism and Philosophical Analysis* (London: Sheldon Press, 1978), 75-77, 96-97.

[50] The fact of *bhakti* influence has never been seriously challenged, although its extent and character has sometimes been disputed; Streeter and Appasamy, *The Sadhu*, 182; Soderblom, 'Christian Mysticism in an Indian Soul', 234-235; Prakash, *Preaching of Sadhu Sundar Singh*, 14; Bookless, 'Water of Life in an Indian Cup', 20-23; Biehl, *Der Fall Sadhu Sundar Singh*, 231-235; Padinjarekuttu, *The Missionary Movement of the 19th and 20th Centuries and its Encounter with India* (Frankfurt: Peter Lang, 1995), 82-83.

[51] Streeter and Appasamy, *The Sadhu*, 239-240; Prakash, *Preaching of Sadhu Sundar Singh*, 14, 28 (n. 44), 296; cf. Heiler, *Gospel of Singh*, 245; Boyd, *Indian Christian Theology*, 107.

rejects Hinduism as a system for its failure to meet the religious needs of India.[52] However, this does not preclude his acceptance of elements of value in either the bhakti framework or in Hinduism as a whole, as his following comments in the same context seem to confirm:

> Among its teachers were many real seekers after truth, and bhaktas, or devotees, who had received some measure of light from that God Who 'left not Himself without witness' among the nations (Acts 14:16-17). Also, some of these devotees, in becoming Sadhus and Sanyasis, renounced not only the world and its luxuries, but even their kingdoms as well, and spent their time in meditation. In the world today it would be difficult to find a people more engrossed in religious observances than the Hindus.[53]

He thus clearly affirms the presence of "some measure of light" from God in Hinduism despite his rejection of Hinduism as a religious system. Moreover, the term *bhakta* in the above quotation is used most naturally for devotees within the *bhakti* tradition,[54] and could indicate a more positive attitude towards the *bhakti* tradition than to Hinduism in general. We are, however, hard-pressed to find any statement in which Sundar Singh explicitly claims to have adopted the *bhakti* framework in his interpretation of the Christian faith. The case for the *bhakti* influence upon his thought is not based on any overt assertion of Sundar Singh in this regard, but rather on evidence of his Christian experience being subconsciously shaped by *bhakti* elements imbibed during his pre-Christian formative years, some of which were appropriated later in his Christian theological formation.

Our task in establishing the validity of this hypothesis is twofold. We first need to suggest why primacy is ascribed to the *bhakti* conditioning among various possible influences upon his formation, and, second, evaluate the textual evidence for the purported *bhakti* influence.

We have earlier noted how his mother's religious devotion within the *bhakti* tradition of Hinduism and Sikhism critically influenced Sundar Singh's spiritual formation.[55] Although Sundar Singh made a number of acquaintances in the years following his conversion, the only other individual who exercised any significant influence upon him was the London Missionary Society (LMS) missionary, Mrs. Rebecca Parker, whom he regarded as his "spiritual mother" and his closest advisor.[56] We have seen that nineteenth century British

[52] Singh, *Search After Reality*, in *Christian Witness*, 141-152.
[53] Singh, *ibid.*, 141-142.
[54] Klostermaier, *Survey of Hinduism*, 212-224.
[55] See p.140-141; cf. Singh, *With and Without Christ*, in *Christian Witness*, 393; Bookless, 'Water of Life in an Indian Cup', 12.
[56] The evidence is in the form of 300 letters written by Sundar Singh to Mrs. Parker between 1918 and 1929 preserved in the LMS. archives, School of Oriental and African Studies, London; Bookless, 'Water of Life in an Indian Cup', 6, n. 14.

Protestant missionary theology was predominantly shaped by the beliefs of the Evangelical Awakening.[57] His formal instruction in the Christian faith was limited to the daily Bible lessons at the American Presbyterian school at Rampur, the brief Bible instruction prior to his baptism, and the few months he spent at Seminary.[58] Mrs. Parker was, hence, most likely the principal avenue of evangelical influence upon Sundar Singh's thought.[59]

Sundar Singh's sadhu lifestyle gave him little exposure to any other sustained human influence, or opportunities for advancing his knowledge through normal avenues of learning. His eagerness to preach kept him from completing his high school education. He regarded human learning of no avail in enhancing one's knowledge of God.[60] On one occasion when asked if he read books, he replied: "I am reading two books, which I can never, never finish... one is the Holy Bible, and second one is the Nature."[61]

This negative attitude to learning in general, along with Sundar Singh's limited knowledge of English and his itinerant lifestyle ensured that he had very limited exposure to western Christian influences.[62] During the latter years of his life, Sundar Singh seems to have given some attention to reading, with a special interest in philosophy, science and medieval western spirituality, and mysticism.[63] The influence, if any, came too late to affect the shape of his mystical orientation, the focal point of his thought world.

The Bible was an influence Sundar Singh consciously imbibed, and he regarded it as a reliable guide to Christ.[64] Sundar Singh had some exposure to the Bible prior to his conversion, but following his adoption of the sadhu life-style, the New Testament became a constant source of inspiration and

---

[57] Marked by an emphasis on the authority of the Bible, the need for conversion to Christ, and the importance of personal religious experience. However, dissonant with evangelical orthodoxy were some affinities of Sundar Singh's mystical experience with the spiritualism of the eighteenth century seer, Swedenborg; Sharpe, 'The Legacy of Sadhu Sundar Singh', 164-165; 'Sadhu Sundar Singh and Swedenborg', in *The Indian Christian* (1929), available in the Library Archives of the United Theological College, Bangalore, India (VPC SSS.5).

[58] Appasamy, *Sundar Singh*, 20, 22-23.

[59] For instance, she seems to have neutralized Gandhi's possible influence on Sundar Singh towards political involvement; see Bookless, 'Water of Life in an Indian Cup', 15-16.

[60] Appasamy, *Sundar Singh*, 176. He placed little value on formal theological study in the early years, but later designated significant amounts from his Trust Fund as scholarships for theological students; Prakash, *Preaching of Sadhu Sundar Singh*, 135.

[61] Vincent David in *The Cowley Evangelist*, Oxford (December 1918), available in the Library Archives of the United Theological College, Bangalore, India (VPC SSS.1).

[62] Bookless, 'Water of Life in an Indian Cup', 16-17.

[63] Appasamy, *Sundar Singh*, 176, 210; cf. Andrews, *Personal Memoir*, 190.

[64] Sadhu Sundar Singh, *At the Master's Feet*, in *The Christian Witness of Sadhu Sundar Singh: A Collection of His Writing*, ed. T.D. Francis (Madras: CLS, 1989), 35-36.

companion on his travels: he spent many hours in private Bible reading and meditation.[65]

The two principal influences upon Sundar Singh's mystical formation were thus his pre-conversion Hindu and Sikh *bhakti* formation, and his biblical reflection, especially on the New Testament. The influence of the Bible on Sundar Singh's experience of Christ was intentional and explicit. The *bhakti* conditioning, on the other hand, was more subliminal, but significant for two reasons. First, it enables us to identify the underlying impulses and thus make sense of many aspects of Sundar Singh's thought. Second, it provides a framework for relating Sundar Singh's experience of Christ to his pre-Christian religious consciousness.

Before we can consider the evidence for *bhakti* influence on Sundar Singh's mystical framework, we need to introduce briefly the *bhakti* tradition, focusing on those aspects relevant to our present discussion.

The existence of different schools of thought within the broader *bhakti* tradition makes its precise definition difficult. Based on the most likely derivation of the term from the root *bhaj-*, its meaning is rendered variously as service, worship, loyalty, homage, and loving devotion to God. *Bhakti* is thus used in its broad sense to denote adoration of and loving devotion to the deity.[66] The phenomenon of *bhakti* has had a pervading influence in Indian religion, due to which recent studies have preferred to describe *bhakti* as a religious process based on "...a set of flexible axioms and practices accumulated over centuries..." which includes most of the principal aspects of Indian religion, and expresses the devotional element in terms of an intimate relationship between a human being and a personal God based on mutual love.[67]

The essential core of *bhakti* thus includes the idea of a personal God who can be loved and worshipped, and remains distinct from the *bhakta* (devotee). The object of the *bhakta*'s total emotional abandonment and singular devotion is her *ishtadevata*, the deity of her choice, who bestows his grace upon and fills her with his *anand*, indescribable peace and bliss.[68] The *bhakta* suffers the agony of separation until through single-minded devotion her soul finds ultimate realization in union with God.[69]

Our concern with Sundar Singh's *bhakti* orientation requires us to dwell briefly on those aspects of the *bhakti* movement relevant to our analysis of the sources of his thought. Although the influence of *bhakti* upon his framework is

---

[65] Appasamy, *Sundar Singh*, 146; Heiler, *Gospel of Singh*, 195-197.
[66] G.M. Bailey and I. Kesarcodi-Watson, eds., *Bhakti Studies* (New Delhi: Sterling Publishers, 1992), 2; Majumdar, *Bhakti Renaissance*, 3.
[67] Bailey and Kesarcodi-Watson, *Bhakti Studies*, 1, 4-7; J. Miller, 'Bhakti and the Rg Veda – Does it Appear There or Not?' in *Love Divine: Studies in Bhakti and Devotional Mysticism*, ed. Karel Werner (Richmond Surrey: Curzon Press, 1993), 1.
[68] Scott, *Kabir's Mythology* (Delhi: Bharatiya Vidya Prakashan, 1985), 23).
[69] Scott, *ibid.*, 22.

quite pronounced, it is difficult to identify his approach with any one particular strand of the *bhakti* tradition.

Among the various Hindu scriptures Sundar Singh was exposed to in his early years, the *Bhagavadgita*, which he had memorised by the age of seven, had pride of place.[70] Although the beginnings of *bhakti* may be traced in the hymns of the Rgveda, the earliest extensive teaching on *bhakti* is to be found in the *Bhagavadgita*.[71] The centrality of *bhakti* to the message of the *Bhagavadgita* is acknowledged within the wide diversity of interpretations regarding its significance.[72] In summarising the basic impulse of the *Bhagavadgita*, Radhakrishnan maintains that it: "...teaches a method which is within the reach of all, that of *bhakti*, or devotion to God."[73] After indicating its importance as a "seminal text" for much of Vaisnava Sanskrit devotional theology, Lipner asserts that "...the *Gita* is a genuinely devotional text, telling of the soul's immortality and of a caring God's saving and reassuring love for each individual..."[74]

Sundar Singh's brief discussion of the message of the *Bhagavadgita*[75] reflects a reasonable measure of familiarity with its content:

> In the Bhagavad *Gita* the attempt has been made to reconcile the Sankhya, Yoga and Vedanta systems of philososphy with the doctrine of *Bhakti* (devotion), and evidence is not lacking that it was now and again influenced by the teaching of St. John's Gospel...[76]

His view recognizes that the *Bhagavadgita* represents an eclectic compilation, but also reflects acquaintance with a prevailing school of thought, which detected Christian influence in it. It is thus natural for us to expect the *Bhagavadgita* to have in some way influenced Sundar Singh's *bhakti* mystical orientation.

Sundar Singh's thought is viewed by some as grounded in the *Visistadvaita* scheme of Ramanuja,[77] who provided the Vaisnava *bhakti* stream with a constructive and elaborate philosophical framework, and thus emerged as the

---

[70] Heiler, *Gospel of Singh*, 37.

[71] Miller, 'Bhakti and the Rg Veda, 6, 21-24, 31 traces the roots of the *bhakti* impulse in the *Rg* vedic hymns, although she distinguishes this early, incipient expression of *bhakti* from its later post-Vedic connotations of fervent devotion to a personal god.

[72] Klostermaier, *Survey of Hinduism*, 95-96.

[73] Radhakrishnan, *Indian Philosophy* (London: George Allen & Unwin Limited, 1962), 519-520; cf. Walker, *Hindu World*, vol. 1, 136.

[74] Lipner, *Hindus: Their Religious Beliefs and Practices* (London: Routledge, 1998), 134-135.

[75] Singh, *Search After Reality*, in *Christian Witness*, 149-152.

[76] Singh, *ibid.*, 151.

[77] Bichl. *Der Fall Sadhu Sundar Singh*, 230-235 makes a strong case for Ramanuja's influence; cf. Padinjarekuttu, *The Missionary Movement*, 82.

chief protagonist of the medieval *bhakti* movement.[78] Based on the three foundations of Vedantic theology, the *Upanishads*, the *Bhagavadgita*, and the *Brahma Sutras*, and fed by the *bhakti* spirituality of the *Alvars*, Tamil Vaisnava mystic-saints who flourished between the seventh and tenth centuries A.D., Ramanuja's system was clearly developed to counter the *advaita* philosophy of Sankara.[79]

A critical concern of Ramanuja's theology is the relationship between Brahman and the world/individual, and he expresses this relationship as a distinctive identity-in-difference (*visistadvaita*), based on a description of the world as Brahman's body, in the sense of something that Brahman fully sustains and controls and which serves the divine purpose.[80] Ramanuja's scheme thus accepts the ultimate reality of a single, supreme Self, Brahman, but recognizes a real identity-in-difference between this divine Self and three entities which have a derived existence: individual subjects, the world in which we live, and God or *Isvara*.[81]

According to Ramanuja, salvation involves a union with Brahman, which does not necessitate dissolution of the individual's self-identity, as in the advaitic vision, but rather its perfection through communion with the Supreme.[82] For Ramanuja, the path to salvation or *bhakti* was devotion grounded in a God-centred integration of knowledge and works, requiring disciplined submission to a complex and rigorous path of spiritual ascent or Yoga.[83]

Sundar Singh's reference to the teaching of Ramanuja emerges in the context of his contrasting of Ramanuja's affirmation of the reality of creation with the denial of its reality in the *maya* doctrine of Sankara's *advaita* Vedanta.[84] The influence of Ramanuja on Sundar Singh's thought is most evident in his application of the Ramanujan body-soul analogy to the relation between God and creation, and in the distinction he affirms between the individual self and God in the experience of mystical union. However, to identify Sundar Singh's theological framework with this one strand of *bhakti* tradition is to go beyond the evidence.

A third strand of *bhakti* thought which influenced Sundar Singh's religious consciousness was that in Sikhism. Sikhism is widely regarded as a child of the

---

[78] G.M. Bailey, and I. Kesarcodi-Watson, eds., *Bhakti Studies* (New Delhi: Sterling Publishers, 1992), 110-111; Majumdar, *Bhakti Renaissance*, 1-6.

[79] Lipner, *The Face of Truth: A Study of Meaning and Metaphysics in the Vedantic Theology of Ramanuja* (Basingstoke: Macmillan, 1986), 4-6.

[80] For a detailed analysis, see Lipner, *The Face of Truth*, 120-142.

[81] Raghavachar 'The Spiritual Vision of Ramanuja', in *Hindu Spirituality: Vedas through Vedanta*, ed. K. Sivaraman (1989; repr., Delhi: Motilal Banarsidass, 1995), 261-273; Bailey and Kesarcodi-Watson, eds., *Bhakti Studies*, 110-146.

[82] Raghavachar, 'The Spiritual Vision of Ramanuja', 262.

[83] Raghavachar, *ibid.*, 264-270.

[84] Singh, *Search After Reality*, in *Christian Witness*, 142-146.

medieval religious renaissance in north India affected by the *sufi* and *bhakti* movements.[85] *Bhakti* elements constituted the principal contribution to the synthesis of Vaisnava bhakti, Nath Yogi, and Sufi elements in the Sant tradition of North India, which provided the primary basis of Guru Nanak's thought.[86]

Guru Nanak's mystical vision was grounded in his understanding of the nature of God as the one, sovereign, ineffable, personal, eternal, formless, creator and sustainer, and the meaning and purpose of human existence was, for him, wholly centred in this vision.[87] Sikh religion is essentially a religion of experience: the ultimate purpose of all life and religion is an inward union with God resulting in eternal bliss. However, humankind, separated from God by an impure heart (*man*) and corrupted by sin (*haumai*) due to the temptations of this world (*maya*), remains a prisoner to the cycle of transmigration.[88]

The gracious initiative (*Nadar*) of God is humankind's only hope for salvation. Nature reveals God's nature to the person who is sensitive to the voice of God (*Guru*) mystically uttered within the inner recesses of the human soul. The enlightened one thus comprehends the Word (*Sabad*) of God in the world and in his inner experience. He responds in loving adoration, meditates on the revealed nature and qualities of God, and thus draws nearer to God, finally reaching the supreme bliss of consummate union.[89]

Sharpe finds little trace of Sikh influence on Sundar Singh's spiritual formation.[90] This may be due to the fact that Sundar Singh himself emphasised the importance given to Hindu teaching in his home during his formative years.[91] Sharpe, however, fails to take into account medieval Hindu *bhakti* impulses which nourished the Sikh tradition or the evidence of Sikh influence on Sundar Singh's formation. Earlier commentators generally regarded the Sikh and Hindu *bhakti* traditions as each having an equal role in Sundar Singh's pre-Christian formation.[92] Heiler viewed Sikhism as the principal influence – a *paidagogos eis Christon*, and Bookless also presupposes the primacy of the Sikh *bhakti* influence.[93]

---

[85] C.O. McMullen, 'Operative Sikh Beliefs and Practices', *Dharma Deepika* 35 (1998): 15.

[86] W.H. McLeod, *Guru Nanak and the Sikh Religion* (Oxford: Clarendon Press, 1978), 151-153, 157-161.

[87] The following summary of Guru Nanak's religious framework relies heavily on chapter five of McLeod's work; McLeod, *Guru Nanak*, 148-226.

[88] McLeod, *Guru Nanak*, 148-151, 177-187.

[89] McLeod, *ibid.*, 196-199, 204-207, 213-226.

[90] Sharpe, 'The Legacy of Sadhu Sundar Singh', 162, 166, n. 7.

[91] Singh, *With and Without Christ*, in *Christian Witness*, 393.

[92] A.J. Appasamy, ed., *The Cross is Heaven* (London: Lutterworth Press, 1956), 7; Boyd, *Indian Christian Theology*, 92.

[93] Heiler, *Gospel of Singh*, 36; Bookless, 'Water of Life in an Indian Cup', 20-22.

Given that Sundar Singh was not primarily a trained theologian or systematic thinker, it should not surprise us if his framework represents a synthesis of elements from different strands of the *bhakti* tradition. Our analysis hence yields elements specific to either the Sikh *bhakti* or the Vaisnava *bhakti* framework, and others common to both or to the *bhakti* tradition in general. Katz's thesis referred to earlier, which insists on the essentially mediated nature of all mystical experience, highlights the importance of this analysis.

Katz does not deny that mystical experience does shape an individual's belief and consciousness, but wants the philosophical investigation of mysticism to take into account the reverse direction of the process. He thus argues that mystical experiences themselves are culturally and ideologically conditioned: "...beliefs shape experience, just as experience shapes belief."[94] The mystic thus brings to his experience a certain interpretative framework, a world of beliefs, images, symbols, and values, which condition the nature and form of his actual experience. The various factors that condition mystical experience linguistically and cognitively include the cumulative sum total of all our faculties, traits, prior experiences, and our expectation of what will be experienced.[95]

This important insight of Katz furnishes us with a helpful hermeneutical key for understanding how Sundar Singh's pre-Christian *bhakti* mystical consciousness conditioned his conversion and subsequent Christian experience. It thus provides us with a grid for analysing how his *bhakti* orientation functioned as an underlying framework of continuity for his appropriation of the fulfilment concept.

Bhakti Mysticism as a Framework of Continuity in Sundar Singh's Fulfilment View

In considering the influence of *bhakti* upon Sundar Singh's theological framework, we are especially concerned with those aspects of his pre-Christian *bhakti* religious consciousness, which conditioned his conversion experience, and then subsequently became incorporated into his Christian world-view. As noted earlier the influence of the New Testament on Sundar Singh's thought is fairly explicit; what is in question is the fact and nature of *bhakti* influence. The following analysis will focus, accordingly, on aspects of Sundar Singh's framework most likely to have been conditioned by Singh's pre-Christian *bhakti* consciousness. The possibility of specifically biblical or Christian influence in the shaping of those elements is thereby not precluded. It is in fact presupposed, except with respect to those features expressly relating to his pre-

94 Katz, 'Language, Epistemology, and Mysticism', 30.
95 Katz, *ibid.*, 46.

Christian consciousness, such as, for instance, the source of his pre-conversion aspirations prior to exposure to Christian sources.

Our analysis thus does not seek to prove that Sundar Singh borrowed certain elements from various *bhakti* strands within his Christian framework, as much as to demonstrate continuity – that elements in his pre-Christian consciousness are likely to have contributed to his Christian theological framework. We will succeed in demonstrating this continuity if we discern some elements of his Christian framework that are distinctively *bhakti*, and others that may be common to both the *bhakti* and Christian traditions. The elements of continuity thus identified will help us affirm a framework of continuity between Sundar Singh's *bhakti* and Christian experience. We focus on three critical components: (1) his conception of God, (2) his understanding of divine revelation, and (3) his view of salvation.

GOD

Sundar Singh's understanding of God is compatible with the Sikh and Vaisnava Hindu *bhakti* conceptions of God at several points. He echoes a facet of Sikh mystical theology when he speaks of God as ineffable and ultimately incomprehensible in essence, transcending all human categories and powers of expression: "No man has ever seen or heard God as He is in Himself…."[96] He thus occasionally uses abstract terms such as Reality or Truth to address God.[97] This emphasis on God as Truth or the True One resonates deeply with the Sikh view as observed in the opening words of the *Japji*:[98]

> There is but one God whose name is true, the Creator, devoid of fear and enmity, immortal, unborn, self-existent; by the favour of the Guru. The True One was in the beginning; the Truc One was in the primal age. The True One is now also, O Nanak; the True One also shall be.[99]

In keeping with the emphasis in both Sikh and Vaisnava *bhakti*,[100] however, the Truth or Reality which Sundar Singh refers to is clearly a personal being,

---

[96] Sadhu Sundar Singh, *Spiritual Life*, in *The Christian Witness of Sadhu Sundar Singh: A Collection of His Writings*, ed. T.D. Francis (Madras: CLS, 1989), 223, 201-202; Singh, *At the Master's Feet*, in *Christian Witness*, 29; cf. McLeod, *Guru Nanak*, 172-173.

[97] Singh, *Reality and Religion*, in *Christian Witness*, 112-113.

[98] The *Japji*, composed by Guru Nanak, the founder of Sikhism, is one of the most important hymns in the *Adi Granth* or *Guru Granth Sahib*, the religious book of the Sikhs.

[99] M.A. Macauliffe, *The Sikh Religion: Its Gurus, Sacred Writings and Authors* (New Delhi: S. Chand, 1985), 195.

[100] Although in Sikhism God is both *nirguna*, impersonal and without attributes, as well as *saguna*, personal and with attributes, the nature of God as *nirguna* receives little attention. God is conceived of as essentially a personal God to whom man responds in love; McLeod, *Guru Nanak*, 168-169, 165. The personal aspect of Brahman, *Isvara*, is

an object of worship and devotion: "God Himself is pleased when we pray. He rejoices in our worship. Yes, God and the soul long for each other. God needs our prayer, just as a mother does not feel well if her baby does not lie on her bosom and drink."[101]

Although he most commonly uses the biblical image of God as FatherorHeavenly Father, he also uses other personal terms such as Creator, Spiritual Mother or Heavenly Mother-Father to address God.[102] The inclusive language of God as Father and Mother would have been viewed as a radical innovation by the Christian community of Sundar Singh's time; this emphasis on the motherhood of God was thus almost certainly influenced by the Vaisnava *bhakti* tradition Sundar Singh had imbibed in his formative years.[103]

The conception of God as love is at the heart of the *bhakti* framework, and, for Sundar Singh, God is supremely and above all else perfect, pure, self-giving love.[104] The phrase "God is love" occurs frequently and expresses Sundar Singh's favourite description of God:

> God is the source of love. The force of gravity... [is] the manifestation in matter of that spiritual force of gravity, which is love and whose source is God... God's love is infinite... God's capacity for love is without limit and, therefore, is sufficient for all.[105]

Infinite love flows out unceasingly from God's presence: God not only draws man to himself, he also desires the perfect happiness of the beings he has created.[106] God needs love and fellowship from human beings as much as they need to express love to God through prayer and worship.[107] This emphasis on love may both explain as well as be an outcome of his deep affinity for the Gospel of John.[108] Thus prominent in his thought is an idea integral to both

---

identified as the creator and lord of the universe and worshipped as Visnu in his various forms by Vaisnavites; Klostermaier, *Survey of Hinduism*, 377.

101 Quoted in Heiler, *Gospel of Singh*, 138.

102 Singh, *At the Master's Feet*, in *Christian Witness*, 32, 54; Singh, *Reality and Religion*, in *Christian Witness*, 99, 113.

103 Dasgupta, *Hindu Mysticism*, 144. Others who have incorporated this divine motherhood imagery from within a Christian *bhakti* framework include H.A. Krishna Pillai and N.V. Tilak; see Heiler, *Gospel of Singh*, 138; Prakash, *Preaching of Sadhu Sundar Singh*, 203.

104 Singh, *At the Master's Feet*, in *Christian Witness*, 33-34, 39, 41, 48-49.

105 Singh, *Reality and Religion*, in *Christian Witness*, 99.

106 S ingh, *Spiritual World*, in *Christian Witness*, 287.

107 Sadhu Sundar Singh, *Real Life*, in *The Christian Witness of Sadhu Sundar Singh: A Collection of His Writings*, ed. T.D. Francis (Madras: CLS, 1989), 324.

108 Streeter and Appasamy, *The Shadhu*, 197; Boyd, *Indian Christian Theology*, 101.

Sikh and Vaisnava *bhakti* theology, of God as the divine lover whose love is unconquerable and indefatigable.[109]

Sundar Singh makes a significant departure from Sikh *bhakti* in his acceptance of the possibility of an incarnation or *avatara*, a concept integral to Vaisnava *bhakti.*[110] His pre-Christian *avatara* aspiration was fulfilled in his experience of Christ, seen clearly in his full affirmation of Christ as "the Word incarnate... [and] God incarnate in whom 'dwelleth all the fullness of the Godhead bodily' (Col.2:9)."[111] Sundar Singh thus does not hesitate to use the term *avatara* to describe the incarnation, illustrating it vividly and frequently in his writings.[112]

The love of God moves him to create, an expression of his power to give life and desire to impart true happiness to man.[113] The personhood of the Creator-God, a prominent feature in the Sikh doctrine of creation, and the reality of the created world are both important emphases in Sundar Singh's framework.[114] The only instance when he explicitly cites Ramanuja, draws attention to his teaching concerning the reality of creation: "Ramanuja and his followers deny the Maya teaching, and hold that the creation is as real as God Himself."[115] Although the intention is clearly to base his teaching upon the New Testament, he alludes to Ramanuja's doctrine in his assertion that the Creator-God is both distinct from and yet dwells within man and the natural world, his creation:

> The truth is that there is one True, Almighty and Eternal God, and that this world is His creation. This material world is not Maya or Illusion, as the Vedantists and Sophists believe, but is real existence. The creation is neither God Himself, nor is the creation separate from Him. His life-giving presence is present in all creatures, because 'in Him we live, and move, and have our being' (Acts 17:28).[116]

Although Sundar Singh does not explicitly refer to it, Ramanuja's idea of the world as the body of God, which he is distinct from and yet indwells, most likely constitutes the background to this description. In Ramanuja the body-soul analogy is employed to show the identity-in-difference between Brahman

---

[109] McLeod, *Guru Nanak*, 213; Dasgupta, *Hindu Mysticism*, 131-137. There is a consequent lack of emphasis on the fear of God and divine judgment in his thought, in striking contrast to the strong emphasis on the lostness of man in the evangelical theology of the nineteenth century; for instance, Nehemiah Goreh wrote a tract of a 126 pages on the doctrine of eternal punishment, Boyd, *Indian Christian Theology*, 51.

[110] Sikhism explicitly rejects the *avatara* doctrine; McLeod, *Guru Nanak*, 167, 172, 214.

[111] Sadhu Sundar Singh, *Reality and Religion*, in *The Christian Witness of Sadhu Sundar Singh: A Collection of His Writings*, ed. T.D. Francis (Madras: CLS, 1989), 89.

[112] Singh, *Search After Reality*, in *Christian Witness*, 166; Heiler, 1989:148-149.

[113] Singh, *Reality and Religion*, in *Christian Witness*, 88.

[114] McLeod, *Guru Nanak*, 168-169.

[115] Singh, *Search After Reality*, in *Christian Witness*, 145.

[116] Singh, *ibid.*, 142, 137.

and the created world and individual subjects he indwells, just as the soul is distinct from the body, and indwells and controls it as its inner ruler.[117] This idea is echoed in Sundar Singh's simple but vivid description of the relation between God and the created world:

> I asked, 'Whence is Life?' I was told that the one source of Life is behind everything. Our clothes are warm, because the body which they conceal is warm. There is no heat in the clothes; that comes from the body within. Just so the life in all living creatures is derived from the one source of Life behind. Their life is from the Giver of life. Again, just as our body is hidden by our clothes, but the shape of the clothes as well as the heat comes from the body inside, so all the vegetables and animals that we see are but the outward forms upheld by the Giver of life.[118]

There are plausible if limited grounds for recognizing the broad influence of Ramanuja on Sundar Singh's understanding of God and creation, but not enough evidence to suggest a detailed dependence on the *Visistadvaita* framework.[119]

Sundar Singh's conception of God was thus both conditioned by and continuous with *bhakti* sources, including the idea of God as pure and perfect love prominent in the broader *bhakti* tradition, the concepts of Divine motherhood and *avatara* from the Vaisnava *bhakti* tradition, and broad resonance with the teaching of Ramanuja in his understanding of God and creation.

Divine Revelation

According to Sundar Singh, God is always present in his creation, and every aspect of God's creation, visible and invisible, animate and inanimate, in some way reflects the nature and attributes of God.[120] The God who has never been seen or heard as he is in himself reveals something of his wisdom, power and glory through his creation: "In heaven and in earth God proclaims His power and wisdom and glory in His wonderful handiwork…"[121]

Sundar Singh, consequently, possessed an extraordinary fascination for nature, the handiwork and reflection of the Creator-God. He loves the beauty of nature, it enhances his communion with God, and he draws great enjoyment

---

[117] Ramanuja, *Sribhasyam on 1:4:27* in J. Pereira, *Hindu Theology: Themes, Texts and Structures* (Delhi: Motilal Banarsidass, 1991), 287; Kesarcodi-Watson, Bailey and Kesarcodi-Watson, eds., *Bhakti Studies*, 144-145; cf. Lipner, *Face of Truth*, 120-142.

[118] Quoted in Streeter and Appasamy, *The Sadhu*, 131-132.

[119] The textual evidence for Sundar Singh's dependence on Ramanuja is simply inadequate and Biehl's case seemingly overstated; Biehl, *Der Fall Sadhu Sundar Singh*, 231-235.

[120] Singh, *Spiritual Life*, in *Christian Witness*, 227.

[121] Singh, *With and Without Christ*, in *Christian Witness*, 384; cf. Singh, *Spiritual Life*, in *Christian Witness*, 223-224.

from reading the great truths of God in the "book of nature".[122] He takes the revelation of God in nature very seriously, frequently juxtaposing the "Book of nature" alongside the Bible:

> The Bible and the Book of Nature are both written in spiritual language by the Holy Spirit. The Holy Spirit being the author of life, all Nature, instinct with life, is the work of the Holy Spirit, and the language in which it is written is spiritual language. Those who are born again have the Holy Spirit for their mother. So to them the language of the Bible and of nature is their mother tongue, which they easily and naturally understand...[123]

The Bible and the "Book of nature" both have the same author, the Holy Spirit, and use the same spiritual language of the Spirit, which only those who are "born again" understand. The difference is that: "The message of the Bible is simple, direct and straightforward, whereas the message of the Book of Nature has to be spelt out carefully letter by letter."[124]

How does man read this "Book of nature" and discern signs of God's presence in creation? To what extent is the revelation of God in creation self-evident and accessible to human reason? There is some ambiguity in Sundar Singh's thought at this point. We have seen that sometimes he seems to suggest that only those who are born again can understand the language of the Holy Spirit in which the Bible and the "book of nature" have both been written. To a question regarding the difference, if any, between the vedic and Christian seers' reading of the "book of nature", Sundar Singh replied in an obvious reference to the *advaitic* school, that whereas the Hindu mystic loses God in Nature – "...thinks that God and Nature are the same", the Christian mystic finds God in Nature – "…knows that there must be a Creator who has created the creation."[125]

In one of his visions, he suggests that people may go astray without the special "spiritual insight" necessary for the reading of God's "book of nature".[126] There is, thus, no value in using "feeble arguments of our limited intellects" to try and prove the existence of God.[127] At other times, however, Sundar Singh appeals to common reason in trying to establish the existence of God:

> It is not possible that matter came into existence in space by its own creative power, or that living organisms should spring from lifeless matter. Consequently,

---

[122] An expression he frequently uses to describe the revelation of God in nature, Streeter and Appasamy, *The Sadhu*, 191.
[123] Quoted in Streeter and Appasamy, *The Sadhu*, 193-194.
[124] Quoted in *ibid.*, 194.
[125] Quoted in *ibid.*, 194-195.
[126] Singh, *At the Master's Feet*, in *Christian Witness*, 36.
[127] Singh, *Spiritual Life*, in *Christian Witness*, 223.

> when we find order and design in the universe, it is a proof of the existence of an Almighty and All-knowing Being…[128]

Sundar Singh's belief concerning the divine self-expression deeply resonates with the Sikh *bhakti* teaching that the created world has been designed to enable the perceptive person to discern the Creator's nature expressed in it.[129] According to the Sikh and Vaisnava *bhakti* teaching, the God who is immanent in all creation is especially immanent within the human heart. In the Sikh *bhakti* scheme, this teaching provides for the possibility of unmediated communication and relationship between God and man.[130] In keeping with this Sikh emphasis, Sundar Singh is convinced that man has a natural intuitive awareness of God's existence. This intuitive mystical knowledge transcends human reason and ordinary sensory perception: "...the heart has a conception of Reality which is independent of the intellect and whose aptness cannot be understood by the intellect."[131]

This *a priori* revelation of God in the depths of the human soul enables all human beings to recognise the evidence of God's presence elsewhere in creation, and to interpret the language of nature:

> Man is a part of the Universe and is a mirror reflecting it. Therefore creation, seen and unseen, is imaged in him. In this world, he is the only being who can interpret creation. He is, so to speak, the language of Nature. Nature speaks, but silently. Man puts into words these silent utterance [*sic*] of Nature.[132]

Thus, although Sundar Singh seems to allow for the place of reason in arriving at a knowledge of God, this notion of a natural intuitive knowledge of God is the basic conviction underlying his understanding of how human beings appropriate God's self-revelation in nature. However, he apparently admits a quantitative differentiation in this universal intuitive knowledge – while all have the inner capacity for processing the data of natural revelation, some have it to a lesser degree than others. Consequently, those who possess this intuitive knowledge in lesser measure require special "spiritual insight" or illumination by the Holy Spirit. This is the closest Sundar Singh comes to distinguishing between a natural and supernatural knowledge of God.

Sundar Singh's Sikh background had also prepared him for the acceptance of the Bible as authoritative written revelation as emphasised in the evangelical missionary tradition he encountered prior to and immediately after his conversion. This is because Sikhism gives a high degree of importance to its

---

[128] Singh, *Search After Reality*, in *Christian Witness*, 136-137.
[129] McLeod, *Guru Nanak*, 150, 165, 168.
[130] McLeod, *ibid.*, 174-175, 189.
[131] Singh, *Reality and Religion*, in *Christian Witness*, 110; cf. Singh, *Search After Reality*, in *Christian Witness*, 135.
[132] Singh, *Reality and Religion*, in *Christian Witness*, 110.

written scriptures, the *Granth Sahib*, viewing it as a *Guru*, the means to divine guidance and a channel of communication between God and man.[133]

According to Boyd, Sundar Singh "...was steeped in the New Testament and all his teaching is rooted there..."[134] Baago, on the other hand, regards the Bible as possessing "no ultimate significance" for Sundar Singh, which in the context represents Sundar Singh as treating the Bible as ultimately dispensable.[135] Some of Sundar Singh's comments could be construed as depreciating the importance of the written word, as, for instance: "If He [Christ] had written something in a book, men would have bowed down and worshipped it, instead of worshipping the Lord Himself."[136]

Sundar Singh's experience of Christ was of definitive significance for him. However, to suggest that the Bible was ultimately dispensable for him is to go beyond the bounds of evidence. There can be little doubt that Sundar Singh gave the Bible, and the New Testament, in particular, central importance.[137] Of greater significance is the fact that he regarded the Holy Spirit as the "true Author" of the Bible, which he consequently described as "the Word of God", "inspired", "given by the Divine Spirit" and "the word of the Saviour which has vital power".[138]

Sundar Singh's words and practice thus leave us in little doubt that he regarded the Bible as the divinely revealed word of God. According to his distinctive view of the inspiration of the Bible, however, the meaning of the biblical text can only be discerned as one enters the ecstatic spiritual state experienced by the inspired authors of scripture.[139] Thus, although his Sikh conditioning prepared Sundar Singh for the idea of an authoritative written Word, his views regarding inspiration and interpretation are both thoroughly mystical:

> Christ speaks: "If you do not understand Me, you cannot understand the Word of God. In order to understand it rightly you do not need to know any Greek or Hebrew, but you must be in the communion of the Holy Spirit, of that Holy Spirit through whom the apostles and prophets wrote. The language of the Word of God is spiritual; only he who is born of the Spirit can rightly and completely understand it, whether he is a scholar or a child."[140]

---

133 McLeod, *Guru Nanak*, 217.

134 Boyd, *Indian Christian Theology*, 108-109; cf. Sharpe, 'The Legacy of Sadhu Sundar Singh', 163.

135 Baago, *Pioneers of Indigenous Christianity*, 62.

136 Quoted in Heiler, *Gospel of Singh*, 194-195; this comment may reflect a reaction to the Sikh tendency to accord honour and reverence to the *Guru Granth Sahib* almost akin to worship; Singh, *Reality and Religion*, in *Christian Witness*, 96.

137 See p.140.

138 Quoted in Heiler, *Gospel of Singh*, 195-198.

139 Heiler, *Gospel of Singh*, 198-199.

140 Quoted in Heiler, *Gospel of Singh*, 199.

Sundar Singh's roots in the Sikh *bhakti* tradition gave him a distinctive understanding of how God reveals himself to humankind, but helped him relate readily to the Christian view of divine revelation. He viewed the created world as a reflection of God's nature and attributes; humans are a part of this reflection of God in nature, and uniquely and intuitively endowed with the capacity to interpret God's revelation in nature. Human beings thus have a capacity for unmediated communication and relationship with God, which special divine illumination can enhance. Sikhism had also prepared Sundar Singh for the Christian idea of an authoritative written divine revelation, the Bible.

SALVATION

Sundar Singh's understanding of salvation is strongly conditioned by the *bhakti* mystic quest for union with the divine. His view of the self in its relation to God is consonant with Vaisnava *bhakti* spirituality, which regards mystical union with the divine as communion between two free personalities rather than absorption in the absolute:[141]

> God is our Creator and we are His creatures; He is our Father, and we are His children.... If we want to rejoice in God we must be different from Him; the tongue could taste no sweetness if there were no difference between it and that which it tastes.... To be redeemed does not mean to be lost or absorbed into God. We do not lose our personality in God; rather we find it.[142]

Man's deep desire for union with God is an intuitive impulse, expressed in a search for true peace and happiness.[143] The thirst in the soul for true happiness and peace implies that real happiness and peace exists. This craving of the soul is fulfilled only when it attains real communion with God, a conviction clearly grounded in Sundar Singh's own spiritual experience.[144]

A closer examination of certain aspects of Sundar Singh's conversion experience offers several points of insight into the influence of his pre-Christian religious consciousness upon his conversion and understanding of

---

[141] This distinction between God and the individual self is not as clearly expressed in Sikh *bhakti* as in Ramanuja. The essentially monotheistic Sikh *bhakti* framework is qualified by certain monistic elements, especially in its vision of the final consummation of man's mystical ascent to God; McLeod, *Guru Nanak*, 164-165, 224-225; cf. J.V. David, 'Hindrances to Communicating the Christian Message among Sikhs', *Dharma Deepika* 35 (1998): 34.

[142] Quoted in Heiler, *Gospel of Singh*, 242; cf. Raghavachar, 'The Spiritual Vision of Ramanuja', 262, 267-268.

[143] Singh, *With and Without Christ*, in *Christian Witness*, 413.

[144] Singh, *At the Master's Feet*, in *Christian Witness*, 74-75; Singh, *With and Without Christ*, in *Christian Witness*, 345, 360.

salvation.[145] First, we have some indication of the reasons for his spiritual restlessness and pre-conversion aspirations. The human predicament, according to Sundar Singh, is determined by sin: "...to cast aside the will of God and to live according to one's own will, deserting that which is true and lawful in order to satisfy one's own desires".[146] The strong moral content in this understanding of sin suggests its roots in the Sikh concept of *haumai*, the condition of unregenerate man living in wilful disobedience to God, being led astray by the delusion of *maya.*[147]

Furthermore, just as *maya* has no real existence of its own, but denotes a distorted and deluding interpretation of the nature and purpose of creation permitted by God himself, for Sundar Singh, sin or evil is "...simply a delusive and destructive state of being... not a self-existent thing, but simply the absence or non-existence of good."[148] The concept of *karma,*[149] likewise, though not specifically a feature of *bhakti*, also conditions Sundar Singh's view of sin. Like *karma*, sin brings with it its own effects, including hardening of a person's character, a process of moral degeneration, and consequent retribution.[150] The influence of the Sikh *maya* concept and *karma* must be seen in sharp contrast to the Calvinistic emphasis on total depravity and sin as a positive principle of evil which characterised much of nineteenth century evangelical theology.[151]

Again, in contrast to the doctrine of total depravity, Sundar Singh insists that the human nature has a divine spark that is never inclined towards sin, and is never destroyed regardless of how depraved the human heart or conscience may become.[152] How is this idea of an impeccable and indestructible divine spark within the human nature reconciled with Sundar Singh's view of sin as

---

[145] Sundar Singh offers several accounts of his conversion: Singh, *With and Without Christ*, in *Christian Witness*, 399-400; Singh, *Life in Abundance*, in *Christian Witness*, 479-480, 484, 502-503, 527.

[146] Singh, *At the Master's Feet*, in *Christian Witness*, 38.

[147] *Maya* in Sikh thought is not the cosmic illusion of classical Vedanta, but essentially untruth (as opposed to truth) and its expression in the world, resulting in delusion concerning the true nature and purpose of creation; McLeod, *Guru Nanak*, 181-184, 185-187.

[148] Singh, *At the Master's Feet*, in *Christian Witness*, 38; cf. Singh, *Spiritual Life*, in *Christian Witness*, 215; Sadhu Sundar Singh, *Real Pearl*, in *The Christian Witness of Sadhu Sundar Singh: A Collection of His Writings*, ed. T.D. Francis (Madras: CLS, 1989), 444.

[149] The Hindu "principle of universal causality resulting from action", broadly defined as "a cosmic law of debit and credit for good and evil; a law of moral retribution, eternally recurring"; Walker, *Hindu World*, vols. 1 and 2, 529-530.

[150] Singh, *Spiritual Life*, in *Christian Witness*, 218-219; Singh, *At the Master's Feet*, in *Christian Witness*, 40-41; Singh, *Spiritual World*, in *Christian Witness*, 269, 272-273.

[151] Cracknell, *Justice, Courtesy and Love: Theologians and Missionaries Encountering World Religions, (1846-1914)* (London: Epworth, 1995), 20.

[152] Singh, *Spiritual Life*, in *Christian Witness*, 224-225; Singh, *Real Pearl*, in *Christian Witness*, 454-455.

moral evil? In Ramanuja's doctrine of immanence, the individual souls of men are regarded as the body of God, and thus distinguished from Brahman who indwells them as inner controller and support. As a result, while the individual soul is subject to sorrow and evil depending on its *karma*, Brahman is free from all evil, devoid of sin, knows all, and remains the self-existent and supreme cause of all.[153] Sundar Singh's conception of an immaculate and indestructible spark thus fits well with this aspect of Ramanuja's framework.

Baago locates the point of departure for Sundar Singh's spiritual experience in the Upanishadic intuition that the soul of man does not really belong in the temporary and unreal world of space, time, and matter where it remains deluded by *maya*. It must ultimately free itself from its bondage to *karma* and return to its eternal home in heaven and be reunited with God. This experience of emancipation from *haumai* was what Sundar Singh seems to have been thirsting for from his childhood. His failure to discover this through yoga and other religious pursuits led to a religious crisis manifested in spiritual depression and unrest of soul.[154]

Sundar Singh's expectation on the occasion of his conversion appears to have been conditioned by the Vaisnava *bhakti* conception of *avatara*, implicit in his admission that he anticipated a manifestation of Krishna, or Buddha, or some other Hindu *avatara*.[155] Thus, the form of his conversion experience was broadly within the framework of his Vaisnava *bhakti* aspirations, although the content – his vision of Christ – was by his own confession, far removed from his conscious expectations.

When we turn to the event itself we see that in phenomenological terms, the most significant feature appears to have been the increasing bright radiance that accompanied his vision of Christ. Light not uncommonly characterises the immediate vision of the ultimate reality in Hinduism,[156] but the correspondence between Sundar Singh's experience and the description of the direct vision of God in some forms of Vaisnavite *bhakti* mysticism is striking:

> This *aparoksa jnana* or the direct vision of God... is accompanied by a kind of brilliance unique to itself. The magnitude of this brilliance goes on increasing according to the receptive capacity of each seeker. Starting from the magnitude of ten lamps it goes beyond the magnitude of a hundred suns. It is against the background of this flood of light that God reveals himself to the seeker.[157]

---

[153] A.J. Appasamy, *The Theology of Hindu Bhakti* (CLS: Madras, 1970), 61-66.

[154] Baago, *Pioneers of Indigenous Christianity*, 55-60; Prakash, *Preaching of Sadhu Sundar Singh*, 294-295.

[155] Singh, *With and Without Christ*, in *Christian Witness*, 399.

[156] See *Mundaka Upanishad II: 2, 10-11*, in *Hindu Scripture*, ed. and trans. R.C. Zaehner (New Delhi: Rupa, 1995), 190.

[157] I. Pandurangi, 'Vedanta as God-Realization (Madhva)', in *Hindu Spirituality: Vedas through Vedanta,* ed. K. Sivaraman (1989; repr., Delhi: Motilal Banarsidass, 1995), 314.

In addition to the manifestation of light, Sundar Singh also received a word of revelation from Christ.[158] This is in keeping with the expectation in the Sikh tradition of the divine communication coming as the Word or *Sabad*, imparted to man by the *Guru*. The inexpressible joy and peace which accompanied Sundar Singh's life-transforming conversion, continued to mark his subsequent spiritual experience. It became for him a critical indicator of the presence of Christ and freedom from the power of sin.[159] We have here close correspondence to representations of the spiritual bliss that constitute the climax of both Vaisnava and Sikh forms of *bhakti* experience.[160] The positive moral content of this experience is also consonant with Vaisnava and Sikh *bhakti* teaching, for when sinners turn to Christ, "...He uproots the evil from their souls, and gives them new life, and they become new creatures like Himself."[161]

A further feature that bears closer scrutiny is Sundar Singh's understanding of God's gracious initiative in salvation. Following his conversion Sundar Singh seems to have been convinced that salvation is not the result of natural human goodness or human effort, but comes as the free gift of a gracious and merciful God.[162] In exploring the possible sources of this influence in Sundar Singh's pre-Christian religious consciousness, we observe that the gracious initiative of God in the work of salvation is a crucial theme in Sikhism.[163] In the human quest for salvation there is a point beyond which human understanding cannot proceed; it is at God's gracious initiative (*Nadar*) that man receives the gift of illuminating perception (*Guru*) through which he understands the need and the means of obtaining salvation. This understanding of the gracious divine initiative most likely conditioned Sundar Singh's prayer for a special revelation at the climax of his religious crisis.

The concept of *prapatti*, or self-surrender, in the Vaisnava *bhakti* tradition also denotes a form of grace. It enables a person who is unable to fulfil the requirements of the way of *bhakti* to surrender the burden and responsibility for God-attainment to God himself once and for all.[164] This sense of total

---

[158] Singh, *With and Without Christ*, in *Christian Witness*, 399.

[159] A recurring theme in his writings and sermons, Singh, *At the Master's Feet*, in *Christian Witness*, 46-47; Singh, *Reality and Religion*, in *Christian Witness*, 91-92, 113; Singh, *Spiritual Life*, in *The Christian Witness*, 229; Singh, *Life in Abundance*, in *Christian Witness*, 476-478, 488, 510, 526-527; 'Salvation through the Cross', 'The Cross is Heaven', in *The Cross is Heaven*, ed. Appasamy, 39-40, 46-48, 53-54.

[160] Raghavachar, 'The Spiritual Vision of Ramanuja', 268; McLeod, *Guru Nanak*, 224, 226.

[161] Singh, *Spiritual Life*, in *Christian Witness*, 220-221.

[162] Singh, *At the Master's Feet*, in *Christian Witness*, 46-47; Singh, *Reality and Religion*, in *Christian Witness*, 113-114.

[163] Macauliffe, *Japji* 7, in *Sikh Religion*, vol. 1, 199.

[164] Dasgupta, *Hindu Mysticism*, 127; Raghavachar, 'The Spiritual Vision of Ramanuja', 72.

dependence on God conveyed by *prapatti* is clearly reflected in Sundar Singh's abandonment to God just prior to his conversion. His understanding of God's gracious intervention in salvation thus may have had its roots in the Sikh concept of *Nadar* and the Vaisnava *bhakti* teaching of *prapatti*, reinforced subsequently by the Christian teaching on divine grace.

We thus summarize our assessment of the *bhakti* influence upon Sundar Singh's theological framework. First, we have identified some distinctively *bhakti* elements in Sundar Singh's framework, and several points at which his pre-Christian *bhakti* religious consciousness was likely to have conditioned his Christian experience, all subsequently assimilated into his Christian world-view. His appropriation of the *bhakti* sources within his framework represents an eclectic synthesis of elements specific to the Vaisnava and Sikh *bhakti* traditions, as well as other heterogenous elements, rather than adoption of any one strand of *bhakti* tradition.

Second, our analysis of Sundar Singh's religious experience provides further confirmation of Katz's thesis that there is no such thing as unmediated mystical experience; all religious experience is mediated. Despite Sundar Singh's attempt to consciously represent a *pure* Christian mystical framework, there is clear evidence that his conversion experience was conditioned by his pre-Christian *bhakti* consciousness.

Katz's thesis thus provides a framework for understanding how Sundar Singh's pre-Christian religious consciousness could connect with his subsequent Christian experience in a preparation-fulfilment relationship. The elements of continuity we have indicated thus enable us to sketch some features of the interpretative framework Sundar Singh brought to his conversion experience, providing us with a framework of continuity for understanding his fulfilment approach.

Third, in specific terms, Sundar Singh's pre-Christian *bhakti* framework prepared him for his experience of Christ at a number of significant points: the view of God as a loving, personal creator, distinct from and yet immanent in his creation; the acceptance of the possibility of the incarnation; the understanding of nature as a channel of divine revelation; the recognition of the divine authority of the written Word; the conception of sin as moral evil and salvation as the fulfilment of the soul's quest for union with God resulting in moral perfection of the soul; and the recognition that salvation comes at the gracious initiative of God.

These aspects of Sundar Singh's *bhakti* framework served as a preparation for his reception of the Christian faith. All these components of a possible framework of continuity in Sundar Singh's fulfilment approach find convergence at one crucial point: the soul's need to fulfil its quest for salvation through mystical union with God. This leads us then to consider how Sundar Singh saw the aspirations of his *bhakti* experience finding their convergence and fulfilment in Christ.

Fulfilment of the Bhakti Religious Quest

Sundar Singh's most explicit statement regarding his fulfilment approach is in the form of the following famous and oft-quoted analogy: "Christianity is the fulfilment of Hinduism. Hinduism has been digging channels. Christ is the water to flow through these channels."[165] What are these "channels" Hinduism has been digging, and how does Christ serve as the water that flows through these channels?

We have noted that a framework of continuity provided by Sundar Singh's pre-Christian *bhakti* mystical orientation had prepared him for the specific Christian revelation. In keeping with his fulfilment ideal, these points of contact within the *bhakti* religious consciousness constitute the channels of objective truth Hinduism has been digging in preparation for Christ, the water, to flow through these channels. The crucial point of convergence in his conception of this preparation-fulfilment relationship, however, is the need for fulfilment of the *bhakti* quest for union with God.

For Sundar Singh, the subjective spiritual impulse for union with God within the *bhakti* mystical consciousness constituted a preparation for Christ, evidence that: "...every race, in every age, has in some form or other shown its deep craving for God", and that the individual soul is "...burdened by the sense of its separation from the Eternal God."[166] A recurring theme in his thought is that this deep and natural craving in the human heart can only be satisfied in God:

> From our experience we know how strong is the desire for God that is born in our hearts. As the hart is distressed till it finds the water-spring in the jungle, so the heart of man thirsts for God, and is restless till it finds Him. Although, in many ways, man tries to satisfy this inborn longing of his heart, yet his desire is never satisfied till he finds God.[167]

This deep longing for communion with God is a characteristic of both Vaisnava and Sikh forms of *bhakti*. According to Sundar Singh, this impulse is a reflection of God's nature hidden within the nature of humanity, causing the unregenerate soul to be burdened by the sense of its separation from God and long for fellowship with him.[168]

---

165 Quoted in Streeter and Appasamy, *The Sadhu*, 232; cf. A. Goodwin, *Sadhu Sundar Singh in Switzerland*, ed. A.F. Thyagaraju (1989; repr., Chennai: CLS, 1997), 38.

166 Singh, *Search After Reality*, in *Christian Witness*, 140.

167 Singh, *Spiritual Life*, in *Christian Witness*, 197; cf. 209, 223; Singh, *At the Master's Feet*, in *Christian Witness*, 53; Singh, *Reality and Religion*, in *Christian Witness*, 112; Singh, *Real Life*, in *Christian Witness*, 332; Singh, *Real Pearl*, in *Christian Witness*, 429, 453.

168 Singh, *Reality and Religion*, in *Christian Witness*, 97; Singh, *Search After Reality*, in *Christian Witness*, 140.

He makes essentially the same assertion using a different metaphor: "As in the flint there is fire, so in the heart of man there is the yearning for communion with God."[169] Every human desire has been bestowed with a special purpose; hence, human beings would not have had the desire for God if that desire could not be fulfilled. He illustrates this in the following testimony of a seeker: "I realized that this impulse and this satisfaction of heart had both come from the Living Christ, in whom all my restless strivings have now found rest."[170]

Sundar Singh's *bhakti* fulfilment view may be represented concisely as follows: if the essential aspiration of all sincere seekers is for a mystical experience of communion with God, the fulfilment of this aspiration may be found in a personal mystical experience of communion with God through Christ. The central issue in our search for a clear understanding of his fulfilment approach is thus: How does he see Christ fulfilling the *bhakti* seeker's quest for a mystical experience of union with God? For further clarity on this issue, we need to examine closely his attitude to non-Christian religious experience.

Christ and Non-Christian Religious Experience

Sundar Singh freely testifies in his public addresses that he had discovered in Christ a peace and fulfilment that he had failed to find in his ancestral religion. He does not, however, attack or vilify non-Christian religion in his preaching and teaching.[171] His views concerning non-Christian religious experience are found primarily in *Search after Reality* and *With and Without Christ*.

In *Search after Reality* he defines the goal of religion as "to obey the commands", "to worship wholeheartedly", and "to enjoy the fellowship" of God, the Creator and Lord of the universe. He explains the gradual progression from idolatry to the worship of God as a spiritual being in terms of an evolutionary development: "A progressive revelation of Reality that fits the need, capacity and state of development of every man and every age."[172] Reality remains the same undifferentiated constant, but different religions result from varying human perceptions and experiences of this Reality. Elsewhere, in language that echoes the relativism of Ramakrishna,[173] he

---

[169] Singh, *Spiritual Life*, in *Christian Witness*, 223; cf. Singh, *Real Pearl*, in *Christian Witness*, 453.

[170] Singh, *With and Without Christ*, in *Christian Witness*, 360; Singh, *Spiritual Life*, in *Christian Witness*, 201.

[171] *The Lamp* 10 (June 29, 1918), VPC SSS.3; cf. Parker, 1996:80; Francis, ed., *Christian Witness*, 14-15.

[172] Singh, *Search After Reality*, in *Christian Witness*, 130-131.

[173] Ramakrishna Paramahamsa, a famous mystic from Bengal, was the centre of a nineteenth-century Hindu renaissance. Based on his personal experience of self-realisation through various *sadhanas* (spiritual disciplines), he regarded all religions as

declares, "Truth is one; but different men may attain it by different paths."[174] Sundar Singh does use language with relativistic overtones when he illustrates how followers of different religions view "Reality" in terms of three men seeing the same white flower through different coloured glasses:

> To each the flower appears to be of a different colour. All are agreed on the basic truth of the existence of the flower. Their whole argument is about the colour, and as soon as they take off their glasses the real colour of the flower is seen by them all. The beliefs and senses of men are like glasses through which they estimate and examine all existing things. But they cannot understand the Reality as they should, until their hearts have been enlightened by God. For those, however, who are real seekers after truth, He who is the light of the world 'which lighteth every man coming into the world' (John 1:9; 8:12), will lead them on to Reality.[175]

That the relativism is only apparent is indicated by the assertion that "the light of the world" enables sincere seekers after truth to grasp Reality as it really is. Different human religious perceptions represent various stages in a progressive movement towards "full recognition of Reality";[176] our partial knowledge of Reality is appropriate to the needs of each phase of our spiritual progress. Honest seekers of all religions will arrive eventually at a full knowledge of God if they live true to the light they already possess.[177]

In subsequent chapters, Sundar Singh assesses the extent to which each of the world's great religions have succeeded in satisfying the universal human craving for God. Hinduism, Buddhism and Islam ("Muhammadanism") are each, in turn, examined briefly and found wanting. His discussion of these religions does not reflect the sophisticated grasp of a specialist scholar, but represents his reflection on operative beliefs encountered in the course of practical engagement with various expressions of the religious consciousness in India. The following account notes Sundar Singh's views on each of the religions without commenting on the soundness of his evaluations.

He concedes that there were many sincere seekers after truth among the teachers of Hinduism, and many devotees who had received some measure of light. However, he regards Hinduism as having failed essentially to meet the

---

essentially the same under different forms and names, different paths to the same goal; Walker, *Hindu World,* vol. 2, 282-284.

[174] Streeter and Appasamy, *The Sadhu*, 116; cf. Singh, *Reality and Religion*, in *Christian Witness*, 112-113. Baago's comparison of Sundar Singh and Ramakrishna's mystical experiences is oversimplified and forced; Sundar Singh consciously distanced himself from the advaitic mysticism which Ramakrishna represented; Baago, *Pioneers of Indigenous Christianity*, 64-66; cf. Singh, *At the Master's Feet*, in *Christian Witness*, 32; Singh, *Reality and Religion*, in *Christian Witness*, 100.

[175] Singh, *Search After Reality*, in *Christian Witness*, 132.

[176] Singh, *ibid.*, 132-133.

[177] Singh, *ibid.*, 134; Singh, *Spiritual Life*, in *Christian Witness*, 201.

religious needs of India.[178] His critique of Vedanta is focused primarily on Sankara's *advaita*, arguing that its teaching on transmigration of the soul and emancipation through reabsorption into Brahman fails to fulfil man's real need for communion with God. In his brief discussion of the teaching of the *Bhagavadgita*, he contrasts Krishna with Christ at one main point: whereas Krishna came to save the righteous and destroy sinners, Christ came to save sinners.

Buddhism is, likewise, found to be inadequate, since the Buddhist vision of *nirvana*, the extinction of all desire, denies the reality of man's vital relation to the created order, and the legitimacy of certain God-given desires essential to life.[179] It results ultimately in the destruction of life rather than salvation. His discussion of Islam focuses essentially on the Quranic designation of Christ as '*Ruh allah*' or "Spirit of God",[180] based on which he disputes the Muslim rejection of the divine sonship of Christ. Sufism is also rejected on the same grounds as parallel ideas in Vedanta and Buddhist philosophy. Islam is thus accorded the most cursory treatment, and dismissed summarily as lacking originality of thought.[181]

His more extensive discussion of the Christian faith in the concluding chapter attempts to demonstrate the sufficiency of Christ to satisfy the human spirit's thirst for God.[182] The proofs he lists are designed to show that Christian faith is "a true, living and soul-satisfying religion", which alone enables man to reach his final destination: moral perfection through mystical communion with God.[183] Sundar Singh thus does not regard all religions as equally legitimate ways to God: he views the vision of God in Christ as completing what was lacking in the other religions of the world.

In *With and Without Christ*, Sundar Singh compares real life experiences of Christians and non-Christians, distinguishing four categories of people: non-Christians without Christ, non-Christians with Christ, Christians with Christ, and Christians without Christ.[184] Sundar Singh's starting point is that "Christians and non-Christians are equally the creation and sons of one God". Christians have a true knowledge of God, are being transformed into his likeness, and have become heirs of eternal life through Jesus Christ. Non-Christians are those who are "walking in the dim light of the truth as they know

---

[178] Singh, *Search After Reality*, in *Christian Witness*, 141-152.
[179] Singh, *ibid.*, 153-159.
[180] Singh, *ibid.*, 160.
[181] Singh, *ibid.*, 160-162.
[182] Singh, *ibid.*, 163-188.
[183] Singh, *Search After Reality*, in *Christian Witness*, 167-172, 184-188.
[184] This classification is revealing in the possibility it assumes of those outside the church having a valid experience of Christ and some within not having any relationship with Christ; our primary concern is with the two categories of non-Christian religious experience.

it", but in choosing to stray away from it, forfeit the blessings that are available in Christ.[185]

Sundar Singh recounts real-life encounters with several non-Christians "without Christ", highlighting their sense of futility when they fail to find God apart from Christ. Despite the light of truth followers of different religions possess, "...without the touch of the Living Christ their lives have no abiding peace and hope". They are unable to satisfy their deepest spiritual needs by their own natural goodness or human effort.[186]

Non-Christians "with Christ" include those who secretly believe in Christ as their saviour, as well as those more deeply influenced by Christ than by their own religions or teachers. In the latter category, Sundar Singh includes Hindu reformers who, despite their overt antagonism to Christianity, have reinterpreted their ancestral religion in the light of the teachings of Christ.[187] His focus here is on the first group, secret disciples, "...who, not having dissociated themselves from their non-Christian environment, still seek to follow Christ in their lives".[188] These secret disciples are those who have accepted Christ as their Saviour and are baptized, but have never publicly identified themselves with the visible organised Church, but worship and serve him in secret.[189]

In justifying the legitimacy of this phenomenon, he insists that "...the quickening work of the Living Christ is not confined to our organized Churches, but is going on among non-Christians far in excess of what is commonly known...",[190] illustrating this fact with several testimonies from his own experience of Hindu, Muslim, and Sikh "non-Christians with Christ".[191] Thus in Sundar Singh's view, while a relationship with Christ is indispensable for salvation, identification with the visible Church seems nonessential.

Sundar Singh acknowledges the presence of a dim measure of the light of truth among the followers of different religions. If honest seekers of all religions live true to the light they already possess, God gives them more light, and they will arrive eventually at a full knowledge of God. Sundar Singh's view in this regard was significantly conditioned by his deep affection and respect for his mother, who seems to represent for him an archetype of the non-

---

[185] Singh, *With and Without Christ*, in *Christian Witness*, 344.

[186] Singh, *ibid.*, 345-355.

[187] Sundar Singh does not elaborate, but Thomas expounds this thesis in some detail; M.M. Thomas, *The Acknowledged Christ of the Indian Renaissance* (Madras: CLS, 1976).

[188] Singh, *With and Without Christ*, in *Christian Witness*, 356-357. Due to this focus we are left without any explanation concerning the participation in Christ of those who have been influenced by Christ unknowingly.

[189] Singh, *ibid.*, 357-358, 362, 364-365, 367.

[190] Singh, *ibid.*, 368.

[191] Singh, *ibid.*, 360-368.

Christian seeker after truth. In a conversation with the Archbishop of Uppsala, he offers the following description of his mother's religious devotion:

> People call us heathen.... Just fancy! My mother a heathen! If she were alive now she would certainly be a Christian. But even while she followed her ancestral faith she was so religious that the term 'heathen' makes me smile. She prayed to God, she served God, she loved God, far more warmly and deeply than many Christians...[192]

He applies essentially the same observation in a broader contrast between the ardent and sincere spiritual passion of Indian seekers after truth and his perception of the religious superficiality in many quarters of western Christianity:

> So far as I can see, there are many more people among us in India who lead a spiritual life than in the West, although they do not know or confess Christ. They live truly according to the light which God has given them.... Among us in India there are many, many, who lead a holy life.... The 'heathen' [Indians] do not seek for days or months only, they go on seeking earnestly and anxiously for the truth for years at a time.... Idol-worshippers seek the truth, but people over here, so far as I can see, seek pleasure and comfort.[193]

He thus regards the worship of idols by sincere seekers after truth as representing a limited but authentic encounter with God.[194] Although there is no consoling power in the stone idol, it is useful as "a means of concentration on God" and may provide devotees divine consolation depending on their measure of faith.[195] Sundar Singh thus concurs closely with Farquhar in his willingness to grant significant amount of validity to non-Christian religious experience.[196]

Is the encounter with God mediated through non-Christian religious experience essentially continuous with or qualitatively different from the experience of God in Christ? Sundar Singh seems to emphasise essential continuity rather than difference when he suggests that there are sincere seekers who may know Christ without knowing his name: "There... are, in India men who live in God without knowing Christ; that is, they do not know His Name."[197] This is made more explicit when he clarifies that non-Christians, who need "the fullest light" that Christ gives, already have some access to the Holy Spirit and to the light of Christ, "the Sun of righteousness":

---

[192] Quoted in Heiler, *Gospel of Singh*, 217.
[193] Quoted in Heiler, *Gospel of Singh*, 217.
[194] Singh, *Spiritual World*, in *Christian Witness*, 261-262.
[195] Singh, *Spiritual Life*, in *Christian Witness*, 224.
[196] See p.89.
[197] Quoted in Heiler, *Gospel of Singh*, 218.

> Non-Christian thinkers also have received light from the Sun of righteousness. The Hindus have received of the Holy Spirit. There are many beautiful things in Hinduism, but the fullest light is from Christ. Every one is breathing air. So every one, Christian as well as non-Christian, is breathing the Holy Spirit, though they do not call it by that name. The Holy Spirit is not the private property of some special people.[198]

There is thus no "nature-grace" distinction in Sundar Singh's theological scheme, no qualitative differentiation between the light of God given to all mankind and the light of God in Christ, the difference being clearly one of degree rather than kind. Consequently, he finds it difficult to deny the possibility of salvation to non-Christians.[199] In one of his ecstatic visions, he received the following response to his anxiety regarding the fate of non-Christians:

> Very few will be lost but many will be saved.... If there were no hope for all the non-Christians in the world and all the Christians who die in sin, God would stop creating men. We must do our part here on earth to save sinners, but if they refuse we need not be without hope for them.[200]

How is Sundar Singh able to hold to this view of unlimited grace and hope for the non-Christian within the fundamental Christocentric framework of his thought? By offering universal access to the Holy Spirit and to the light of Christ to Christians and non-Christians alike, Sundar Singh affirms a basic underlying continuity in God's revealing activity, and his view of salvation is set within this understanding of a universal economy of revelation.

Sundar Singh is convinced that because of his infinite grace and mercy, God does not judge an individual based on the correctness of his beliefs; rather, he rewards genuineness in the heart of the sincere seeker by a fuller revelation of the truth as it really is.[201] Non-Christians will have opportunity in the after-life to have their false and partial views of truth corrected:

> When people earnestly desire to live lives pleasing to God, the readjustment of their views and the renewal of their lives begin in this world. Not only does the Spirit of God teach them directly, but in the secret chamber of their hearts they are helped by communion with the saints, who, unseen by them, are ever at hand to assist them towards the good. But, as many Christian believers, as well as non-

---

[198] Quoted in Streeter and Appasamy, *The Sadhu*, 232; cf. Heiler, *Gospel of Singh*, 218.
[199] Heiler, *Gospel of Singh*, 218.
[200] Quoted in Streeter and Appasamy, *The Sadhu*, 129-130.
[201] Singh, *Spiritual Life*, in *Christian Witness*, 203; cf. Singh, *Real Pearl*, in *Christian Witness*, 435.

Christian seekers after truth, die while still holding false and partial views of truth, their views are corrected in the world of spirits...[202]

He records one of his visions in which he witnessed the experience in the world of spirits of a sincere seeker after truth who worshipped idols. When the person admitted the error of his ways, and asked to be enlightened concerning the truth, a full revelation of Christ was given to him and others who had just arrived in the world of spirits.[203]

This is a graphic illustration of how Sundar Singh attempts to hold together the universalist and Christocentric poles of his soteriological framework by employing the device of his post-mortem hope of salvation for the non-Christian. Jesus Christ is for him the only light of truth and saviour from sin, for both Christian and non-Christian alike: "Christ is a Universal Saviour. As there is only one sun that shines in East and West alike, so there is only one 'Light that lighteth every man coming into the world'... there is only one who can completely satisfy the needs of all men…."[204] Non-Christians who have not been offered the choice of salvation through Christ in this life, will be presented with that opportunity after death.

Sundar Singh thus recognises that the light of truth is present in all religions. Religions are conditioned perceptions of Reality but genuine expressions of the human search for God, representing different stages within a progressive movement towards a fuller knowledge of God. He acknowledges the provisional role of non-Christian religious experience in enabling man to have communion with God and affirms its qualitative continuity with Christian experience.

However, he clearly regards non-Christian religions as basically inadequate, rejecting them as systems. They are not salvific in themselves, only provisionally adequate. Christian faith alone is living, satisfying, and fully adequate, because Christ alone completes what is lacking in the other religions of the world. He accordingly makes provision for the sincere non-Christian seeker to receive post-mortem clarity of revelation and the opportunity for salvation through Christ in the after-life.

---

[202] Singh, *Spiritual World*, in *Christian Witness*, 260-261. For Sundar Singh, "world of spirits" describes an intermediate state that disembodied souls of human beings enter after death, following which they are led by good angels into heaven or by evil spirits into outer darkness. Beyond this realm is "the third heaven", where the soul experiences a direct vision of God along with the angels, and experiences "communion with the saints", the fellowship of all those around the throne of Christ. Sundar Singh claimed to have access into both these dimensions of the unseen world through his ecstatic experiences; Singh, *Spiritual World*, in *Christian Witness*, 254-256; cf. Heiler, *Gospel of Singh*, 185-189; Scott, 'Sadhu Sundar Singh: Church of the Sadhu Ideal', 268-269.

[203] Singh, *Spiritual World*, in *Christian Witness*, 261-262.

[204] Singh, *With and Without Christ*, in *Christian Witness*, 76.

Christ as Fulfilment

We have noted that the critical point of convergence in Sundar Singh's conception of the preparation-fulfilment relationship is the *bhakti* quest for salvation through mystical fulfilment. Sundar Singh's view of salvation must, however, be analysed in the context of its location between two poles: God's concern for the salvation of all humankind, and the decisiveness of Christ in God's plan of salvation.

Sundar Singh's overwhelming sense of the love and mercy of God causes him to affirm strongly that God wills the salvation of all men and women. God's continuing concern for people ensures his ongoing commitment to their well-being and happiness. Sundar Singh, hence, has a very optimistic view of God's posture towards unregenerate humanity, grounded in a theology of creation in which God's intent in creating man for fellowship with him must be fulfilled ultimately:

> Man did not create his own spirit, nor can he kill it. The Creator formed every creature for some particular purpose, and as neither man nor God will destroy the spirit of man or the divine seed that is in him, the purpose for which he was created will one day be fulfilled. He may go astray and be lost, but eventually he will return to the one in whose image he has been made, because this is his destiny.... As God created man to live in His presence and fellowship it is impossible that he should become separated from Him for ever.[205]

Consequently, we can never be without hope for any person. This is one of several indicators in Sundar Singh's writings of a strong inclination towards universalism. There is a certain degree of ambiguity in Sundar Singh's teaching in this regard. On one hand, he speaks of judgment and hell in terms that affirm the Church's traditional doctrine of everlasting punishment. The consequences of sin are described variously as falling into "the darkness of hell", experiencing "the wrath to come", or rushing into "eternal destruction".[206] Disobedient Christians having no relationship to Christ will be "thrust out" of the kingdom of God.[207] He warns sternly that there is no possibility of salvation in the hereafter: "no second chance", "no escape" from the "eternal death" which awaits those who reject the opportunity of salvation in this life.[208]

The judgment and punishment awaiting hardened sinners is described more explicitly elsewhere. Evil-doers are consigned to the darkness of "the bottomless pit... Hell", where they "remain in torment for ever", if they are not restored by true repentance and the grace of God.[209] Sundar Singh's firm faith

---

[205] Singh, *Real Pearl*, in *Christian Witness*, 455; cf. Singh, *Spiritual Life*, in *Christian Witness*, 224-225.

[206] Singh, *At the Master's Feet*, in *Christian Witness*, 39, 41.

[207] Singh, *With and Without Christ*, in *Christian Witness*, 369f, 379.

[208] Quoted in Heiler, *Gospel of Singh*, 190.

[209] Singh, *Spiritual World*, in *Christian Witness*, 272-273.

in the unyielding grace of God manifests itself in the intimation in this passage that there is hope for the sinner even in hell.

It is not God who sends the sinner to hell: people have of their own free will turned their faces away from God and made hell for themselves.[210] God's love and grace active even in hell, and the help of the saints already in heaven, enable those in hell to receive light in increasing measure until they are finally able to enter heaven.[211] Sundar Singh thus leaves us in little doubt concerning his belief in the final salvation of all men, clearly negating his teaching on everlasting punishment.[212] Hell is thus more a form of painful purgatory in which the sinner is prepared by the grace of God to enter heaven, rather than a place of eternal pain and torture.[213]

The other pole of Sundar Singh's view of salvation is the conviction that God's incarnation and redemption in Christ constitute the climax of his loving response to man's longing for communion with him. In explaining Sundar Singh's strong Christocentricity, Baago observes that the realization of his quest for union with God came with his vision of Christ at the climax of his religious search, and consequently: "...his answer to the Hindu quest for illumination was always Christ. Through Christ and Christ alone could man be released and reach *moksha*."[214] Thus, despite the value he ascribes to the revelation of God in nature and to the intuitive divine awareness within the human heart, he remains convinced that God is most fully revealed in Christ.

Although Sundar Singh does not use the term *Logos* extensively, the idea of the *Logos*-Christ is a prominent aspect of his thought. In a brief commentary on John 1:1, 3, Sundar Singh expounds the role of the *Logos* as the agent of creation.[215] The *Logos* is God's creative power and the means by which humanity received the breath of life. Evidence of the *Logos*' presence may be seen in all creation and within the recesses of the human soul, but revealed most fully in Jesus Christ:

> We in India... knew already that God is good. But we did not know that He was so good that Christ was willing to die for us. There is much that is beautiful in Hinduism, but the highest light comes from Christ.[216]

---

[210] Singh, *ibid.*, 266; Singh, *At the Master's Feet*, in *Christian Witness*, 41; 'The Lord of the Cross' in Appasamy, *The Cross is Heaven*, 32.

[211] Singh, *Spiritual World*, in *Christian Witness*, 261-262.

[212] Francis suggests that Sundar Singh's universalism may have remained "a concealed foundation" of his evangelistic preaching emphasising repentance and judgement", Francis, *Christian Witness*, 14.

[213] Singh, *At the Master's Feet*, in *Christian Witness*, 80.

[214] Baago, *Pioneers of Indigenous Christianity*, 60.

[215] Singh, *Reality and Religion*, in *Christian Witness*, 88-89.

[216] Quoted in Heiler, *Gospel of Singh*, 219.

The incarnation was the supreme manifestation of God's infinite love hidden from all eternity.[217] Man's finiteness prevents him from seeing the infinite God, but the love of God moved him to take on finite human form so that that man might be able to see God and find satisfaction in him.[218] He thus plainly asserts that there is no knowledge of God apart from Christ:

> We do not know God apart from Christ. God is love only when we see Him in the Person of Christ. He has revealed Himself nowhere excepting in Him, in such a way that we can see His Heart and His Will. Let no one persuade thee that thou canst find God anywhere save in the Lord Christ.... Shut thine eyes and say: I will know no other God save my Lord Christ.[219]

This strong Christocentricity, however, exists alongside the universalist tendency within his framework. On one hand, non-Christians possess some knowledge of God and may even have an authentic experience with God that is salvific; on the other hand, no one can know God apart from Christ. This tension in Sundar Singh's thought comes into sharp focus in his understanding of the relation between the historical Christ and the Christ of experience.

Sundar Singh accepts the historical facts concerning the earthly life of Christ quite literally.[220] More real to him than the Jesus of history, however, is the risen Christ who lives among us, and whom we encounter mystically in our devotional experience:

> [O]ur spiritual eyes must be opened, then we shall see that Jesus Christ is the Son of God; go to some quiet place and there He will reveal Himself.... It is not enough to know about Jesus Christ, you must know Him. I am quite sure if you will pray He will reveal Himself to you and you will know who Jesus Christ is... pray to Him, find a quiet time to be with Him every morning...[221]

Only those who know Christ "personally" and have communion with him through prayer can become convinced of the essential truths of the gospel.[222] Belief in the deity of Christ was for Sundar Singh essential to Christian faith, but those who fail to enter into personal mystical communion with Christ have only a theoretical knowledge of him:

> They...know Christ only from theology or from the standpoint of history. Therefore they can only regard Him as a holy man, a moral teacher of great

217 Singh, *Spiritual World*, in *Christian Witness*, 287.
218 Singh, *At the Master's Feet*, in *Christian Witness*, 33, 39.
219 Quoted in Heiler, *Gospel of Singh*, 146.
220 See, for instance, his treatment of the New Testament material in Singh, *Search After Reality*, in *Christian Witness*, 163-184.
221 Singh, 'Christ Manifests Himself', in *Life in Abundance*, in *Christian Witness*, 501, 503.
222 Heiler, *Gospel of Singh*, 160.

> eloquence and magnetism, or perhaps an outstanding religious genius.... they cannot believe in His Divinity. They cannot see in Him the Divine Redeemer. But to those who desire it and ask for it God will give the power to see this truth.[223]

Likewise, salvation through the atonement of Christ must be experienced if it is to be believed:

> Nowadays many people don't believe in the Atonement because they have no experience of the salvation in Jesus Christ. Those who have experience [*sic*] know it is true, that through Jesus Christ we receive new life.... there are many people, learned people, who believe, but they give their heads, not their hearts.[224]

Christ's substitutionary atonement includes both forgiveness of sin as well as the destruction of the sinful tendency within the regenerated human heart.[225] When the seeker enters into mystical communion with God through Christ, his whole being is renewed and he becomes conformed to the image of Christ.[226] Christ's deity and vicarious redemption are thus, for Sundar Singh, an integral part of the Christian faith;[227] his faith in these doctrines rests primarily not on the testimony of Scripture, church tradition, or any form of objective factual truth, but on personal experience of the risen Christ.

Some commentators have thus concluded that it was the "living", "inward" or "risen" [228] Christ and not the "historic Jesus" which was the primary object of Sundar Singh's faith.[229] Heiler, for instance, sees this emphasis as indicative of Sundar Singh's fundamental mystical orientation:

> Like many Christian mystics, he [Sundar Singh] regards the working of Christ in the individual soul as on a higher plane than His activity during His appearance upon earth. Not history, but the deep inward life, is Christ's peculiar sphere of revelation, His most sacred sphere of activity.[230]

How valid is this assessment of Sundar Singh's Christology? The evidence appears convincing. Firstly, Sundar Singh insists that it was the revelation of

---

[223] Quoted in Heiler, *Gospel of Singh*, 159.

[224] Singh, 'True Salvation', in *Life in Abundance*, in *Christian Witness*, 507-508.

[225] Appasamy, ed., 'Salvation through the Cross', in *The Cross is Heaven*, 42-43; Singh, *At the Master's Feet*, in *Christian Witness*, 43-44; Singh, *Real Pearl*, in *Christian Witness*, 450.

[226] Singh, *At the Master's Feet*, in *Christian Witness*, 54-55.

[227] "The Deity of Christ and Redemption are absolutely fundamental truths. Without them Christianity has no message left…"; quoted in Heiler, *Gospel of Singh*, 160.

[228] Terms he uses to denote the Christ of mystical experience as distinct from the historical Christ.

[229] Baago is convinced that Sundar Singh's view of Christ is docetic, but his argument based essentially on Sundar Singh's sermon illustrations is forced, and fails to take all the evidence into account; Baago, *Pioneers of Indigenous Christianity*, 62-63.

[230] Heiler, *Gospel of Singh*, 158.

the living Christ, not the story of the historical Jesus, which affected his conversion:

> When people ask me, 'What made you a Christian?' I can only say: 'Christ Himself made me a Christian.' When He revealed Himself to me I saw His glory and was convinced that He was the Living Christ. I do not believe in Jesus Christ because I have read about Him in the Bible – I saw Him and experienced Him and know Him in my daily experience. Not because I read the Gospels, but because of Him of whom I read in the Gospels, have I become what I am.[231]

The compelling concern for this emphasis may have been to move beyond intellectual, cognitive assent to experiential appropriation of the living Christ as an immanent present reality. However, some comments could imply that he regarded the historical witness of the New Testament as ultimately inconsequential to his experience of Christ: "...From the standpoint of history it is important to know the Bible. But even if the Bible were to disappear no one could take away my peace; I would still have my Christ."[232]

Some thus conclude that the Gospel accounts of the life and teaching of Jesus were of no real significance to Sundar Singh, since his inward fellowship with the living Christ was the real foundation of his faith.[233] Sundar Singh's earlier remarks in the same context, however, clearly contradict this inference: "Of course one has to know the Bible. I love the Bible, for it is that which has led me to the Saviour, to the Saviour who is independent of history.... From the standpoint of history it is important to know the Bible."[234]

He thus does not undermine the historicity of the Christ-event, but is concerned with establishing the priority of his inner experience of the living Christ, rather than the historical fact of Christ, as the basis of his faith. This is clarified in his response to his father's inquiry regarding the way to know Christ:

> If you want to know about Him, you must read the Bible; but if you want to know Him, you must pray, because reading only is not enough. There are many infidels and heathen who read the Bible and never know Him. Prayer is the only key, the real key that will open the truth to you.[235]

He thus clarifies that the historical facts are important for a knowledge of Christ, but an inner experience of the living Christ through prayer is essential for a personal relationship with him. The priority Sundar Singh ascribes to his inner mystical experience of Christ is clearly conditioned by the importance

---

231 Quoted in Heiler, *Gospel of Singh*, 155-156.
232 Quoted in Heiler, *ibid.*, 156.
233 Baago, *Pioneers of Indigenous Christianity*, 63.
234 Quoted in Heiler, *Gospel of Singh*, 156.
235 Appasamy, 'The Lord of the Cross', in *The Cross is Heaven*, 34.

accorded to the direct mystical apprehension of reality within his *bhakti* framework. However, the historical facts concerning the life and ministry of Jesus as recorded in the New Testament do have a vital role in ensuring continuity between his "inner Christ" of experience and the Christ of tradition.

The evidence would thus seem to confirm that the "living inward Christ" of experience does have priority over the "historic Jesus" in Sundar Singh's view of Christ as fulfilment. The *bhakti* mystical quest is thus fulfilled in an experience of mystical encounter with the "living inward Christ", in which the seeker's heart is transformed, set free from sin, and finds true inner peace and bliss. We will need to return to this issue in our analysis of Sundar Singh's fulfilment approach, but our understanding of his view remains incomplete until we have evaluated the significance of his appropriation of the sadhu ideal.

Fulfilment and the Sadhu Ideal

Sundar Singh was acutely conscious of the importance of indigenization, and the need for incorporating concordant elements of his pre-Christian religious tradition within his interpretation of the Christian faith. In a famous illustration of this principle, Sundar Singh relates an incident in which a high caste Brahmin collapsed on a station platform on account of extreme heat and thirst, but refused a drink of water offered to him in a china cup. When water was brought to him in his own brass vessel, however, he accepted it gladly.[236] His application of this incident is perhaps one of his best-known sayings: "Indians greatly need the Water of Life, but they do not want it in European vessels".[237]

We have already observed some evidence of the *bhakti* conditioning of his theological framework, but Sundar Singh's willingness to appropriate aspects of the Hindu tradition is most clearly evident in his adoption of the sadhu life-style,[238] an integral aspect of his expression of Christian discipleship. But was his adoption of the sadhu life-style only a pragmatic evangelistic device for facilitating acceptance of the Christian gospel among religious Hindus, or did he regard it as in some way incorporating one or more aspects of the gospel in an indigenous form of expression? Our investigation will require us to examine Sundar Singh's distinctive interpretation of the sadhu ideal against the background of the Hindu ascetic tradition.[239]

Ghurye identifies two principal features in his characterization of the Hindu ascetic tradition within which he locates the Indian sadhu ideal: austerity (*tapas*, one aspect of which is celibacy), and the practice of yogic techniques as

---

[236] Streeter and Appasamy, *The Sadhu*, 228.
[237] Heiler, *Gospel of Singh*, 232.
[238] Prakash, *Preaching of Sadhu Sundar Singh*, 50-51; Heiler, *Gospel of Singh*, 55-56.
[239] Sikhism does not favour the *sadhu* ideal, but rather recommends the role of a hard-working householder. Sundar Singh's adoption of the *sadhu* lifestyle was thus clearly inspired by the Vaisnava ideal of wandering saint or *bhakta*, McLeod, *Guru Nanak*, 211.

a means of experiencing the ecstatic trance state.[240] The term *tapas* designates all kinds of austerities, including keeping silence, frequent bathing, sleeping on the floor, begging alms, fasting and sexual continence.[241] Austerity, based on self-control and self-mortification, is thus an essential mark of the sadhu life-style, and in his quest for salvation, a true sadhu renounces the world with all its pleasures and comforts, has no home of his own, lives on alms, undergoes various penances, and endures all kinds of hardships.[242]

To all external appearances there was little to distinguish Sundar Singh's practice of the sadhu ideal. He had left his home and adopted the life-style of a wandering mendicant with the attendant physical hardships, practised various forms of self-denial, and remained celibate all his life. Sundar Singh's distinctiveness is to be found in the significance he ascribed to these ascetic austerities rather than their specific forms.

In the first place, while the sadhu in the Hindu tradition embraces the suffering of self-restraint and renunciation to gain *moksa* (salvation), Sundar Singh did not attach any salvific merit to ascetic practices:

> My ideal has never been renunciation for the sake of renunciation. There is no merit attached to renunciation. Everything in the world has been created by God, and whatever God has created is good. The harm comes, not when we use God's gifts, but when we misuse them…[243]

He thus contrasts the understanding of renunciation and austerity in the Hindu ascetic tradition with his own positive attitude towards the created world:

> This is where I entirely disagree with the Hindu idea of renunciation. I do not call myself a Sannyasi, for a Sannyasi means one who renounces. He renounces the world because he thinks everything in it is evil, but I think that all is good. The world is all the property of my Father, and is therefore my property. If I renounce the world I renounce some of the gifts which my Heavenly Father gives me out of His Love. Therefore I do not renounce the world, but only the evil in it.[244]

Secondly, Sundar Singh unites the Indian ideal of renunciation as a pathway to self-realization with the Christian ideal of renunciation for the purpose of selfless service to mankind.[245] His friend and biographer, C.F. Andrews expresses it thus:

---

[240] Ghurye, *Indian Sadhus*, 15-26 lists a total of four traits: ecstasy, austerity, concentration, and celibacy; cf. Dhavamony's description; M. Dhavamony 'The Sadhu Ideal as Realized by Hindu Saints', *Studia Missionalia* 35 (1986): 203-219.

[241] Ghurye, *Indian Sadhus*, 17; Klostermaier, *Survey of Hinduism*, 170-171.

[242] Dhavamony, 'The Sadhu Ideal', 204.

[243] Appasamy, *Sundar Singh: A Biography*, 210-211.

[244] Streeter and Appasamy, *The Sadhu*, 88-89.

[245] Parker, *Call of God*, 3, 6; Prakash, *Preaching of Sadhu Sundar Singh*, 46-47.

> In the ancient Indian ideal, the human spirit goes forth in utter detachment from human society in order to find God. With St. Francis [of Assisi], on the other hand, God Himself is found through the service of the poor. …Sundar... made a very brave attempt to combine these two ideals. He loved solitude with all his soul; but he sought to unite it with the love of those who suffered pain.[246]

Although Sundar Singh did not become formally involved in any organization of human service for any length of time, for a short period he was involved in serving those stricken with the smallpox and plague, as well as caring for leprosy patients and the physically handicapped.[247] His love for mankind and his ideal of joyful service was for the most part expressed through his courageous evangelistic and missionary endeavours. The cross, which denotes vicarious redemptive suffering, became the focal point of Sundar Singh's reinterpretation of this aspect of suffering renunciation within the sadhu ideal. A symbol of pain, suffering, and persecution, it represented the pathway to victory, glory and life eternal.[248]

The second principal feature Ghurye designates is the practice of yogic techniques as a means of attaining the ecstatic state. In Upanishadic thought, *yoga* denotes a spiritual union achieved at the highest stage of absolute sense-restraint – "a state in which the five senses, thought, intellect, and mind all cease to operate".[249] Dhavamony defines *yoga* in this sense as "a method or a way of disciplined activity whereby an end is achieved."[250] *Yoga* as a system of physical and mental discipline is usually an integral part of the ascetic practice of a sadhu.[251]

Sundar Singh's practice of the sadhu ideal bears the marks of yogic influence in several aspects. Sundar Singh possessed to a remarkable degree the yogic ability to bear stoically the bodily wants of hunger, thirst, heat, and cold.[252] Furthermore, certain techniques of *yoga* Sundar Singh had learned in the years before his conversion significantly conditioned his approach to prayer and meditation. Andrews and Surya Prakash both confirm that Sundar Singh never seems to have given up the discipline of meditation he had acquired through Yoga: "Although he found these practices unsatisfying when he

---

[246] Andrews, *Personal Memoir*, 101.

[247] Andrews, *ibid.*, 101, 106; cf. Streeter, and Appasamy, *The Sadhu*, 27-28.

[248] Singh, *At the Master's Feet*, in *Christian Witness*, 67-68; Singh, *Reality and Religion*, in *Christian Witness*, 104-105.

[249] Dasgupta, *Hindu Mysticism*, 62; it can also refer to a metaphysical system of thought within philosophical Hinduism.

[250] In this generic sense, the term may be applied generally to Hindu ascetics who exercise restraint and discipline of body and mind in striving for union with the Absolute; Dhavamony, 'The Sadhu Ideal', 204-206.

[251] Ghurye, *Indian Sadhus*, 19-21.

[252] Dasgupta, *Hindu Mysticism*, 73-74.

became a Christian, he did not abandon them altogether, but rather sought to transform them and use them in Christ's service."[253]

Meditation is an important component in the Sikh understanding of the way of salvation. Salvation depends upon the gracious divine initiative expressed through the Word of God communicated through the *Guru*. The individual must, however, grasp the salvation offered through disciplined meditation on the Word of God, by which he is cleansed of all evil and ultimately attains union with God.[254] Meditation thus played an important role in Sundar Singh's pre-Christian religious formation and continued to be the focal point of his subsequent spiritual experience.

Yogic meditation techniques appear to have been a means of entrance into his mystical experience, often characterised by ecstasy and accompanied by visions. He attached a great deal of value to these ecstatic experiences, which helped him persevere with the sadhu life-style.[255] Sharpe regards Sundar Singh's ecstatic experiences as his greatest distinguishing feature, comparing them with the Hindu experience of *samadhi*.[256]

Sundar Singh himself distinguished his Christian experience of ecstasy from his pre-Christian experience of yoga. He regarded these ecstatic experiences as gifts, and valued them highly, but did not believe they should be sought after or induced.[257] But why were they of such great importance to him? Within his theological framework, people have direct intuitive and mystical access to the Logos-Christ and to the Holy Spirit. Furthermore, the essential *bhakti* aspiration for union with God is fulfilled in a mystical encounter with the "living inward Christ" of experience. Sundar Singh's experiences of mystical ecstasy were important as the means by which he connected with the unseen spiritual world and received divine messages of spiritual illumination:

> The brain is a very subtle and sensitive instrument, furnished with many fine senses which, in meditation, receive messages from the unseen world and stimulate ideas far above normal human thought. The brain does not produce these ideas, but receives them from the spiritual, invisible world above and interprets them in terms of the conditions and circumstances familiar to men. ...in real prayer, light streams out from God and illumines the innermost, sensitive part of the soul... the man of meditation touches the heart, as it were, of such realities and enjoys their bliss, as his soul and the spiritual world, from which they come, are closely akin.[258]

---

[253] Andrews, *Personal Memoir*, 249; cf. Prakash, *Preaching of Sadhu Sundar Singh*, 19.
[254] McLeod, *Guru Nanak*, 207-208.
[255] Streeter and Appasamy, *The Sadhu*, 109.
[256] Sharpe, 'The Legacy of Sadhu Sundar Singh', 162.
[257] Soderblom, 'Christian Mysticism in an Indian Soul', 233.
[258] Singh, *Reality and Religion*, in *Christian Witness*, 94.

It was thus Sundar Singh's employment of the yogic technique in his practice of meditation that helped mediate his experience of the Christian vision of union with Christ. It is finally only in the practice of prayer and meditation, through which the seeker encounters the "living inward Christ" in the world of mystical experience that fulfilment in Christ reaches its actual consummation.

There is thus a mutuality in fulfilment implicit in Sundar Singh's appropriation of the sadhu ideal. On one hand, the ideals of renunciation and suffering find their fulfilment in the cross and the Christian conception of vicarious suffering. The mystical quest for union with God is also fulfilled in the seeker's encounter with the "living inward Christ" of experience. In the reverse trajectory of fulfilment, we see Christian ideals finding fulfilment in some aspects of the sadhu ideal. In Sundar Singh's pursuit of Christian discipleship, the cross, the ideal of suffering, and selfless service, finds unique fulfilment in the sadhu ideal of self-denial and renunciation for the purpose of God-realization. Likewise, the sadhu practice of the yogic technique of meditation helps lead the seeker to mystical fulfilment through an encounter with the "living inward Christ".

We thus conclude that Sundar Singh's adoption of the sadhu ideal was not just a pragmatic evangelistic device designed to make Christ culturally acceptable and attractive to the Hindu. It was rather a spontaneous but conscious attempt to represent the Christian gospel in a form of living expression that represented the highest ideal of Hindu religion, both in terms of speculative thought as well as practical devotion.

A Critical Analysis of Sundar Singh's Understanding of Fulfilment

The main difficulty in understanding Sundar Singh's view of fulfilment is the lack of any systematic or detailed treatment of the concept in his writings. His style does not lend itself to sustained discussion of any one theme, and hence his understanding of fulfilment must be constructed from fragments of thought scattered all through his writings, and an integrated pattern drawn from ideas implicit in his teaching. The fulfilment concept was, nonetheless, an integral aspect of his theological framework. His fulfilment view was not a theoretical construct as much as a practical approach emerging from his actual engagement with the sources of the various religious traditions, as well as authentic evangelistic and dialogical encounters with representatives of these traditions.

Sundar Singh's fulfilment approach has the *bhakti* quest for salvation as its point of convergence. His pre-Christian religious consciousness, shaped by *bhakti* sources, aroused in him a deep longing for an authentic experience of mystical communion with God. His quest was satisfied in a mystical encounter with the "risen" Christ, conditioned by his *bhakti* consciousness and his exposure to the New Testament sources. His personal experience thus determined the essential contours of his fulfilment view.

Our critique first examines Sundar Singh's conviction regarding the pedagogical value of Hindu religious experience; second, his concept of revelation, especially the notion of an intuitive mystical knowledge, his device for affirming continuity between Hindu and Christian religious experience; and, third, the adequacy of his conception of the "inner" Christ of mystical experience for affirming the decisiveness of Christ.

The Pedagogical Value of Hindu Religious Experience

Sundar Singh manifests a dialectical attitude towards Hinduism. On one hand, he rejects Hinduism as a system, regarding it as having failed essentially to meet the religious needs of India. At the same time, he is sympathetic with the basic religious impulse of Hinduism, in particular the *bhakti* quest, for union with God.

Sundar Singh clearly does not believe in the equal validity of all religions and, in fact, offers a measured critique of some of the major religions that despite its lack of sophistication, ascribes differing degrees of value to them. In one instance he seems to interpret the pedagogical function of the Hindu tradition in terms of the evolutionary theory of the development of religion.[259] In this context he appears to perceive Reality, or God as he really is, as the ultimate destination of humanity's progressive spiritual journey.[260] Various religions of the world represent different partial human perceptions of Reality, intermediate stages in a continuum of progressive movement towards reality, which has Christ at the end.

In humanity's progressive journey towards the truth, sincere seekers are headed in the right direction, and will be divinely guided towards a perfect apprehension of Reality, which they encounter in the risen Christ. The intent of Sundar Singh's scheme is to demonstrate that while non-Christian religious experience has some validity, Christian faith alone fulfils the longings of the human spirit for communion with God. Although the idea is not developed in detail nor mentioned elsewhere, this distinct allusion to the evolutionary theory of religion is worth noting.[261] The Hindu tradition is viewed as possessing partial but authentic intimations of truth, a provisional stage along a continuum of evolutionary movement towards the full knowledge of God found in Jesus Christ.

Sometimes Sundar Singh makes the Hindu tradition serve as an Old Testament to the Hindu community in relation to the Christian faith. In one such instance, he recounts the testimony of a Hindu *pandit* who had been

---

[259] See p.168.
[260] Singh, *Search After Reality*, in *Christian Witness*, 132-133.
[261] Singh, *ibid.*, 136.

convinced by two Christian sadhus that Christ was the sinless incarnation promised in the Hindu scriptures and the only saviour.[262] In their explanation, they compared the function of the law of *karma* in the Hindu religion to the Law in other religions.[263] They accordingly compared the role of the ancient Hindu *rishis* who served as mediators of the Law in the Indian context, to Moses' role in mediating the Law of God to the Jews.

The sadhus further pointed out that the Law does not make anyone righteous: it only helps us distinguish between right and wrong. Its function is to emphasize humanity's need for righteousness, and since no one is able to fulfil the Law, all are without hope of salvation. Christ meets humanity's need for righteousness by becoming human, fulfilling the Law on humanity's behalf, and by giving his life on behalf of sinners, has provided salvation for all people.[264] This is clearly an attempt to apply the Pauline argument in Romans to the Hindu law of *karma*. The argument lacks both detail and depth, and we fail to find a more elaborate exposition of the same argument elsewhere in his writings. This is, however, an illustration of one way in which Sundar Singh may have viewed the Hindu tradition as an Old Testament in relation to fulfilment in Christ.

We observe a different expression of essentially the same posture to the Hindu tradition in one of Sundar Singh's public addresses. A report of his visit to Tiruvella, Kerala, records a synopsis of his address, which compared the Christian idea of salvation with salvation in other religions, especially Hinduism. His approach is summarised as follows:

> Very clearly did the speaker then point out that the great Purusha or Prajapati of the Hindu Vedas who sacrificed himself for the Salvation of the world was no other than the crucified and enthroned Lord Jesus whom the Christians adore as their Saviour and Lord. It matters not, said he, whether we call him Jesus or Prajapati, provided we believe in him and receive him into our hearts as king and master.[265]

This summary clearly reflects resonance with the vedic fulfilment view of K.M. Banerjea. Unfortunately, again, the evidence for Sundar Singh's view of Jesus as *Prajapati* is very meagre, and raises several difficult questions: How accurate is this reporter's representation of Sundar Singh's view? Did Sundar Singh have any prior acquaintance with Banerjea's work, or did he arrive at a similar conclusion independently? Is the positive tone of his identification of

---

262 Singh, *With and Without Christ*, in *Christian Witness*, 360-368.

263 His subsequent application of the reference here to "religions" suggests that he may have had Judaism primarily in mind.

264 Singh, *With and Without Christ*, in *Christian Witness*, 362-363.

265 'Sadhu Sundar Singh at Tiruvella', in *The Christian Patriot* (August 10, 1918), available the in Library Archives of the United Theological College, Bangalore, India (VPC SSS.3).

Jesus with *Prajapati* another indication of the lack of importance given to the historical Christ in his theological scheme?

Heiler's reference to Sundar Singh's acquaintance with a *pandit* in north India suggests one way by which he may have acquired this view. Sundar Singh reports that this *pandit* used to give lectures on the sacred books of India, and on one occasion shared the following astonishing conclusion:

> The Vedas reveal to us the necessity of redemption from sin, but where is the Redeemer? Prajapati, of whom the Vedas speak, is Christ, who gave His life as a ransom for sinners.... I have greater faith in the Vedas than you have because I believe in Him whom the Vedas reveal, even in Jesus Christ.[266]

While the lack of adequate elaboration of this idea in Sundar Singh's writings does not allow for a searching analysis or critique, it does illustrate another way in which he may have viewed the Hindu tradition as providing a pedagogy to Christ. Thus, although Sundar Singh rejected Hinduism as a system, he did regard it as containing objectively some elements of the true knowledge of God.

In explaining the nature and source of this "true knowledge" that non-Christians have access to, Sundar Singh emphasises God's fairness towards people of every race, based on the assertion in Acts [14:17] that God has not left himself without witness anywhere in the world.[267] He thus emphasises the universality of God's covenantal concern for humanity:

> This Reality supplies all human needs and necessities everywhere. As one sun shines and illumines the world, provides light and life for all the inhabitants living therein, just so the Sun of Righteousness (Mal.4:2) gives spiritual light and life to all, heals them and teaches them...[268]

Elsewhere Sundar Singh distinguishes this general "spiritual light" of truth from the "full light of truth" revealed in Christ.[269] The precise nature or channel of the pre-Christian "light of truth" remains unspecified, but he maintains that genuine seekers after truth follow Christ, "the full light", while others who reject him remain in darkness. The conclusion is, thus, unmistakeable: the light and satisfaction provided by Hindu religious experience is of a provisional nature; only in Christ can full light and true fulfilment be found.

What, then, is the value of the partial and provisional knowledge of God that Hindus have access to apart from Christ? Sundar Singh is more a mystic than a theologian, and accordingly has little to say regarding the objective knowledge of God in other religions. On the other hand, he is vitally concerned about their

---

[266] Quoted in Heiler, *Gospel of Singh*, 220.
[267] Singh, *With and Without Christ*, in *Christian Witness*, 344-345.
[268] Singh, *Real Life*, in *Christian Witness*, 340.
[269] Singh, *With and Without Christ*, in *Christian Witness*, 345.

subjective value in testifying to the fervent desire within the human heart for mystical union with God. For Sundar Singh, Hindu religious experience represents an authentic expression of mankind's search for truth, and sincere *bhakta*s' appropriation of some measure of the universal light of God. It serves primarily as a witness and reminder of humanity's spiritual restlessness and incompleteness: the love of God both places this deep longing for communion with God within the soul of man, and makes provision for it to be fulfilled.

By conceding Christians and non-Christians equal access to the light of Christ and the Holy Spirit, Sundar Singh clearly does not distinguish qualitatively between the knowledge of God in natural revelation and the knowledge of God in Christ. This considerably strengthens the theological continuity between Christian and non-Christian religious experience, but dilutes the aspect of transcendence within his fulfilment framework, a significant weakness of his approach.

Revelation and the Intuitive Knowledge of God

Sundar Singh takes the revelation of God in nature very seriously: the created world is a reflection of God's nature and attributes, and as part of this reflection of God in nature, man is intuitively endowed with a capacity for mystical knowledge which enables him to interpret God's revelation in nature. As wonderful as the revelation of God in the natural order is, his revelation in the heart of man is much greater.[270] It enables man to intuitively discern God's presence in the world, and also creates a desire for more of God's presence in a heart positively attuned to him.[271]

Like other mystics, Sundar Singh is somewhat distrustful of rational reflection and speculative reasoning: "The realization of God and spiritual insight do not depend on the knowledge of this world.... Real spiritual knowledge comes only through prayer and meditation, because God then speaks to man in the secret chamber of the heart...."[272] "Reality" does not yield its secrets to barren philosophical argument or abstract intellectual inquiry; immediate perception of reality is obtained through mystical experience when "intuition", the sensory faculty of the soul, is exercised.[273] He also uses the term "spiritual intuition" to denote this mystical apprehension of reality:

> Religious truths cannot be perceived by the head, but by the heart. Through the understanding alone we cannot find Christ ...Religion is a matter of the heart.... Spiritual intuition is as delicate as the sense of touch; it feels the reality of the Presence of God as soon as it is touched by Him. The soul cannot account for this

[270] Heiler, *Gospel of Singh*, 144.
[271] Singh, *With and Without Christ*, in *Christian Witness*, 359-360.
[272] Singh, *With and Without Christ*, in *Christian Witness*, 373.
[273] Singh, *Search After Reality*, in *Christian Witness*, 169; Singh, *Reality and Religion*, in *Christian Witness*, 102.

> logically, but it reasons thus: I am perfectly satisfied; such peace can only come from Divine Reality, therefore I have found Divine Reality. The heart has reasons of which the mind knows nothing.[274]

Thus, although the mystical apprehension of reality is distinct from the logical or rational process, as the above quotation illustrates, he does not hesitate to employ simple, common sense appeals to logic and reason. Recourse to such logical argument is not uncommon in his writings, although the argument may at times appear to be relatively unsophisticated.[275] He also commends positive and useful intellectual inquiry in the service of God, and is thus not totally opposed to the use of logic or reason.[276]

In the final analysis, however, spiritual intuition clearly remains the ultimate authority in matters of religious truth and experience. Truth and reality ultimately transcend all human expression, are beyond the rational human process and ordinary sensory perception, hence, intuitively grasped and communicated:

> We know much more than we can ever put into words, because we can never explain the whole of our inner consciousness. Something is always left unexpressed. We have experiences which are beyond our powers of expression, but are not beyond our comprehension. At times we have an intuition, and lofty thoughts suddenly flash into our minds. These we have not learned from any one... nor have we been able to gain knowledge of them in the visible world through our senses.[277]

What is the source of this intuitive knowledge and the means by which it comes to us? Sundar Singh indicates the possibility of a mystical connection between individual souls and the unseen spiritual world in the following terms:

> How have we been able to come to know these hidden things? I would say that the proof of this is that our souls are connected with the spiritual and unseen world whose light, without our being aware of it, is reflected in our inner selves. By means of our inner perceptions some truths from that other world come to us, but their proof will be possible by experience which we now see as in a glass darkly.[278]

---

[274] Quoted in Heiler, *Gospel of Singh*, 133-134.

[275] See his use of a form of the teleological argument for the existence of God, and his argument against the doctrine of *maya*; Singh, *Search After Reality*, in *Christian Witness*, 136f, 142; cf. 167f; see also his arguments against atheism and agnosticism in Singh, *Real Pearl*, in *Christian Witness*, 432f.

[276] Singh, *Real Pearl*, in *Christian Witness*, 436; this is striking given his own limited formal education; cf. Streeter and Appasamy, *The Sadhu*, 182.

[277] Singh, *Search After Reality*, in *Christian Witness*, 135.

[278] Singh, *Search After Reality*, in *Christian Witness*, 135-136.

Sundar Singh does not explain clearly the connection between "the spiritual and unseen world" and the souls of men, but the indwelling *Logos*-Christ, which makes the knowledge of God through nature possible, is probably also the source of this mystical knowledge of God in the depths of the human soul.[279] This mystical intuitive awareness of God offers man the possibility of unmediated communion with God, and creates a longing for a fuller revelation of the truth and deeper fellowship with God.

In natural theology the knowledge of God comes as the logical outcome of reason applied to facts observed in the natural order. Thus, for Banerjea and Goreh, the inner witness that enables man to discern truth is the light of reason.[280] In contrast, Sundar Singh is convinced that humanity has a natural intuitive capacity to discern God's revelation in the world based on an inner mystical capacity for knowing.[281] The Sikh and Vaisnava *bhakti* emphasis on the special immanence of God in the human heart may have conditioned Sundar Singh's thought at this point.

Sundar Singh makes no attempt to justify this notion of a universal intuitive mystical knowledge biblically or theologically. This idea of a universal self-validating mystical knowledge, however, resonates deeply with the Sikh mystical notion of *Guru*, the illuminating voice of God spoken in the inner recesses of the human soul. Thus while the *Logos* conception may undergird his notion of an intuitive mystical knowledge that is universal and epistemologically self-validating, its affinity to Sikh *bhakti* sources is more pronounced.

This concept of a universal intuitive mystical knowledge is the device Sundar Singh employs in including different expressions of non-Christian religious experience within a cosmic salvation-history scheme, and extending the scope of divine grace manifested in Christ to people of all faiths. His proposal assumes that underneath all the diversity in the world lies a common unifying reality embedded deep within the soul of man: an intuitive mystical awareness of God, which is an extension of God himself. The nature of this divine presence within the human soul is defined in terms of *bhakti* rather than advaitic non-duality. This intuitive knowledge of God enables people of all faiths to discern God's self-expression in his creation, as well as to appropriate the revelation of God in Christ.

---

[279] Heiler, *Gospel of Singh*, 146.

[280] Boyd, *Indian Christian Theology*, 56-57.

[281] "Almost everyone has an inner capacity – some more, some less – to sense spiritual truths without knowing how they have attained them"; Singh, *With and Without Christ*, in *Christian Witness*, 411.

The Logos-Christ of Mystical Experience

Christ is central to Sundar Singh's fulfilment theological framework. His dramatic conversion to Christianity was the direct result of a vision of Christ, and thereafter, Christ remained the focus of his religious experience. He is convinced that it is in Christ alone that God is fully revealed, and that we have no knowledge of God or salvation apart from him. Is the decisiveness of Christ adequately affirmed in the priority he gives to the mystical Christ of experience over the historical Christ?

Sundar Singh's *bhakti* mystical orientation ensures that the *Logos*-Christ of mystical experience has priority over the historical Jesus as the object of his faith. This emphasis enables him to universalize the Christ of experience and hold together the two main poles of his salvation scheme: God's universal salvific concern and the decisiveness of Christ.

Sundar Singh's conception bears some formal correspondence with the *Logos*-Christ notion of K.C. Sen.[282] While Christ is the centre of both their religious experiences, the historical Jesus appears to be of less consequence than the *Logos*-Christ. The focus of Sen's experience was the "spirit-Christ" or "all-pervading" Logos-Christ; for Sundar Singh it was the "risen", "living", or "inward" Christ. Both concur with the early fathers in owning truth wherever it may be found as God's truth and thus seeing traces of God's revelation and the *Logos*-Christ in non-Christian religious experience, philosophy, science, poetry, and art.[283] The various fragments of truth are brought together in Christ, in whom alone the *Logos*-light is manifested in full measure.

There is, however, significant divergence between Sen and Sundar Singh in the value each ascribes to the historical Jesus. For Sen, Christ was primarily the universal *Logos*-Christ who may be appropriated through mystical experience in the context of all cultures and religions. Although the Christ of mystical experience is extremely important to Sundar Singh's scheme, the objective facts of the Christ-event also have considerable value. Sen rejected what he termed the "narrow", "smaller" or "little" Christ of history, since he regarded the objectivity and historicity of the Christ-event as of little consequence. On the other hand, for Sundar Singh, the historical figure of Christ has critical significance.

Thus, in attempting to prove Christ's true identity as the incarnate God, Sundar Singh bases his apologetic on the Old Testament prophecies which foretold his coming, and the New Testament account of his sufferings, death, and bodily resurrection, the uniqueness of his ethical teaching and moral example.[284] The difficulty with Sundar Singh's Christology is that although the Christ of history and the *Logos*-Christ of experience are both concepts integral to his thought, the two are never adequately linked. His intention may have

---

[282] For Sen's conception of Logos fulfilment, see pp.28-30.
[283] Singh, *Spiritual Life*, in *Christian Witness*, 227; cf. Heiler, *Gospel of Singh*, 219.
[284] Singh, *Search After Reality*, in *Christian Witness*, 163-184.

been to make the Christ of mystical experience function as a means of empirical epistemological verification of the essential Christian affirmations. The end result, however, is the subordination of the Christ of tradition to the Christ of experience.

What, then, is the significance and function of Sundar Singh's *Logos*-Christ conception? The *Logos* theology of the early fathers served as a means for demonstrating that divine revelation is not restricted to the historical Jesus, even within a scheme of uncompromising Christocentricity. Recognizing the *Logos* as the agent and sustainer of the created world, present and active in it since the time of creation, they ground their approach in a Christological interpretation of creation, discerning the illuminating action of the *Logos* in glimpses of revelation, faith and grace outside of the specific revelation in Christ.

Sundar Singh is not a systematic theologian and hence his *Logos* theology bears the weaknesses of his limited conceptual apparatus. Although it lacks the depth and sophistication of the early fathers, his fulfilment approach does resonate with theirs in its attempt to provide an explanation for the universal revelatory activity of the *Logos*. In a strategy that echoes the Ramanujan body-soul analogy, he explains how God indwells the world and the soul of man as the *Logos*, the means by which the revelation of God is received in the depths of the soul. He remained convinced, however, that although the illuminating power of the *Logos* enlightened every corner of the world, his light was most sharply focussed in the incarnate Christ of history, now the living, resurrected Lord of Christian faith:

> The Wise Men followed the Star to Bethlehem. But when they reached Bethlehem they no longer needed the Star, for they had found Christ, the Sun of Righteousness. When the sun rises the stars lose their radiance.... In India we have many genuine truth-seekers, who faithfully follow their Star; but it is only starlight which guides them. But you Christians have the glory of the Sun... Hinduism and Buddhism have dug canals, but they have no living water to fill them. In this sense I was prepared to receive the Living Water from Christ. Christianity is the fulfilment of Hinduism.[285]

Sundar Singh's theological intentions are thus unmistakable. The pre-Christian light of the *Logos* is only starlight, in contrast to the blazing light of Christ, "the Sun of Righteousness", before whose glory the starlight fades. The *Logos*-light only prepares channels, and is distinguished from the light the living Christ brings as the "Living Water" which must flow through these channels. He thus seeks to affirm the decisiveness of God's revelation in the Christ-event.

---

[285] Quoted in Heiler, *Gospel of Singh*, 220.

But like Sen, and in contrast to the fathers, Sundar Singh's Christological trajectory seems to operate in the reverse direction, with the Christ of mystical experience as the focal point, and the Christ of tradition a separate parallel concept. Thus, although he affirms the decisiveness of Christ, the Christ he affirms is primarily the "living inward Christ" of his experience. Although this conception of Christ is shaped by his experience of the Holy Spirit's mediation of the New Testament witness, it is not overtly and unmistakably subservient to the biblical sources.

Summary Evaluation

We have observed that Sundar Singh was primarily a mystic-saint and evangelist rather than a thinker. His theology has, hence, sometimes been perceived as simplistic and elementary, and given cursory treatment.[286] Others have, on the other hand, hallowed him as an original and creative mystical genius.[287] In conclusion, we first examine the distinctiveness of his fulfilment approach, and then assess its importance and value for our ongoing discussion.

In investigating Sundar Singh's fulfilment view, we have been able to identify elements of all three models of fulfilment described in our typology in chapter one. The preparatory value of the Hindu tradition is seen in its possessing partial but authentic intimations of reality as a provisional stage along a continuum of evolutionary movement towards the full knowledge of God. His attempt to treat some aspects of the Hindu tradition as an Old Testament in relation to the Hindu community follows the lines of a prophetic fulfilment scheme.

However, neither of these strands is developed in any degree of depth or consistency in Sundar Singh's writings. Although he believes that the Hindu tradition does possess "the light of truth" in an objective sense, he is more concerned with the subjective intimations within Hinduism and other religions, which point to a universal need for mystical union with God. The allusions to evolutionary and prophetic fulfilment must thus be treated as illustrations of an essentially undeveloped conviction regarding the presence of objective divine truth in other religions.

Sundar Singh's fulfilment approach has its basic impulse in the *bhakti* mystical quest for a personal experience of communion with God. God who is pure and self-giving love, has revealed this love especially in the incarnation and redemption accomplished by Christ. Humanity's need for communion with

---

[286] Scott, 'Sadhu Sundar Singh: Church of the Sadhu Ideal', 267; Sharpe, 'The Legacy of Sadhu Sundar Singh', 166.

[287] Heiler, *Gospel of Singh*, 222; Sundar Singh inspired and influenced a whole generation of Christian leaders; the most prominent among them was Bishop A.J. Appasamy, who provided theological clarity to many of his ideas; Boyd, *Indian Christian Theology*, 108, 119; cf. Francis, *Christian Witness*, 17.

God is fulfilled through a mystical encounter with the living Christ, which results in transformation of heart and discovery of true peace and happiness. The universality of God's concern for the salvation of humanity and the particularity of the means he employs in Christ are thus held together in a form of the *Logos* fulfilment view.

The device Sundar Singh uses to establish continuity between Christian faith and *bhakti* consciousness is the concept of a universal intuitive mystical knowledge within the human heart, giving humanity the capacity for unmediated revelatory and relational access to God. An incipient *Logos* theology thus undergirds Sundar Singh's formulation of this view, but the biblical and theological resources employed in the development of this concept are inadequate. Sundar Singh strongly affirms the particularity of salvation in Christ. His view of the Christ of history is biblically orthodox and grounded in tradition, but developed alongside his conception of the "living inward Christ" of mystical experience, to which he gives priority due to his *bhakti* mystical orientation.

Sundar Singh's appropriation of the sadhu ideal complements his version of *Logos* fulfilment. Not only are *bhakti* aspirations fulfilled in Christ, in the reverse trajectory of fulfilment, some aspects of Christian faith also find fulfilment in the sadhu ideal. The sadhu lifestyle was a childhood ideal that Sundar Singh instinctively identified as a means of deepening his Christian discipleship in its potential for fulfilment of certain Christian beliefs and values.

This emphasis echoes Westcott's dual consummation view of fulfilment, in which he not only saw other religions finding fulfilment in Christianity, but also perceived prospects in them for the enhancement of the Church's understanding and appropriation of truths hitherto obscured within the Gospel. Sundar Singh's intimations in this regard resonate deeply with one of his theological contemporaries in India, P. Chenchiah, who was convinced that there were aspects of Hinduism that could contribute positively to the development of Christian thought and experience, and recommended strengthening the channels of mutual influence and fulfilment.[288] We have observed a similar emphasis in Farquhar's fulfilment approach as well.[289]

Sharpe has compared Sundar Singh's influence during the crucial years leading up to India's independence to that of Rabindranath Tagore and Mahatma Gandhi: "From Tagore came an aesthetic challenge, from Gandhi an ethical challenge, and from Sundar Singh a spiritual challenge…", and Indian and Western Christians both felt compelled to react to all three.[290] Sundar Singh's exceptional influence upon the religious world of the 1920s was largely due to his discovery and successful embodiment of a form of Indian

---

288 See p.42, n.204.

289 See p.63.

290 Sharpe, 'Sadhu Sundar Singh and His Critics', 63.

Christianity that penetrated the heart of the gospel, and yet "appeared to have access to the innermost chambers of Indian spirituality".[291]

The greatest strength of Sundar Singh's fulfilment view was its emergence as his spontaneous attempt to interpret Christ from the highest point in his pre-Christian consciousness, the Hindu sadhu ideal of supreme renunciation and self-denial for the purpose of mystical God-realisation. His fulfilment approach was shaped essentially by an integral aspect of this ideal, the longing for mystical union with God. Thus, the most significant achievement of Sundar Singh's fulfilment approach is that it is grounded in the highest ideal in the Hindu tradition, the ideal of religious experience.

A second strength of Sundar Singh's fulfilment view is that it is grounded in operative Hindu beliefs and empirical data of religious experience, rather than the theoretical sources of the Hindu tradition. Hence, his fulfilment view is, more than an abstract construct, a practical dialogical approach forged in the context of his grass-roots engagement with people of other faiths. This feature greatly enhances the appeal of his approach and may be one reason for the widespread popularity of his writings.[292]

Sundar Singh's approach also represents an essentially irenic and inclusivist view of non-Christian religious experience. The light of truth is present in all religions; hence, non-Christian religions represent provisional but authentic expressions of the human search for God. Although Christ completes what is lacking in the other religions of the world, and is alone the universal saviour, non-Christians will have the opportunity for a clearer revelation and for salvation through Christ in the after-life.

Sundar Singh's fulfilment approach does, however, have several theological weaknesses. Although he maintains that non-Christian religious experience has some pedagogical value, he fails to outline criteria for identifying objectively elements of truth outside of the Christian revelation. He is also unsuccessful in differentiating adequately between Christian and pre-Christian participation in the *Logos*, and while this strongly affirms theological continuity between Christian and non-Christian religious experience, it dilutes the transcendence feature of fulfilment.

It is hard to understand why serious assessments of Sundar Singh's theological contribution have been so few and far between, especially during the latter half of the twentieth century. The theological inadequacies of Sundar Singh's fulfilment view are easily explained given that it represents the efforts of an unsophisticated convert-mystic to relate his experience of Christ to the *bhakti* mystic quest. His fulfilment approach must, however, be commended

---

[291] Sharpe's expression; 'The Legacy of Sadhu Sundar Singh', 161; cf. Heiler, *Gospel of Singh*, 231; Soderblom, 'Christian Mysticism in an Indian Soul', 238.

[292] In 1966, Appasamy observes that his writings had been translated into forty different languages and mentions pending requests for translation into other languages' Singh, 'Introduction', *Real Pearl*, in *Christian Witness*, 421.

for its originality, creativity of insight, and, most of all, its indigenous quality. Nicol Macnicol perhaps best captures the significance of Sundar Singh's theological genius: "He is India's ideal of the disciple of Christ.... In him Christianity and Hinduism seem to meet, and the Christian faith stands forth, not as something foreign, but like a flower which blossoms on an Indian stem."[293]

[293] Quoted in Heiler, *Gospel of Singh*, 246.

A Critical Evaluation of the Contributions of Farquhar, Banerjea, and Sundar Singh to Fulfilment Thought

Our study has examined the Christian response to the phenomenon of other religions within a specific tradition of encounter in the Indian context: the fulfilment stream that emerged in the experience and reflection of converts to Christian faith during the critical pre-independence period. The framework we have chosen to evaluate their contribution is provided by J.N. Farquhar's fulfilment approach, which represents the peak of development of nineteenth century Protestant fulfilment theology.

Our critical assessment of Farquhar's fulfilment approach in chapter two exposed the need for further illumination in three areas of the nineteenth century Protestant fulfilment tradition: (1) a verification of its claim concerning the value of the Hindu tradition as a pedagogy to Christ; (2) the adoption of an appropriate theological device for affirming Hindu-Christian continuity; and (3) the formulation of an adequate Christology that responds positively to certain definite aspirations of the Hindu tradition and affirms the central claim of the Christian faith, the decisiveness of the Christ-event. This three-fold concern provided the framework for our analyses of the fulfilment notions of Banerjea and Sundar Singh in chapters three and four, guided our assessment of their approaches, and indicated points at which their proposal confirms and complements the nineteenth century Protestant fulfilment tradition.

In the following comparative evaluation of the fulfilment approaches of Farquhar, Banerjea and Sundar Singh, we examine the cumulative response of Indian converts to the main questions that emerged in our analysis of Farquhar's view. This enables us to outline a fulfilment proposal that incorporates the cumulative contributions of all three subjects of our study, which we then evaluate in our concluding chapter.

The Socio-political Impulse for the Emergence of Fulfilment Approach in Pre-independence India

As a prelude to our comparison of the three fulfilment approaches, we need to distinguish the principal common contextual impulse that prompted the rise of various fulfilment approaches within pre-independence India. Farquhar's fulfilment approach was forged in response to the prevailing perception of Christianity as a foreign, denationalising influence and Christian mission as a destructive invasion of the traditional culture of India.[1] His apologetic response thus attempted to assert the relevance of Christ to India against the charge that the Christian message was an assault on the spirit of nationalism. This led him then to a serious investigation of the Hindu religious sources in search of a way for affirming continuity between the Christian faith and the Hindu tradition. His approach sought to distinguish between universal and context-specific elements in the Christian gospel, and so provide a basis for distinguishing the evangelistic mandate of sharing the message of Christ from the imperialistic enterprise.

Most of the Indian fulfilment contributions considered in this study were also forged in response to the common rejection of the Christian message, based not on religious or philosophical grounds, but on the perception of it being foreign. Although they drew their insights from different sources, Sen, Goreh, Upadhyay, and Tilak were all concerned essentially with refuting the charge of cultural foreignness and irrelevance of the Christian faith. Sen thus speaks of Christ coming to India as an "Asiatic in race" and "Hindu in faith", and despite his deep attraction to Christ, remained within the Hindu fold all his life. Goreh consciously resisted western influence upon his traditional culture and life-style, and despite the influence of rationalism and western orthodoxy, affirmed the presence of divine light within the Hindu tradition.

Essentially, the same impulse is expressed in Upadhyay's life-long quest for a Hindu-Catholic theology and identity, as a result of which he remained a patriotic nationalist all his life. Tilak claimed that his quest for an ideal religion that would provide the spiritual foundation for a prosperous India led him to Christ. His deep love for his Hindu spiritual heritage and life-long attempt to free the person and message of Christ from western cultural forms, led him eventually to launch a culturally indigenous Christian movement.

We find this same impulse prominent in Banerjea and Sundar Singh. Banerjea devotes a significant opening segment of *Dialogues* to a series of arguments countering the Hindu opposition to Christianity as a foreign religion, destructive of the Indian way of life. The ultimate objective of *Arian Witness* was to refute the charge that Christianity was a foreign religion and that Hindu converts to Christianity had betrayed their ancestral faith. Banerjea's overriding concern thus seems to have been to redeem the Christian faith from the charge of foreignness, and to demonstrate that Hindu converts could remain loyal to their ancestral culture even as disciples of Christ.

---

[1] The thesis that the nineteenth century Christian missionary enterprise was part of the British imperialist programme of political, economic, and cultural conquest continues to influence the Hindu response to Christianity even a century later; see A. Shourie, *Missionaries in India: Continuities, Changes Dilemmas* (New Delhi: ASA, 1994), and response by V. Mangalwadi, *Missionary Conspiracy: Letters to a Postmodern Hindu* (New Delhi: Good Books, 1996); also G. Studdert-Kennedy, *British Christians, Indian Nationalists and the Raj* (Delhi: Oxford University Press, 1998).

In Sundar Singh the impulse is expressed most clearly in his famous saying: "Indians greatly need the Water of Life, but they do not want it in European vessels".[2] Although implied in his attempt to draw lines of pedagogical continuity between the Hindu tradition and Christian faith, this principle is most explicitly applied in his conscious adoption of the *sadhu* lifestyle. We have seen that in Sundar Singh this was not just a pragmatic evangelistic device, but an attempt to represent the Christian gospel in a form of living expression that represented the highest ideal of Hindu religion.

Thus, like Farquhar, the Indian thinkers clearly go to great lengths to distinguish their theological task from the imperialistic project with which the Christian mission was frequently confused. We will respond to the charge of imperialism as it relates to the fulfilment tradition in due course. For the moment, we observe that the fulfilment approach emerged essentially as a solution to the need for inculturation or contextualization in the gospel-culture encounter in the Indian context.[3] This inculturation impulse led them to explore the Hindu tradition for resources to affirm meaningfully the universal relevance of Christ within the Hindu context. Their research yielded various elements in the Hindu tradition and experience that could be regarded as a pedagogy to Christ. The following comparative theological assessment thus begins with an evaluation of the fulfilment claim regarding the pedagogical value of Hinduism.

A Comparative Theological Assessment of the Fulfilment Conceptions of Farquhar, Banerjea and Sundar Singh

Fulfilment and the Pedagogical Value of Hinduism

Farquhar discovered elements in the Hindu tradition and experience that led him to express the pedagogical value of Hinduism in both objective and subjective terms. Objectively, he was able to identify fragments of truth and light that anticipate the fuller truth and light revealed in Christ and by which they are clarified, corrected, and completed. Subjectively, he was able to discern expressions of basic human religious needs and instincts underlying various Hindu beliefs and practices, unfulfilled aspects of which seemed to point beyond to ultimate satisfaction in Christ. Hogg's criticism that Christianity does not fulfil any need intrinsic to Hinduism thus struck at the root of Farquhar's fulfilment view.[4]

---

[2] See p.180.

[3] In this discussion, the terms inculturation and contextualization are used interchangeably in their broadest sense to denote the means by which the Christian faith takes on indigenous expression in any given culture.

[4] For our initial response to Hogg's criticism.

While indicating the theological inconsistency of Hogg's criticism at this point, we had suspended judgment pending evaluation of the empirical evidence. The experience and reflection of converts provides appropriate data for evaluating the conflicting claims of Farquhar and Hogg, but two common misconceptions frequently arising from Hogg's criticism must first be clarified.

First, Hogg's contention that in Farquhar's fulfilment approach Hinduism represents only unfulfilled "needs", only a "seeking" and no "finding", is misplaced. Farquhar insists that Hinduism represents an authentic revelation from God and possesses priceless religious treasures. The Hindu is mystically related to Christ, is filled with the life that is in Christ, and although he is saved only through Christ, may be accepted by God apart from explicit knowledge of the Christian gospel.

Second, Farquhar's fulfilment view does not necessarily imply, as Hogg's criticism suggests, that there must be a widespread religious dissatisfaction among Hindus, consciously searching for what is offered in Christ. To apply this as a test of Farquhar's view is no more legitimate than to expect that the justification of Jesus' claim to have fulfilled Old Testament messianic expectations should require that the majority of the Jews of his time accept the validity of his claim. Farquhar's fulfilment approach is a conscious attempt to apply the Jewish-Christian fulfilment model to the relationship between Hinduism and Christianity. The plausibility of the Jewish-Christian fulfilment model rests upon the New Testament testimony of a small group of ethnic Jews, convinced by Jesus' claim to have fulfilled the Old Testament messianic expectations. The verification of the fulfilment claim sought from those rooted within the Hindu tradition must thus be commensurable with the first century Jewish-Christian response.

The crucial question then is: Do the fulfilment approaches of Indian converts we have considered indicate any resources in the Hindu tradition or impulses in Hindu religious experience that witness to the presence of a genuine anticipation of and need for that which is offered in Christ? We first summarise the responses considered in chapter one.

Observing the presence of fragments of truth within the Hindu tradition, Sen sees the Hindu scriptures as pointing prophetically to the coming of Christ. He thus applies Jesus' words in Matthew 5:17 to Christ's fulfilment of Hindu aspirations, making him the first Indian to describe the relationship of Christ to other religions in terms of fulfilment. Goreh's essentially negative attitude to Hinduism does not prevent him from recognising the light of general revelation in the Hindu tradition in certain ideas that point beyond to fulfilment in Christ. He sees the deepest Hindu anticipations and yearnings for union with God fulfilled through participation in the Christian Eucharist.

Within the natural-supernatural framework of Upadhyay's form of *Logos* fulfilment, natural religion reaches its highest form of expression in the Vedantic conception of Brahman as *Saccidananda*. The supernatural revelation of God in Christ fulfils this high point in the Hindu tradition in the doctrine of the Trinity, viewed as a fuller description of the nature of God as *Saccidananda*. Tilak clearly regarded the Hindu devotional literature and the writings of the bhakti poet-saints as serving as an Old Testament for Hindus in India. Tilak's own spiritual journey convinced him that the Hindu scriptures anticipated and prepared Hindus to receive the message of Christ.

Thus, contra Hogg, the responses of Indian Christian converts during the pre-independence period broadly attest to the presence of authentic intimations of Christ within the Hindu religious tradition. We observe further convincing evidence of resources for a pedagogy to Christ within the Hindu tradition and experience in our more detailed investigation of the views of Banerjea and Sundar Singh. In continuity with Farquhar's identification of objective and subjective aspects of the pedagogy to Christ in Hinduism, Banerjea focuses on objective pointers to Christ in the vedic texts, whereas Sundar Singh primarily discerns a subjective testimony to Christ in Hindu religious experience.

Banerjea was convinced that the Vedas offered greater potential for a meeting point between Hinduism and Christianity than the later philosophical schools. He discovered germs or fragments of truth in them, which seemed to affirm what he considered the essentials of Christian faith. He saw a prophetic prediction of Christ in the recognition of sacrifice as the great remedy for sins in certain vedic texts, and more specifically, in the vedic self-sacrificing divine figure of *Prajapati*.

Sundar Singh's view of the anticipation of Christ within the Hindu tradition is aptly summarised in his metaphor of Christ as 'the Water of Life' that flows through the channels dug by Hinduism. Based on his personal experience and various encounters with other Hindu mystics, Sundar Singh maintained that the impulse for union with God within the *bhakti* mystical consciousness constituted a preparation for Christ. He was convinced that this aspiration was fulfilled in a personal mystical experience of communion with God through Christ.

Banerjea and Sundar Singh's views are consistent with the broad direction of Indian theological reflection on this issue during this period. The Indian fulfilment approaches we have considered provide a strong empirical affirmation of Farquhar's thesis, and clearly undermine the force of Hogg's objection at this point.

The recognition of a pedagogy to Christ in Hindu or other traditions raises an important question. Given that this pedagogy to Christ in non-Christian traditions is identified through a Christic reading of their sources, what are the grounds for such a reading of non-Christian texts? The search for a pedagogy to Christ within the Hindu tradition was motivated, at least initially, by the inculturation impulse. The method employed was a Christological reading of the non-Christian texts and, at this point, we are concerned with a biblical evaluation of this procedure.

The theological basis for the Christian reading of non-Christian texts is grounded originally in the constitutive claim of Christian faith – both assumed and explicitly stated in the New Testament – that the coming of Christ fulfilled the messianic expectations of the Jewish scriptures.[5] The significance of the key text, the record of Jesus' words in Matthew 5:17, 18, has been variously interpreted, giving rise to diverse opinions regarding the early Jewish Christian attitude to the Old Testament.[6]

The interpretation most consistent with the context of the passage and with the antitheses that follows illustrating Jesus' fulfilment of the Law, views Jesus as "fulfilling" the Law by teaching the eschatological will of God anticipated by it.[7] The Old Testament as a whole is viewed as the promise component in a promise-fulfilment scheme of salvation history.[8] Jesus is seen as affirming that his teaching is in essential continuity with the Old Testament against rumours that he has come to overthrow Jewish tradition. Rather than abolishing the Law and the prophets, his teaching brings the Old Testament to its intended eschatological climax. The continuing validity of the Old Testament is asserted, but as interpreted in terms of Jesus' own fulfilment of it.[9] The New Testament account of Jesus' promise-fulfilment approach to the Law thus indicates that the early Jewish Christian community regarded his attitude to the Old Testament as marked by a tension between elements of continuity and discontinuity.[10]

On one hand, the New Testament records Jesus' deep commitment to the essentials of Jewish faith and the substantial continuity of his teachings with the Old Testament. He frequently appeals to the Old Testament, quotes, alludes to, and interprets the Jewish scriptures, and also uses various common Jewish concepts and phraseology.[11] On the other hand, as evidenced in the tone of the six antitheses in Matthew 5:21-48, for instance, Jesus is viewed as Lord of the Law itself. He asserts his independent authority by his implicit abrogation of several commandments and his manner of announcing God's will for his followers without support from any other source. This element of newness in Jesus' message brought him into confrontation with some aspects of his Jewish

---

[5] J. Goldingay, *Approaches to Old Testament Interpretation* (Leicester: Apollos, 1990), 115.

[6] D. Moo, *The Wycliffe Exegetical Commentary: Romans 1-8* (Chicago: Moody Press, 1991), 457 lists five distinct interpretations; cf. V. Poythress, *The Shadow of Christ in the Law of Moses* (Brentwood: Wolgemuth & Hyatt, 1991), 264-267, 363-377.

[7] "Law" in this discussion can be taken to refer to the entire Old Testament; Poythress, *Shadow of Christ*, 264.

[8] Moo, *Wycliffe Exegetical Commentary*, 457. According to Goldingay, *Old Testament Interpretation*, 117-118, the theme of promise and fulfilment is both "the centre of OT thinking and… the key link between the two Testaments".

[9] Poythress, *Shadow of Christ*, 268.

[10] Moo, *Wycliffe Exegetical Commentary*, 458-459; cf. M. Blanchard, 'Christianity as Fulfilment and Antithesis', *The Indian Journal of Theology* 17 (1968), 8-10.

[11] C.A. Evans, 'Old Testament in the Gospels' in *Dictionary of Jesus and the Gospels,* J.B. Green, S. McKinght, and I.H. Marshall, eds. (Leicester: InterVarsity Press, 1992), 579-581; Moo, *Wycliffe Exegetical Commentary*, 453.

tradition, since he implicitly judged it in his claim to have come to "fulfil" the Old Testament.[12]

This promise-fulfilment model thus involved both substantial continuity with the Old Testament Jewish faith, and a transcending of the old by reinterpretation and reorientation, with Jesus replacing the Law as the locus of God's word to his people. Based on this Jewish Christian promise-fulfilment tradition, the Jewish scriptures, interpreted Christologically, became the bedrock of New Testament faith and theology. Hence, when addressing Jews or those influenced by Jewish tradition, the apostolic writers always grounded their teaching in the Old Testament.[13] However, features of discontinuity, such as new elements in their message and their heralding of a new dispensation, caused their message to be rejected by the Jews.[14]

In examining the New Testament use of the Old Testament, Longenecker points out that, in contrast to the approach of mainline Jewish exegetes of the first century, the primary intent of the apostolic writers was to highlight the theme of fulfilment. He maintains that their understanding of fulfilment began from outside the biblical materials and they used the biblical texts mainly to support their extrabiblical stance. The distinctive stance at the heart of their exegetical methodology was their Christocentric perspective shaped by their experience of and reflection on the Christ-event. This perspective led them to take Jesus' own use of the Old Testament as normative, gave them a new understanding of their place in redemptive history, and caused them to view the Old Testament as promise/preparation for Christ, the fulfilment.[15]

The Jewish Christian impulse to affirm continuity of Jesus' person and message with the Jewish scriptures parallels the inculturation impulse of Indian Christian converts in relation to the Hindu tradition. This New Testament promise-fulfilment approach has served as a model for subsequent approaches

---

[12] Moo, *Wycliffe Exegetical Commentary*, 454-456, 459.

[13] M.R. Wilson, *Our Father Abraham: Jewish Roots of the Christian Faith* (Grand Rapids, Eerdmans, 1989), 112-113.

[14] Wilson, *Our Father Abraham*, 107-127; Goldingay, *Old Testament Interpretation*, 29-37.

[15] R.N. Longenecker, *Biblical Exegesis in the Apostolic Period* (Grand Rapids: Baker Book House, 1999), xxvi-xxx, 185-193. He points out that the apostolic writers were not so much concerned with commentaries on biblical texts or their contemporary application as in demonstrating redemptive fulfilment in Christ. Convinced that the fullness of divine revelation was expressed in Christ, their Christocentric interpretation of the Old Testament was more charismatic than scholastic. Consequently, New Testament writers' interpretations of Old Testament texts often totally eclipse, if not distort their original meaning. Introducing a compendium of essays which address various facets of this issue, Beale observes: "...there is a consensus among the significant group of New Testament scholars, if not a majority, that the New Testament uses the Old without regard for its original meaning"; G.K. Beale, ed., *The Right Doctrine from the Wrong Texts? Essays on the Use of the Old Testament in the New* (Grand Rapids: Baker, 1994), 9.

to the Christological reading of non-Christian religious texts. Illustrated originally in the apologetic writings of the early fathers, it seems to have also definitively influenced the fulfilment approaches of Indian converts in the pre-independence period.

To what extent is it legitimate to transpose this procedure of a Christological interpretation of the Jewish scriptures to the reading of other non-Christian texts? Paul's address to the Greeks at Athens in Acts 17:22-31 offers an illustration of the Christian use of non-Christian texts outside the Jewish context.[16] Paul avoids any direct reference to the Old Testament, but makes use of several concepts of distinct pagan origin.[17] The first is the inscription on the altar to the "unknown god", probably one of several such altars at Athens integral to the religious consciousness of the Athenians.[18] It served as a point of contact – a text Paul used to launch his speech. Although the ignorance rather than the worship is underlined, Paul clearly intended to convey that he was now making known to them this "unknown god" whom they worshipped in ignorance.[19]

Paul's speech also employs two consecutive quotations from Greek poets to illustrate his argument: "in him we live and move and have our being" – a reference traced back to the sixth century B.C. poet, Epimenides, the Cretan, and "for we are indeed his offspring" – a citation from a third century B.C. poet, Aratus of Cilicia (Acts 17:28).[20] A further reference to pagan sources is

---

[16] The authenticity of Paul's Areopagus address and its significance for the Christian witness to people of other faiths has been the subject of much debate. Our discussion assumes that it represents the Lucan record of Paul's pattern of gospel presentation to a Gentile audience; F.F. Bruce, *Commentary on the Book of Acts* (Grand Rapids: Eerdmans, 1987), 354-355; L. Legrand, 'The Unknown God of Athens: Acts 17 and the Religon of the Gentiles', *The Indian Journal of Theology 30* (1981), 161-162; L. Legrand, 'The Missionary Significance of the Areopagus Speech' in *God's Word Among Men*, ed. G. Gispert-Sauch (Delhi: Vidyajyoti, 1973), 60-63.

[17] P. Hacker, *Theological Foundations of Evangelization* (St Augustin: Steyler Verlag, 1980), 28-30.

[18] Acts 17:23; F.F. Bruce, *The Acts of the Apostles* (Grand Rapids: Eerdmans, 1990), 380-381.

[19] Bruce, *Commentary on the Book of Acts*, 356; Legrand, 'The Missionary Significance of the Areopagus Speech', 67-69. Munck sees Paul's thought here related to his stated conviction in Rom. 1:19-23, that God is known through his creation; J. Munck, *The Acts of the Apostles, Anchor Bible*, vol. 31 (New York: Doubleday, 1986), 172; for an opposing view which sees "...no real connection between 'an unknown god' and the true God" in Paul's strategy, see I.H. Marshall, *The Acts of the Apostles* (Leicester, InterVarsity Press, 1980), 286.

[20] For details of background, see C.J. Hemer, *The Book of Acts in the Setting of Hellenistic History* (Tubigen: Mohr, 1980), 116-118, and Bruce, *The Acts of the Apostles*, 384-385. Legrand, 'The Unknown God of Athens', 158, n. 1 points out that such quotations from non-biblical religious texts are not only extremely rare in the New Testament, this combination represents a unique occurrence.

the allusion to Stoic philosophy in the expression "men should seek God, in the hope that they might feel after him" (Acts 17:27).

According to Hemer, Paul is here interacting with the specific traditions of Athenian religion.[21] The inculturation impulse is evident in his selection and employment of specific non-Christian notions familiar to his Gentile audience. In their original context, none of these pagan concepts used by Paul expressed pure, Christian knowledge of God. But the fact that each of them contained an element of truth is recognized by him, and utilized to relate the Christian gospel to such knowledge of God as they possessed. These fragments of truth are, however, identified on the basis of Christological criteria, loosened from their original context, and reoriented in the communication of the Christian message.[22]

Paul's desire to affirm continuity and his recognition of elements of truth in Gentile religion does not make him overlook elements of discontinuity. Concerning the grammatical construction of this passage, Legrand notes that the positive clauses are subordinate to the more prominent negative clauses, suggesting that in Paul's view, the religion of the Gentiles represents a mixture of truth and aberration.[23] His reference to the "unknown god" was designed to convey that although the quest for God expressed in their worship was legitimate, their mode of worship – their polytheistic idolatry – was not.[24] Likewise, Paul's acceptance of truth in the Stoic assertion that God is "not far from each one of us", does not imply his approval of the Stoic pantheistic framework.[25]

The recognition of elements of a true knowledge of God and legitimate human spiritual aspirations in Paul's use of non-Christian texts was complemented by an assertion of the transcendent element of Christian newness. This necessitated a radical reinterpretation and reorientation of these elements towards a Christological frame of reference. The reinterpreted text takes on a significance that is both new and, at the same time, continuous with its pre-Christian meaning. The dialectic corresponds to that found in the New Testament promise-fulfilment approach to the Jewish scriptures, and similar to that observed in the Christological reading of Hindu texts in Indian fulfilment approaches.

Banerjea's Christological reading of the Vedas begins by accepting the textual witness of the Vedas concerning the importance of the institution of sacrifice and its value as the remedy for sins. His identification of the figure of

---

[21] Hemer, *The Book of Acts*, 118.

[22] Hacker, *Theological Foundations of Evangelization*, 29, 30.

[23] Legrand, 'The Unknown God of Athens', 166; cf. Hacker, *Theological Foundations of Evangelization*, 30.

[24] Hacker, *Theological Foundations of Evangelization*, 28, 29; J.R.W. Stott, *The Message of Acts* (Leicester: InterVarsity Press, 1990), 278-279; cf. Legrand, 'The Unknown God of Athens', 165.

[25] Hacker, *Theological Foundations of Evangelization*, 29.

Prajapati and his interpretation of its self-sacrifice as a prophetic prefigurement of Christ constitutes a Christological reorientation of the concept, since the criteria employed are clearly derived from the Christian discourse. Consequently, even though this understanding of *Prajapati* bears some continuity with its original significance, the specific Christological connotation Banerjea gives to it is distinctly new.

A similar dialectic takes on a wide range of nuances in Farquhar's interpretation of Hindu texts. At one end, concepts such as sacrifice and the incarnation are essentially affirmed because of their seeming proximity to corresponding ideas in Christian teaching. He describes the incarnation idea as "one of the most powerful forces" within Hinduism, and its widespread influence as "the strongest possible testimony to the religious value it possesses for the Hindu and the Asiatic spirit."[26] On the other hand, he clearly highlights the inadequacies of the Hindu ideal in a comparative assessment with the incarnation in Christ.[27]

At the other end of the spectrum are concepts remote to nineteenth century evangelical Christianity such as the doctrine of *karma*, the caste system, Vedanta philosophy and image-worship. Here Farquhar highlights a fundamental flaw in the belief or practice, but then discerns one or more valid aspirations within each that finds fulfilment in Christ. For instance, although he denounces the practice of image-worship, he also sees it as embodying an important truth that immediate and direct access to God is available at all times. This valid sentiment, expressed in some unhealthy superstitious practices in Hinduism, finds its fullest spiritual satisfaction in Christ.

Farquhar's manner of reference to fragments of truth in the Hindu scriptures seems to parallel Banerjea's citation of Vedic texts. Although Banerjea views the light in the Vedas very seriously, he takes care to distinguish the recollections of a primitive revelation in them from the inspiration of the Hebrew prophets. His attitude to the Hindu scriptures thus differs from Farquhar's undifferentiated view and is more analogous to the early fathers' approach to Greek philosophy, in the careful theological distinction he draws between divine revelation in the Vedas and the Old and New Testaments.

To summarise: (1) the Christian commitment to the theological principle of inculturation/contextualization constitutes an essential impulse for a Christian reading of non-Christian texts; (2) the continuity-discontinuity dialetic is a feature we observe in the New Testament promise-fulfilment pattern of reading the Jewish scriptures, and in the use of non-Christian texts in New Testament apostolic preaching; (3) we may derive biblical and theological justification for Farquhar and Banerjea's inculturation efforts by observing a similar dialectic in their Christological readings of Hindu texts.

---

[26] Farquhar, *Crown of Hinduism*, 421.
[27] Farquhar, *Crown of Hinduism*, 429-444.

Indian converts such as Banerjea, Sundar Singh, and others are thus in a position comparable to the early Jewish Christians and Gentile converts, who could legitimately claim the right to interpret their ancestral religious tradition from the perspective of their Christian experience. This entitlement became an obligation in the light of the contextualization impulse and the need to justify their conversion to Christ against the charge of national and religious apostasy.

Fulfilment and Continuity-Discontinuity

Our acceptance of the pedagogical value of the Hindu tradition raises another set of critical questions relating to truth and divine revelation in Christian faith and other religions. Do the sacred books of other religions offer only a human discourse about God or a human word addressed to God in anticipation of a divine response? Or can we regard them as containing a 'ord from God to the people of those religions and even to all humankind? If it is in some sense the latter, then how are we to understand the relationship between the divine word contained in the sacred scriptures of various religious traditions and what Christians regard as the decisive Word of God in Jesus Christ as recorded in the New Testament?

The answers to these questions are critical for the fulfilment approach, since essential to it is some theological explanation of continuity between the particular revelation-salvation history of Christians and the history of God's dealings with peoples of other faiths. Our response to these questions will draw on Jacques Dupuis' introduction to a theology of religions in which he proposes a scheme for locating revelation in other religions within a Christian Trinitarian framework.[28]

Our comparison of the continuity schemes of the subjects of our study will first need to take into account their qualitative evaluation of the truth content in other religious traditions. Do they regard the existence of elements of truth and light in other religious traditions as evidence that they contain an authentic word from God?

According to Farquhar, the authors of the sacred books of Hinduism and Islam clearly heard a divine message, which was subsequently corrupted in its communication by the thoughts of the messengers. His understanding of the progress of revelation through history treats the revelation in other religions as qualitatively the same as that in Old Testament Judaism. The earlier religions possess more primitive forms and the later religions more sophisticated expressions of revelation, but all express the natural longings of the human religious consciousness and must be interpreted in the light of the teaching of Christ. His scheme enables him to draw only a quantitative distinction between

[28] Our assessment in this section owes much to chapter nine of J. Dupuis, *Toward a Christian Theology of Religious Pluralism* (New York: Orbis, 1997), 235-253.

the fragmentary revelation in other religions and the brighter and fuller revelation in Christ.

Banerjea's understanding of divine revelation in the Hindu tradition is based on his view of a universal primeval revelation, an original communication of the divine will to all humankind at the dawn of history. He also has a belief in natural revelation implanted by God in human nature, although the relation between these related ideas is not clarified. What seems clear is that for him, primeval revelation involved some form of supernatural communication distinct from natural revelation or the knowledge of God accessible to human reason. In his view, the Hindu tradition, and the Vedas in particular, do contain an authentic word from God.

Farquhar's view of revelation includes a subjective aspect, a mystical God-awareness he alludes to but which remains largely undeveloped in his thought. This aspect is further illuminated in Sundar Singh's understanding of revelation in the Hindu tradition. Sundar Singh was convinced that Hindus have access to the Holy Spirit and to the light that the *Logos*-Christ gives. The location of this revelation, however, is not religious texts but the deepest recesses of the human heart, the realm of mystical experience. The light of truth is, thus, present in all religions as they provide conditioned and nuanced perceptions of Reality and mediate a limited but authentic encounter with God. A genuine word from God is, thus, mediated within Hindu religious experience.

Acceptance of the presence of divine revelation in other religions leads the subjects of our study to suggest various schemes of continuity. The evolutionary hypothesis served as the formal framework for Farquhar's understanding of the development of religion as a historical process, involving the progressive unfolding of truth. But Jesus' discipleship principle of life through death expressed for him the theological core of the idea of progressive revelation. It encapsulated the dialectic involved in inculturation, and also summarised how God's revelation in Christ was related to the revelation in Hinduism.

The negative component of the metaphor highlights the transcendent aspect of the relationship: the Hindu tradition is tested against the criterion of Christ's person and teachings, and the elements that are excluded must be left behind and allowed to die. It also makes room for continuity: it emphasises the ongoing life and relevance of a reborn Hinduism with Christ at its centre, so that all that is of value in the Hindu heritage may continue to live on. Farquhar was convinced that this scheme enabled Christianity to function as a universal religious system while providing freedom for application to specific national and cultural contexts.

Farquhar's scheme of continuity was based essentially on the New Testament promise-fulfilment tradition, and he was criticised for transposing what was uniquely applicable to the Jewish Christian context to a non-Jewish context. In justifying his approach, Farquhar drew several points of correspondence between Jewish-Christian and Hindu-Christian fulfilment. His arguments, however, stop short of a theological explanation of revelational continuity between the Hindu tradition and Christian faith. It is at this point that the contributions of Banerjea and Sundar Singh have the potential to complement Farquhar's fulfilment approach.

Banerjea's solution was his view of a universal primeval revelation. Originally in unwritten form, recollections of this primitive revelation have been transmitted through oral tradition, eventually recorded in the Vedas, and recognised as such on the basis of Christological criteria. This primal revelation was qualitatively the same as that given to the authors of the Old Testament: supernatural, eternal and infallible in nature, and continuous with and possessing the same authority as the supernatural revelation in Christ.

For Banerjea, the idea of primeval revelation is a device to justify his main hypothesis of a primordial vedic concept of divine self-sacrifice as a prefigurement of Christ. Although he does not expressly employ the concept of covenant, a cosmic covenant is implied by his ideas of a universal primeval revelation and a primordial redemptive sacrifice. These notions are designed to emphasise the universal scope of God's covenant in Christ, and include vedic Hindu religion within the sweep of a cosmic salvation-history scheme with redemption in Christ as its focus and fulfilment.

In contrast to Farquhar's view, there is no hint of progression in Banerjea's view of revelation. The two loci of supernatural communication seem to be the primordial revelation at the time of creation and the supernatural revelation given to the authors of the Christian scriptures. Banerjea's clearer scheme of theological continuity, however, indicates a more convincing basis for extending the scope of the divine covenant to include the Hindu tradition within a universal salvation-history scheme. The universality of salvation-history is thus grounded in his concept of an original primeval revelation, and the cosmic scope of the divine covenant clearly affirmed in his view of a primordial divine sacrifice fulfilled in the redemptive sacrifice of Christ.

Sundar Singh's device for continuity is the revelational knowledge of God within the human heart. This intuitive mystical awareness embedded within the soul of man is a common unifying reality and an extension of God himself. Although not explicitly described as such, a form of *Logos* theology is intimated in his attempt to incorporate various expressions of non-Christian experience within a cosmic salvation-history scheme on the basis of this universal mystical knowledge. The essential continuity thus affirmed between Christian and non-Christian religious experience makes no qualitative differentiation between divine revelation in Christ and that available to all humanity.

Although the solutions of Banerjea and Sundar Singh lack detail and sophistication, they provide original indigenous resources for framing theological continuity between revelation in Christian and other religious traditions. Banerjea's scheme offers a counterpoint to those who object to the application of the Jewish-Christian fulfilment model to the Christian relation to other religions. His view affirms continuity on the basis of a theory of revelatory and redemptive continuity. It corroborates Farquhar's application of the New Testament promise-fulfilment tradition to other religious contexts, but its basis in an empirical study of the Hindu texts also allows it to stand as an independent validation of the fulfilment principle of continuity.

Farquhar ascribes some value to Hindu religious experience by placing it at an earlier stage on a scale of evolutionary development with Christ as the climax, but is unable to define theologically its relation to the revelation in Christ. Sundar Singh's intuitions regarding continuity help complement Farquhar's tentative recognition of the revelatory value of Hindu religious experience, confirming the plausibility of a *Logos* framework for explaining Christian revelational continuity with other faiths.

Banerjea and Sundar Singh's ideas concur with and corroborate many aspects of Jacques Dupuis' explanation of how divine revelation in other religious traditions can be related to the Christian trinitarian revelation. Dupuis' theological scheme thus offers a helpful framework for locating the seminal insights of Sundar Singh and Banerjea in this regard.[29]

Dupuis grounds his investigation of revelation in non-Christian religious experience in Avery Dulles' typology of models of revelation.[30] Dupuis' preference is for "inner experience" and "new consciousness" models of revelation which by acknowledging the revelatory work of God in all cultures, provide adequate scope for revelation in other religions.[31] Dupuis, like Dulles, bases his explanation of how other religions can in different degrees bear witness to a divine self-revelation, on Rahner's conception of the supernatural existential, an internal ontological dimension of every human being, which enables one to have a supernatural connection and communication with God.

This understanding of the mystical dimension of the divine self-communication and illuminating grace, described as the primordial revelation of grace is, according to Rahner, epistemologically prior to any form of propositional revelation.[32] The universality of this divine self-disclosure provides a basis for recognising the interpersonal divine-human encounter in non-Christian religious experience as an authentic location for divine

---

[29] Dupuis' scheme takes into consideration data gleaned from a fairly thorough overview of Christian attitudes to other faiths, and includes in its purview an evaluation of non-Christian revelatory experience.

[30] The five models are: (1) revelation as propositional doctrine; (2) revelation as history; (3) revelation as mystical experience; (4) revelation as dialectical presence; and, (5) revelation as new consciousness; A. Dulles, *Models of Revelation* (New York: Images Books, 1985), 174-192.

[31] Dulles, *Models of Revelation*, 182-185, 187-189; cf. Dupuis, *Toward a Christian Theology*, 238.

[32] Dupuis, *Models of Revelation*, 239; cf. M. Ruokanen, *The Catholic Doctrine of Non-Christian Religions: According to the Second Vatican Council* (Leiden: E.J. Brill, 1992), 29-32.

revelation, so that "...other religions too can, in different degrees, bear witness to a self-revelation of God."[33]

Dupuis compares the predominant "revelation in experience" traditions of the eastern mystical religions, and the "special" revelation within the prophetic Judeo-Christian traditions, concluding that although the theological content of non-Christian experience remains incomplete, provisional, and essentially pre-Christian, the experience and revelation of the divine mediated is authentic.[34] His intent is to show that the cosmic revelation within the mystical religious tradition and the historicalrevelation of the prophetic tradition spring ultimately from the same source. He bases the theological justification of his proposal on the unity of God: the same God who acts in history speaks to human beings in the depths of their hearts: "There is only one Reality, one Truth, whether it is known through the experience of the cosmos and the human soul or through encounter with a historic event."[35]

Dupuis proposes a trinitarian framework for understanding how divine revelation operates. God had already spoken through the divine *Logos* prior to the incarnation, and the light of this same *Logos* shines through the elements of truth present in non-Christian religious traditions.[36] Likewise, the Spirit's activity in divine self-disclosure is also universal, and operative in the sacred texts of other religious traditions.[37]

This recognition of the universal revelatory activity of the Word and the Spirit leads Dupuis to acknowledge that God has spoken to the nations through the religious experience of their sages or prophets recorded in their sacred books. However, he adds the caveat:

> What is suggested here is not tantamount to saying that the *whole* content of the sacred scriptures of the nations is the word of God in the words of human beings... many elements may have been introduced that represent only human words concerning God. Still less are we suggesting that the words of God contained in the scriptures of the nations represent God's decisive word to humankind...[38]

Dupuis clarifies the decisive significance of the fullness of revelation in Jesus Christ and the normative status of the New Testament witness to the

---

[33] Dupuis, *Models of Revelation*, 239; cf. K. Rahner, 'Christ in the non-Christian Religions' in *God's Word Among Men,* ed. G. Gispert-Sauch, ed. (Delhi: Vidyajyoti, 1973), 99f.

[34] Dupuis, *Models of Revelation*, 239-241.

[35] Dupuis, *ibid.*, 242.

[36] Bouquet, 'Revelations and the Divine Logos', in *The Theology of the Christian Mission*, ed. G.H. Anderson (London: SCM, 1961), 191-193 also extrapolates the possibility of revelatory activity amongst non-Christian prophets and sages from the concept of a universalized *Logos* at work in the world since creation.

[37] Dupuis, *ibid.*, 242-244.

[38] Dupuis, *ibid.*, 247.

Christ event, and as a prelude to the statement of his main thesis, summarises his view of "an open theology of revelation and sacred scriptures":

> [W]hile uttering his decisive word in Jesus Christ, and besides speaking through the prophets of the Old Testament, God has uttered initial words to human beings through the prophets of the nations – a word whose traces can be found in the sacred scriptures of the world's religious traditions.[39]

Dupuis thus understands the relation between biblical and extra-biblical revelation in terms of a progressive, differentiated, and complementary divine revelation, within which he distinguishes three stages. The first is cosmic, in which God speaks "a secret word" to the hearts of ancient seers, traces of which may be found in the non-Christian sacred scriptures. In the second stage, God speaks to Israel through his prophets; the Old Testament records both this word and human responses to it. The divine word in both these preliminary stages is oriented toward the third stage: God's decisive, plenary revelation in Christ, of which the New Testament is the official record.[40] Within this framework Dupuis suggests that concepts such as "word of God", "sacred scripture", and "inspiration" may be applied analogically to the various stages of progressive, differentiated revelation.[41]

Dupuis' scheme illuminates our discussion and advances our argument at three important points. Firstl, Dupuis' analysis of non-Christian religious experience concurs closely with Sundar Singh's understanding of a universal intuitive divine awareness within the human soul, which serves as the basis for affirming religious continuity with people of other faiths. Dupuis' scheme thus confirms and helps locate Sundar Singh's intuition within a coherent theological hypothesis of the relationship between revelation in non-Christian religious experience and in Christ. Conversely, Sundar Singh's observations in practical engagement with other faiths contribute towards the empirical verification Dupuis regards as essential for corroborating his hypothesis.

Dupuis and Sundar Singh's views, however, both manifest a common inadequacy in their lack of criteria for evaluating religious experience. Thus, although Dupuis makes allowance for the imperfect or incomplete apprehension of God in non-Christian experience, he nevertheless insists that: "...a Christian theology of religious experience cannot but interpret the experience as in all circumstances involving the self-disclosure and self-gift of the one God who fully manifested himself in Jesus Christ."[42]

The position as stated presents at least two difficulties. First, it does not seem to make provision for a self-critique of religious experience within the religious traditions themselves. Could there be instances when Christian or

---

[39] Dupuis, *ibid.*, 250.
[40] Dupuis, *ibid.*, 250.
[41] Dupuis, *ibid.*, 251-252.
[42] Dupuis, *ibid.*, 241.

non-Christian religious experience may be judged to be unauthentic on the basis of criteria internal to the tradition within which they occur? Is every claim of mystical encounter with the divine necessarily genuine in and of itself, regardless of the resulting claims and fruits? Neither Dupuis nor Sundar Singh spell out criteria for a discernment of spirits that takes adequate account of the possible influence of human depravity and cosmic moral evil upon religious experience.

Second, especially evident in Sundar Singh's evaluation of non-Christian religious experience, is a dilution of the element of Christian transcendence. In discussing the complementarity of revelation within and outside the Judeo-Christian tradition, Dupuis does assert that for the Christian: "...the normative criterion for such a discernment is unmistakably the mystery of the person and event of Jesus Christ.... Whatever is in contradiction with him who is "*the* Word" cannot come from the God who sent him."[43] This qualification does not, however, emerge clearly in his evaluation of non-Christian experience, nor is it developed as a sustained argument, and hence appears inconsistent with his earlier assertion.

The second point at which Dupuis' hypothesis helps us is in providing a theological framework for describing Banerjea's view of primeval revelation and its relation to the revelation in Christ. Whereas Banerjea was unable to provide a coherent theological scheme that could adequately explain his empirical observations or justify his view, his notion of primeval revelation fits well within the first stage of Dupuis' progressive and differentiated scheme of revelation.

Finally, Dupuis' scheme succeeds in bringing together the two streams of revelation that emerged in the principal subjects of our study: the prophetic stream in Banerjea's thought and the mystical stream in Sundar Singh's reflections. Dupuis makes a strong case for theological continuity between the streams of prophetic-historical revelation of the Judeo-Christian religions and the cosmic-mystical revelation in the eastern religions, suggesting that they both spring from the same source. His argument may be applied appropriately to the continuity schemes of Banerjea and Sundar Singh: despite the difference in the avenues of revelation they stress, the source [God] and agency [the Spirit] remain common. Thus, the complementarity that Dupuis proposes between revelation within and outside the Christian tradition pertains more closely to these two Indian Christian notions of revelatory continuity.

Dupuis' hypothesis provides a coherent theological explanation for Banerjea and Sundar Singh's insights on continuity, but does not adequately emphasise the other pole of the dialectic. It provides a coherent complement to Farquhar's view of progressive revelation without the attendant weight of the evolutionary theory, and offers theological justification for both Banerjea and Sundar

---

[43] Dupuis, *ibid.*, 252.

Singh's continuity schemes. Conversely, the insights of Banerjea and Sundar Singh help substantiate the plausibility of Dupuis' hypothesis.

Fulfilment and the Decisiveness of Christ

A third main issue requiring closer attention in our comparative evaluation is: Are there Christological resources for relating the central fact of the Christian faith, the incarnation, to the Hindu tradition in a way that acknowledges aspirations within it and also affirms the decisiveness of the Christ-event? We have already noted the weakness of Farquhar's view at this point. His implicit *Logos* Christology leaves some critical questions unanswered and thus stops short of providing a viable Christology for the fulfilment approach. Banerjea's attempt to relate Hinduism and Christianity in a preparation-fulfilment relationship on the basis of the vedic prefigurement of Christ as *Prajapati* has considerable potential in this regard. Substantial points of correspondence emerge when we compare Banerjea's use of *Prajapati* with the Johannine concept of *Logos*.

The use of *Logos* in the prologue of John's Gospel has been the object of much discussion and scholarly investigation.[44] The growing consensus among scholars is that while the seedbed of the *Logos* concept is probably located in Old Testament and other Jewish antecedents, the Greek tradition exercised the most significant influence within the continuity discerned between the *Logos* concept and parallel conceptions in various religious and philosophical traditions outside of Israel.[45] The process of development of the *Logos* concept is summarised by one interpreter as follows:

> Here then we have a fascinating example of an ancient religious tradition from the area in which Israel's faith was cradled, accomodated to the monotheistic and historic nature of the revelation in Israel, spread through the Western world and taken up in its developing religious and philosophical traditions, and finally given a new orientation within the Gospel.[46]

---

[44] For detailed bibliographies, see D.H. Johnson, 'LOGOS' in *Dictionary of Jesus and the Gospels*, ed. S. McKnight and I.H. Marshall (Leicester: InterVarsity Press, 1992), 484; G.R. Beasley-Murray, *Word Biblical Commentary: John*, vol. 36 (Waco, Word Books, 1987), 1; see p.9, n. 29. Concerning the background, it is sufficient for our purpose to note that while earlier Johannine scholarship emphasized the Hellenistic background, most modern treatments tend to give priority to the influence of Old Testament and Jewish strains of thought, without denying Greek associations of the term; D.A. Carson, *The Gospel according to John* (Leicester, InterVarsity Press, 1991), 9-60; L. Morris, *The Gospel according to John* (Grand Rapids: Eerdmans, 1995), 104.

[45] Beasley-Murray, *Word Biblical Commentary*, 8, 9-10; Morris, *The Gospel according to John*, 102, n. 132.

[46] Beasley-Murray, *Word Biblical Commentary*, 9.

When John used the term *Logos*, it undoubtedly aroused certain specific religious and philosophical associations among his readers, whatever their background. For both Jew and Gentile alike, the *Logos* represented the ruling fact of the universe, the self-expression of God and the starting-point of all things.[47] It was a term that would be widely recognized by his Gentile audience, and strike familiar chords among Greek readers in particular.[48] Thus, based on the prevailing understanding of the *Logos* as "the Self-Expression of Ultimate Divinity" which gave unity to the whole cosmos, the author of the Fourth Gospel and some early patristic writers employed it in communicating the truth of the incarnation to the Greek world. The Church endorsed the specific Christian significance assigned to this term.[49]

Like the *Logos* concept, the *Prajapati* ideal is rooted originally outside the Christian tradition, possessing distinct religious and philosophical connotations within the Hindu tradition. In both instances, while some nuances of meaning may be remote to the original notion, other senses overlap with the idea being conveyed. The early Christian theologians, nevertheless, used the term *Logos* in a way that was continuous with its prior significance and yet extended its meaning, making it do something new in order to express a Christian reality. Banerjea's similar strategy with the concept of *Prajapati* can thus draw justification from John's approach.

An important difference, however, is that the term *Prajapati* is not as widely known, nor its connotations as widely understood in the Indian context, as *Logos* in the first century Near Eastern context. Furthermore, while John's usage became part of scripture and was endorsed by the Early Church, Banerjea's employment of *Prajapati* has not had widespread acceptance within the Indian church. The reasons for this are somewhat complex, and may be linked to the decline in influence of the fulfilment tradition as a whole. These differences do not, however, reduce the force of our argument that Banerjea's strategy has a theological precedent in the New Testament *Logos* concept.

A more significant point of contrast is that whereas the *Logos* concept served as a prefigurement primarily of the person of Christ, the *Prajapati* figure that Banerjea discovered in the Vedas anticipated both the person and the sacrificial atonement of Christ. Banerjea's case for Christ's fulfilment of the vedic concept of the self-sacrificing *Prajapati* was set forth after demonstrating the importance and value of sacrifice for the atonement of sins in the vedic texts.

Banerjea's strategy may appear to place undue theological constraint on our understanding of the work of Christ by focussing on one soteriological metaphor, sacrifice. The importance of this metaphor in the Church's

---

[47] Morris, *The Gospel according to John*, 108; Carson, *The Gospel according to John*, 116.

[48] Carson, *The Gospel according to John*, 103.

[49] Bouquet, 'Revelation and the Divine *Logos*', 189-190.

interpretation of the atoning work of Christ can hardly be contested: the centrality of the Eucharist in the worship liturgy of the Church is perhaps the strongest historical witness to this fact. Moreover, the establishment of theological continuity through the sacrificial metaphor does not preclude the possibility or necessity for extending its application to include other Christological metaphors.

Two facts add credence to the theological viability of Banerjea's use of *Prajapati* as a prefigurement of Christ. First, the principal arguments of Banerjea's thesis have not been adequately responded to to-date. Second, it is difficult to find alternative proposals of a similar prophetic prefigurement of Christ in the Hindu scriptures. None of the later notions of "unknown Christ", "acknowledged Christ" and "unbound Christ", of which Banerjea's conception of Christ as *Prajapati* was a precursor, are as ingenious in conception or as rooted in the Hindu texts.

Banerjea's Christological proposal merits a legitimate place within the Indian fulfilment tradition, due to its historical primacy and enduring influence. Despite its relative marginalization in some quarters, his view continues to have abiding attraction especially for Hindu converts. For a significant number of Hindu Christians, who have arrived at corresponding conclusions independent of Banerjea's influence, *Prajapati* continues to function as a prophetic prefigurement of Christ.

Banerjea does not explicitly employ the *Logos* theology of the early fathers, but his fulfilment Christology approaches their view at one crucial point, and departs from it at another. He affirms elements of continuity and discerns aspects of discontinuity between Christian faith and the vedic tradition based on a strategy similar to that of the early fathers. The early fathers discerned fragments of truth in Greek philosophy based on Christological criteria, which they then identified with the activity of the *Logos* in its pedagogical function towards the Greeks. Banerjea, likewise, employs Christological criteria to distinguish the "diamonds" from "dust" within the Vedas, a procedure that led to his identification and use of the concept of *Prajapati* as a vedic pedagogy to Christ. *Prajapati* thus performs a similar Christological function in relation to the Hindu vedic tradition as the *Logos* concept does for Greek philosophy.

On the other hand, the early fathers' *Logos* Christology helped ground their notions of revelation and redemption in one unified concept, whereas the corresponding concepts of primeval revelation and *Prajapati* develop and remain separate in Banerjea's thought. Despite this weakness, Banerjea's Christology may be viewed as in essential continuity with the fulfilment impulses of the New Testament and the early fathers.

The Christocentric focus of Sundar Singh's view of religious experience informs and complements Farquhar's fulfilment Christology in a different direction. His emphasis on the living, inward Christ of mystical experience enables him to extend the salvific concern of God to the whole world, and yet affirm Christ's decisiveness. Here again, as in Banerjea, we observe a convergence with some aspects of the early fathers' *Logos* Christology without an explicit appropriation of their strategy.

The theological pioneers in the Indian context faced a task comparable to that which the early fathers encountered. The newness of Christianity was easily asserted based on the uniqueness of the Incarnation; the fathers' real challenge was to demonstrate the universal continuity of Christian faith. They did this by employing a cosmic salvation-history scheme, which viewed God as preparing the world for the incarnation since creation by means of the revealing agency of the *Logos*.[50] The fathers' teaching on the revealing activity of the *Logos* apart from the incarnation finds verification in Sundar Singh's explanation of how divine revelation is received in the depths of the soul – consequent on God indwelling the world and the soul of a person. He thus offers a plausible account of how the universal revelatory activity of the *Logos* in other religions functions as a pedagogy to Christ.

Ruokanen points out that the early fathers' view of universal grace did not recognize any clear distinction between nature and grace, so that creative, redemptive, and sanctifying grace were all regarded as inseparable aspects of the Triune God: "...part of the ontological constitution of every human being".[51] Likewise, Sundar Singh's framework, though less sophisticated, does not seem to recognize any "nature-grace' distinction or qualitative differentiation between the universal light given to all mankind and God's special revelation in Christ. Despite this common starting point, however, the idea develops in divergent directions in Sundar Singh and the early fathers.

The fathers recognized real participation in the reality of Jesus Christ in the revelation, faith, and grace observed among the Greeks, but regarded non-Christian participation in the *Logos* as a temporary and provisional stage in an ongoing movement towards perfection and fulfilment in Christ.[52] According to Saldanha, this distinction by the fathers was a result of their biblical Christocentricity.[53] Sundar Singh's commitment to the decisiveness of Christ enables him to draw a degree of distinction between the light of the pre-incarnate *Logos*, a "preparation", and the full light of the incarnate *Logos*, the "fulfilment". He is, however, unable to maintain the "transcendent" pole of the dialectic convincingly, since the dominance of the mystical element allows him little room for a salvation-history orientation. The subordination of the historical to the mystical in his Christology thus conditions his assertion of the decisiveness of Christ.

The Christologies of Banerjea and Sundar Singh are not in themselves theologically cohesive constructs. Their value consists in the originality of their

---

[50] C. Saldanha, *Divine Pedagogy: A Patristic View of Non-Christian Religions* (Rome: Las, 1984), 161, 176-180.
[51] Ruokanen, *Catholic Doctrine of Non-Christian Religions*, 12.
[52] Saldanha, *Divine Pedagogy*, 179, 186.
[53] Saldanha, *Divine Pedagogy*, 151, 167.

intuitive insights, which provide components for a form of *Logos* theology that resonates deeply with essential New Testament and patristic impulses. Their provisional reflections thus represent a significant complement to Farquhar's fulfilment Christology.

Farquhar's identification of objective elements of truth in Hindu religious texts on the basis of Christological criteria thus finds focussed expression in Banerjea's vedic prefigurement of Christ as *Prajapati*. Sundar Singh's distinctive contribution to the *Logos* Christology scheme in the Indian context is in confirming its application in the realm of religious experience. Substantial resources for a concordant *Logos* Christology thus emerge at the convergence of these two streams of fulfilment Christology.

Banerjea's notion of Christ as *Prajapati*, identifies him as "the Lord and supporter of the Creation", the "*Purusha* begotten before the world", and the "*Viswakarma*, the Author of the universe", all of which assign a role to *Prajapati* in creation comparable to that accorded to the *Logos* in early church tradition. Sundar Singh expounds the role of the *Logos* as the creative power of God, which brought all things into existence and indwells all of creation, but is most fully revealed in Jesus Christ, the incarnate Son of God. It appears that Sundar Singh also accepted the idea that the vedic ideal of *Prajapati* as the self-sacrificing Saviour was fulfilled in Christ. While he may have concurred with the objective identification of the self-sacrificing *Prajapati* as a prefigurement of Christ, his distinctive conviction was that the Hindu seeker's quest for an authentic experience with God is satisfied when he enters into mystical communion with Christ. The content of this fulfilment experience includes an apprehension of Christ's deity and his vicarious atoning sacrifice.

For Sundar Singh, appropriation of Christ's sacrificial atonement rests not on any form of objective testimony either in Scripture or other doctrinal formulations, but on mystical experience, the content of which is clarified in the Christian discourse. Thus, Banerjea's objective identification of *Prajapati* as a creator-redeemer figure on the basis of a *Logos* Christology, seems to coincide broadly with Sundar Singh's account of his experiential appropriation of Christ as *Logos* within a *bhakti* mystical framework.

In summary, first, the fulfilment tradition emerged in the Indian context with the desire of converts to demonstrate that it was possible to follow the way of Christ with integrity and remain faithful to what was true and good within their ancestral religion and culture. This basic impulse for indigenity was shaped by their experience of Christ as mediated through the Christian tradition and their nationalist concerns, and to a lesser extent, by other factors such as the theory of evolution.

Second, this urge to demonstrate cultural relevance led the subjects of our study to explore the dominant pre-Christian tradition in India for a possible pedagogy to Christ, a strategy most likely patterned after the New Testament promise-fulfilment tradition. We evaluated the challenge to Farquhar's claim that Hinduism can serve as a pedagogy to Christ, and concluded that it can be justified on both biblical and empirical grounds. This quest for a pre-Christian pedagogy to Christ within the pre-Christian tradition of converts must, in fact, be regarded as an inevitable obligation in the light of the original fulfilment concern to assert cultural indigenity. Furthermore, we observed a dialectic in Farquhar and Indian converts' approaches to Hindu texts similar to that observed in the Jewish Christian reading of the Jewish scriptures and in the use of non-Christian texts in apostolic preaching.

Third, the dialectic in the fulfilment reading of non-Christian texts raises a fundamental theological question that leads to the heart of the fulfilment conception. If there is a legitimate pedagogy to Christ in the Hindu tradition, how are we to define theologically its relation to what Christians regard as the decisive Word of God in Christ, recorded in the New Testament? Farquhar's understanding of progressive revelation, Banerjea's conception of primeval revelation, and Sundar Singh's view of mystical revelation, seem to offer divergent solutions to the problem, yet share an important common insight. Their empirical observations lead them to concur that the Hindu tradition contains an authentic divine revelation. They do not, however, offer an adequate theological framework for explaining the continuity they affirm between revelation in Christ and the Hindu tradition.

Jacques Dupuis' trinitarian understanding of the relation between biblical and extra-biblical revelation as a progressive, differentiated and complementary divine revelation provides a scheme within which the conceptions of Farquhar, Banerjea, and Sundar Singh may be readily incorporated. His framework provides theological justification for Sundar Singh's intuition concerning revelation in non-Christian religious experience, and Banerjea's notion of a universal primeval revelation, but needs to make provision for a more consistent preservation of the Christ-centred dialectic in the evaluation of non-Christian religious experience.

Finally, we evaluated the Christological resources underlying the fulfilment schemes of Indian converts. Although the Christological constructs of Banerjea and Sundar Singh are not in themselves adequate, their intimations represent a significant complement to Farquhar's fulfilment Christology, and resonate deeply with New Testament and some patristic impulses. We are thus able to identify a point of convergence between Banerjea's identification of the creator-redeemer figure of Prajapati in the vedic texts and Sundar Singh's form of Logos Christology.

A Cumulative Description of the Fulfilment Proposal

We have observed how the fulfilment insights of converts in pre-independence India complement the weaknesses of the nineteenth century fulfilment tradition at three crucial points. Our observations now enable us to outline the contours of a cumulative fulfilment proposal that incorporates some of the essential impulses of the Protestant fulfilment tradition in pre-independence India.

The fulfilment approaches of the three subjects of our study seem to follow a broad pattern of contextualization, which begins with the normativity of Christ as a fundamental premise, based on which it then engages in a selective and transforming critique of the dominant religion and culture. We thus begin our cumulative description with an analysis of the theological method employed by our principal subjects. Gavin D'Costa's application of Hans Frei's typology of Christian theology to inculturation in the Indian context offers a suitable framework for such an analysis.[54]

D'Costa highlights the complexity of the task of contextualization in a Hindu context by drawing upon Frei's grid of five types of theological method, which he then employs in testing the inculturation reflections of the contemporary Indian theologian, Felix Wilfred. Frei's types are arranged along an axis, one pole of which represents the view that Christian theology is entirely subordinated to the dominant culture which dictates the "general criteria of intelligibility, coherence, and truth that it must share with other academic disciplines"; at the other end of the axis, theology is extrapolated on the basis of the internal coherent character of Christianity itself: "it is the Christian community's second-order appraisal of its own language and actions under a norm or norms internal to the community itself".[55]

In Frei's scheme, type 1 gives the first pole priority, whereby theology becomes a philosophical discipline, essentially culturally determined with little attention paid to the Christian community's self-description. Type 5 is the other "fideist" extreme, with little or no concern for external cultural interpretation or relevance. Types 2, 3 and 4 represent inculturation strategies that attempt to take both poles into consideration and are located along the axis on the basis of their proximity to one or other pole. Type 2 thus still allows the culture to dictate the criteria in translating the Christian message, and type 3 tries to give both poles autonomy in the correlation process.[56] Frei's preference is for type 4 in which: "the practical discipline of Christian self-description governs and limits the applicability of general criteria of meaning in theology, rather than vice versa."[57]

D'Costa's proposal is that Indian inculturation attempts could be located variously within the different types along this axis, but following Frei, prioritises type 4 and illustrates the method in his critique of the Indian theologian, Felix Wilfred.[58] Frei's preference is based on his judgment that type 4 best reflects the meaning of the *sensus literalis* of Scripture. First, this

[54] G. D'Costa, 'Inculturation, India and Other Religions: Some Methodological Reflections', *Studia Missionalia* 44 (1995), 121-147; H. Frei, *Types of Christian Theology* (New Haven: Yale University Press, 1992).

[55] Frei, *Types of Christian Theology*, 2.

[56] Chapter 1 sets forth the typology; chapter 4 illustrates the typology by offering a representative analysis of each type; Frei, *Types of Christian Theology*, 2-5, 28-55.

[57] Frei, *Types of Christian Theology*, 4.

[58] D'Costa, 'Inculturation, India and Other Religions', 130-147.

denotes, that the literal sense has priority over other legitimate readings in New Testament interpretation, and, second, that this sense is thoroughly Christological in that Jesus is "the *ascriptive* subject of the descriptions or stories told about and in relation to him", "the subject matter of these stories is not something or someone else", and "the rest of the canon must in some way or ways... be related to this subject matter or at least not in contradiction to it".[59]

The task of Christian theology in Frei's type 4 is to redescribe the text in different contexts rather than to discover "the text as symbolic representation of something else more profound".[60] The process of redescription – which we may legitimately characterise as inculturation or contextualization – requires the employment of vocabulary, thought forms, and conceptual frameworks from the prevailing philosophy and culture outside the Church. In the form of inculturation prescribed in type 4, the use of philosophy and culture is controlled by the Christological *sensus literalis* of the text; the Christian self-description is not definitively governed by the autonomous logic of the vocabulary and forms derived from the cultural context.[61]

When we evaluate the contextualization efforts of our three principal subjects in the light of Frei's analysis, we observe the clear dominance of type 4 features in their fulfilment approaches. Essential to Farquhar's scheme is his definition of Christianity "as it springs living and creative from Christ Himself", not in any of its provincial cultural expressions. Christ is clearly "the full and final revelation", and his supreme authority mediated through the New Testament, the normative revelation, "the central sun in the light of which everything must be read and estimated."[62] His exploration of the Hindu tradition was thus governed by a view of contextualization as essentially redescription.

Likewise, for Banerjea, the biblical witness to Christ clearly serves a normative function in the redescription of the Christian revelation in the Hindu context. Thus, the preparatory and provisional nature of primeval revelation and the prophetic function of the vedic figure of *Prajapati* are both defined on the basis of his determinative point of reference, the New Testament description of Christ as God and man, and his sacrifice for sin as the means of humanity's reconciliation with God.

The correspondence of Sundar Singh's formulation with type 4 is less explicit, but can nevertheless be demonstrated. The ambiguity arises from the priority Sundar Singh gives to the inward Christ of mystical experience over the historical Jesus. This would constitute a significant obstacle to his location

---

[59] D'Costa, 'Inculturation, India and Other Religions', 129; cf. Frei, *Types of Christian Theology*, 5.
[60] Frei, *Types of Christian Theology*, 44.
[61] D'Costa, 'Inculturation, India and Other Religions', 127-129.
[62] See pp.81.

within type 4 if this indicates the determinative influence of the *bhakti* tradition logic. This feature of Sundar Singh's thought should, however, be viewed in the context of the stated impulse of his project: to present Christ, the Water of life in an Indian cup. The priority he ascribes to the Christ of experience does not negate the privilege he accords to the objective New Testament record of the person and teachings of Christ. Sundar Singh's fulfilment approach may thus also be regarded as a form of type 4 inculturation, since it reflects an attempt to redescribe the normative Christian revelation within the Hindu cultural context.

Our locating of the three central figures of our study in type 4 is helpful for the light it casts on the process of contextualization shaping their fulfilment approaches. In type 4, the theologian is obligated to relate the Christian self-description to the general criteria of the dominant culture, but must allow Christological norms to guide his redescription of the Christological revelation and to determine definitively how it interprets and reshapes his cultural context. D'Costa summarises this understanding of inculturation as follows: "...inculturation cannot be an uncritical adoption of culture, but must always be a Christologically shaped transformation of culture which will therefore imply both continuity and discontinuity with its pre-Christian form."[63]

This understanding of inculturation requires that the fulfilment view be grounded in the particular Christian discourse, the decisive moment of which was the incarnation event. The significance of this decisive moment could be stated in various ways, but the central constitutive claim of the Christian faith, that in the person and event of Jesus Christ God has spoken and acted decisively for the benefit of the whole world, must be normative in this method of Christian self-description.

This premise will need to be justified subsequently against what is undoubtedly the most serious and persistent criticism of fulfilment theology, that it always pre-judges the issue of religious truth by its commitment to the normativity of the Christ-event.[64] It must, however, be recognized that for the fulfilment thinkers we have considered in this study, the constitutive event of Christian faith was decisive in shaping the logic and presuppositions of their theological discourse. The decisiveness of Christ thus became the starting point in their definition of normative truth and in the truth criteria they formulated for evaluation of truth claims. From this starting-point we are able to distinguish three key trajectories within a broader trinitarian movement towards eschatological fulfilment in and through Christ.[65]

---

[63] D'Costa, 'Inculturation, India and Other Religions', 141.

[64] A. Race, *Christians and Religious Pluralism* (New York: Orbis, 1982), 62-69.

[65] The following description is developed on the basis of ideas derived from the fulfilment approaches of Farquhar, Banerjea and Sundar Singh. Although the language and frame of reference at many points are not explicitly theirs, the categories we

The 'Cosmic' Trajectory

The first of these trajectories is retrospective, and points to the fulfilment movement as originating in God, the Creator and Ruler of the universe, actively engaged in the re-establishment of his liberating rule over a fallen world. God's loving concern to bring all things together in himself, and his redemptive activity in the world come to a climax in the incarnation of Christ. This trajectory is expressed, first, in the recognition of a universal cosmic covenant, a concept that is frequently assumed and undergirds the fulfilment approach, although the term itself is not prominent.

God's revelatory and salvific dealings with the human race are set in a universal covenantal framework, within which the Old Testament covenant is treated as a sub-set and the new covenant regarded as the climax and fulfilment. Fulfilment thinkers thus apply a conception of salvation history that seeks to incorporate the histories of other religious traditions within the particular history of God's revealing and saving activity recorded in the Old Testament and climaxing in Christ.

Farquhar emphasises the universal fatherhood of God: God has a relationship with adherents of all faiths, and people from every nation have genuine access to him. Every human being is in some way a participant in the divine economy of progressive revelation reaching its climax in Christ. According to Farquhar, this participation ensures that they could obtain salvation on the basis of their faithfulness to the light of revelation they possess, even apart from explicit knowledge of Christ.

The existence of an original cosmic covenant is implied in Banerjea's concept of primeval revelation, an original universal communication of the divine will, focusing on God's plan of salvation through the self-sacrifice of the Lord of creation. Although his view is grounded specifically in the vedic Hindu tradition, it seeks to incorporate the Hindu religious tradition within a cosmic covenant/universal history scheme, and to affirm salvation-history continuity with its fulfilment in Christ.

In Sundar Singh's thought the cosmic covenantal relationship is expressed in existential terms of the soul's inner mystical awareness of God and its inner longing for fuller experiential knowledge of God. This awareness is both mediated and nurtured by religious experience prior to and apart from the specific revelation in Christ. In all three approaches we have considered within this pre-incarnation trajectory, the revelatory and salvific actions of God in other religions have a function corresponding to that of the Old Testament: they have a provisional and pedagogical role in fulfilling the kingdom purpose of God.

---

introduce are derived from notions inherent in their thought, which we have extended by logical inference.

Whereas the first trajectory offers a normative Christological explanation of the meaning of history prior to the incarnation, two distinct but complementary fulfilment trajectories proceed proleptically from the incarnation event, which then prescribe God's pattern of dealing with humankind subsequent to the incarnation.

The 'Word' Trajectory

The second trajectory springs from the definitive disclosure of Christ as the normative criterion of truth, and reflects the fulfilment impulse towards the pursuit of truth wherever it may be found. The movement is from the particular to the universal, from the truth as revealed in the particular event of the incarnation towards the cultures and religions of the world. Based on the truth as defined in Christ, the various cultures and religions of the world are sifted for evidence of the presence and activity of the *Logos*. Elements of truth thus identified on the basis of Christological criteria are incorporated within a progressive Christic movement towards eschatological fulfilment.

This movement involves deepening and complementing the Christian appropriation of Christ, as elements from new receptor cultures are introduced into and augment the internal Christian discourse. It thus provides the theological basis for the ongoing inculturation/contextualization project of the Church, enabling the gospel to be expressed in contextually relevant community life and enriching its universal ecclesial expression.

We have observed this impulse in all the subjects of our study. It inspired missionary thinkers like Farquhar to carefully explore the sources of Hinduism and other traditions, not just for points of weakness to be exploited, but to discover and celebrate signs of the presence and activity of the *Logos*. Converts like Banerjea and Sundar Singh were intuitively motivated in a similar direction. Convinced that the Vedas were the most ancient and reliable sources of Hindu tradition, Banerjea studied them closely, winnowing vedic texts for divine truths identified on the basis of Christological criteria.

This trajectory directed towards the discovery or recovery of truth wherever it may be found in the cultures and religions of the world, also finds expression in a form of reverse fulfilment in Farquhar and Sundar Singh. Farquhar was convinced that the rich religious tradition of India had a positive contribution to make towards a fuller understanding of Christ's universal Lordship. The Indian tradition would contribute truths that are not discontinuous with the Christ-event and are yet distinctively new, which complement truths already known but have not as yet reached fullest expression in the Church. As the inculturation process advances, elements of truth in other religions and cultures will enrich and complement aspects of Christian truth and bring them to their full expression.

In Sundar Singh, this reverse fulfilment takes concrete expression in his appropriation of a distinctly Hindu ideal, the sadhu life-style. He clearly viewed the Christian virtues of suffering and selfless service as finding deeper fulfilment in his pursuit of the sadhu ideal of self-denial, renunciation, and mystic meditation. This was the consequence of his conscious attempt to find indigenous expression for his understanding of Christian discipleship. The end-result of such a Christ-centred process of contextualization, according to Farquhar, is that rather than destroying what is of value in the Hindu culture and religion, Christ becomes the restorer of the national heritage.

The 'Spirit' Trajectory

The third trajectory also originates in the Christ-event, but its derived impulse is the disclosure of God's universal concern to redeem humanity and restore the world back to himself in and through Christ. The movement is from the universal to the particular, seeking to discern and affirm the authentic activity of the Spirit in the world of religious experience. The criteria employed in this evaluation are also Christological, as various religious experiences are judged on the basis of their orientation towards Christ. If the second trajectory is a Christic movement, this is essentially a movement of the Spirit as the "Spirit of Christ", presenting Christ as the fulfilment of the religious aspirations of people of all faiths and cultures.

The fulfilment thinkers we have considered recognise the Christ-event as the decisive moment of the disclosure of God's universal redemptive concern, and his purpose to redeem all humanity in Christ. But they also recognise the universal illuminating and revealing action of the Spirit in the world prior to and apart from the Christ-event. This trajectory thus provides the theological basis for the Church's evangelistic mandate, as the Spirit enables and guides the Church in its announcement of the good news of the kingdom, and actively draws people to God and to Christ.

In Banerjea's approach this movement takes the shape of an explicit invitation to be incorporated into the Church. In Farquhar, the emphasis is on participation in the kingdom as represented and focused in Christ. For Sundar Singh it involves entering into personal, mystical communion with God through Christ. In each case the movement of the Spirit draws people of all faiths towards eschatological fulfilment in a relationship of loving communion with Christ and the Father through the Spirit. The same Christ-event that manifests God's universal redemptive concern thus also represents the prophetic focus and medium of God's redemptive action.

This does not imply that pre-Christian religious experience has no validity whatsoever. The Spirit's activity in pointing to Christ is discerned even in the Christ-ward movements among people of other faiths or no faith, but interpreted in relation to the New Testament account of Christ and the Spirit. Non-Christian religious experience is thus evaluated on the basis of its Christ-ward orientation. For instance, every pre-Christian religious sentiment is given value in Farquhar's scheme. But although he is prepared to extend the possibility of saving grace to those non-culpably ignorant of Christ, he insists that God accepts them only on the basis of Christ.

Sundar Singh also views non-Christian religious experience as mediating a limited but authentic encounter with God through the Spirit. But while his scheme allows people of other faiths universal access to the Holy Spirit and to the light of Christ, their knowledge of God is only completed by a post-mortem encounter with Christ. Thus, although pre-Christian mediations of the Spirit are real, they are provisional and preparatory in nature. This Spirit trajectory thus points beyond and directs these intimations to their ultimate eschatological fulfilment.

Here again reverse fulfilment may be observed, as certain aspects of non-Christian religious experience enrich and complement the Christian experience of the Spirit. This is illustrated in some aspects of Sundar Singh's conversion experience as well as in his appropriation of yogic meditative practices in his devotional life.

Convergence

These three trajectories are distinct but not exclusive. The Christic and pneumatic movements converge primarily in the Church, in an ongoing trinitarian movement towards eschatological fulfilment in the realisation of the kingdom. The Church, as a sign and sacrament of the kingdom, is in a real sense the locus of fulfilment. However, the trajectory of the fulfilment movement should extend beyond the Church, as Christological criteria are applied in discerning elements of truth, beauty, goodness, and justice in the world which are then brought into the service of the kingdom mission.

The impact of this movement may be observed in the specific Christian contributions to the self-critique and reformation of other faiths, in its facilitation of movements of the Spirit towards health, peace, justice, and equality in our world, and in the enrichment of the Church's self-understanding through its encounter with other religions. Thus, by judicious application of Christological criteria in "the discerning of spirits", the presence of the *Logos* and the Spirit's activity can be identified and celebrated even outside the Church, and employed to advance God's Kingdom purposes in the world.

We may thus speak of three moments of fulfilment. First, we recognise a provisional level of potential kingdom fulfilment in the world, in which although there is no explicit acknowledgment of Christ's lordship, signs of Christic or pneumatic movements towards eschatological fulfilment may be discerned on the basis of Christological criteria. Second, there is a more overt and evident locus of fulfilment within the Church, where an explicit acknowledgment of Christ's Lordship results in the experience of a self-conscious, fuller measure of fulfilment. This is, however, only an anticipation of the third and final moment of consummation – eschatological fulfilment at the *parousia*.

In our concluding chapter, we evaluate the fulfilment proposal outlined here in the light of our central thesis question.

Christ and the Other Religions in Fulfilment Theology

The fulfilment proposal outlined at the end of the previous chapter needs to be evaluated for its adequacy as a response to the problem our thesis question poses: to what extent does it affirm the particular truth claims of the Christian tradition and ascribe genuine value to non-Christian religious experience? Our procedure will first seek to demonstrate the coherence and viability of the fulfilment proposal in the light of problems which come to light in the course of comparison with two common alternative solutions. Second, our assessment will attempt to justify a fundamental methodological premise of the fulfilment proposal: commitment to the normativity of the Christ-event. Third, we will also evaluate and respond to two important criticisms of fulfilment theology. Finally, we will reflect on some of the reasons for the decline of Protestant fulfilment theology in the twentieth century, and consider the possible implications of our study for its revitalization and recovery.

An Evaluation of the Fulfilment Proposal

Gavin D'Costa's radical critique exposes the logical incoherence of the dominant typology that has framed the theology of religions discussion in recent decades.[1] He argues that it obscures the real issues: the justification and clarification of various truth claims and the examination of how they relate to other truth claims. For D'Costa, the central question in Christian theological terms is: "...what is revelation, in what way do we come to know it and how do we relate it to other truth claims that we encounter?"[2]

Our description of the Word and Spirit trajectories of the fulfilment proposal thus leads us to the critical theological issues at each end of the dialectic. In the Word trajectory of fulfilment, we observed that the disclosure of Christ as the normative criterion of truth provides the impetus for actively pursuing truth in the cultures and religions of the world. The fulfilment proposal here challenges the tendency in some approaches, which in seeking to affirm the finality of Christ, seem to discount *a priori* the truth claims of other religious traditions.

---

[1] G. D'Costa, 'The Impossibility of a Pluralist View of Religions', *Religious Studies* 32: 223-232; cf. G. D'Costa, *The Meeting of Religions and the Trinity* (Edinburgh: T&T Clark, 2000), 19-24.

[2] D'Costa, 'Impossibility of a Pluralist View', 232.

Our discussion of the Spirit trajectory, on the other hand, raises questions from the opposite end of the dialectic, challenging the assumptions in some constructs that seek to legitimise movements of the Spirit without attention to the need for Christological criteria. The problem stated simply is: how does one define what is Christian without reference to Christ? Is there any way Christians can evaluate and identify genuine movements of the Spirit apart from the normative self-disclosure in Christ? We take up each of these issues in turn. Our consideration of the second will entail justification of a fundamental commitment of fulfilment theology to the normativity of the Christ-event.

Fulfilment and the Religions

The anti-religions posture of the nineteenth century Protestant missionary tradition continues to be expressed within some quarters of evangelical Protestantism today. Representatives of this attitude evidence a passionate commitment to the absolute truthfulness of the gospel of Christ, but often adopt a pre-formed ideological stance towards other religions. We offer three illustrations of how fair and careful research fails to precede judgments on other faiths.

In seeking to address some concerns of liberation theology to the contemporary theology of religions debate, Andrew Kirk exposes some of the logical, theological, and ethical difficulties of pluralism.[3] His justification of the claim that Jesus Christ constitutes the definitive norm of truth is built on the twofold premise that religion is on the whole harmful and oppressive and that Christianity must not be categorised as a religion.[4] Kirk is critical of the frequent unqualified appreciation of religion in the pluralist discourse, but in trying to demonstrate the essential incompatibility of Christ and the religions, unfairly prejudges other religions. He thus contends that the closer we get to the centre of another faith, we depart proportionately away from the historic Christian faith.[5] The following generalization perhaps best illustrates this point:

> The heart of God is supremely and finally manifested in Jesus' cry of dereliction on the cross. Yet, the suffering of God in the pain and sin of humankind as it is borne by Jesus Christ is a notion universally rejected by all other faiths. How, then, does one suppose that they manifest something of the truth of God? If God is truly at work, revealing himself as he is among people of religious faith, why do they not readily recognise that God was in Christ reconciling the world to himself?[6]

---

[3] J.A. Kirk, *Loosing the Chains: Religions as Opium and Liberation* (London: Hodder & Stoughton, 1992), 30-50.

[4] Kirk, *ibid.*, 94-121.

[5] Kirk, *ibid.*, 180-182.

[6] Kirk, *ibid.*, 186.

Kirk's assertion fails to take into account the testimony of a long line of Hindu converts, that their ancestral tradition does bear such a witness to Christ, on which they base their evangelistic appeal to the Hindu community. Tilak's vigorous witness to his Hindu compatriots was based on his claim to have come to Christ "over the bridge" of the renowned Hindu poet-saint, Tukaram. Banerjea invited his Hindu audience to Christ on the grounds that their common vedic ancestors possessed a tradition of the self-sacrificing Lord of creation, *Prajapati*, and loyalty to the vedic testimony should cause them to embrace Christ who fulfils this tradition.

Dewi Hughes' treatment of religious pluralism offers a critique of fulfilment theology, in which he makes the following contentious observation:

> It may be possible to argue that there is a longing in the heart of everyone for the true God who comes in Jesus, but that there is no evidence of such a longing in the religion which has developed in India. In the experience of missionaries the opposite is true – Hindu religion is the greatest hindrance to the acceptance of Jesus as the true and final revelation of God.[7]

This comment follows his observation of differences within the seeming compatibility between the *bhakti* Hindu tradition and Christianity. His willingness to concede a universal "longing in the heart...for the true God" is presumably based on *a priori* grounds, but his inability to find the slightest expression of this sentiment in India's religious tradition of several millennia is inexplicable given the weight of evidence to the contrary.

Hughes' categorical verdict purportedly based on missionary experience simply does not fit with what we have discovered in our investigation, and at best, may be expressing a missionary viewpoint especially dominant in the early nineteenth century. But beginning with Ziegenbalg's early admission of "a small light of the gospel" within Hinduism, and reaching its peak in the early years of the twentieth century, a distinct missionary fulfilment tradition has recognised and celebrated distinct anticipations of Christ within Hinduism.

Our final example is from Harold Netland's defence of Protestant evangelical restrictivism. He presents a rejoinder to the suggestion that those inculpably ignorant of the Christian gospel may be saved apart from explicit faith in Christ on the same basis as Old Testament saints.[8] Netland bases his rejection of this comparison partly on Carl F. Henry's assertion that Old Testament saints were saved on the basis of "a divinely approved sacrifice... which focuses on the Mediator-Messiah... if only in an elementary and preparatory sense."[9] Netland thus concludes: "The Old Testament sacrificial system anticipated and foreshadowed the perfect sacrifice of Christ and thus

---

[7] D.A. Hughes, *Has God Many Names?* (Leicester: Apollos, 1996), 228-229.

[8] H. Netland, *Dissonant Voices: Religious Pluralism and the Question of Truth* (Grand Rapids: Eerdmans, 1991), 266.

[9] Netland, *Dissonant Voices*, 267.

propitiated God," a requirement which non-Christians inculpably ignorant of the gospel could not fulfil since they did not have the Old Testament revelation.[10]

A strand of Indian Christian tradition beginning with Banerjea identifies within the ancient vedic texts all the elements that Netland regards as essential for non-Christians inculpably ignorant of the gospel to be judged on the same basis as Old Testament saints. Awareness of this Indian tradition would thus presumably convince those holding Netland's viewpoint to concede the possibility of salvation for inculpably ignorant Hindus, who fulfil the conditions for the salvation of Old Testament saints by accepting the vedic anticipations of the perfect sacrifice of Christ.[11] The intent of this counter observation is not to score a point for inclusivism over exclusivism as much as to highlight the tendency to hasty and injudicious *a priori* judgments on other religions among some who have legitimate concerns about upholding the decisiveness of Christ.

The three authors we have quoted are all representatives of the Protestant evangelical tradition from within which the nineteenth century fulfilment discussion first emerged in the Indian context. This tendency to dismiss without trial the fact of religions reflects, first, the influence of Kraemer's "discontinuity" theory on the Protestant attitude to other religions in the post-Tambaram era. Second, it reveals an unfortunate inconsistency within the theological framework of a segment of Protestant evangelicals committed to the decisiveness of Christ.

An *a priori* rejection of religion as a possible locus of revelation does not rest well with commitment to Christ as the normative truth. The lack of a coherent framework for explaining Christologically attested truths in other religions and cultures makes the assertion of Christ's decisiveness self-contained and insular. It eliminates motivation for the empirical study of religions, and weakens prospects for developing an effective apologetic.

In contrast, fulfilment theologians' commitment to the decisiveness and normativity of Christ expands rather than constricts their notion of Christ's Lordship. Their commitment to pursue truth wherever it may be found finds impetus and is proscribed by their allegiance to the normative prescription of truth in the Christ-event. This leads them to a posture of critical openness towards all religions and cultures.

---

[10] Netland, *Dissonant Voices*, 267.

[11] In a subsequent work, Netland does seem to display a more irenic attitude, conceding that other religions are capable of manifesting "the capacity for religious awareness, reflection and expression… a gift of God's creation and revelation", but eventually goes on to essentially concur with Kraemer's negative, pessimistic verdict on the phenomenon of religions; Harold Netland, *Encountering Religious Pluralism: The Challenge to Christian Faith & Mission* (Downers Grove: InterVarsity Press, 2001), 344-345.

Fulfilment and Christ

We frequently encounter a different problem at the other end of the dialectic in approaches that take the fact of other religions seriously. Michael Barnes' Spirit-centred theology of religions is a good illustration, since it provides the context for our justification of two important elements in the fulfilment proposal: its fundamental premise of commitment to the normativity of Christ, and the importance of Christological criteria in discerning the Spirit's activity.

Barnes' objection to the fulfilment approach is based on his estimation of it as a purely internal, confessional theology.[12] He finds it inadequate in that it only addresses the old problematic, by explaining the phenomena of other religions in Christian terms; it does not attend to the new problematic concerned with exploring the religions' self-understanding of their theological significance.[13] He censures fulfilment theology for "relativizing" other religions:

> No longer can we be content to relativize the world religions in the light of Christian faith; such an interpretation ends up as a projection of Christianity on to the other. Almost all Christian theologies which are still dealing with the old problematic – using the language of 'natural' and 'supernatural', 'implicit' and 'explicit', 'provisional' and 'perfect', etc. – see the relationship of religions in terms of fulfilment. They produce an interpretation of the other in the light of Christian faith.[14]

What alternative strategy does Barnes propose? Barnes' treatment must be commended for the skilful manner in which the significant issues are clearly delineated and synthetically approached. Taking exception with the view of a common transcendental experiential source for all religiosity, Barnes makes George Lindbeck's theory of religion as a comprehensive cultural-linguistic interpretative scheme the starting point for his own construct. He faults Lindbeck for ignoring the transcendent dimension in religion and implicitly reducing religion to culture: "Our human creativity is always seeking to transcend the boundaries that culture puts on religion. …religion always has a transcendent as well as an integrative function."[15]

Rather than searching for a common essence of religion, Barnes insists that all religions have a common dialectical or dialogical structure. The structure he proposes consists of a transcendent-prophetic-parabolic element at one pole, and an integrative-institutional-mythical element at the other. For him, this theory best explains the elements of continuity and change in religion and the

---

[12] M. Barnes, *Christian Identity and Religious Pluralism: Religions in Conversation* (Nashville: Abingdon, 1989), 66.

[13] Barnes, *ibid.*, 13, 20-22.

[14] Barnes, *ibid.*, 83.

[15] Barnes, *ibid.*, 93-100, 102.

cultural conditioning of religious faith; most importantly, it provides a common framework for inter-religious relationship and discourse.[16]

Despite his rejection of religion as grounded in a common essence or transcendental experience, we find an essentialist view of religion at the heart of Barnes' own proposal. He distinguishes a universal "faith" which is present and recognized in all religions – "...the human response to the transcendent dimension in religion",[17] from beliefs – "the intellectual and cultural forms which faith takes within a particular tradition."[18] This distinction between "universal" faith and "particular" beliefs is critical to Barnes' proposal, for his adoption of Panikkar's theory of the interpenetration of religions requires accepting that, despite differing belief structures, one person's belief performs the same function for her as the Christian belief does for the other.[19]

Barnes, consequently, has difficulty with the notion of a "*Christian* meaning of other religions", and prefers to base his theology of interpenetration upon a Spirit-centred rather than a Christocentric scheme. This proposal safeguards the revelatory quality of other religions in the manner indicated in our discussion of the Spirit trajectory of fulfilment.[20] But despite his intent to place his proposal within a Christian trinitarian framework, his theology of interpenetration permits no distinction between Christian and non-Christian valuations of the meaning of Christ, thus producing an unresolved tension in his framework with regard to the particularity of Christ. Although he acknowledges that Christianity is based on a particular historical revelation centred in Christ, he looks for a "more self-consciously inter-religious" starting-point that is trinitarian, yet not grounded in the historical Christ.[21]

The importance of the faith-belief distinction for Barnes' Spirit-centred theology of the interpenetration of religions becomes evident at this point. Faith represents the universal transcendent dimension, the shape of grace in the common dialogical structure of all religions; beliefs represent the different symbol systems that express and communicate the key faith experiences. The Spirit's activity in all religions is discerned on this basis, and the central concern not how other religions are related to Christ, but to examine how the Spirit of Christ is active in revealing the mystery of what God is doing in the world.[22]

Barnes' view acknowledges the Spirit's activity prior to and apart from Christ. But he regards a Christocentric theology as restricting the Spirit's

---

[16] Barnes, *ibid.*, 93, 100-107.

[17] Barnes, *ibid.*, 127.

[18] Barnes, *ibid.*, 126; On page 133, n. 16 and 17, Barnes clearly acknowledges his dependence on Cantwell Smith and Panikkar in making this distinction; cf. Hogg's similar distinction, 68.

[19] Barnes, *ibid.*, 130.

[20] Barnes, *ibid.*, 135, 137.

[21] Barnes, *ibid.*, 139-141.

[22] Barnes, *ibid.*, 143.

sphere of action, and would like to move away "...from talk about the Spirit to talk about Christ."[23] There is, however, no device indicated for distinguishing between what is legitimately the activity of the Spirit of Christ and what is not? In what follows, we focus first on Barnes' principal point of contention with the fulfilment approach, and then on the issue of the Spirit's activity.

Barnes' alternative rests on Cantwell Smith's tenuous distinction between faith and belief, a strategy which recent scholarship has seriously questioned.[24] Heim makes evident that Smith's abstraction of faith as the common thread between different religious traditions is empty of any real content: "Many... argue that the 'faith' Smith describes is not the foundational substrate in all religious traditions, which his historical acuity has allowed him to discover, but itself a conditioned notion in whose terms each tradition can be construed, and by the construal changed."[25]

Barnes' attempt to distance himself from any explicitly Christian criteria thus results in his proposal reflecting the weakness of other pluralist approaches. The shared misconception is that it is possible to formulate a set of transcendent, theologically neutral criteria – an epistemological helicopter above all of the religions – based on which religious truth claims can be evaluated. D'Costa has argued convincingly that there is no such privileged high ground in any theological evaluation of religious truth claims, showing that pluralist truth claims are in fact controlled by exclusivist logic, and do not have real autonomy since the claims made are inevitably tradition-specific.[26]

Newbigin presents a logically coherent case for the epistemological validity of prior commitment to the normativity of the Christ-event as a prerequisite for Christian theological reflection.[27] His starting-point is the submission that the Christian proclamation that: "...in the ministry, death, and resurrection of Jesus God has acted decisively to reveal and effect his purpose of redemption for the whole world",[28] must be regarded as an epistemological "given" of the

---

[23] Barnes, *ibid.*, 148.

[24] M. Heim, *Salvations: Truth and Difference in Religion* (New York: Orbis, 1997), 64-65.

[25] Heim, *ibid.*, 65-66; D'Costa points out the impossibility of idealizing or reifying faith "out of the socio-historical reality which shapes it"; D'Costa *Christian Uniqueness Reconsidered: The Myth of a Pluralistic Theology of Religions* (New York: Orbis Books, 1990), 18.

[26] D'Costa, 'Impossibility of A Pluralist View', 225-226; also D'Costa, *Meeting of Religions and the Trinity*, 19-47; others have also highlighted the ideological exclusivism inherent in the pluralistic position, some of whom Vanhoozer cites in support of his own view; *The Trinity in a Pluralistic Age: Theological Essays on Culture and Religion* (Grand Rapids: Eerdmans, 1997), 55f.

[27] Newbigin, *The Gospel in a Pluralist Society* (Grand Rapids: Eerdmans, 1989), 1-13, 27-115; also the discussion of Newbigin's thesis in Yates, *Christian Mission in the Twentieth Century* (Cambridge: Cambridge University Press, 1994), 239-244.

[28] Newbigin, *The Gospel in a Pluralist Society*, 5.

Christian faith. In explaining how this functions as an essential "presupposition of all valid and coherent Christian thinking", he says:

> This proclamation invites belief. It is not something whose truth can be demonstrated by reference to human experience in general. Rather, it is that by the acceptance of which all human experience can be rightly understood. It is the light by which things are seen as they really are, and without which they are not truly seen. It rests on no authority beyond itself.[29]

Newbigin's case draws heavily on Michael Polanyi's explanation of how the notion of personal knowledge operates in scientific enquiry. A vital point in Newbigin's argument is his appeal to Berger's concept of "plausibility structures", the patterns of belief and practice accepted within a given society that determine its notion of what constitutes reasonable belief. According to Newbigin, human reason does not function in total autonomy, but is conditioned and shaped by the tradition within which it is located. The Church serves as the plausibility structure which the Christian gospel creates and indwells, and which the Church in turn legitimises. This does not imply that Christians possess all the truth and are closed to avenues of learning outside their plausibility structure, but it does signify that the Christian quest for truth is guided by a tradition that has been decisively shaped by the Gospel.[30]

Addressing this issue from a different direction, Jacques Dupuis insists that religious faiths are fundamentally distinct and inherently demand the total faith-commitment of their adherents. Theology can only operate from within the presuppositions of a particular faith, and hence Christian theology can only function consistently in accordance with Christianity's own internal logic, as a way of faith and of life. The confessional nature of a theology need not, however, make it insular or parochial, rather it can and should adopt a universal horizon, and create space for other "confessional" theologies of religions.[31]

Barnes' basic premise in attempting to formulate the Christian tradition in a way that is faithful to the Church and "open" to the other runs aground at this point:

> My basic premise is that the ground of all Christian theologising is trinitarian as much as it is Christological. That is to say that we begin not with the historical Jesus Christ who points the way to the Father but with the *Spirit* of Christ through

[29] Newbigin, *ibid.*, 6.

[30] Newbigin, *ibid.*, 8-13; cf. Ramachandra's application of this argument in his critique of Samartha's privileging of mystical experience; V. Ramachandra, *The Recovery of Mission* (Carlisle: Paternoster, 1996), 21-23.

[31] Dupuis, *Toward a Christian Theology of Religious Pluralism* (New York: Orbis, 1997), 6-7; cf. Hastings, *Kraemer Towards Tambaram: A Study in Hendrik Kraemer's Missionary Approach* (Uppsala: Gleerup, 1990), 235-236.

which the world was brought into being and who continues the work of God's ever-present self-revelation to humankind.[32]

This attempt to make the "*Spirit* of Christ" the starting-point of a trinitarian theology seems to overlook the fact that the Christian doctrine of the Trinity is itself contingent on the historical fact of the incarnation. Any trinitarian formulation that does not derive from the early Christian experience of and testimony to the divinity of Christ must be regarded as theologically inadequate, despite its use of trinitarian vocabulary and various triadic constructs.[33] The consequence of not grounding the trinity in the Christ-event is that the notion of Spirit also remains vague.

The issue Barnes poses as one of the "enormous difficulties" of the Christocentric position: "Why should not the Word of God be spoken other than in historical Christianity – and even elsewhere than in the historical Jesus of Nazareth?" thus begs the real question.[34] The more critical questions would seem to be: Is the "Word of God" the only word that is being spoken and heard in the world? Is the Spirit of God the only spirit at work in the world, or are there other spirits whose words may also be heard? Does one need to be able to distinguish between authentic and specious claims of divine revelation, or must all claims be accepted as equally valid?

It is at this point that the normative Christocentricity of fulfilment theology calls into question Christian attempts to legitimise movements of the Spirit apart from Christocentric evaluative criteria. The adoption of an explicit Christocentric starting-point is a theologically coherent way of employing a Christian trinitarian framework in evaluating other religions. This procedure does not preclude *a priori* the legitimacy or value of truth claims in other religious traditions, instead provides a credible theological basis for recognising the presence of the *Logos* and the activity of the Spirit in them.

Criticisms of the Fulfilment Proposal

Our concluding assertion in the previous section is liable to a criticism: Does not fulfilment theology by its commitment to specifically Christian criteria thereby merely subsume all religions within the Christian dispensation and negate their distinct identity?[35] This leads us to consider two expressions of this criticism of fulfilment theology: the more universal charge of imperialism, and the Dalit objection from within the Indian context. Both of these are forms of rejection of the kingdom-continuity inherent within the fulfilment scheme.

---

[32] Barnes, *Christian Identity and Religious Pluralism*, 174, 136.
[33] Ramachandra, *The Recovery of Mission*, 93-94.
[34] Barnes, *Christian Identity and Religious Pluralism*, 175.
[35] Barnes, *ibid.*, 91.

Criticism 1: Fulfilment Theology is a Form of Imperialism

The imperialist allegation has various shades of expression. We are concerned primarily with the form it takes as an aspect of cultural imperialism associated with colonial Christianity and the western missionary enterprise.[36] This is an issue explored in some degree of depth in Ingleby's study of the relation of cultural change to Christian missionary education in India, in which he also evaluates the influence of fulfilment theology upon the changing missionary approach to education.[37]

Ingleby distinguishes two main approaches. The first, patterned after Duff's original strategy, presupposed the inherent superiority and normative quality of western culture, and saw the eradication of oriental culture as the ultimate goal of the western missionary enterprise. Under the influence of fulfilment theology and beginning with Miller's diffusion theory,[38] a second approach developed which sought for and affirmed the positive elements of oriental culture: truth already possessed by these cultures was regarded as the starting point for further instruction.[39] Ingleby maintains that the charge of cultural imperialism may be applied legitimately to the first of these approaches but is unjustified in the second.[40]

From the early stages of this study we have provided evidence to corroborate the above conclusion. In fact the essential impulse of nineteenth century fulfilment theology in India was the desire to affirm cultural indigenity and continuity with the ancestral religious heritage.[41] The charge of imperialism is, however, also directed at another level, perhaps best summarised in Race's summary criticism of fulfilment theology:

> In an age that values the historical and empirical, to say that one religion contains the fullest expression of religious truth and value, without any recourse to the

---

[36] Richard, 'A Survey of Protestant Evangelistic Efforts among High Caste Hindus in the Twentieth Century', *Missiology: An International Review* 25 4 (1997): 422; see also pp.45.

[37] Ingleby, 'Education as a Missionary Tool: A Study in Christian Missionary Education by English Protestant Missionaries in India with Special Reference to Cultural Change' (Ph.D. thesis, Oxford Centre for Mission Studies, 1998), 327-404.

[38] William Miller's philosophy of missionary higher education viewed its primary role as the gradual 'diffusion' of Christian ideas and principles through Hindu society rather than proselytization; Sharpe, *Not to Destroy but to Fulfil: The Contribution of J.N. Farquhar to Protestant Missionary Thought in India before 1914* (Uppsala: Swedish Institute of Missionary Research, 1965), 83-85.

[39] Ingleby, 'Education as a Missionary Tool', 290-327, 347-368.

[40] Ingleby, *ibid.*, 400-404; D'Costa, illustrates how the charge of cultural imperialism may sometimes be used to render a particular contextual theological interpretation impervious to criticism; G. D'Costa, 'Inculturation, India and Other Religions: Some Methodological Reflections', *Studia Missionalia* 44 (1995): 136, 144.

[41] Aloysius Pieris, an opponent of fulfilment theology, tacitly acknowledges this fact; A. Pieris, *An Asian Theology of Liberation* (New York: Orbis, 1988), 60.

empirical data of the other religions themselves, is tantamount to an unjustified theological imperialism.[42]

According to Brian Stanley, Christian claims regarding Christ's decisiveness and universal lordship make Christianity an "inherently imperial religion". He views the term "imperialism" as connoting essentially "control by an alien national or racial group... primarily political or economic".[43] Acceptance of Stanley's view would extend the charge of imperialism to all Christians, not just fulfilment theologians. The term "imperialism", with its distinct geo-political overtones involving the use of coercive power in suppression or eradication of the other, may be applied justifiably to some aspects of Christian missionary history. But to what extent is it germane to the theology of fulfilment?

Our first consideration is epistemological, as we clarify the nature of fulfilment theology's privilege of interpreting the fact of religious plurality from a Christocentric perspective. Are all claims to universal truth in themselves imperialistic? Mortimer Adler argues that human progress in science, historical research, and philosophy is made on the basis of a fundamental recognition of the unity of truth and the trans-cultural testing and communication of truth-claims.[44] Adler concedes that when it comes to religion and culture, aspects belonging to the sphere of taste are merely a matter of local preference, but those components belonging to the sphere of truth – having to do with "the way things are" – are trans-culturally prescriptive.[45]

In this sense every attempt to offer a theological interpretation of reality or religious phenomena on the basis of a privileged interpretive framework may be dubbed theologically imperialist, and all the major religions regarded as imperialist inasmuch as they are universal in vision.[46] But this connotation is remote to the original significance of the term. There is thus no *a priori* reason why the claim of Christianity – or any other faith or ideology – to have access to universal truth, should be regarded as imperialist, unless it asserts this claim coercively and denies the same privilege to others.

---

[42] A. Race, *Christians and Religious Pluralism* (New York: Orbis, 1982), 68; cf. Samartha, *One Christ – Many Religions: Toward a Revised Christology* (New York: Orbis, 1991), 99; P.F. Knitter, *No Other Name? A Critical Survey of Christian Attitudes to World Religions* (New York: Orbis, 1985), 9.

[43] B. Stanley, *The Bible and the Flag: Protestant Missions and British Imperialism in the Nineteenth and Twentieth Centuries* (Leicester: Apollos, 1990), 184, 34.

[44] M.J. Adler, *Truth in Religion: The Plurality of Religions and the Unity of Truth* (New York: Macmillan, 1990), 115-128.

[45] Adler, *Truth in Religion*, 2-5, 101-106.

[46] D'Costa, *Christian Uniqueness Reconsidered* , ix; cf. Vanhoozer, *The Trinity in a Pluralistic Age*, 56; J. Milbank, 'The End of Dialogue' in *Christian Uniqueness Reconsidered: The Myth of a Pluralistic Theology of Religions*, ed. G. D'Costa (New York: Orbis Books, 1990), 180-181.

Our second consideration has to do with the theological content of the fulfilment claim itself. The dual-consummation dimension of fulfilment insists that the Christian tradition remain ever open to insights from other religions and cultures, resulting in its ongoing enrichment and transformation. This idea is further corroborated in John Cobb's view of a radical pluralism of religious traditions, within which he sees the need for each religion "...in faithfulness to its past to be enriched and transformed in its interaction with the other traditions".[47] Cobb's main argument is that Christocentricism provides the deepest and fullest reason for openness to other religions, since the future orientation toward the kingdom as embodied in Jesus opens Christians to the many possibilities of the kingdom manifested in the world and through other religions.[48] He clarifies the nature of this claim as follows:

> It is not a claim that Christians are better people than others, or that Christian history has made a more positive contribution to the planet than have other traditions, or that Christian institutions are superior. The claim is only that a tradition in which Jesus Christ is the center has in principle no need for exclusive boundaries, that it can be open to transformation by what it learns from others, that it can move forward to become a community of faith that is informed by the whole of human history, that its theology can become truly global.[49]

To what extent is the charge of imperialism valid? Although fulfilment theology assumes its original impetus in God's initiative to re-establish his kingdom rule over humankind, God's rule need not be interpreted in terms of a coercive elimination of human freedom or religio-political conquest. The New Testament narrative discloses the nature of God as Trinity in terms of three divine subjects in loving interpersonal relationship. This mutual divine fellowship is open towards the world, so that the love of God takes priority over his rule. The Trinity discloses the rule of God as a rule of love seeking communion without repressing freedom.[50]

The term imperialism thus has connotations of political hegemony and power alien to the theology of fulfilment. The charge is especially untenable when the indigenisation process involved in fulfilment is essentially an "intra-Christian" reflection not forced upon the non-Christian,[51] and which does not

---

[47] J. B. Cobb, 'Beyond "Pluralism"' in *Christian Uniqueness Reconsidered: The Myth of a Pluralistic Theology of Religions*, ed. G. D'Costa (New York: Orbis Books, 1990), 92.
[48] Cobb, *ibid.*, 90-91.
[49] Cobb, *ibid.*, 92-93.
[50] J. Moltmann, *The Trinity and the Kingdom of God*, trans. M. Kohl (London: SCM Press, 1981), 174-176; cf. Bauckham, 'Jurgen Moltmann's The Trinity and the Kingdom of God and the Question of Pluralism' in *The Trinity in a Pluralistic Age: Theological Essays on Culture and Religion*, ed. K. Vanhoozer (Grand Rapids: Eerdmans, 1997), 155-158.
[51] D'Costa, *Christian Uniqueness Reconsidered*, 25.

deny people of other faiths or no faith the right to proffer alternative readings of the Christian tradition.[52]

Criticism 2: Fulfilment theology is a theology of and for the high castes

A sub-altern theological tradition within India, Dalit theology, presents what may be described as a counter-tradition to the caste converts' fulfilment tradition highlighted in this study.[53] A major hindrance to the growth in acceptance of fulfilment theology in India is the common perception that it is a theology of and for the high castes. The reasons for this are largely historical, in that Hindu religious discourse within India has largely been limited to the privileged high castes, and located primarily in the Brahmanical Sanskrit tradition. The Dalits in India, who have suffered under the oppressive aspects of Brahmanical Hinduism, thus tend to reject any form of continuity with the Hindu tradition such as implied in fulfilment theology.

The historical and sociological factors involved in this religious marginalization of the Dalits require more complex analysis than we are able to provide within the scope of this study. We will restrict our comments to justifying our inability to address the relevant issues within the scope of this project, and explaining why the Dalit experience does not thereby invalidate the fulfilment thesis.

First, our study has been located within the mainstream Indian theological tradition in the pre-independence period. Although the origins of the Dalit Christian consciousness can be traced to the closing years of the eighteenth century, Dalit contributions to nineteenth century Indian theological reflection on other religions have been negligible, and hence could not be taken into account.

Second, in a careful documentation and analysis of the history of two Dalit Christian communities, Jayakumar shows that the missionaries were extremely successful in their preferred confrontational approach, contrasting the absolute superiority of Christianity to the popular Hinduism practised by the Dalits. He also points out that the missionaries sometimes adopted a more fulfilment type evangelistic strategy in their approach to the high caste Hindus.[54] The conversion experiences of Dalits and the role of their pre-Christian religious

---

[52] Fulfilment theology thus does not deny the prerogative of another religious tradition like Hinduism to include Christianity in a fulfilment scheme, based on an interpretation of other religions in the light of its own criteria; Cobb, 'Beyond "Pluralism"', 84.

[53] Dalit theology may be broadly defined as a form of Indian theology of the oppressed, which draws its inspiration from the historical and cultural self-consciousness of the "untouchables" or scheduled castes of India; Jayakumar, *Dalit Consciousness and Christian Conversion: Historical Resources for a Contemporary Debate* (Delhi: ISPCK, 1999), 4-34.

[54] Jayakumar, *Dalit Consciousness*, 168-169.

consciousness thus need to be examined more carefully before their perspectives on fulfilment theology can be properly evaluated.

Our investigation of the Dalit conversion experience would thus need to include an interrogation on the following lines. First, was the Dalit pre-Christian consciousness essentially Hindu or non-Hindu? While the Dalit castes have been included within the Hindu community in terms of their sociological grouping, whether this classification is religiously or theologically valid is at best a moot point. Jayakumar thus argues strongly for distinguishing the Dalits from the Hindu social order.[55] More importantly, since these groups were religiously marginalized by the higher castes, Hindu religious resources could not have exercised a positive influence upon their religious consciousness. On the other hand, if some form of primal religion shaped their religious consciousness, the fulfilment impulse should be examined within the framework of that expression of pre-Christian consciousness.

A second critical question is: what aspects of the Dalit pre-Christian consciousness resonated positively with the Christian gospel message? The primary motif in the Dalit consciousness is clearly oppression, and the dominant aspirations include the desire for dignity, freedom, equality, and social justice. Were these aspirations shaped by their primal religious consciousness, through their experience as outcastes in the Hindu social system, or were they shaped exclusively by the Christian gospel proclamation?

The Dalit scepticism of fulfilment theology arises in part from the perception that it reinforces the legitimacy of a Brahmanical tradition inherently oppressive towards the Dalits. In this light an issue that needs further exploration is the extent to which the pre-Christian experience of Hindu converts to Christ included a questioning of caste, and the way in which conversion affected their attitude to it. Some aspects of the Hindu reform movement that arose as a response to the Christian gospel did include a rejection of caste discrimination and oppression. But the Indian fulfilment tradition needs to be evaluated more closely in the light of this question.

The Christian mandates of evangelization and inculturation provide sound theological reasons for exploring the possibility of a fulfilment approach in the Dalit context. But pending informed judgment on the above and other related questions, we must conclude that while the Dalit rejection of fulfilment theology as an elitist formulation has some ethical justification, the grounds for a theological judgment are inadequate, pending further investigation.

Conclusion: Towards a Recovery of Protestant Fulfilment Theology

The broad concern of this study has been to evaluate the adequacy of fulfilment theology as an explanation of the relation between Christian particular truth-claims of God's decisive revealing/redemptive action in Christ, and the

---

55 Jayakumar, *Dalit Consciousness*, 9-16.

evidence in non-Christian religious tradition and experience of God's universal revealing/redemptive action towards all humankind. We explored this concern in relation to a specific "tradition of encounter", the fulfilment approaches of converts in the pre-independence period in India, focussing especially on the fulfilment views of K.M. Banerjea and Sadhu Sundar Singh.

In what way do the fulfilment approaches of Banerjea and Sundar Singh complement the claim of the nineteenth century Protestant fulfilment tradition to offer a coherent and satisfactory explanation of how the particular truth claims of the Christian faith relate to non-Christian religious experience?

First, Banerjea and Sundar Singh furnish significant empirical confirmation of the fulfilment claim that there are elements in the Hindu tradition and experience that can serve as a pedagogy to Christ. Their discernment of this pedagogy was, however, based on a dialectic consisting of elements of continuity and discontinuity, analogous to the Jewish Christian reading of the Jewish scriptures, and the use of non-Christian texts in New Testament apostolic preaching.

Second, Banerjea and Sundar Singh also each suggest a theological basis for affirming continuity between the Christian revelation and light in the Hindu religious tradition. Although their perspectives are distinct, they are not incompatible and may be incorporated within a broader trinitarian scheme of progressive, differentiated, and complementary divine revelation.

Third, Banerjea and Sundar Singh provide material for a theologically coherent Christology to undergird the fulfilment proposal. Banerjea's original conception of the creator-redeemer figure of *Prajapati* provides a useful objective complement to Sundar Singh's rudimentary *Logos* theology, both ideas resonating deeply with New Testament and patristic impulses.

Our comparative assessment of the fulfilment approaches of Farquhar, Banerjea, and Sundar Singh enabled us to outline a cumulative fulfilment proposal, with the decisiveness of the Christ-event as the starting premise. From this starting-point the fulfilment impulse follows a trinitarian movement: a retrospective cosmic trajectory traces God's pre-incarnational covenant dealings with mankind; a Word trajectory winnows the world's religions and cultures for signs of the *Logos*'s presence; and a Spirit trajectory evaluates various religious movements through a disclosure of and invitation to Christ. These three trajectories converge in a kingdom movement towards eschatological fulfilment expressed in three distinct but interrelated moments: within the world, in the Church and at the *parousia*.

Our evaluation of this fulfilment proposal argued for the epistemological legitimacy of its commitment to normative Christocentricity as a fundamental starting premise, and indicated how this commitment results in expanded rather than constricted notions of Christ's Lordship and the kingdom of God. The doctrine of the trinity is a consequence of this Christological affirmation and provides the basis for discerning the activity of God both within and outside the Church. Truth is thus identified and celebrated wherever it may be found in the different cultures and religions of the world, yet in a manner that affirms the particular truth claims of Christian faith. In the ongoing movement towards eschatological fulfilment the Christian faith is enriched as it incorporates Christologically attested reflections of truth discovered in other religions. Conversely, other religions and cultures are winnowed, purified, and transformed through prophetic engagement as elements of truth and goodness are affirmed and their meaning extended on the basis of a Christocentric interpretive framework. The fulfilment proposal thus addresses coherently the concerns at both ends of the universality-particularity dialectic as articulated in our thesis question.

In considering the implications of our study, we need to attend to a final pending question: the reasons for the decline in influence of Protestant fulfilment theology in the twentieth century. We have already drawn attention to the negative consequences of the dependence of fulfilment theology on the evolutionary model, the ebb in its influence resulting in the fulfilment tradition being undermined.[56] Fulfilment theology received firm endorsement from the Protestant missionary community at Edinburgh 1910, and continued to exercise influence until the Tambaram missionary conference of 1938, when it was buried under the weight of Kraemer's discontinuity broadside. Kraemer's position emphasised the *sui generis* quality of the Christian gospel and its essential discontinuity with any aspect of human religion.[57]

There were, however, socio-political and economic factors that contributed to the rise in influence of dialectical theology, dominant in the Protestant theological environment within which Kraemer's view found favourable acceptance.[58] The erosion of optimism and loss of confidence in the Christian vision in the wake of the two world wars thus resulted in the growth in influence of dialectical theology and the negative verdict on human culture and religion of some of its proponents. Consequently, the Protestant attitude to other religions in the post-war era became deeply polarized between pro-Tambaram and pro-dialogical positions.

This polarization reached its peak at the Fifth Assembly of the World Council of Churches at Nairobi in 1975, and was reflected again at its Vancouver Assembly in 1983.[59] Kraemer's discontinuity thesis and the reaction to it thus contributed significantly to the marginalization of the fulfilment tradition in Protestant circles. On the other hand, the Roman Catholic Church post-Vatican II has appropriated the theology of fulfilment more explicitly than

---

[56] See p.79-80, and n. 200.

[57] For analyses of Kraemer's view of religions and opposition to fulfilment theology, see Sharpe, *Faith Meets Faith: Some Christian Attitudes to Hinduism in the Nineteenth and Twentieth Centuries* (London: SCM Press Ltd., 1977), 89-101; S.W. Ariarajah, *Hindus and Christians: A Century of Protestant Ecumenical Thought* (Grand Rapids: Eerdmans, 1991), 77-79.

[58] Sharpe, *Faith Meets Faith*, 89.

[59] Ariarajah, *Hindus and Christians*, 168.

before and has continued to give it reasoned and creative theological expression.[60]

The retreat of fulfilment theology in India in the second half of the twentieth century was due to certain contextual factors. Lipner indicates the first of these in his general assessment of the indigenizing activity in India in the nineteenth century. He observes that its uncoordinated nature adversely affected the dissemination of theological ideas, suggesting that this hindered continuity of thought and the development of a tradition, a situation that persists up to the present.[61]

Our study confirms the validity of this observation as it relates to the development of the fulfilment tradition in India. The frequent, spontaneous and persistent emergence of the fulfilment motif in India affirmed its plausibility. However, the lack of coordination in its development made it difficult for fulfilment thinkers to complement and build on one another's insights, thus contributing significantly to its decline.

A second factor was the altered composition of the Indian Church. The early and middle years of the nineteenth century witnessed the conversion of a significant number of Brahmins. Thus, Banerjea, Goreh, Upadhyay, and Tilak represented a class of educated Brahmin converts thoroughly versed in Sanskrit, with an intimate grasp of the Hindu religious texts.[62] Christian mission to the high castes in the years following the Hindu renaissance thus required serious engagement with the sources of Hindu tradition.

The middle years of the nineteenth century, however, saw Christianity become increasingly a lower caste option, with the rapid growth of the Christian Church among the backward castes and tribal groups. Subsequent generations, moreover, saw fewer converts from the high-caste Hindu community from within which the fulfilment tradition had earlier emerged and had its primary appeal.[63] We have observed that the Dalit communities responded more favourably to an apologetic approach that was negative towards the high-caste Sanskritic tradition.

---

[60] Pope John Paul II, *Post-Synodal Apostolic Exhortation: Ecclesia in Asia* (New Delhi, November 1999), 22-23, 28. This description of broad trends in Protestant and Roman Catholic thought does not discount the fact that there are individual theologians of both persuasions who hold positions that may not fit the above general characterization.

[61] Lipner, 'A Modern Indian Christian Response' in *Modern Indian Responses to Religious Pluralism*, ed. H.G. Coward (Albany: State University of New York, 1987), 311.

[62] Sharpe, *Not to Destroy but to Fulfil: The Contribution of J.N. Farquhar to Protestant Missionary Thought in India before 1914* (Uppsala: Swedish Institute of Missionary Research, 1965), 38.

[63] Sharpe, *ibid.*, 94. Manilal Parekh (see p.43) thus lamented the fact that Indian Christianity no longer had the power to attract high-caste Hindus into its ranks, since it was almost completely a low-caste church; W.W. Emilsen, *Violence and Atonement: The Missionary Experiences of Mohandas Gandhi, Samuel Stokes and Verrier Elwin in India before 1935* (Frankfurt: Peter Lang, 1994), 205.

A third factor that adversely affected the influence of the fulfilment approach in India in the twentieth century was the transformed socio-economic context following independence. Issues of Christians and nationalism, nation-building and church union took precedence over the question of the relation to other faiths. Subsequently, the predominantly Dalit composition of the Church has brought issues of Dalit identity, theology, and spirituality to the fore. When the issue of religious pluralism eventually returned to the Indian theological agenda in the closing decades of the twentieth century, it began to be addressed with little reference to the earlier fulfilment tradition.

At the close of his survey of Christian attitudes to Hinduism in the modern period, Sharpe suggests that the retreat of a theory is sometimes accidental, not due to advanced knowledge or maturity of insight, as much as factors extraneous to the theory itself.[64] The foregoing observations confirm the relevance of this insight to the fulfilment tradition in India, making way for the possibility of a fresh appraisal. Our study brings to light several compelling reasons for the recovery of the fulfilment tradition, and in considering these we will also indicate possible avenues for further research.

First, we have seen that the Indian fulfilment tradition emerged as part of the religious narrative of Hindu converts seeking to incorporate their ancestral tradition within their appropriation of Christ. This insight helps correct the perception that pre-independence Christian perspectives were defined exclusively by essentially negative missionary attitudes towards Hinduism. Despite a measure of western influence, the Indian fulfilment tradition is an authentically indigenous theological development. The pioneers of this tradition laid the foundations for "a genuine Indian theology of encounter,"[65] with great promise for the future of the Indian Church.

Responsible stewardship of this vital Indian indigenous tradition of encounter demands that it be recovered, carefully investigated, and promising insights thoroughly explored. Three areas in particular warrant further research. This study has focussed on the contributions of two representatives of the Indian fulfilment tradition, Banerjea and Sundar Singh. There are a number of other theological pioneers, some referred to in this study and others, whose fulfilment views need to be examined in detail, and our present conclusions tested, corrected, and refined accordingly. A second area of critical need is for the development of a Christian hermeneutics of non-Christian texts. Our study has suggested a broad theological framework for a Christian approach to the textual sources and religious experience of people of other faiths. Christians, however, need more detailed guidelines on how to read the scriptures of other faiths. The concept of *Prajapati* has much potential both for the development of an authentic Indian Christology and as a point of contact in Christian-Hindu

64 Sharpe, *Faith Meets Faith*, 132.
65 Sharpe, *Not to Destroy*, 94.

engagement. Research on this theme has not been adequate thus far, and the potential not fully explored.

A second reason for recommending the recovery of the fulfilment approach is its potential contribution to the broader Protestant fulfilment tradition. The credibility and resilience of fulfilment theology is seen in the persistent emergence of the concept in the history of Christian thought. However, whereas the fulfilment motif continues to influence conservative Roman Catholic approaches to other religions, it has been relatively marginalised in Protestant quarters.

In introducing this project, we defined its scope in relation to the Church's broader mandate of exploring its accumulated experience of inter-faith engagement as found in various traditions of encounter in diverse cultures and times. This study has examined one such tradition of encounter, but contemporary Protestant reflection on the issue must continue to be informed by research and recovery of other similar indigenous traditions in other eras and regions of the world.

The investigation of particular contextual stories of encounter must be complemented by attention to another task essential to the future vitality of Protestant fulfilment theology. We have seen that integral to fulfilment theology is the conviction that the local narratives of diverse human communities can be woven together into a single grand metanarrative, a cosmic salvation-history scheme focussed and fulfilled in Christ. The advent of postmodernism has signalled the arrival of a radical new paradigm of discourse that strongly resists any claim to universality, and its incredulity toward the metanarrative strikes at the heart of the fulfilment claim.[66] This is an issue for which subsequent research will need to articulate a convincing response.

The recovery of this tradition is important, thirdly, because of its value for contemporary reflection on the Christian approach to Hinduism. At the outset of our project we observed that the original context in which the issue of the Christian relation to other religions emerged was mission. In recent years, Christian mission has been the focus of acrimonious debate between Christians and Hindu nationalists. Much of the opposition to mission has centred on the perception that it poses a threat to the integrity of India's ancient religious and

[66] See, for instance Lyotard, *The Postmodern Condition: A Report on Knowledge*. trans. Geoff Bennington and Brian Massumi (Minneapolis: University of Minnesota, 1984), xxiii-xxiv, 82. The postmodern rejection rests essentially on the perception that metanarratives have frequently been used as instruments of oppression to marginalize local narratives. This is, however, not a necessary effect of the metanarrative, which is often capable of exercising antitotalizing and emancipating influence; Watson, *Text, Church and World: Biblical Interpretation in Theological Perspective* (Grand Rapids: Eerdmans, 1994), 124-153; J.R. Middleton and B.J. Walsh, *Truth is Stranger than it Used to Be: Biblical Faith in a Postmodern Age,* (Downers Grove: InterVarsity Press, 1995), 87-107.

cultural heritage. This anxiety is frequently justified in cases where missionary efforts are not undergirded by a sound theology of inter-religious engagement.

There is, at the same time, increasing evidence in India of growing numbers of "non-baptised believers in Christ", who remain integrated within the Hindu community, yet believe in Jesus Christ as Lord and Saviour in accordance with the *ishta devata* principle, or in even more orthodox terms.[67] A preliminary assessment suggests that this phenomenon is the outcome of the fulfilment impulse at work among Hindus drawn to Christ, and their spontaneous attempts to incorporate their experience of Christ within their ancestral culture and tradition.[68] The depth and quality of these inculturation efforts could be considerably enhanced by the recovery of the Indian fulfilment tradition, which offers an early prototype of converts' Christ-centred reading of their religious and cultural heritage.

The contemporary phenomenon we have just described needs to be investigated more thoroughly. It is critically important that the conclusions of our study be tested in the light of the living experience of Hindu followers of Christ. If our conclusions are confirmed, it would not only strengthen the broader case for fulfilment theology, it would also help alleviate some of the Hindu nationalist apprehensions regarding Christian mission.

Christian mission need never envisage the destruction of Hinduism, or any other religion or world-view, which has a right to exist if it continues to meet the needs of people in our world. Fulfilment theology enables the Church to be faithful to its stewardship of the story of God's decisive word and action in Christ, while demonstrating that there is nothing intrinsic to Christian faith that threatens the future of any indigenous cultural heritage. It can provide, moreover, a basis for the Church to cooperate with people of all faiths in furthering the kingdom purpose of God for a better world free of poverty, injustice, and strife.

As long as allegiance to Christian faith entails asserting the universal lordship of Christ over all cultures and traditions, some form of fulfilment theology which predicates continuity with them seems inevitable, challenging what is deficient and affirming what is of value in every religion, including Christianity. The potential of fulfilment theology has, however, yet to be fully realised, pending work at several points in its complex and multi-faceted proposal. The present study endeavours to make a modest contribution towards this broader project.

---

[67] A statistical survey of this phenomenon in Madras city in 1983 suggests that the number of these Hindu followers of Christ at least equals if not exceeds the ten percent official Christian population of Madras; H.E. Hoefer, *Churchless Christianity* (Madras: Gurukul Lutheran Theological College and Research Institute, 1991), 109.

[68] Hoefer, *Churchless Christianity*, 64, 205-214.

Bibliography

Primary Sources

Banerjea, K.M. *The Arian Witness: or Testimony of Arian Scriptures in Corroboration of Biblical History and the Rudiments of Christian Doctrine, including dissertations on the original home and early adventures of Indo-Arians.* Calcutta: Thacker, Spink, 1875.

_______. *Two Essays as Supplements to the Arian Witness.* Calcutta: Thacker, Spink, 1880.

_______. *Dialogues on Hindu Philosophy Comprising the Nyaya, Sankhya and Vedant; to which is added a Discussion of the Authority of the Vedas.* 1861. Reprint, London: Williams and Norgate, 1903.

_______. *On the Relation between the Hindu and Buddhistic Systems of Philosophy and the Light which the History of One Throws on the Other.* 1861. Reprint in T.V. Philip, *Krishna Mohan Banerjea: Christian Apologist*. Madras: CLS, 1982, 131-158.

_______. *The Claims of Christianity on British India.* 1864. Reprint in T.V. Philip, *Krishna Mohan Banerjea: Christian Apologist*, 159-180. Madras: CLS 1982.

_______. *The Relation between Christianity and Hinduism*. 1881. Reprint in T.V. Philip, *Krishna Mohan Banerjea: Christian Apologist*, 181-201. Madras: CLS, 1982,

Farquhar, J.N. *The Crossbearer: Being Extracts from the Gospel according to St. Matthew, Translated, Analysed and Explained in a Brief Commentary.* Calcutta: Methodist Publishing House, 1990.

_______. 'The Science of Religion as an Aid to Apologetics', *Harvest Field* 12 (1901): 369-374.

_______. *Christ and the Gospels: A Letter to the Thinking Men of Calcutta.* Calcutta, 1901.

_______. *Criticism and Christianity: A Letter to the Thinking Men of Calcutta and Bengal*. Calcutta, 1901.

_______. *Gita and Gospel.* Calcutta, 1903.

_______. *Permanent Lessons of the Gita.* Madras, 1903.

_______. *The Age and Origin of the Gita.* Madras, 1904.

_______.'How to Present the Response in the Christian Faith to Hindu Religious Aspirations'. *The Harvest Field* 15:12 (1904): 461-472.

_______. 'Missionary Study of Hinduism'. *The Harvest Field* 16:5 (1905): 166-178.

_______. 'Christianity in India'. *The Contemporary Review* 93 (1908): 597-

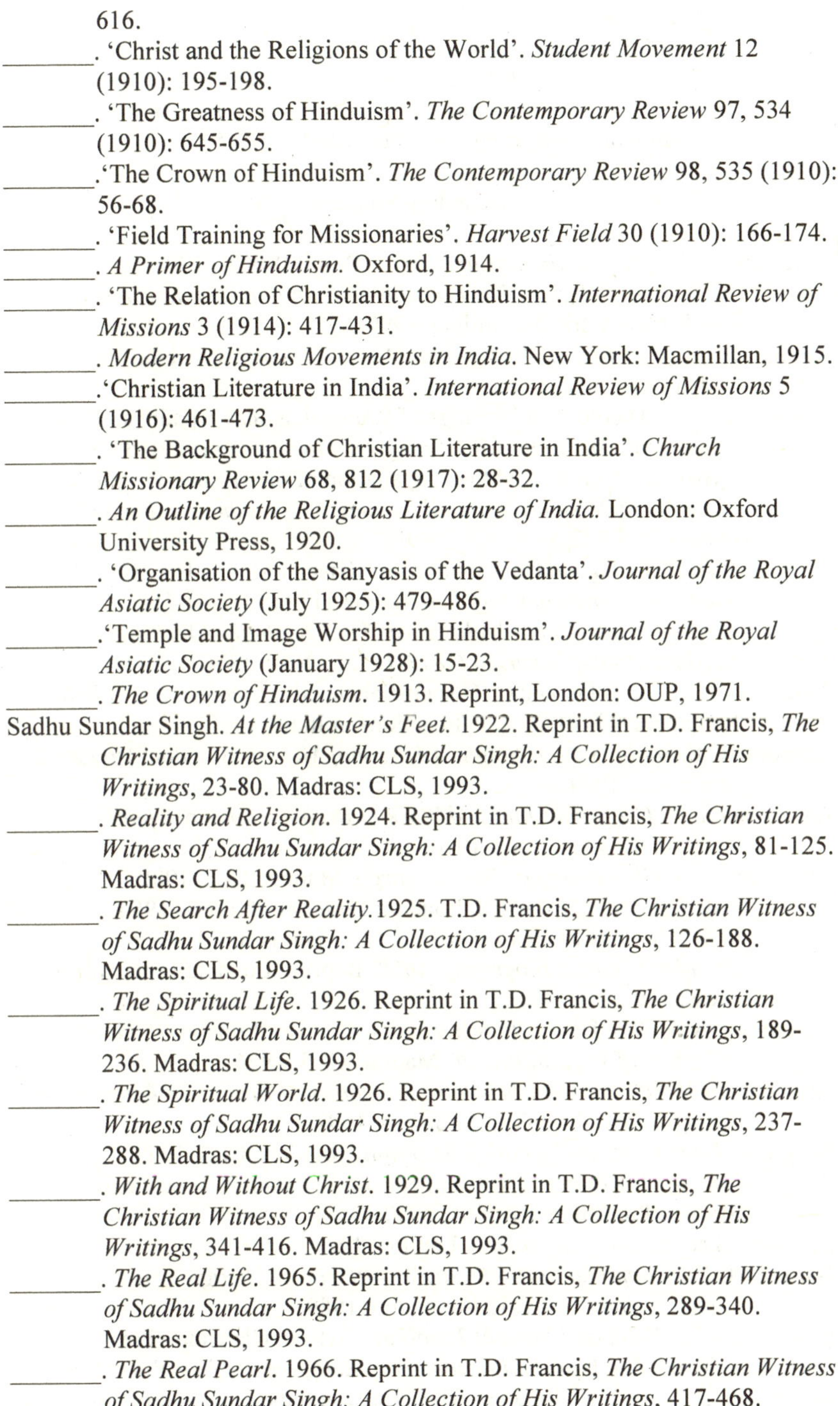

616.

_______. 'Christ and the Religions of the World'. *Student Movement* 12 (1910): 195-198.

_______. 'The Greatness of Hinduism'. *The Contemporary Review* 97, 534 (1910): 645-655.

_______.'The Crown of Hinduism'. *The Contemporary Review* 98, 535 (1910): 56-68.

_______. 'Field Training for Missionaries'. *Harvest Field* 30 (1910): 166-174.

_______. *A Primer of Hinduism.* Oxford, 1914.

_______. 'The Relation of Christianity to Hinduism'. *International Review of Missions* 3 (1914): 417-431.

_______. *Modern Religious Movements in India*. New York: Macmillan, 1915.

_______.'Christian Literature in India'. *International Review of Missions* 5 (1916): 461-473.

_______. 'The Background of Christian Literature in India'. *Church Missionary Review* 68, 812 (1917): 28-32.

_______. *An Outline of the Religious Literature of India.* London: Oxford University Press, 1920.

_______. 'Organisation of the Sanyasis of the Vedanta'. *Journal of the Royal Asiatic Society* (July 1925): 479-486.

_______.'Temple and Image Worship in Hinduism'. *Journal of the Royal Asiatic Society* (January 1928): 15-23.

_______. *The Crown of Hinduism*. 1913. Reprint, London: OUP, 1971.

Sadhu Sundar Singh. *At the Master's Feet.* 1922. Reprint in T.D. Francis, *The Christian Witness of Sadhu Sundar Singh: A Collection of His Writings*, 23-80. Madras: CLS, 1993.

_______. *Reality and Religion*. 1924. Reprint in T.D. Francis, *The Christian Witness of Sadhu Sundar Singh: A Collection of His Writings*, 81-125. Madras: CLS, 1993.

_______. *The Search After Reality.*1925. T.D. Francis, *The Christian Witness of Sadhu Sundar Singh: A Collection of His Writings*, 126-188. Madras: CLS, 1993.

_______. *The Spiritual Life*. 1926. Reprint in T.D. Francis, *The Christian Witness of Sadhu Sundar Singh: A Collection of His Writings*, 189-236. Madras: CLS, 1993.

_______. *The Spiritual World.* 1926. Reprint in T.D. Francis, *The Christian Witness of Sadhu Sundar Singh: A Collection of His Writings*, 237-288. Madras: CLS, 1993.

_______. *With and Without Christ*. 1929. Reprint in T.D. Francis, *The Christian Witness of Sadhu Sundar Singh: A Collection of His Writings*, 341-416. Madras: CLS, 1993.

_______. *The Real Life*. 1965. Reprint in T.D. Francis, *The Christian Witness of Sadhu Sundar Singh: A Collection of His Writings*, 289-340. Madras: CLS, 1993.

_______. *The Real Pearl*. 1966. Reprint in T.D. Francis, *The Christian Witness of Sadhu Sundar Singh: A Collection of His Writings*, 417-468.

Madras: CLS, 1993.
_______. *Life in Abundance: Sermons of the Sadhu recorded by Alys Goodwin in Switzerland, March 1922*. ed. A.F. Thyagaraju 1980. Reprint in T.D. Francis, *The Christian Witness of Sadhu Sundar Singh: A Collection of His Writings*, 469-562. Madras: CLS, 1993.

Secondary Sources

Abraham, K. *Prajapathi, the Cosmic Christ.* Delhi: ISPCK, 1997.
Adler, M.J. *Truth in Religion: The Plurality of Religions and the Unity of Truth.* New York: Macmillan, 1990.
Aguilar, H. *The Sacrifice in the Rgveda (Doctrinal Aspects).* Delhi: Bharatiya Vidya Prakashan, 1976.
Aleaz, K.P. 'The Theological Writings of Brahmabandhav Upadhyay Re-Examined'. *The Indian Journal of Theology* 28:2 (1979): 55-77.
_______. 'Bishop's College and the Propagation of the Gospel: Origin and Growth of a Vision'. *National Council of Churches Review* 115 (1995): 916-922.
_______. 'The Theological Contributions of Krishna Mohun Banerjea'. *National Council of Churches Review* 117 (1997): 41-56.
_______. *From Exclusivism to Inclusivism: The Theological Writings of Krishna Mohun Banerjea (1813-1885).* Delhi: ISPCK, 1998.
Amaldoss, M., T.K. John, and G. Gispert-Sauch, eds. *Theologizing in India.* Bangalore: Theological Publications in India, 1981.
Andrews, C.F. *Sadhu Sundar Singh: A Personal Memoir.* London: Hodder & Stoughton, 1934.
Animananda, B. *The Blade: Life and Work of Brahmabandhav Upadhyay.* Calcutta: Roy and Sons, 1946.
Appasamy, A.J. *Christianity as Bhakti Marga.* Madras: CLS, 1930.
_______, ed. *The Cross is Heaven.* London: Lutterworth Press, 1956.
_______. *The Theology of Hindu Bhakti.* CLS: Madras, 1970.
_______. *Sundar Singh: A Biography.* 1958. Reprint, London: Lutterworth Press, 1996.
Appasamy, A.S. *Fifty Years' Pilgrimage of a Convert.* London, 1924.
_______. *The Use of Yoga in Prayer.* Madras: CLS. 1926.
Ariarajah, S.W. *Hindus and Christians: A Century of Protestant Ecumenical Thought.* Grand Rapids: Eerdmans, 1991.
Baago, K. *Pioneers of Indigenous Christianity.* Madras: CLS, 1969.
Bailey, G.M. and I. Kesarcodi-Watson, eds. *Bhakti Studies.* New Delhi: Sterling Publishers Pvt. Ltd., 1992.
Banerjea, S.N. *A Nation in Making.* London, 1925.
Barnes, M. *Christian Identity and Religious Pluralism: Religions in Conversation.* Nashville: Abingdon, 1989.
Barr, J. *Biblical Faith and Natural Theology.* Oxford: Clarendon Press, 1993.
Barrows, J.S., ed. *The World's Parliament of Religions II.* New York, 1893.
Bauckham, R. 'Jurgen Moltmann's The Trinity and the Kingdom of God and

the Question of Pluralism.' In *The Trinity in a Pluralistic Age: Theological Essays on Culture and Religion*, edited by K. Vanhoozer. Grand Rapids: Eerdmans, 1997.

Beale, G.K., ed. *The Right Doctrine from the Wrong Texts? Essays on the Use of the Old Testament in the New.* Grand Rapids: Baker, 1994.

Bearce, G.D. *British Attitudes towards India 1784-1858.* London: Oxford University Press, 1961.

Beasley-Murray, G.R. *Word Biblical Commentary, John.* Vol. 36. Waco: Word Books, 1987.

Bediako, K. *Theology and Identity: The Impact of Culture upon Christian Thought in the Second Century and in Modern Africa.* Oxford: Regnum Books, 1992.

Biehl, M. *Der Fall Sadhu Sundar Singh–Theologie zwischen den Kulturen.* Frankfurt: Peter Lang, 1990.

Blanchard, M. 'Christianity as Fulfilment and Antithesis', *The Indian Journal of Theology* 17 (1968): 5-20.

Bookless, D. 'The Water of Life in an Indian Cup: Sadhu Sundar Singh and the Indigenisation of Christianity in India'. M.A. dissertation, Cheltenham & Gloucester College of Higher Education, 1990.

Bouquet, A.C. *The Christian Faith and Non-Christian Religions.* Welwyn: James Nisbet, 1958.

_______. 'Revelation and the Divine *Logos*'. In *The Theology of the Christian Mission*, edited by G.H. Anderson. London: SCM, 1961.

Boyd, A.J. *Christian Encounter*. Edinburgh: Saint Andrew, 1961.

Boyd, R. *Manilal C. Parekh; Dhanjibhai Fakirbhai.* Madras: CLS, 1974.

_______. *An Introduction to Indian Christian Theology*. 1969. Reprint, Delhi: ISPCK, 1991.

Braaten, C.E. *No Other Gospel: Christianity among the World's Religions.* Minneapolis: Fortress, 1992.

Brockington, J. *Hinduism and Christianity.* Basingstoke: Macmillan, 1992.

Bruce, F.F. *Commentary on the Book of the Acts*. Grand Rapids: Eerdmans, 1987.

_______. *The Acts of the Apostles*. Grand Rapids: Eerdmans, 1990.

Carson, D.A. *The Gospel according to John.* Leicester: InterVarsity Press, 1991.

Choong, C.P. 'Issues in the Hindu-Christian Debate during the Nineteenth Century Bengal Renaissance'. *Evangelical Review of Theology* 19, 4 (1995): 387-392.

Clark, A. and B. Winter, eds. *One God, One Lord: Christianity in a World of Religious Pluralism*. Grand Rapids: Baker Book House, 1993.

Clarke, Sathianathan. 'The Jesus of Nineteenth Century Indian Christian Theology'. In *Studies in World Christianity*, Vol. 1. Part 1, edited by James P. Mackey, 32-46. Edinburgh: Edinburgh University Press, 1999.

Cobb, J.B. 'Beyond "Pluralism".' In *Christian Uniqueness Reconsidered: The Myth of a Pluralistic Theology of Religions*, edited by G. D'Costa.

New York: Orbis Books, 1990.
Cook, F.C. *The Origins of Religion and Language*. London, 1884.
Copley, A. 'The Conversion Experience of India's Christian Elite in the Mid-Nineteenth Century', *The Journal of Religious History* 18, 1 (1994).
_______. *Religions in Conflict: Ideology, Cultural Contact and Conversion in Late-Colonial India.* Oxford: Oxford University Press, 1997.
Cottrell, J. *Mission and Meaninglessness: The Good News in a World of Suffering and Disorder*. London: SPCK, 1990.
Cottrell, J., and S.E. Burris. 'The Fate of the Unreached: Are They Lost Without Special Revelation?' *International Journal of Frontier Missions* 10:2 (1993): 67-72.
Coward, H.G., ed. *Modern Indian responses to Religious Pluralism*. Albany: State University of New York, 1987.
_______. *Hindu-Christian Dialogue: Perspectives and Encounters*. Delhi: Motilal Banarsidass Publishers, 1993.
Cracknell, K. *Justice, Courtesy and Love: Theologians and Missionaries Encountering World Religions (1846-1914)*. London: Epworth, 1995.
Danielou, J. *Holy Pagans of the Old Testament*. London: Longman, Green, 1957.
Das, H. 'The Rev. K.M. Banerjea'. *Bengal Past and Present* 37, 73 (1929): 133-144.
Das, S.K. *The Shadow of the* Cross. New Delhi: Munshiram Manoharlal, 1974.
Das, R.C. *How to Present Christ to a Hindu.* Allahabad: North India Tract & Book Society, 1951.
_______. *Convictions of an Indian Disciple*. Bangalore: CISRS, 1966.
Dasgupta, S.N. *Hindu Mysticism*. Delhi: Motilal Banarsidass, 1996.
Davey, C.J. *The Story of Sadhu Sundar Singh: The Yellow Robe*. Chicago: Moody Press, 1963.
David, J.V. 'Hindrances to Communicating the Christian Message among Sikhs'. *Dharma Deepika* 35 (1998): 31-43.
David, M.D. *The YMCA and the Making of Modern India: A Centenary History*. New Delhi: National Council of YMCAs of India, 1992.
David, S.I., ed. *Christianity and the Encounter with Other Religions: A Select Bibliography*. Bangalore: United Theological College, 1988.
D'Costa, G. *Theology and Religious Pluralism*. Oxford: Basil Blackwell, 1986.
_______. *John Hick's Theology of Religions: A Critical Evaluation*. Lanham: University Press of America, 1987.
_______, ed. *Christian Uniqueness Reconsidered: The Myth of a Pluralistic Theology of Religions*. New York: Orbis Books, 1990.
_______. 'One Covenant or Many Covenants? Toward a Theology of Christian-Jewish Relations', *Journal of Ecumenical Studies* 27 (1990): 441-452.
_______. 'Other Faiths and Christianity'. In *The Blackwell Encyclopedia of Modern Christian Thought*, edited by A.E. McGrath. Oxford: Blackwell, 1993.

_______. 'Inculturation, India and Other Religions: Some Methodological Reflections'. *Studia Missionalia* 44 (1995): 121-147.

_______. 'The Impossibility of a Pluralist View of Religions'. *Religious Studies* 32 (1996): 223-232.

_______. *The Meeting of Religions and the Trinity*. Edinburgh: T&T Clark, 2000.

De Wolf, L.H. 'The Interpenetration of Christianity and the Non-Christian Religions'. In *The Theology of the Christian Mission*, edited by G.H. Anderson. London: SCM, 1961.

Deshmukh, P.S. *The Origin and Development of Religion in Vedic Literature*. London: Oxford University Press, 1933.

Dewick, E.C. *The Christian Attitude to Other Religions*. Cambridge: Cambridge University Press, 1953.

Dhavamony, M. 'The Sadhu Ideal as realized by Hindu Saints'. *Studia Missionalia* 35 (1986): 199-224.

_______. 'The Cosmic Christ and World Religions'. *Studia Missionalia* 42 (1993): 179-181.

Dulles, A. *Models of Revelation*. New York: Image Books, 1985.

Dunn, J.D.G. *Word Biblical Commentary: Romans 1-8*. Vol. 38A. Dallas: Word Books, 1988.

Dupuis, Jacques. *Toward a Christian Theology of Religious Pluralism*. New York: Orbis, 1997.

Dupuis, James. 'The Cosmic Influence of the Holy Spirit and the Gospel Message'. In *God's Word Among Men*, edited by G. Gispert-Sauch. Delhi: Vidyajyoti, 1973.

Emilsen, W.W. *Violence and Atonement: The Missionary Experiences of Mohandas Gandhi, Samuel Stokes and Verrier Elwin in India before 1935*. Frankfurt: Peter Lang, 1994.

Evangelical Alliance (UK). 'The Salvation of the Gentiles: Implications for Other Faiths'. *Evangelical Review of Theology* 15, 1 (1991): 36-43.

Evans, C.A. 'Old Testament in the Gospels'. In *Dictionary of Jesus and the Gospels*, edited by J.B. Green, S. McKnight, and I.H. Marshall, 579-590. Leicester: InterVarsity Press, 1992.

Fenger, F. *A History of the Tranquebar Mission*. Tranquebar: Evangelical Lutheran Mission Press, 1863.

Fernando, A. *The Christian's Attitude toward World Religions*. Wheaton: Tyndale House, 1987.

Firth, C.B. *An Introduction to Indian Church History*. Madras: CLS, 1989.

Flanagan, K. 'Theological Pluralism: A Sociological Critique'. In *Religious Pluralism and Unbelief: Studies Critical and Comparative*, edited by I. Hamnett London: Routledge, 1990.

Flemming, Dean. 'Contextualizing the Gospel in Athens: Paul's Areopagus Address as a Paradigm for Missionary Communication'. *Missiology* 30, 2 (April 2002): 199-214.

Francis, T.D. *The Christian Witness of Sadhu Sundar Singh: A Collection of His Writings*. Madras: CLS, 1993.

Frei, H. *Types of Christian Theology*. New Haven: Yale University Press, 1992.

Gardner, C.E. *Life of Father Goreh*. London: Longman's, 1900.

Ghosha, R. *A Biographical Sketch of the Rev. K.M. Banerjea.* 1893. Reprint, Calcutta 1980.

Ghurye, G.S. *Indian Sadhus*. Bombay: Popular Prakashan, 1964.

Gispert-Sauch, G. 'The Sanskrit Hymns of Brahmabandhav Upadhyay'. *Religion and Society* 19 (1972): 60-79.

Goldingay, J. *Approaches to Old Testament Interpretation*. Leicester: Apollos, 1990.

Goodwin, A. *Sadhu Sundar Singh in Switzerland*. Edited by A.F. Thyagaraju. 1989. Reprint, Chennai: CLS, 1997.

Goreh, N. *A Rational Refutation of the Hindu Philosophical Systems*. Calcutta: Bishop's College Press, 1862; (original Hindi title, *Shaddarshana Darpana*, 1860).

Grafe, H. 'Hindu Apologetics at the Beginning of the Protestant Mission Era in India'. *Indian Church History Review* 6, 1 (1972): 44-50.

Gray, G.F.S. 'Sadhu Sundar Singh and the Non-Christian Religions'. *International Review of Mission* 60 (1959): 421-426.

Gulliford, H. 'Christ the Fulfiller of Hinduism'. *Harvest Field* 34 (1914): p. 365f.

Gundry, R. 'Salvation According to Scripture: No Middle Ground'. *Christianity Today* 22 (1977): 14-16.

Hacker, P. *Theological Foundations of Evangelization*. St. Augustin: Steyler Verlag, 1980.

Hall, W.P. and R.G. Albion. *A History of England and the British Empire*. Boston: Ginn & Co., 1937.

Hallencreutz, C.F. *Kraemer Towards Tambaram: A Study in Hendrik Kraemer's Missionary Approach*. Uppsala: Gleerup, 1966.

Hastings, A. 'Pluralism: the relationship of theology to religious studies'. In *Religious Pluralism and Unbelief: Studies Critical and Comparative*, edited by I. Hamnett. London: Routledge, 1990.

Hedges, P.M. 'A History and Study of Fulfilment Theology in Modern British Thought'. Ph.D. thesis, University of Wales, 1999.

_______. *Preparation and Fulfilment: A History and Study of Fulfilment Theology in Modern British Thought in the Indian Context*. Bern, Peter Lang, 2001.

Heiler, F. *The Gospel of Sadhu Sundar Singh.* Translated by Olive Wyon. 1927. Reprint, London: Allen & Unwin 1989.

Heim, M. *Salvations: Truth and Difference in Religion.* New York: Orbis, 1997.

Hemer, C.J. *The Book of Acts in the Setting of Hellenistic History*. Tubigen: Mohr, 1989.

Hick, J., and P. Knitter, eds. *The Myth of Christian Uniqueness: Towards a Pluralistic Theology of Religions*. New York: Orbis, 1987.

Hoefer, Herbert E. *Churchless Christianity.* Madras: Gurukul Lutheran Theological College and Research Institute, 1991.

Hogg, A.G. 'The Crown of Hinduism, and Other Volumes'. *Madras Christian College Magazine* 13 (1914): 423f.

_______. 'The Crown of Hinduism, and Other Volumes'. *International Review of Mission* 3, 9 (1914): 171-173.

_______. *The Christian Message to the Hindu.* London: SCM Press, 1947.

_______. *Karma and Redemption: An Essay Toward the Interpretation of Hinduism and the Restatement of Christianity.* 1909. Reprint, Madras: CLS, 1970.

Hooker, R.H. *Themes in Hinduism and Christianity: A Comparative Study.* Frankfurt: Peter Lang, 1989.

Hughes, D.A. *Has God Many Names?* Leicester: Apollos, 1996.

Ingleby, J.C. 'Education as a Missionary Tool: A Study in Christian Missionary Education by English Protestant Missionaries in India with Special Reference to Cultural Change'. Ph.D. thesis, Oxford Centre for Mission Studies, 1998.

Jacob, P.S. *The Experiential Response of N V. Tilak.* Bangalore/Madras: CISRS/ CLS, 1979.

_______. 'Interfaith Dialogue: N.V. Tilak's Experiential Model'. *Indian Church History Review* 27, 2 (1993): 107-120.

Jathanna, O.V. *The Decisiveness of the Christ-event and the Universality of Christianity in a World of Religious Plurality: with special reference to Hendrik Kraemer and Alfred George Hogg as well as to William Ernest Hocking and Pandipeddi Chenchiah.* Berne: Peter Lang, 1981.

Jayakumar, S. *Dalit Consciousness and Christian Conversion: Historical Resources for a Contemporary Debate.* Delhi: ISPCK, 1999.

Johnson, D.H. '*LOGOS*'. In *Dictionary of Jesus and the Gospels*, edited by J.B. Green, S. McKnight and I.H. Marshall, 481-484. Leicester: InterVarsity, 1992.

Katz, S.T. 'Language, Epistemology, and Mysticism'. In *Mysticism and Philosophical Analysis*, edited by S.T. Katz. London: Sheldon Press, 1978.

Keller, C. 'Mystical Literature'. In *Mysticism and Philosophical Analysis*, edited by S.T. Katz. London: Sheldon Press, 1978.

Kirk, J.A. *Loosing the Chains: Religion as Opium and Liberation.* London: Hodder & Stoughton, 1992.

Klostermaier, K.K. *A Survey of Hinduism.* New Delhi: Munshiram Manoharlal Publishers, 1990.

Knitter, P.F. *No Other Name? A Critical Survey of Christian Attitudes to World Religions.* New York: Orbis, 1985.

Kopf, D. *British Orientalism and the Bengal Renaissance: The Dynamics of Indian Modernization: 1773-1835.* Berkeley: University of California, 1969.

_______. *The Brahmo Samaj and the Shaping of the Modern Indian Mind.* Princeton: Princeton University Press, 1979.

Kraemer, H. *The Christian Message in a Non-Christian World.* New York: Harper & Brothers, 1938.

_______. *Religion and the Christian Faith*. London: Lutterworth, 1956.
Kristiansen, R.E. 'World Religions in Christian Perspective'. *Areopagus* 5, 2 (1992): 17-21.
Kung, H. *Christianity and the World Religions: Paths of Dialogue with Islam, Hinduism and Buddhism.* Translated by P. Heinegg. London: Collins, 1987.
Kuttianimattathil, J. *Practice and Theology of Interreligious Dialogue: A Critical Study of the Indian Christian Attempts since Vatican II.* Bangalore: Kristu Jyoti Publications, 1995.
Legrand, L. 'The Missionary Significance of the Areopagus Speech'. In *God's Word Among Men*, edited by G. Gispert-Sauch. Delhi: Vidyajyoti. 1973.
_______. 'The Unknown God of Athens: Acts 17 and the Religion of the Gentiles'. *The Indian Journal of Theology* 30 (1981): 158-167.
Lehmann, E.A. *It Began at Tranquebar: The Story of the Tranquebar Mission and the Beginnings of Protestant Christianity in India Published to Celebrate the 250th Anniversary of the Landing of the First Protestant Missionaries at Tranquebar in 1706.* Madras: CLS, 1956.
Lewis, G.R., and B.A. Demarest. 'Divine Revelation to All People of All Times'. In *Integrative Theology*. Grand Rapids: Zondervan, 1996.
Lewis, J.F., and W.G. Travis. 'Toward an Evangelical Theology of Religions'. In *Religious Traditions of the World.* Grand Rapids: Zondervan, 1991.
Lindbeck, G. *The Nature of Doctrine: Religion and Theology in a Post Liberal Age.* London: SPCK, 1984.
Lipner, J. 'Christians and the Uniqueness of Christ'. *Scottish Journal of Theology* 28 (1975): 359-368.
_______. 'Being One, Let Me Be Many: Facets of the Relationship between the Gospel and Culture'. *International Review of Mission* 74 (1985): 158-168.
_______. *The Face of Truth: A Study of Meaning and Metaphysics in the Vedantic Theology of Ramanuja*. Basingstoke: Macmillan, 1986.
_______. 'A Modern Indian Christian Response'. In *Modern Indian Responses to Religious Pluralism*, edited by H.G. Coward, 291-314. Albany: State University of New York, 1987.
_______. *Hindus: Their Religious Beliefs and Practices*. London: Routledge, 1998.
_______. *Brahmabandhab Upadhyay: The Life and Thought of a Revolutionary.* New Delhi: OUP, 1999.
Lipner, J., and G. Gispert Sauch, eds. *The Writings of Brahmabandhab Upadhyay (Including a Resume of his Life and Thought).* Vol. 1. Bangalore: UTC, 1991.
Longenecker, R.N. *The Christology of Early Jewish Christianity*. Grand Rapids: Baker Book House, 1970.
_______. *Biblical Exegesis in the Apostolic Period.* Grand Rapids/Vancouver: Eerdmans/ Regent College, 1999.

Lubac, H. de. *The Church: Paradox & Mystery*. Shannon, Ireland: Ecclesia Press, 1969.

Lucas, B. 'Not to Destroy, but to Fulfill'. *Harvest Field* 34 (1914): 422-424.

Lucas, B., C. Wohlenberg, and H. Gulliford. 'Not to Destroy, but to Fulfil', I, II, & III. *Harvest Field* 34, 12 (1914): 451-464.

Lyotard, J.F. *The Postmodern Condition: A Report on Knowledge.* Translated by Geoff Bennington and Brian Massumi. Minneapolis: University of Minnesota, 1984.

Macauliffe, M.A. *The Sikh Religion: Its Gurus, Sacred Writings and Authors*. New Delhi: S. Chand, 1985.

Macdonald, K.S. *The Vedic Religion or the Creed and Practice of the Indo-Aryans three thousand years ago.* London: James Nisbet, 1881.

Macdonell, A.A. 'Vedic Religion'. In *Encyclopedia of Religion and Ethics.* Vol. 12. Edited by J. Hastings. Edinburgh: T&T Clark, 1921.

Mackichan, D. 'A Present-Day Phase of Missionary Theology'. *International Review of Mission* 3 (1914): pp 243-254.

Macnicol, N. 'Farquhar, John Nicol'. In *Dictionary of National Biography 1922-1930*. London: Oxford University Press, 1937: p. 296.

Majumdar, A.K. *Bhakti Renaissance*. Bombay: Bharatiya Vidya Bhavan, 1979.

Malieckal, L. *Yajna and Sacrifice: An Inter-religious Approach to the Theology of Sacrifice*. Bangalore: Dharmaram Publications, 1989.

Mangalwadi, V. *Missionary Conspiracy: Letters to a Postmodern Hindu*. New Delhi: Good Books, 1996.

Marshall, I.H. *The Acts of the Apostles*. Leicester: InterVarsity Press, 1980.

Martin, P. *Missionary of the Indian Road: The Theology of Stanley Jones*. Bangalore: Theological Book Trust, 1996.

Mattam, J. 'Interpreting Christ to India Today: The Calcutta School'. *The Indian Journal of Theology* 23 (1974): 191-205.

_______. 'Modern Catholic Attempts at Presenting Christ to India'. *The Indian Journal of Theology* 23 (1974): 206-218.

Maw, M. *Visions of India: Fulfilment Theology, the Aryan Race Theory, and the Work of British Protestant Missionaries in Victorian India.* Frankfurt: Peter Lang, 1990.

McDermott, J.G.R. *God's Rivals: Why has God Allowed Different Religions? Insights from the Bible and the Early Church.* Downers Grove: InterVarsity Press, 2007.

McLeod, W.H. *Guru Nanak and the Sikh Religion*. Oxford: Clarendon Press, 1978.

McMullen, C.O. 'Operative Sikh Beliefs and Practices'. *Dharma Deepika* 35 (1998): 13-22.

Mead, R.T. 'A Dissenting Opinion about Respect for Context in Old Testament Quotations'. In *The Right Doctrine from the Wrong Texts? Essays on the Use of the Old Testament in the New*, edited by G.K. Beale. Grand Rapids: Baker, 1994.

Metcalf, T.A. *Ideologies of the Raj.* Cambridge: Cambridge University Press, 1996.

Middleton, J.R., and Walsh, B.J. *Truth is Stranger than it used to be: Biblical Faith in a Postmodern Age.* Downers Grove: InterVarsity Press, 1995.

Milbank, J. 'The End of Dialogue'. In *Christian Uniqueness Reconsidered: The Myth of a Pluralistic Theology of Religions*, edited by G. D'Costa. New York: Orbis Books, 1990.

Miller, J. *The Vision of Cosmic Order in the Vedas*. London: Routledge & Kegan Paul, 1985.

_______. 'Bhakti and the Rg Veda – Does it Appear There or Not?' In *Love Divine: Studies in Bhakti and Devotional Mysticism*, edited by Karel Werner. Richmond Surrey: Curzon Press, 1993.

Mitra, H. 'Banerjee, Krishnamohun'. In *Dictionary of National Biography*, Vol. 1: 118-120, edited by S.P. Sen. Calcutta: Institute of Historical Studies, 1972.

Moltmann, J. *The Trinity and the Kingdom of God.* Translated by M. Kohl. London: SCM Press, 1981.

Monier-Williams, M. *Indian Wisdom*. London: William H. Allen, 1875.

_______. *Modern India and the Indians*. London: Trubner, 1878.

_______. *The Holy Bible and the Sacred Books of the East, 4 addresses*. London: SPCK, 1900.

Montgomery, H.H., ed. *Mankind and the Church: An attempt to estimate the Contribution of great races to the fulness of the Church of God (by seven bishops).* London: Longmans, Green, 1907.

Moo, D. *The Wycliffe Exegetical Commentary: Romans 1-8*. Chicago: Moody Press, 1991.

Mookenthottam, A. *Indian Theological Tendencies: Approaches and Problems for further Research as seen in the works of some leading Indian Theologians.* Berne: Peter Lang, 1978.

Morris, L. *The Gospel according to John*. Grand Rapids: Eerdmans, 1995.

Moses, D.G. *Religious Truth and the Relations between Religions*. Madras: CLS, 1950.

Muir, J. *An Essay on Conciliation*. Calcutta, 1849.

Muller, F.M. *Chips from a German Workshop I*. London: OUP ,1867-1875.

_______. *Lectures on the Origin and Growth of Religion as illustrated by the Religions of India*. London: Longmans, Green, 1878.

_______. *Biographical Essays*. London: Longmans, Green, 1884.

_______. *The Life and Letters of the Rt. Hon. Friedrich Max Muller, Edited by his Wife, II*. London: Longmans, Green, 1902.

_______. *Physical Religion*. New Delhi: Asian Educational Services, 1979.

Munck, J. *The Acts of the Apostles, Anchor Bible.* Vol. 31. New York: Doubleday, 1986.

Neil, S. *Christian Faith and Other Faiths: The Christian Dialogue with Other Religions.* London: Oxford University Press, 1961.

_______. *Bhakti: Hindu and Christian*. Madras: CLS, 1974.

Netland, H. *Dissonant Voices: Religious Pluralism and the Question of Truth.* Grand Rapids: Eerdmans, 1991.

Newbigin, L. 'Religious Pluralism and the Uniqueness of Jesus Christ', *International Bulletin of Missionary Research* 13, 2 (1989): 50-54.

_______. *The Gospel in a Pluralist Society*. Grand Rapids: Eerdmans, 1989.

O'Flaherty, W.D. ed. and trans. *Textual Sources for the Study of Hinduism.* Manchester: University Press, 1988.

Oldenberg, H. *The Religion of the Veda.* Translated by S. . Shrotri. Delhi: Motilal Banarsidass, 1988.

Padinjarekuttu, I. *The Missionary Movement of the 19th and 20th Centuries and its Encounter with India.* Frankfurt: Peter Lang, 1995.

Pandurangi, K.T. 'Vedanta as God-Realization (Madhva)'. In *Hindu Spirituality: Vedas through Vedanta*, edited by K. Sivaraman. Delhi: Motilal Banarsidass, 1995.

Panikkar, R. *The Vedic Experience: Mantramanjali.* Pondicherry: All India Books, 1989.

Pape, W.R. 'Keshub Chunder Sen's Doctrine of Christ and the Trinity: A Rehabilitation'. *The Indian Journal of Theology* 25 (1976): 55-71.

Paradkar, B.A.M. *The Theology of Nehemiah Goreh.* Bangalore: CISRS, 1969.

Parekh, M.C. *Brahmarshi Keshub Chunder Sen.* Rajkot, 1931.

Parker, R.J. *Sadhu Sundar Singh: Called of God.* 1918. Reprint, Madras: CLS, 1996.

Pathak, S.M. *American Missionaries and Hinduism.* Delhi: Munshiram Manoharlal, 1967.

Pathil, K. *Indian Churches at the Crossroads.* Rome/Bangalore: CIIS/ Dharmaram, 1994.

Paul, R.D. *Chosen Vessels: Lives of Ten Indian Christian Pastors of the Eighteenth and Nineteenth Centuries.* Madras: CLS, 1961.

Pereira, J. *Hindu Theology: Themes, Texts and Structures.* Delhi: Motilal Banarsidass, 1991.

Philip, T.V. 'Krishna Mohan Banerjea and Arian Witness to Christ: Jesus Christ the True Prajapati'. *Indian Journal of Theology* 29, 2 (1980): 74-80.

_______. *Krishna Mohan Banerjea: Christian Apologist.* Madras: CLS, 1982.

Phillips, M. *The Teaching of the Vedas.* 1894. Reprint, Delhi: Low Price Publications, 1995.

Phillips, W.G. 'Evangelicals and Pluralism: Current Options'. *The Evangelical Quarterly* 64 (1992): 229-244.

Pieris, A. *An Asian Theology of Liberation.* New York: Orbis, 1988.

Pinnock, C. *A Wideness in God's Mercy.* Grand Rapids: Zondervan, 1992.

Poddar, A. *Renaissance in Bengal: Quests and Confrontations: 1800-1860.* Shimla: Indian Institute of Advanced Study, 1970.

Pope John Paul II. *Post-Synodal Apostolic Exhortation: Ecclesia in Asia.* New Delhi, November 1999.

Potdar, K.R. *Sacrifice in the Rgveda: Its Nature, Influence, Origin and Growth.* Bombay: Bharatiya Vidya Bhavan, 1953.

Poythress, V. *The Shadow of Christ in the Law of Moses*. Brentwood: Wolgemuth & Hyatt, 1991.

Prakash, P.S. *The Preaching of Sadhu Sundar Singh.* Bangalore: Wordmakers, 1991.

Puthenkalam, X.J. *Hindu Christian Bhakti: An Indian Concept and Style of Discipleship*. Kottayam: Oriental Institute of Religious Studies, 1990.

Puthiadam, I. 'Diversity of Religions in the context of Pluralism and Indian Christian Life and Reflection'. In *Theologizing in India*, edited by M. Amaldoss, T.K. John, and G. Gispert-Sauch. Bangalore: Theological Publications in India, 1981.

Race, A. *Christians and Religious Pluralism*. New York: Orbis, 1982.

Radhakrishnan, S. *East and West in Religion*. London, 1933.

_______. *Indian Philosophy*. London: George Allen & Unwin Limited, 1962.

Raghavachar. 'The Spiritual Vision of Ramanuja'. In *Hindu Spirituality: Vedas through Vedanta*, edited by K. Sivaraman. Delhi: Motilal Banarsidass, 1989.

Rahner, K. 'Christ in the Non-Christian Religions'. In *God's Word Among Men*, edited by G. Gispert-Sauch. Delhi: Vidyajyoti, 1973.

Ramachandra, V. *The Recovery of Mission*. Carlisle: Paternoster, 1996.

Richard, H.L. *Christ-Bhakti: Narayan Vaman Tilak and Christian Work among Hindus.* Delhi: ISPCK, 1991.

_______. 'The Aryan Witness Recalled: Vedic Sacrifice and Fulfilment Theology'. *To All Men All Things* 3, 3 (1993): 1-7.

_______. 'The Aryan Witness Recalled: Vedic Sacrifice and Fulfilment Theology'. *To All Men All Things* 4, 1 (1994): 1-5.

_______. *R.C. Das: Evangelical Prophet for Contextual Christianity.* Bangalore/Delhi: CISRS/ISPCK, 1995.

_______. 'A Survey of Protestant Evangelistic Efforts among High Caste Hindus in the Twentieth Century'. *Missiology: An International Review* 25, 4 (1997): 419-445.

Ruether, R.R. *To Change the World: Christology and Cultural Criticism.* London: SCM, 1981.

Ruokanen, M. *The Catholic Doctrine of Non-Christian Religions: According to the Second Vatican Council.* Leiden: E.J. Brill, 1992.

Saldanha, C. *Divine Pedagogy: A Patristic View of Non-Christian Religions.* Rome: Las. 1984.

Samartha, S.J. *The Hindu Response to the Unbound Christ.* Bangalore: CISRS, 1974.

_______. *One Christ – Many Religions: Toward a Revised Christology.* New York: Orbis, 1991.

Samuel, V.K. 'Mission in the Context of World Religions'. In *A.D. 2000 and Beyond: A Mission Agenda*, edited by V.K. Samuel and C. Sugden. Oxford: Regnum Books, 1991.

Sanders, J. *An Investigation into the Destiny of the Unevangelized.* Grand Rapids: Eerdmans, 1992.

Sanneh, L. *Encountering the West: Christianity and the Global Cultural Process: The African Dimension*. London: Marshall Pickering, 1993.

Sarkar, S. *Bengal Renaissance and other Essays*. New Delhi, 1970.

Satthianathan, S. *Sketches of Indian Christians*. Madras: CLS, 1896.

Scott, D.C., ed. *Keshub Chunder Sen*. Madras: CLS, 1979.

_______. *Kabir's Mythology*. Delhi: Bharatiya Vidya Prakashan, 1985.

_______. 'Sadhu Sundar Singh: Church of the Sadhu Ideal'. *Jeevadhara* 17 (1987): 267-280.

Selvanayagam, I. *Vedic Sacrifice: Challenge and Response*. New Delhi: Manohar, 1996.

Sharma, K. *Bhakti and the Bhakti Movement: A New Perspective*. New Delhi: Manoharlal. 1987.

Sharpe, E.J. *J.N. Farquhar: A Memoir*. Calcutta: YMCA, 1962.

_______. *Not to Destroy but to Fulfil: The Contribution of J.N. Farquhar to Protestant Missionary Thought in India before 1914*. Uppsala: Swedish Institute of Missionary Research, 1965.

_______. 'Christ the Fulfiller'. *Bangalore Theological Forum* 3, 1 (1969): 1-11.

_______. *John Nicol Farquhar and the Missionary Study of Hinduism*. Aberdeen: Scottish Institute of Missionary Studies, 1971.

_______. *The Theology of A.G. Hogg*. Bangalore/Madras: CISRS/CLS, 1971.

_______. *Comparative Religion: A History*. London: Gerald Duckworth, 1975.

_______. 'Sadhu Sundar Singh and His Critics: An Episode in the Meeting of East and West'. *Religion* 6 (1976): 48-66.

_______. *Faith Meets Faith: Some Christian Attitudes to Hinduism in the Nineteenth and Twentieth Centuries*. London: SCM. Press Ltd, 1977.

_______. 'The Legacy of J.N. Farquhar'. *Occasional Bulletin of Missionary Research* 3, 2 (1979): 61-64.

_______. 'The Legacy of Sadhu Sundar Singh' *International Bulletin of Missionary Research* 14 (1990): 161-167.

_______. 'J.N. Farquhar 1861-1929: Presenting Christ as the Crown of Hinduism'. In *Mission Legacies: Biographical Studies of Leaders of the Modern Missionary Movement*, edited by G.H. Anderson, et. al. New York: Orbis, 1995.

_______. *The Riddle of Sadhu Sundar Singh*. New Delhi: Intercultural Publications, 2004.

Shourie, A. *Missionaries in India: Continuities, Changes, Dilemmas*. New Delhi: ASA, 1994.

Slater, T.E. *The Higher Hinduism in Relation to Christianity*. London, 1903.

Smith, G. *The Life of Alexander Duff*. London, 1853.

Soderblom, N. 'Christian Mysticism in an Indian Soul'. *International Review of Mission* 11 (1922): 226-238.

Staffner, H. *Jesus Christ and the Hindu Community*. Anand: Gujarat Sahitya Prakash, 1988.

Stanley, B. *The Bible and the Flag: Protestant Missions and British Imperialism in the Nineteenth and Twentieth Centuries*. Leicester: Apollos, 1990.

_______. *The World Missionary Conference, Edinburgh.* Studies in the History of Christian Missions. Grand Rapids: Eerdmans, 2009.

Stott, J.R.W. *The Message of Acts*. Leicester: InterVarsity Press, 1990.

Streeter, B.H. and A.J. Appasamy. *The Sadhu: A Study in Mysticism and Practical* Religion. 1921. Reprint, Delhi: Mittal Publications; London: Macmillan, 1987.

Studdert-Kennedy, G.*British Christians, Indian Nationalists and the Raj.* Delhi: Oxford University Press, 1991.

Studdert-Kennedy, G. *Providence and the Raj: Imperial Mission and Missionary Imperialism,* New Delhi, Sage, 1998.

Sugden, C. *Seeking the Asian Face of Jesus: The Practice and Theology of Christian Social Witness in Indonesia and India 1974-1996*. Oxford: Regnum Books, 1997.

Sukhtankar, V.A. 'The Crown of Hinduism'. *The Indian Interpreter* 8, 4 (1914): 171-179.

Sullivan, F.A. *Salvation outside the Church? Tracing the History of the Catholic Response*. London: Chapman, 1992.

Supple, P.C. 'Christians and Religious Pluralism 1830-1914: Changing Attitudes to Other Faiths'. M.Litt. thesis, University of Oxford, 1991.

Surin, K. 'Revelation, Salvation, the Uniqueness of Christ and Other Religions'. *Religious Studies* 19 (1983): 323-343.

_______. 'Towards a 'materialist' critique of religious pluralism'. In *Religious Pluralism and Unbelief: Studies Critical and Comparative*, edited by I. Hamnett. London: Routledge, 1990.

Swidler, L. *Toward a Universal Theology of Religion.* New York: Orbis, 1987.

Taylor, J. *The Go-Between God – The Holy Spirit and the Christian Mission.* London: SCM Press, 1972.

Thachil, J. *The Vedic and the Christian Concept of Sacrifice*. Alwaye: Pontifical Institute of Theology and Philosophy, 1985.

Thangasamy, D.A. *The Theology of Chenchiah.* Bangalore: CISRS, 1967.

Thomas, M.M. *The Acknowledged Christ of the Indian Renaissance*. Madras: CLS, 1976.

_______. *Risking Christ for Christ's sake: Towards an Ecumenical Theology of Pluralism.* Geneva: WCC, 1987.

Thomas, M.M., and P.T. Thomas. *Towards an Indian Christian Theology: Life and Thought of some Pioneers*. Tiruvalla: New Day Publications of India, 1992.

Thomas, O.C. *Attitudes Towards Other Religions: Some Christian Interpretations*. New York: Harper & Row, 1969.

Thompson, A.F. 'Christian Views of Hindu *Bhakti*'. In *Hindu-Christian Dialogue: Perspectives and Encounters*, edited by H.G. Coward, 176-190. Delhi: Motilal Banarsidass, 1993.

Tilak, L. *I Follow After*. Translated by E. Josephine Inkster. Madras: Oxford University Press, 1950.

Tillich, P. *Christianity and the Encounter of the World Religions*. New York: Columbia University, 1963.

Titus, D.P. *Fulfilment of the Vedic Quest in the Lord Jesus Christ*. Nainital: Sat Tal Ashram, 1982.

_______. *The Concept of Divine Sacrifice in the Bible and Vedic Scriptures*. Nainital: Khristadvaita Ashram, 1993.

Tomlinson, W.E. 'The Crown of Hinduism'. *Harvest Field* 34, 1 (1914): 5-11.

Underhill, E. *Mysticism: A Study in the Nature and Development of Man's Spiritual Consciousness*. Cleveland: The World Publishing Company, 1970.

Vanhoozer, K., ed. *The Trinity in a Pluralistic Age: Theological Essays on Culture and Religion*. Grand Rapids: Eerdmans, 1997.

_______. *Is there a Meaning in the Text? The Bible, the Reader and the Morality of Literary Knowledge*. Grand Rapids: Zondervan, 1998.

Vasanthakumar, M.S. 'Expound Christ from Non-Christian Texts'. *Dharma Deepika* 4, 2 (2000): 5-20.

Vaughan, J. *The Trident, the Crescent and the Cross*. London: Longmans, Green, 1876.

Verkuyl, J. 'The Biblical Notion of Kingdom: Test of Validity for Theology of Religion'. In *The Good News of the Kingdom: Mission Theology for the Third Millennium*, edited by C.V. Engen, D.S. Gilliland, and P. Pierson. New York: Orbis, 1993.

Vesci, U.M. *Heat and Sacrifice in the Vedas*. Delhi: Motilal Banarsidass, 1985.

Vetticatil, J. 'Brahmabandhav Upadhyaya'. *Jeevadhara* 17, 100 (1987): 322-343.

Walker, B. *Hindu World: An Encyclopedic Survey of Hinduism*. Vol. II. New Delhi: Munshiram Manoharlal Publishers, 1983.

Walls, A.F. *The Missionary Movement in Christian History: Studies in the Transmission of Faith*. New York/Edinburgh: Orbis/T&T Clark, 1996.

Ward, K. *Religion and Revelation: A Theology of Revelation in the World's Religions* Oxford: Clarendon, 1994.

Watson, F. *Text, Church and World: Biblical Interpretation in Theological Perspective* Grand Rapids: Eerdmans, 1994.

Werner, K., ed. *Love Divine: Studies in Bhakti and Devotional Mysticism*. Richmond Surrey: Curzon Press, 1993.

Whaling, F. *The World's Religious Traditions: Current perspectives in Religious Studies*. Edinburgh: T&T Clark, 1984.

_______. *Christian Theology and World Religions: A Global Approach*. Basingstoke: Marshall Pickering, 1986.

_______. 'Religion, theories of'. In *The Blackwell Encyclopedia of Modern Christian Thought*, edited by A.E. McGrath. Oxford: Blackwell, 1993.

Wilson, M.R. *Our Father Abraham: Jewish Roots of the Christian Faith*. Grand Rapids: Eerdmans, 1989.

Winslow, J.C. *Narayan Vaman Tilak: The Christian Poet of Maharashtra.* Calcutta: Association Press, 1930.
Yates, T. *Christian Mission in the Twentieth Century*. Cambridge: Cambridge University Press, 1994.
Zaehner, R.C. *At Sundry Times: An Essay in the Comparison of Religions.* London: Faber and Faber, 1958.
_______. *Hinduism*. Oxford: Oxford University Press, 1985.
_______, ed. and trans. *Hindu Scriptures*. New Delhi: Rupa, 1995.

Archival Sources

1. *The Inquirer* 3:12 (August 1902) – 5:1 (September 1903), United Theological College Library Archives, Bangalore, India.
2. A large collection of unpublished materials on Sahu Sundar Singh classified as *Various Private Collections about Sadhu Sundar Singh* (VPC SSS) are preserved in seven collection boxes in the United Theological College Library Archives, Bangalore, India.

Box 1 (VPC SSS.1): *Correspondence of Sadhu Sundar Singh with various people.*
Box 2 (VPC SSS.2): *Correspondence of the Sadhu and others between 1916 to1931.*
Box 3 (VPC SSS.3): *Newspaper and Periodical Cuttings and Notices.*
Box 4 (VPC SSS.4): *Materials from the Hand of Sundar Singh.*
Box 5 (VPC SSS.5): *Materials collected by A.J. Appasamy in connection with the writing of 'Sundar Singh: A Biography'.*
Box 6 (VPC SSS.6): *Correspondence of A.J. Appasamy and Information regarding the Sadhu's preaching tours in Australia and Denmark.*
Box 7 (VPC SSS.7): *General Correspondence in connection with A J. Appasamy's biography on the Sadhu.*

REGNUM EDINBURGH 2010 SERIES
Series Listing

David A. Kerr, Kenneth R. Ross (eds.)
Edinburgh 2010
Mission Then and Now
2009 / 978-1-870345-73-6 / xiv + 343pp (paperback)
2009 / 978-1-870345-76-7 / xiv + 343pp (hardback)

No one can hope to fully understand the modern Christian missionary movement without engaging substantially with the World Missionary Conference, held at Edinburgh in 1910. As the centenary of the Conference approaches, the time is ripe to examine its meaning in light of the past century and the questions facing Christian witness today. This book is the first to systematically examine the eight Commissions which reported to Edinburgh 1910 and gave the conference much of its substance and enduring value. It will deepen and extend the reflection being stimulated by the upcoming centenary and will kindle the missionary imagination for 2010 and beyond.

Daryl M. Balia, Kirsteen Kim (eds.)
Edinburgh 2010
Witnessing to Christ Today
2010 / 978-1-870345-77-4 / xiv +301pp

This volume, the second in the Edinburgh 2010 series, includes reports of the nine main study groups working on different themes for the celebration of the centenary of the World Missionary Conference, Edinburgh 1910. Their collaborative work brings together perspectives that are as inclusive as possible of contemporary world Christianity and helps readers to grasp what it means in different contexts to be 'witnessing to Christ today'.

Claudia Währisch-Oblau, Fidon Mwombeki (eds.)
Mission Continues
Global Impulses for the 21st Century
2010 / 978-1-870345-82-8 / 271pp

In May 2009, 35 theologians from Asia, Africa and Europe met in Wuppertal, Germany, for a consultation on mission theology organized by the United Evangelical Mission: Communion of 35 Churches in Three Continents. The aim was to participate in the 100th anniversary of the Edinburgh conference through a study process and reflect on the challenges for mission in the 21st century. This book brings together these papers written by experienced practitioners from around the world.

Brian Woolnough and Wonsuk Ma (Eds)

Holistic Mission

God's plan for God's people 2010 / 978-1-870345-85-9

Holistic mission, or integral mission, implies God is concerned with the whole person, the whole community, body, mind and spirit. This book discusses the meaning of the holistic gospel, how it has developed, and implications for the the church. . It takes a global, eclectic approach, with 19 writers, all of whom have much experience in, and commitment to, holistic mission. It addresses critically and honestly one of the most exciting, and challenging, issues facing the church today. To be part of God's plan for God's people, the church must take holistic mission to the world.

Kirsteen Kim and Andrew Anderson (Eds)

Mission Today and Tomorrow

2011/978-1-870345-91-0

The centenary of the historic and influential World Missionary Conference held in Edinburgh 1910 presented a unique opportunity for the whole church worldwide to come together in celebration, reflection and recommitment to witnessing to Christ today. Edinburgh 2010 also engaged in serious study and reflection on the current state of world mission and the challenges facing all those who seek to witness Christ today. The results of this research was presented and debated within the context of Christian fellowship and worship at the conference in June 2010. This record of that conference is intended to give the background to that Call, to share the spirit of the conference, and to stimulate informed and focused participation in God's mission in Christ for the world's salvation.

Tormod Engelsviken, Erling Lundeby and Dagfinn Solheim (Eds)

The Church Going Glocal

Mission and Globalisation 2011/978-1-870345-93-4

This book provides thought-provoking and inspiring reading for all concerned with mission in the 21st century. I have been challenged by its contributors to re-think our Gospel ministries in our new local contexts marked by globalisation and migration. With its biblical foundation, its missiological reflection and interaction with contemporary society I warmly recommend this volume for study and pray that it will renew our passion for the Gospel and compassion for people.

REGNUM Studies in Global Christianity

(Previously GLOBAL THEOLOGICAL VOICES series)

Series Listing

David Emmanuuel Singh (ed.)

Jesus and the Cross

Reflections of Christians from Islamic Contexts

2008 / 978-1-870345-65-1 / x + 226pp

The Cross reminds us that the sins of the world are not borne through the exercise of power but through Jesus Christ's submission to the will of the Father. The papers in this volume are organised in three parts: scriptural, contextual and theological. The central question being addressed is: how do Christians living in contexts, where Islam is a majority or minority religion, experience, express or think of the Cross? This is, therefore, an exercise in listening. As the contexts from where these engagements arise are varied, the papers in drawing scriptural, contextual and theological reflections offer a cross-section of Christian thinking about Jesus and the Cross.

David Emmanuuel Singh (ed.)

Jesus and the Incarnation

Reflections of Christians from Islamic Contexts

2011/978-1-870345-90-3

In the dialogue of Christians with Muslims nothing is more fundamental than the Cross, the Incarnation and the Resurrection of Jesus. This book contains voices of Christians living in various 'Islamic contexts' and reflecting on the Incarnation of Jesus. The aim of these reflections is constructive and the hope is that the papers weaved around the notion of 'the Word' will not only promote dialogue among Christians on the roles of the Person and the Book, but, also, create a positive environment for their conversations with Muslim neighbours.

Sung-wook Hong

Naming God in Korea

The Case of Protestant Christianity

2008 / 978-1-870345-66-8 / xiv + 170pp

Since Christianity was introduced to Korea more than a century ago, one of the most controversial issue has been the Korean term for the Christian 'God'. This issue is not merely about naming the Christian God in Korean language, but it relates to the question of theological contextualization—the relationship between the gospel and culture—and the question of Korean Christian identity. This book examines the theological contextualization of the concept of 'God' in the contemporary Korean context and applies the translatability of Christianity to that context. It also demonstrates the nature of the gospel in relation to cultures, i.e., the universality of the gospel expressed in all human cultures.

Hubert van Beek (ed.)
Revisioning Christian Unity
The Global Christian Forum
2009 / 978-1-870345-74-3 / xx + 288pp

This book contains the records of the Global Christian Forum gathering held in Limuru near Nairobi, Kenya, on 6 – 9 November 2007 as well as the papers presented at that historic event. Also included are a summary of the Global Christian Forum process from its inception until the 2007 gathering and the reports of the evaluation of the process that was carried out in 2008.

Paul Hang-Sik Cho
Eschatology and Ecology
Experiences of the Korean Church
2010 / 978-1-870345-75-0/ 260pp (approx)

This book raises the question of why Korean people, and Korean Protestant Christians in particular, pay so little attention (in theory or practice) to ecological issues. The author argues that there is an important connection (or elective affinity) between this lack of attention and the other-worldly eschatology that is so dominant within Korean Protestant Christianity. Dispensational premillennialism, originally imported by American missionaries, resonated with traditional religious beliefs in Korea and soon came to dominate much of Korean Protestantism. This book argues that this, of all forms of millennialism, is the most damaging to ecological concerns.

Dietrich Werner, David Esterline, Namsoon Kang, Joshva Raja (eds.)
The Handbook of Theological Education in World Christianity
Theological Perspectives, Ecumenical Trends, Regional Surveys
2010 / 978-1-870345-80-4/ 759pp

This major reference work is the first ever comprehensive study of Theological Education in Christianity of its kind. With contributions from over 90 international scholars and church leaders, it aims to be easily accessible across denominational, cultural, educational, and geographic boundaries. The Handbook will aid international dialogue and networking among theological educators, institutions, and agencies. The major objectives of the text are (1) to provide introductory surveys on selected issues and themes in global theological education; (2) to provide regional surveys on key developments, achievements, and challenges in theological education; (3) to provide an overview of theological education for each of the major denominational / confessional traditions; and (4) to provide a reference section with an up-to-date list of the regional associations of theological institutions and other resources.

David Emmanuel Singh & Bernard C Farr (eds.)
Christianity and Education
Shaping of Christian Context in Thinking
2010 / 978-1-870345-81-1/ 244pp (approx)

Christianity and Education is a collection of papers published in *Transformation: An International Journal of Holistic Mission Studies* over a period of 15 years. It brings to life some of the papers that lay buried in shelves and in disparate volumes of *Transformation,* under a single volume for theological libraries, students and teachers. The articles here represent a spectrum of Christian thinking addressing issues of institutional development for theological education, theological studies in the context of global mission, contextually aware/informed education, and academies which deliver such education, methodologies and personal reflections.

J.Andrew Kirk
Civilisations in Conflict?
Islam, the West and Christian Faith 2011- 978-1-870345-71-2

Samuel Huntington's thesis, which argues that there appear to be aspects of Islam that could be on a collision course with the politics and values of Western societies, has provoked much controversy. The purpose of this study is to offer a particular response to Huntington's thesis by making a comparison between the origins of Islam and Christianity; the two religions that can be said to have shaped, in contrasting ways, the history of the Western world. The early history of each faith continues to have a profound impact on the way in which their respective followers have interpreted the relationship between faith and political life. The book draws significant, critical and creative conclusions from the analysis for contemporary intercultural understanding, and in particular for the debate about the justification of violence for political and religious ends.

REGNUM STUDIES IN MISSION
Series Listing

Kwame Bediako

Theology and Identity

The Impact of Culture upon Christian Thought in the Second Century and in Modern Africa

1992 / 1-870345-10-X / xviii + 508pp

The author examines the question of Christian identity in the context of the Graeco–Roman culture of the early Roman Empire. He then addresses the modern African predicament of quests for identity and integration.

Christopher Sugden

Seeking the Asian Face of Jesus

The Practice and Theology of Christian Social Witness in Indonesia and India 1974–1996

1997 / 1-870345-26-6 / xx + 496pp

This study focuses on contemporary holistic mission with the poor in India and Indonesia combined with the call to transformation of all life in Christ with micro-credit enterprise schemes. 'The literature on contextual theology now has a new standard to rise to' – Lamin Sanneh (Yale University, USA).

Hwa Yung

Mangoes or Bananas?

The Quest for an Authentic Asian Christian Theology

1997 / 1-870345-25-8 / xii + 274pp

Asian Christian thought remains largely captive to Greek dualism and Enlightenment rationalism because of the overwhelming dominance of Western culture. Authentic contextual Christian theologies will emerge within Asian Christianity with a dual recovery of confidence in culture and the gospel.

Keith E. Eitel

Paradigm Wars

The Southern Baptist International Mission Board Faces the Third Millennium

1999 / 1-870345-12-6 / x + 140pp

The International Mission Board of the Southern Baptist Convention is the largest denominational mission agency in North America. This volume chronicles the historic and contemporary forces that led to the IMB's recent extensive reorganization, providing the most comprehensive case study to date of a historic mission agency restructuring to continue its mission purpose into the twenty-first century more effectively.

Samuel Jayakumar

Dalit Consciousness and Christian Conversion

Historical Resources for a Contemporary Debate

1999 / 81-7214-497-0 / xxiv + 434pp

(Published jointly with ISPCK)

The main focus of this historical study is social change and transformation among the Dalit Christian communities in India. Historiography tests the evidence in the light of the conclusions of the modern Dalit liberation theologians.

Vinay Samuel and Christopher Sugden (eds.)

Mission as Transformation

A Theology of the Whole Gospel

1999 / 0870345133/ 522pp

This book brings together in one volume twenty five years of biblical reflection on mission practice with the poor from around the world. The approach of holistic mission, which integrates proclamation, evangelism, church planting and social transformation seamlessly as a whole, has been adopted since 1983 by most evangelical development agencies, most indigenous mission agencies and many Pentecostal churches. This volume helps anyone understand how evangelicals, struggling to unite evangelism and social action, found their way in the last twenty five years to the biblical view of mission in which God calls all human beings to love God and their neighbour; never creating a separation between the two.

Christopher Sugden

Gospel, Culture and Transformation

2000 / 1-870345-32-0 / viii + 152pp

A Reprint, with a New Introduction, of Part Two of Seeking the Asian Face of Jesus

Gospel, Culture and Transformation explores the practice of mission especially in relation to transforming cultures and communities. - 'Transformation is to enable God's vision of society to be actualised in all relationships: social, economic and spiritual, so that God's will may be reflected in human society and his love experienced by all communities, especially the poor.'

Bernhard Ott

Beyond Fragmentation: Integrating Mission and Theological Education

A Critical Assessment of some Recent Developments in Evangelical Theological Education

2001 / 1-870345-14-2 / xxviii + 382pp

Beyond Fragmentation is an enquiry into the development of Mission Studies in evangelical theological education in Germany and German-speaking Switzerland between 1960 and 1995. The author undertakes a detailed examination of the paradigm shifts which have taken place in recent years in both the theology of mission and the understanding of theological education.

Gideon Githiga

The Church as the Bulwark against Authoritarianism

Development of Church and State Relations in Kenya, with Particular Reference to the Years after Political Independence 1963-1992

2002 / 1-870345-38-x / xviii + 218pp

'All who care for love, peace and unity in Kenyan society will want to read this careful history by Bishop Githiga of how Kenyan Christians, drawing on the Bible, have sought to share the love of God, bring his peace and build up the unity of the nation, often in the face of great difficulties and opposition.' Canon Dr Chris Sugden, Oxford Centre for Mission Studies.

Myung Sung-Hoon, Hong Young-Gi (eds.)

Charis and Charisma

David Yonggi Cho and the Growth of Yoido Full Gospel Church

2003 / 1-870345-45-2 / xxii + 218pp

This book discusses the factors responsible for the growth of the world's largest church. It expounds the role of the Holy Spirit, the leadership, prayer, preaching, cell groups and creativity in promoting church growth. It focuses on God's grace (charis) and inspiring leadership (charisma) as the two essential factors and the book's purpose is to present a model for church growth worldwide.

Samuel Jayakumar

Mission Reader

Historical Models for Wholistic Mission in the Indian Context

2003 / 1-870345-42-8 / x + 250pp

(Published jointly with ISPCK)

This book is written from an evangelical point of view revalidating and reaffirming the Christian commitment to wholistic mission. The roots of the 'wholistic mission' combining 'evangelism and social concerns' are to be located in the history and tradition of Christian evangelism in the past; and the civilizing purpose of evangelism is compatible with modernity as an instrument in nation building.

Bob Robinson

Christians Meeting Hindus

An Analysis and Theological Critique of the Hindu-Christian Encounter in India

2004 / 1-870345-39-8 / xviii + 392pp

This book focuses on the Hindu-Christian encounter, especially the intentional meeting called dialogue, mainly during the last four decades of the twentieth century, and specifically in India itself.

Gene Early

Leadership Expectations

How Executive Expectations are Created and Used in a Non-Profit Setting

2005 / 1-870345-30-4 / xxiv + 276pp

The author creates an Expectation Enactment Analysis to study the role of the Chancellor of the University of the Nations-Kona, Hawaii. This study is grounded in the field of managerial work, jobs, and behaviour and draws on symbolic interactionism, role theory, role identity theory and enactment theory. The result is a conceptual framework for developing an understanding of managerial roles.

Tharcisse Gatwa

The Churches and Ethnic Ideology in the Rwandan Crises 1900-1994

2005 / 1-870345-24-X / approx 300pp

Since the early years of the twentieth century Christianity has become a new factor in Rwandan society. This book investigates the role Christian churches played in the formulation and development of the racial ideology that culminated in the 1994 genocide.

Julie Ma

Mission Possible

Biblical Strategies for Reaching the Lost

2005 / 1-870345-37-1 / xvi + 142pp

This is a missiology book for the church which liberates missiology from the specialists for the benefit of every believer. It also serves as a textbook that is simple and friendly, and yet solid in biblical interpretation. This book links the biblical teaching to the actual and contemporary missiological settings with examples, making the Bible come alive to the reader.

Allan Anderson, Edmond Tang (eds.)

Asian and Pentecostal

The Charismatic Face of Christianity in Asia

2005 / 1-870345-43-6 / xiv + 596pp

(Published jointly with APTS Press)

This book provides a thematic discussion and pioneering case studies on the history and development of Pentecostal and Charismatic churches in the countries of South Asia, South East Asia and East Asia.

I. Mark Beaumont

Christology in Dialogue with Muslims

A Critical Analysis of Christian Presentations of Christ for Muslims from the Ninth and Twentieth Centuries

2005 / 1-870345-46-0 / xxvi + 228pp

This book analyses Christian presentations of Christ for Muslims in the most creative periods of Christian-Muslim dialogue, the first half of the ninth century and the second half of the twentieth century. In these two periods, Christians made serious attempts to present their faith in Christ in terms that take into account Muslim perceptions of him, with a view to bridging the gap between Muslim and Christian convictions.

Thomas Czövek,

Three Seasons of Charismatic Leadership

A Literary-Critical and Theological Interpretation of the Narrative of Saul, David and Solomon

2006 / 978-1-870345484 / 272pp

This book investigates the charismatic leadership of Saul, David and Solomon. It suggests that charismatic leaders emerge in crisis situations in order to resolve the crisis by the charisma granted by God. Czovek argues that Saul proved himself as a charismatic leader as long as he acted resolutely and independently from his mentor Samuel. In the author's eyes, Saul's failure to establish himself as a charismatic leader is caused by his inability to step out from Samuel's shadow.

Jemima Atieno Oluoch

The Christian Political Theology of Dr. John Henry Okullu

2006 / 1-870345-51-7 / xx + 137pp

This book reconstructs the Christian political theology of Bishop John Henry Okullu, DD, through establishing what motivated him and the biblical basis for his socio-political activities. It also attempts to reconstruct the socio-political environment that nurtured Dr Okullu's prophetic ministry.

Richard Burgess

Nigeria's Christian Revolution

The Civil War Revival and Its Pentecostal Progeny (1967-2006)

2008 / 978-1-870345-63-7 / xxii + 347pp

This book describes the revival that occurred among the Igbo people of Eastern Nigeria and the new Pentecostal churches it generated, and documents the changes that have occurred as the movement has responded to global flows and local demands. As such, it explores the nature of revivalist and Pentecostal experience, but does so against the backdrop of local socio-political and economic developments, such as decolonisation and civil war, as well as broader processes, such as modernisation and globalisation.

David Emmanuel Singh & Bernard C Farr (eds.)

Christianity and Cultures

Shaping Christian Thinking in Context

2008 / 978-1-870345-69-9 / x + 260pp

This volume marks an important milestone, the 25th anniversary of the Oxford Centre for Mission Studies (OCMS). The papers here have been exclusively sourced from Transformation, a quarterly journal of OCMS, and seek to provide a tripartite view of Christianity's engagement with cultures by focusing on the question: how is Christian thinking being formed or reformed through its interaction with the varied contexts it encounters? The subject matters include different strands of theological-missiological thinking, socio-political engagements and forms of family relationships in interaction with the host cultures.

Tormod Engelsviken, Ernst Harbakk, Rolv Olsen, Thor Strandenæs (eds.)

Mission to the World

Communicating the Gospel in the 21st Century: Essays in Honour of Knud Jørgensen

2008 / 978-1-870345-64-4 / 472pp

Knud Jørgensen is Director of Areopagos and Associate Professor of Missiology at MF Norwegian School of Theology. This book reflects on the main areas of Jørgensen's commitment to mission. At the same time it focuses on the main frontier of mission, the world, the content of mission, the Gospel, the fact that the Gospel has to be communicated, and the context of contemporary mission in the 21st century.

Al Tizon

Transformation after Lausanne

Radical Evangelical Mission in Global-Local Perspective

2008 / 978-1-870345-68-2 / xx + 281pp

After Lausanne '74, a worldwide network of radical evangelical mission theologians and practitioners use the notion of "Mission as Transformation" to integrate evangelism and social concern together, thus lifting theological voices from the Two Thirds World to places of prominence. This book documents the definitive gatherings, theological tensions, and social forces within and without evangelicalism that led up to Mission as Transformation. And it does so through a global-local grid that points the way toward greater holistic mission in the 21st century.

Bambang Budijanto

Values and Participation

Development in Rural Indonesia

2009 / 978-1-870345-70-5 / x + 237pp

Socio-religious values and socio-economic development are inter-dependant, inter-related and are constantly changing in the context of macro political structures, economic policy, religious organizations and globalization; and micro influences such as local affinities, identity, politics, leadership and beliefs. The three Lopait communities in Central Java, Indonesia provide an excellent model of the rich and complex negotiations and interactions among all the above factors. The book argues that the comprehensive approach in understanding the socio-religious values of each local community is essential to accurately describing their respective identity which will help institutions and agencies, both governmental and non-governmental, to relate to these communities with dignity and respect.

Young-hoon Lee

The Holy Spirit Movement in Korea

Its Historical and Theological Development

2009 / 978-1-870345-67-5 / x + 174pp

This book traces the historical and theological development of the Holy Spirit Movement in Korea through six successive periods (from 1900 to the present time). These periods are characterized by repentance and revival (1900-20), persecution and suffering under Japanese occupation (1920-40), confusion and division (1940-60), explosive revival in which the Pentecostal movement played a major role in the rapid growth of Korean churches (1960-80), the movement reaching out to all denominations (1980-2000), and the new context demanding the Holy Spirit movement to open new horizons in its mission engagement (2000-). The volume also discusses the relationship between this movement and other religions such as shamanism, and looks forward to further engagement with issues of concern in wider society.

Alan R. Johnson

Leadership in a Slum

A Bangkok Case Study

2009 / 978-1-870345-71-2 xx + 238pp

This book looks at leadership in the social context of a slum in Bangkok from an angle different from traditional studies which measure well educated Thais on leadership scales derived in the West. Using both systematic data collection and participant observation, it develops a culturally preferred model as well as a set of models based in Thai concepts that reflect on-the-ground realities. This work challenges the dominance of the patron-client rubric for understanding all forms of Thai leadership and offers a view for understanding leadership rooted in local social systems, contrary to approaches that assume the universal applicability of leadership research findings across all cultural settings. It concludes by looking at the implications of the anthropological approach for those who are involved in leadership training in Thai settings and beyond.

Titre Ande

Leadership and Authority

Bula Matari and Life - Community Ecclesiology in Congo

2010 / 978-1-870345-72-9 xvii + 189pp

This book proposes that Christian theology in Africa can make significant developments if a critical understanding of the socio-political context in contemporary Africa is taken seriously. The Christian leadership in post-colonial Africa has cloned its understanding and use of authority on the Bula Matari model, which was issued from the brutality of colonialism and political absolutism in post-colonial Africa. This model has caused many problems in churches, including dysfunction, conflicts, divisions and a lack of prophetic ministry. Titre proposes a Life-Community ecclesiology for liberating authority, where leadership is a function, not a status, and 'apostolic succession' belongs to all the people of God.

Frank Kwesi Adams

Odwira and the Gospel

A Study of the Asante Odwira Festival and its Significance for Christianity in Ghana

2010 /978-1-870345-59-0

The study of the Odwira festival is the key to the understanding of Asante religious and political life in Ghana. The book explores the nature of the Odwira festival longitudinally - in pre-colonial, colonial and post-independence Ghana - and examines the Odwira ideology and its implications for understanding the Asante self-identity. The book also discusses how some elements of faith portrayed in the Odwira festival could provide a framework for Christianity to engage with Asante culture at a greater depth. Theological themes in Asante belief that have emerged from this study include the theology of sacrament, ecclesiology, eschatology, Christology and a complex concept of time. The author argues that Asante cultural identity lies at the heart of the process by which the Asante Christian faith is carried forward.

Bruce Carlton

Strategy Coordinator

Changing the Course of Southern Baptist Missions

2010 / 978-1-870345-78-1 xvii + 268pp

In 1976, the Southern Baptist Convention adopted its Bold New Thrusts in Foreign Missions with the overarching goal of sharing the gospel with every person in the world by the year 2000. The formation of Cooperative Services International (CSI) in 1985 and the assigning of the first non-residential missionary (NRM) in 1987 demonstrated the Foreign Mission Board's (now International Mission Board) commitment to take the gospel message to countries that restricted traditional missionary presence and to people groups identified as having little or no access to the gospel. Carlton traces the historical development along with an analysis of the key components of the paradigm and its significant impact on Southern Baptists' missiology.

Julie Ma & Wonsuk Ma
Mission in the Spirit:
Towards a Pentecostal/Charismatic Missiology
2010 / 978-1-870345-84-2 xx + 312pp

The book explores the unique contribution of Pentecostal/Charismatic mission from the beginning of the twentieth century. The first part considers the theological basis of Pentecostal/Charismatic mission thinking and practice. Special attention is paid to the Old Testament, which has been regularly overlooked by the modern Pentecostal/Charismatic movements. The second part discusses major mission topics with contributions and challenges unique to Pentecostal/Charismatic mission. The book concludes with a reflection on the future of this powerful missionary movement. As the authors served as Korean missionaries in Asia, often their missionary experiences in Asia are reflected in their discussions.

S. Hun Kim & Wonsuk Ma (eds.)
Korean Diaspora and Christian Mission
2011-978-1-870345-89-7

As a ‘divine conspiracy’ for Missio Dei, the global phenomenon of people on the move has shown itself to be invaluable. In 2004 two significant documents concerning Diaspora were introduced, one by the Filipino International Network and the other by the Lausanne Committee for World Evangelization. These have created awareness of the importance of people on the move for Christian mission. Since then, Korean Diaspora has conducted similar research among Korean missions, resulting in this book. It is unique as the first volume researching Korean missions in Diasporic contexts, appraising and evaluating these missions with practical illustrations, and drawing on a wide diversity of researchers.

GENERAL REGNUM TITLES

Vinay Samuel, Chris Sugden (eds.)
The Church in Response to Human Need
1987 / 1870345045 / xii+268pp

Philip Sampson, Vinay Samuel, Chris Sugden (eds.)
Faith and Modernity
Essays in modernity and post-modernity
1994 / 1870345177 / 352pp

Klaus Fiedler
The Story of Faith Missions
1994 / 0745926878 / 428pp

Douglas Peterson
Not by Might nor by Power
A Pentecostal Theology of Social Concern in Latin America
1996 / 1870345207 / xvi+260pp

David Gitari
In Season and Out of Season
Sermons to a Nation
1996 / 1870345118 / 155pp

David. W. Virtue
A Vision of Hope
The Story of Samuel Habib
1996 / 1870345169 / xiv+137pp

Everett A Wilson
Strategy of the Spirit
J.Philip Hogan and the Growth of the Assemblies of God Worldwide, 1960 - 1990
1997 /1870345231/214

Murray Dempster, Byron Klaus, Douglas Petersen (eds.)
The Globalization of Pentecostalism
A Religion Made to Travel
1999 / 1870345290 / xvii+406pp

Peter Johnson, Chris Sugden (eds.)
Markets, Fair Trade and the Kingdom of God
Essays to Celebrate Traidcraft's 21st Birthday
2001 / 1870345193 / xii+155pp

Robert Hillman, Coral Chamberlain, Linda Harding
Healing & Wholeness
Reflections on the Healing Ministry
2002 / 978-1- 870345-35- 4 / xvii+283pp

David Bussau, Russell Mask
Christian Microenterprise Development
An Introduction
2003 / 1870345282 / xiii+142pp

David Singh
Sainthood and Revelatory Discourse
An Examination of the Basis for the Authority of Bayan in Mahdawi Islam
2003 / 8172147285 / xxiv+485pp

For the up-to-date listing of the Regnum books see www.ocms.ac.uk/regnum

Regnum Books International

Regnum is an Imprint of The Oxford Centre for Mission Studies
St. Philip and St. James Church
Woodstock Road
Oxford, OX2 6HR
Web: www.ocms.ac.uk/regnum